Hebrew

2nd Edition

by Jill Suzanne Jacobs, M.A.

A Wiley Brand

Hebrew For Dummies®, 2nd Edition

Published by: **John Wiley & Sons, Inc.**, 111 River Street, Hoboken, NJ 07030-5774, www.wiley.com

Copyright © 2022 by John Wiley & Sons, Inc., Hoboken, New Jersey

Published simultaneously in Canada

No part of this publication may be reproduced, stored in a retrieval system or transmitted in any form or by any means, electronic, mechanical, photocopying, recording, scanning or otherwise, except as permitted under Sections 107 or 108 of the 1976 United States Copyright Act, without the prior written permission of the Publisher. Requests to the Publisher for permission should be addressed to the Permissions Department, John Wiley & Sons, Inc., 111 River Street, Hoboken, NJ 07030, (201) 748-6011, fax (201) 748-6008, or online at http://www.wiley.com/go/permissions.

Trademarks: Wiley, For Dummies, the Dummies Man logo, Dummies.com, Making Everything Easier, and related trade dress are trademarks or registered trademarks of John Wiley & Sons, Inc. and may not be used without written permission. All other trademarks are the property of their respective owners. John Wiley & Sons, Inc. is not associated with any product or vendor mentioned in this book.

LIMIT OF LIABILITY/DISCLAIMER OF WARRANTY: WHILE THE PUBLISHER AND AUTHORS HAVE USED THEIR BEST EFFORTS IN PREPARING THIS WORK, THEY MAKE NO REPRESENTATIONS OR WARRANTIES WITH RESPECT TO THE ACCURACY OR COMPLETENESS OF THE CONTENTS OF THIS WORK AND SPECIFICALLY DISCLAIM ALL WARRANTIES, INCLUDING WITHOUT LIMITATION ANY IMPLIED WARRANTIES OF MERCHANTABILITY OR FITNESS FOR A PARTICULAR PURPOSE. NO WARRANTY MAY BE CREATED OR EXTENDED BY SALES REPRESENTATIVES, WRITTEN SALES MATERIALS OR PROMOTIONAL STATEMENTS FOR THIS WORK. THE FACT THAT AN ORGANIZATION, WEBSITE, OR PRODUCT IS REFERRED TO IN THIS WORK AS A CITATION AND/OR POTENTIAL SOURCE OF FURTHER INFORMATION DOES NOT MEAN THAT THE PUBLISHER AND AUTHORS ENDORSE THE INFORMATION OR SERVICES THE ORGANIZATION, WEBSITE, OR PRODUCT MAY PROVIDE OR RECOMMENDATIONS IT MAY MAKE. THIS WORK IS SOLD WITH THE UNDERSTANDING THAT THE PUBLISHER IS NOT ENGAGED IN RENDERING PROFESSIONAL SERVICES. THE ADVICE AND STRATEGIES CONTAINED HEREIN MAY NOT BE SUITABLE FOR YOUR SITUATION. YOU SHOULD CONSULT WITH A SPECIALIST WHERE APPROPRIATE. FURTHER, READERS SHOULD BE AWARE THAT WEBSITES LISTED IN THIS WORK MAY HAVE CHANGED OR DISAPPEARED BETWEEN WHEN THIS WORK WAS WRITTEN AND WHEN IT IS READ. NEITHER THE PUBLISHER NOR AUTHORS SHALL BE LIABLE FOR ANY LOSS OF PROFIT OR ANY OTHER COMMERCIAL DAMAGES, INCLUDING BUT NOT LIMITED TO SPECIAL, INCIDENTAL, CONSEQUENTIAL, OR OTHER DAMAGES.

For general information on our other products and services, please contact our Customer Care Department within the U.S. at 877-762-2974, outside the U.S. at 317-572-3993, or fax 317-572-4002. For technical support, please visit https://hub.wiley.com/community/support/dummies.

Wiley publishes in a variety of print and electronic formats and by print-on-demand. Some material included with standard print versions of this book may not be included in e-books or in print-on-demand. If this book refers to media such as a CD or DVD that is not included in the version you purchased, you may download this material at http://booksupport.wiley.com. For more information about Wiley products, visit www.wiley.com.

Library of Congress Control Number: 2022932609

ISBN: 978-1-119-86202-4 (pbk); 978-1-119-86203-1 (ebk); 978-1-119-86204-8 (ebk)

SKY10032664_031222

Contents at a Glance

Table of Contents

Introduction

Hebrew is an incredible language. If you're picking up this book, I'm guessing that you have at least a passing interest in the subject, which thrills me because I think that Hebrew is an amazing, fascinating, and beautiful language. It's the only language in the history of the world to go from a deep freeze to a fully thawed, living, spoken language again. When you speak Hebrew, you're part of that amazing linguistic history. Whether you're interested in Hebrew because you want to communicate with your Israeli cousins, want to brush up on the subject so you can understand prayers and other sacred Jewish literature better, or want to impress your Jewish in-laws, *Hebrew For Dummies* can help.

About This Book

This book is a great place to start regardless of your motivation for picking up or dusting off your Hebrew skills. It won't make you fluent overnight (though wouldn't that be nice?) or turn you into a Biblical scholar, but *Hebrew For Dummies* can give you a solid foundation in both conversational Hebrew and the Hebrew of prayer, sacred texts, and holidays. As if that's not enough, I also share with you my love of things Jewish and the delightful, sometimes quirky culture of the modern State of Israel, where the largest group of Hebrew speakers resides today. But if you aren't planning on taking a trip to the Middle East, don't worry: Hebrew is alive and well all over the world. You can find plenty of opportunities to practice your language skills. (If you're not sure where to turn, I have you covered with some tips on where you can find Hebrew speakers and Hebrew sources right here in North America.) בְּהַצְלָחָה! (beh-*hahtz-lah-*ḥah; *Good luck! Much success to you!*)

This book is only the beginning — but I hope it's a good one! You can pick up a language only through exposure and repetition, so go online and listen to the audio files for this book again and again. Be sure to practice, practice, and (you knew it was coming) practice. Go to places where you hear Hebrew and speak Hebrew in your home and workplace. Teach your favorite Hebrew words and expressions to everyone you know. Before you know it, Hebrew will creep into your mind, soul, and heart, and you'll speak it day and night!

Here are a couple of conventions that I use in this book for your reading pleasure:

>> For this second edition, we're proud to include the Hebrew letters for each word (with vowels), along with the pronunciation (how to say the word) and translation (what the word means in English). In the pronunciations, the stressed syllables are italicized.

>> Because Hebrew language is often gender-specific (with masculine and feminine nouns, verb forms, and so on; see Chapter 2 for an explanation of gender), I've included the following abbreviations wherever necessary:

- Masculine singular (MS)

- Feminine singular (FS)

- Nonbinary singular (NB)

- Masculine plural (MP)

- Feminine plural (FP)

To help you develop your language skills, *For Dummies* language books include

>> **Talkin' the Talk dialogues:** Here's where you get to see Hebrew in action. These relatively short, real-life dialogues use the vocabulary and grammatical concepts that I introduce in the book.

>> **Words to Know blackboards:** Here's where you can find the key words and phrases I introduce. It's all here: the word as it's written in Hebrew, the proh-nun-see-aye-shun, and the translation.

>> **Fun & Games activities:** I'm a teacher; I just can't help myself. So, at the end of each chapter, I include some fun little exercises to help reinforce your newly acquired Hebrew.

Foolish Assumptions

My father taught me never to assume anything. He even had a little ditty about assumptions that I won't repeat here. But my editor said that I had to come up with some assumptions about you, the reader. So here they are:

>> You know no Hebrew — or if you learned Hebrew in religious school, you don't remember a word of it.

» You're not looking for a book that will make you fluent in Hebrew; you just want to know some words, phrases, and sentence constructions so that you can communicate basic information in Hebrew.

» You don't want to have to memorize long lists of vocabulary words or a bunch of boring grammar rules.

» You're inexplicably drawn to all yellow-and-black books.

» You want to have fun and pick up some Hebrew at the same time.

Do any descriptions sound like you? Well, good. I bet you're in good company.

How This Book Is Organized

This book is organized into six parts plus an appendix. The six parts are broken down into chapters. I've organized the chapters around active topics — things you want to do (like go to a bank, go to a restaurant, or go to a synagogue). Each chapter gives you the lowdown on the Hebrew you need to know to get by while doing that activity. And, though I know that you don't want to be bogged down by grammar rules, I sneak a grammatical tidbit or two into each chapter. Don't worry: I make these brief excursions as quick and painless as possible.

Part 1: Getting Started

This part of the book starts with the basics. I introduce you to the Hebrew letters and vowels and give you some basic Hebrew vocabulary. I explain how I represent the Hebrew sounds in English letters (so you don't have to crack your teeth reading the Hebrew, although I encourage you to try). In Part 1, I also give you a basic grounding in Hebrew grammar.

Part 2: Hebrew in Action

Here's where I really get going. In these chapters, I give you basic Hebrew vocabulary to start using in your daily life — when you rise up, when you lie down, in your home, and when you walk (to quote from an important Hebrew prayer). Part 2 gives you the words to meet and greet, flirt and work, eat and drink, and shop 'til you drop. I also give you vocabulary to use when you go out for a night on the town and when you talk about it on the phone the next day. And I give you all the words you need when you're hanging out at home and cleaning up your place after you've made a mess.

Part 3: Hebrew on the Go

Here's where I start to get practical. I cover dealing with money, going to the bank, asking directions, getting around using various forms of transportation (funny thing — I don't mention camels; oh well), and hitting the road for a trip. So, if travel bug has paid you a visit, take a look at Part 3. I give you the words and phrases you need for planning the trip. And I also give you some vocabulary for handling — God forbid — an emergency.

Part 4: Israeli Life

When you travel to Israel or converse with Israelis about Israeli life, you'll need a specialized vocabulary. In these chapters, I've got you covered. You'll learn the names of some Israeli cities and towns, Israel's diverse religious, cultural and ethnic groups, and how to talk about Israel's history, conflicts and quest for peace. There's even a bit of Arabic in these chapters, too.

Part 5: Sacred Hebrew

Where would Hebrew be without Judaism? In this part, I present the sacred side of the Hebrew language. I tell you all about blessings, prayers, and Jewish holidays.

Part 6: The Part of Tens

What would a For Dummies book be without one of these? I'll put my top ten lists up against anyone's. In this section, I give you ten Israeli sayings so you can sound like a real צַבָּר (*tzah*-bahr; native Israeli), plus the top-ten Hebrew sayings heard in the Jewish Diaspora (that's everywhere outside of the Land of Israel). I also give you a list of some great reads about the wonderful, wild, and wacky world of Hebrew. It's all here.

Appendixes

Here's all the nuts and bolts. The cogs that make Hebrew run — verb tables and a Hebrew-English/English-Hebrew dictionary. And it doesn't stop there. I put the answers to the Fun & Games activities (which you find at the end of each chapter) here too. This is the place to go when you want some information, and you want it fast.

Icons Used in This Book

Sometimes, I want to point out something that's especially important or interesting: a grammatical concept, something to remember, a tip to help you with your Hebrew skills, or a bit of insider insight into the wonderful world of Jewish culture. In these cases, I use the following icons, which you can find in the margins.

TIP

This icon accompanies helpful tips for picking up the Hebrew language.

REMEMBER

Think of this icon as that string around your finger that reminds you of all the little things you've gotta do but tend to forget. This icon flags important concepts that you have to keep in mind while you study Hebrew. You know what they say: God is in the details.

CULTURAL WISDOM

This little guy is by far my favorite icon. When you see this icon, you know that I've taken the opportunity to cram in all sorts of interesting information about the Jewish world — religious and secular — in Israel and the Jewish Diaspora (lands outside Israel).

GRAMMATICALLY SPEAKING

Ah, grammar. Can't live with it; can't live without it. This icon alerts you to instances where I point out the quirks of the Hebrew language and all those grammar rules that underlie the language's structure.

The website associated with this book gives you the opportunity to hear Hebrew in action. The site features audio files of native Hebrew speakers bringing to life some of the dialogues from the pages of this book. I bet you'll be amazed by how beautiful Hebrew can sound. Check it out at: `www.dummies.com/go/hebrewfd2e`.

TECHNICAL STUFF

I really tried to make this foray into Hebrew as painless as possible for you, but every now and then, I felt the need to explain things in technical terms. Don't worry — you can skip the paragraphs marked with this icon and still get all the Hebrew you need for basic conversation.

Beyond the Book

In addition to what you're reading right now, this book comes with a free, access-anywhere Cheat Sheet containing tips and techniques for learning Hebrew faster. To get this Cheat Sheet, simply go to `https://www.dummies.com` and type **Hebrew For Dummies Cheat Sheet** in the search box.

Where to Go from Here

First, the good news: You don't have to read this entire book. In fact, you don't have to read any of it. (But if that's the case, you probably wouldn't have bought it.) Anyway, here's my point: This book is organized so that you can read only the chapters that interest you and skip the rest. At no point in the text do I assume that you've read any of my scintillating writing in other chapters or sections, and I won't get insulted if you want to read only certain chapters.

If you're interested in the religious stuff, by all means, go straight to chapters 17, 18, and 19. But if you're interested in the day-to-day stuff, or if you just want to know how to ask that cute Israeli out on a date, Chapter 3 may be your cup of tea. Take a look at the table of contents and turn to the chapter that most interests you. Go ahead and do it! Read this book out of order. Skip chapters. I won't tell anyone. In fact, I'll never know.

All right, all right, I do have to add a few exceptions to the read-anything-you-want rule. You'll probably want to read Chapter 1, which gives you an overview of the book. And if you're a grammar geek, you'll looooove Chapter 2. If you aren't a grammar geek (most people despise the stuff, and I can't say that I blame them), you may want to look at Chapter 2 anyway. Here's a tip from someone who knows: After you understand the basics of Hebrew grammar, picking up the rest of the language is a cakewalk. So, consider checking out Chapter 2.

1

Getting Started with Hebrew

Chapter **1**

You Already Know Some Hebrew

! בָּרוּךְ הַבָּא (*Bah*-rooh Hah-*Bah!*; *Welcome to Hebrew!*) In studying Hebrew, you're joining millions of other Hebrew speakers around the world. Its two centers are Israel (of course) and North America, which is home to many Hebrew newspapers, Hebrew-speaking camps and schools, and institutions. You're also speaking the Bible's original language and one of the most ancient languages still spoken today. Furthermore, you're speaking the only language in the history of the world known to have undergone a revival, returning fully to being a spoken language after hundreds — perhaps even 2,000 — years of being relegated to correspondence, literature, and the sacred world of prayer and the Bible.

Hebrew was once almost exclusively a holy language — a language of prayers and ritual, of the Bible and other sacred texts, and a language above the humdrum of the everyday. That's no longer true. The same ancient and holy tongue is now the language of sunbathing on the beach, eating dinner, going to the doctor, and carrying out the myriad events of everyday life.

All languages are portals — openings to culture and friendship, literature, and ideas. Discover any one of these portals, and a whole new world opens up to you. Discover Hebrew, and a whole Jewish and Israeli world is yours.

Taking Stock of What's Familiar

If you've ever been to a synagogue or had a bit of Jewish education, you probably know a little Hebrew already. But even if you've never walked through a synagogue's door or studied anything Jewish, you probably still know some Hebrew words. You've probably heard the word *amen,* for example. That word is Hebrew! *Amen* comes from a word meaning "faith" or "belief," and people usually say it at the end of a prayer. And the word *Hallelujah?* Hebrew again! The word literally means "Praise God." Even the word *alphabet* derives from the Hebrew words for the first two letters of its alphabet, *aleph* and *bet.* (To see what the Hebrew alphabet looks like, check out "Recognizing Tips to Help You Read Hebrew" later in this chapter.)

You may have heard other Jewish words, of course, such as שלעפ (*shlehp; to drag or pull*) and קוועטשט (*kvehtsh; to complain*), which are actually Yiddish (the language of the Jews of Eastern Europe combining Old High German, Hebrew, and other languages) and are part of the Israeli vernacular today. You may never have thought about other words that have Hebrew roots. Did you know that *cinnamon* is a derivative of the Hebrew word קִנָּמוֹן (kee-nah-*mohn*), which appears in the biblical book The Song of Songs? The English word *dilute* may derive from the Hebrew word דַּל (*dahl*), which means "weak" or "thin" and first appears in the biblical book of Genesis.

Some people claim that Hebrew is the mother of all languages. No matter what its history or origin, Hebrew, a language that has its origins in the Fertile Crescent, has crept into North American spoken English. This process works in reverse, too, as many English words and phrases have crept into the Hebrew language. Interestingly enough, although you as an English speaker may identify some words as English, some of them derive from Italian and French, which shows the universality of certain words. But if you say the following words with an Israeli accent, you're speaking Hebrew!

>> Hamburger

>> Macaroni

>> Pizza

>> Cafe

>> Radio

>> Internet

>> Telephone

Incidentally, The Academy for Hebrew Language, the institute responsible for creating Modern Hebrew words, created an authentic Hebrew word for the telephone. The academy called the telephone a שָׂח-רָחוֹק (sahch-rah-*chohk*), which put together the words for *conversation* and *long distance.* So, *telephone* translated as "long-distance conversation." Pretty clever, huh? This word didn't stick with the Israeli public, however, so טֶלֶפוֹן (*telephone*) it is.

INTRODUCING THE ACADEMY FOR HEBREW LANGUAGE

Hebrew, the language of the Bible, is spoken today in Israel and around the world as a modern language. The question, of course, is where all these modern words come from? Who decides? The answer is הָאָקֶדֶמְיָה לַלָּשׁוֹן הָעִבְרִית, (ha-ah-*kah-dee*-mee-yah la-lh-*shon* hah-*eev*-reett; The Academy for Hebrew Language), an institute founded in Israel in 1953 to oversee the language's development and to create new words as the need arose in a manner consistent with Hebrew's historical development. So, although Hebrew is an ancient biblical language, new words needed to be developed, such as *high tech* (תַּעֲשִׂיָּה עִלִּית; tah-ah see-*yat* ee-*leet*) and *start-up company* (חֶבְרַת הֲזֶנֶק; hehv-*raht* hehz-*nehk*), *surfboard* (גַּלְשָׁן; gahl-*shan*), *jet lag* (יַעֶפֶת; yah-*eh*-feht), and even — when you've had a few too many — *hangover* (חֲמַרְמֹרֶת; ḥah-mahr-*moh*-reht).

Other timely words include נְגִישׁוּת (neh-*shee*-goot; *affordability*), חֲרִיגָנוּת (ḥahr- ree-gahn-oot; *exceptionalism*), נְתוּנֵי עָתֵק (nee-*too*-nee ah-tahk; *big data*), תַּג הַקְבָּצָה (tahg-hahk -*bahk*-tzah; *hashtag*), הַעֲלָמַת זֶהוּת (heet-*ahm*-aht *zah*-hoot; *anonymization*), עִילוּת (ee-*loot*; *gentrification*), אַחֲוָה (ah-vah; *solidarity*), and תַּצְלוּם מָסָךְ (tahtz-loom mahḥ *screen shot*).

The Israeli public doesn't accept all the words the academy invents, of course, although the academy's decisions are binding for government documents and the official Israel Broadcasting Authority.

Israelis aren't above taking matters into their own hands and creating words of their own. In the 1990s, Motorola Israel Corporation introduced wireless phones, coining the new word פֶּלֶא-פוֹן *pela-phone* (meaning "wonder phone)." You can find out more about the academy at: https://hebrew-academy.org.il/. Here's a great video on the Academy (it's in Hebrew, but there are English subtitles); https://www.youtube.com/watch?v=cY62gLh10CM You can even check out their Facebook page and "like" it at www.facebook.com/AcademyOfTheHebrewLanguage.

Speaking Hebrew Like a Native

When speaking a foreign language, you want to sound as authentic as possible. Use the tips in the following sections to start. The most important parts of sounding like a native are persistence and practice — and then some more practice! Listen to the dialogues from this book (available online) as much as possible. Spend as much time listening to Hebrew spoken by native speakers as you can.

Memorizing vocabulary and certain stock phrases and repeating them to yourself until you can say them at quite a clip is also helpful. In no time at all, you may fool people into thinking that you speak Hebrew fluently — or close to fluently, anyway.

Stressing out (not)

The first tip I give you has to do with the way syllables are stressed. In American English, we often stress or place emphasis on the first syllable in each word, as in "When *speak*ing a *for*eign *lan*guage . . . ." But Hebrew often places the emphasis on the last syllable. So, if you were speaking that previous phrase with an Israeli accent, you'd place your emphasis on the last syllable: "When speak*ing* a for*eign* langu*age* . . . ."

GESTURING LIKE THE BEST OF THEM

Gestures provide the flourishing touch to help you seem like a native speaker. Use the following gestures when you're speaking in Israel:

- Holding one hand at about shoulder level with the palm upright and all the fingers cupped together in the center means ! רֶגַע (*reh*-gah; *wait a minute*).

- When you want to catch a cab, point your index finger down at the ground, indicating that you want the cab to stop where you're pointing.

- In Israel, the American thumbs-up sign has traditionally been seen as an unfriendly gesture that means you're בְּרֹגֶז (*broh*-gehz; *mad* or *pissed off at someone*).

  Interestingly, an ad campaign in Israel once encouraged kids to make a thumbs-up sign to drivers when they're crossing the street, with the drivers returning the thumbs-up as an indication that they see the children and will let them cross without running them over. So, thumbs-up is taking on a positive connotation!

Getting out the gutturals

The second piece of advice I'll give you has to do with certain Hebrew letters that are pronounced at the back of the throat. Use these tips to pronounce them:

» ע (eye-*yeen*): This letter makes a barely audible guttural sound in the back of the throat. For practical purposes, this letter is nearly a silent syllable.

» כ (**ḥ***ahf*): This letter makes a sound you don't hear in English. It's a hard H sound, like the one you make when you clear your throat. In this book it is written as an **ḥ**.

» ח (**ḥ***eht*): This letter makes a strong throaty H sound. In this book, this syllable is written as **ḥ**.

» ר (*raysh*): Traditionally this letter makes an R sound as in *round*. To sound like a native, roll this syllable like a Spanish R, and try to produce the sound from the back of your throat.

Find out about the rest of the Hebrew alphabet in "Recognizing Tips to Help You Read Hebrew" later in this chapter.

TECHNICAL STUFF

A PEOPLE DISPERSED, A LANGUAGE INTACT

Hebrew served as the vernacular during the ancient Jewish commonwealth until it was conquered by the Romans in 70 CE (Common Era). Then Jews fanned out across the globe to Asia, Africa, and Europe. Even though they were dispersed, the Jewish people continued to practice their religion (Judaism) and remained literate in their language (Hebrew).

Hebrew continued to be the language of prayer, study, and correspondence for Jewish people. Gradually, Jews adopted the languages of their host countries as their spoken language. They mixed Hebrew with their host countries' languages, giving rise to new Jewish languages such as Ladino, Judeo-Arabic, and Yiddish.

In the 1800s, a movement began to revive Hebrew as a spoken language. Eliezer Ben-Yehuda championed the cause and moved to אֶרֶץ יִשְׂרָאֵל (*eh*-rehtz yees-*rah*-ehl; *the Land of Israel*) to revive Hebrew, writing the first Modern Hebrew dictionary. Today, Hebrew is one of the two official languages in Israel (Arabic being the other) and is a living, spoken language for millions of Israelis and other Hebrew speakers across the globe.

Opening your mouth to say "Ah!"

Third, watch the pronunciation of your vowels. When pronouncing the *ah* sound, pronounce that vowel fully. Open your mouth wide and say "Ah" as though you were at the doctor's office. Hebrew doesn't have a short *i* sound (like the vowel sound in *sit*), so any time you see an *i*, remember to make it a long sound, like the *ee* in *Whoopee!* In Hebrew, *oh* sounds are long, as in *over*.

REMEMBER

Hebrew is a Mediterranean language, and as such, it has a certain nasal quality. More so than in English — but actually a lot like in French — you use your nasal cavity when making sounds. Here's a less-technical tip: When speaking Hebrew, try to fake a French accent. At the very least, your Hebrew will sound better than it does with an American accent!

Counting in Hebrew

Learning how to count is fundamental to the study of any language. Hebrew divides words into masculine and feminine genders (see Chapter 2), and numbers are no different; they have masculine and feminine forms. You may feel a little confused, but don't worry! Table 1-1 gives you the *cardinal numbers* (the numbers you use for counting) from 1 to 10. When you want to count without counting objects, use the feminine form. See "Counting objects" later in this chapter to find out how to incorporate gender into numbers.

TABLE 1-1

Counting from 1 to 10

Number	Masculine	Feminine
1	אֶחָד (eh-*ḥad*)	אַחַת (ah-*ḥat*)
2	שְׁנַיִם (*shnah*-eem)	שְׁתַּיִם (*shta*-yim)
3	שְׁלוֹשָׁה (shloh-*sha*)	שָׁלוֹש h (sha-*lohsh*)
4	אַרְבָּעָה (ahr-bah-*ah*)	אַרְבַּע (*ahr*-bah)
5	חֲמִשָּׁה (ḥah-mee-*shah*)	חָמֵשׁ (ḥah-*mesh*)
6	שִׁשָּׁה (shee-*shah*)	שֵׁשׁ (shesh)
7	שִׁבְעָה (sheev-*ah*)	שֶׁבַע (she-vah)
8	שְׁמוֹנָה (shmoh-*nah*)	שְׁמוֹנֶה (shmoh-neh)
9	תִּשְׁעָה (teesh-*ah*)	תֵּשַׁע (*tey*-sha)
10	עֲשָׂרָה (ah-sah-*rah*)	עֶשֶׂר r (*eh*-sehr)

Counting objects

The gender of the number you use when you want to count something depends on the gender of the noun you're counting. (Sound confusing? Don't worry. You can do it.) Counting objects in Hebrew is easy. Just remember to do the following things:

>> **Figure out the gender of the noun you're counting.** If you want to talk about one book, first you must figure out whether the noun *book* is masculine or feminine. (It's masculine.) So, when you count books, you need to use the masculine form of the number.

>> **Place the number appropriately before or after the noun.** For the number 1, you place the number after the noun. So rather than saying "one book," you say, "book one" (סֵפֶר אֶחָד; *seh*-fehr eh-*chad*). But after you get to the number two, place the number before the noun. In Hebrew, the plural of סֵפֶר is סְפָרִים (sfah-*reem; books*). So, to say "two books," you say שְׁנֵי סְפָרִים (*shnay* sfah-*reem*); for "three books," say שְׁלוֹשָׁה סְפָרִים (shloh-*shah* sfah-*reem*); for "four books," say אַרְבָּעָה סְפָרִים (ahr-bah-*ah* sfah-*reem*); and so on.

TIP

The number 2 in Hebrew is an exception. When you're specifying two of something, say "two boys" (יְלָדִים; yuh–lah–*deem*) or "two girls" (יְלָדוֹת; yuh–lah–*doht*), and drop the last syllable (*im*) of the number 2. So, you get יְלָדִים (*two boys*) and שְׁתֵּי יְלָדוֹת (*two girls*). Drop the *im* regardless of the noun you're counting.

Counting higher

To form the numbers 11–19, place the second number in front of the 10. In the masculine form, for example, 11 is אַחַד עָשָׂר. In the feminine form, 11 is אַחַת עֶשְׂרֵה (ah-*chaht* es-*reh*). Table 1-2 shows the numbers 11–19.

REMEMBER

Use the appropriate gender for the 10 and the additional number that makes up the compound number.

The multiples of ten (10, 20, 30, and so on) are easy because these numbers are gender-neutral. Table 1-3 shows the multiples of 10.

TABLE 1-2 ## Counting from 11 to 19

Number	Masculine	Feminine
11	אַחַד עָשָׂר (eh-*had* ah-*sahr*)	אַחַת עֶשְׂרֵה (ah-*haht* ehs-*reh*)
12	שְׁנֵים עָשָׂר (shnehym ah-*sahr*)	שְׁתֵּים עֶשְׂרֵה (shtehym ehs-*reh*)
13	שְׁלוֹשׁ עָשָׂר (shloh-*sha* ah-*sahr*)	שְׁלוֹשָׁה עֶשְׂרֵה (shlosh-*ehsreh*)
14	אַרְבָּעָה עָשָׂר (ahr-bah-*ah* ah-*sahr*)	אַרְבַּע עֶשְׂרֵה (ahr-*bah* es-*reh*)
15	חֲמִשָּׁה עָשָׂר (**h**ah-mee-*shah* ah-*sahr*)	חָמֵשׁ עֶשְׂרֵה (**h**ah-*mesh* es-*reh*)
16	שִׁשָּׁה עָשָׂר (shee-*shah* ah-*sahr*)	שֵׁשׁ עֶשְׂרֵה (shehsh ehs-*reh*)
17	שִׁבְעָה עָשָׂר (sheev-*ah* ah-*sahr*)	שְׁבַע עֶשְׂרֵה (shvah es-*reh*)
18	שְׁמוֹנָה עָשָׂר (shmoh-*nah* ah-*sahr*)	שְׁמוֹנֶה עֶשְׂרֵה (shmoh-*neh* ehs-*reh*)
19	תִּשְׁעָה עָשָׂר שׁ (teesh-*ah* ah-*sahr*)	תְּשַׁע עֶשְׂרֵה (*tshah*-esreh)

TABLE 1-3 ## Counting Multiples of 10

Number	Hebrew	Pronunciation
20	עֶשְׂרִים	ehs-*reem*
30	שְׁלוֹשִׁים	shloh-*sheem*
40	אַרְבָּעִים	ahr-bah-*eem*
50	חֲמִשִּׁים	**h**ah-mee-*sheem*
60	שִׁשִּׁים	shee-*sheem*
70	שִׁבְעִים	sheev-*eem*
80	שְׁמוֹנִים	shmoh-*neem*
90	תִּשְׁעִים	teesh-*eem*

If you want to say something like "21" or "47," however, you have to pay attention to gender again. (See Table 1-4.) The pattern for making these numbers is to state the number in the tens, such as עֶשְׂרִים (ehs-*reem*; 20) and then add the word for and (וְ; *veh*), followed by the single number, such as אֶחָד (eh-*chad*; one). So, 21 would be עֶשְׂרִים וְאֶחָד (ehs-*reem* veh-eh-*chad*).

TABLE 1-4

Counting from 21 to 29

Number	Masculine	Feminine
21	עֶשְׂרִים וְאֶחָד (ehs-*reem* veh-eh-*ḥahd*)	עֶשְׂרִים וְאַחַת (ehs-*reem* veh-ah-*ḥat*)
22	עֶשְׂרִים וּשְׁנַיִם (ehs-*reem* oosh-*nah*-yim)	עֶשְׂרִים וּשְׁתַּיִם (ehs-*reem* ush-*tah*-yeem)
23	עֶשְׂרִים וּשְׁלוֹשָׁה (ehs-*reem* oosh-loh-*sah*)	עֶשְׂרִים וְשָׁלוֹשׁ (ehs-*reem* veh-shah-*lohsh*)
24	עֶשְׂרִים וְאַרְבָּעָה (ehs-*reem* veh-ahr-bah-*ah*)	עֶשְׂרִים וְאַרְבַּע (ehs-*reem* veh-ahr-bah)
25	עֶשְׂרִים וַחֲמִשָּׁה (ehs-*reem* vah-*ḥah*-mee-*shah*)	עֶשְׂרִים וְחָמֵשׁ (ehs-*reem* veh-*ḥah*-mesh)
26	עֶשְׂרִים וְשִׁשָּׁה (ehs-*reem* veh-sheev- ah)	עֶשְׂרִים וְשֵׁשׁ (ehs-*reem* veh-shehsh)
27	עֶשְׂרִים וְשִׁבְעָה (ehs-*reem* veh-sheev- ah)	עֶשְׂרִים וְשֶׁבַע (ehs-*reem* veh-sheh-vah)
28	עֶשְׂרִים וּשְׁמוֹנָה (ehs-*reem* ush-moh-*nah*)	עֶשְׂרִים וּשְׁמוֹנֶה (ehs-*reem* ush-moh-*neh*)
29	עֶשְׂרִים וְתִשְׁעָה (ehs-*reem* veh-teesh-ah)	עֶשְׂרִים וְתִשַׁע (ehs-*reem* veh-*the*-sha)

If you can count to 30, you can count to a million! For all the numbers, you follow the same pattern as in Table 1–4. First, state the number that's the multiple of 10 (20, 30, 40, and so on); then add וְ (*veh; and*) plus the single digit: שְׁלוֹשִׁים וְאֶחָד (shloh-*sheem* veh-eh-*ḥahd; 31*), אַרְבָּעִים וְאֶחָד (ahr-bah-*eem* veh-eh-*chahd; 41*), and so on.

To count by hundreds, first say the feminine number of the quantity of hundreds, such as *four* (אַרְבַּע), and then add the word for *hundreds* (מֵאוֹת). This pattern continues until a thousand:

100	מֵאָה	may-*ah*
200	מָאתַיִם	mah-*tah*-yeem
300	שְׁלוֹשׁ מֵאוֹת	*shlohsh*-meh-oht

To count by thousands, first you say the feminine number of the quantity of thousands and then follow it with the word for *thousands*, אֲלָפִי (ah-lah-*feem*). This pattern continues to 1 million. The Hebrew word for *1,000* is אֶלֶף (eh-*lehf*), and the word for *2,000* is אַלְפַּיִם (ahl-*pah*-yeem):

1,000	אֶלֶף	*eh*-lehf
2,000	אַלְפַּיִם	ahl-*pah*-eem
3,000	שְׁלֹשֶׁת אֲלָפִים	*shloh*-sheht ah-lah-*feem*
10,000	עֲשֶׂרֶת אֲלָפִים	ah-*seh*-reht ah-lah-*feem*
1,000,000	מִלְיוֹן	meel-*yohn*

Several chapters in this book give you an opportunity to practice using numbers. Check out Chapter 9 to find out how to ask for and give phone numbers. Also see Chapter 14, which is all about money. Don't you love counting money?

Recognizing Tips to Help You Read Hebrew

Hebrew is no ordinary language. Quite the contrary. Hebrew dates back more than 3,500 years to antiquity, and the Hebrew alphabet is quite possibly the first alphabet known to humankind. Hebrew was the language of King David and King Solomon, and the Bible's original language. Furthermore, ancient people called the Phoenicians based their alphabet on the Hebrew alphabet. The Greeks based their alphabet on the Phoenicians' letters. And the Latin letters you're reading right now are derived from the Greeks' letters! So, although the Hebrew language may look a little different, only four degrees separate it from what you're used to.

TECHNICAL STUFF

In Jewish circles, using the terms CE (Common Era) and BCE (Before the Common Era) instead of the terms AD (*Anno Domini,* or year of our Lord) and B. (Before Christ) is customary. In Hebrew, you say לְפְנֵי הַסְּפִירָה (leef-*nahy* hah-sfee-*rah; before the counting*) and אַחֲרֵי הַסְּפִירָה (ah-chah-*ray* hah-sfee-*rah; after the counting*). 2021/22 is 5782, dated from the time of Creation, placed at 3761 BCE.

Figuring out the Hebrew alphabet's shapes, sounds, and stories

The Hebrew alphabet is one of the oldest alphabets still in use today. Even though the letters look different from the Latin characters that comprise the English alphabet, don't be intimidated! Just spend some time memorizing the shapes and sounds of these Hebrew letters and reading Hebrew will be easier!

Like many ancient alphabets, the Hebrew alphabet is written from right to left. Hebrew consists of 22 letters, all of which are consonants. Vowels aren't written within the consonant letters; rather, they're written in the form of dots and dashes below the consonant letters. For a more complete discussion of Hebrew vowels, see "Those dots and dashes they call vowels" later in this chapter.

The pronunciation I provide in this book is the Sephardic (Mediterranean) pronunciation, which is spoken in Israel today. Ashkenazi (European) pronunciation differs slightly; the vowels, for example, have different pronunciations, and a few consonants are different as well. I use Sephardic pronunciation in this book.

Deciphering the consonant letters

Table 1-5 shows the Hebrew letters and their sounds.

TABLE 1-5   **The Hebrew Alphabet**

Name of the Letter	Pronunciation	Hebrew Character	The Sound It Makes
Aleph	*ah*-lehf	א	Makes no sound.
Bet	*beht*	בּ	Makes a B sound as in *boat*.
Vet	*veht*	ב	Makes a V sound as in *veterinarian*.
Gimmel	*gee*-mehl	ג	Makes a G sound as in *girl*.
Dalet	*dah*-leht	ד	Makes a D sound as in *door*.
Hey	*hey*	ה	Makes a soft H sound as in *hello*.
Vav	*vahv*	ו	Also makes a V sound as in *veterinarian*. (Don't ask me why.)
Zayin	*zah*-een	ז	Makes a Z sound as in *zipper*.
Chet	*ḥeht*	ח	Makes a strong guttural H"sound. In this book, this letter is represented as **ḥ**.
Tet	*teht*	ט	Makes a T sound as in *teaspoon*.
Yod	*yohd*	י	Makes a Y sound at the beginning of a word, as in *young*. This letter also behaves like a vowel at times. I discuss it in "Those dots and dashes they call vowels" later in this chapter.
Kaf	*kahf*	כּ	Makes a K sound as in *kite*.
Khaf	*khahf*	כ	Makes a strong guttural H sound. This letter is represented in this book as kh.
Lamed	*lah*-mehd	ל	Makes an L sound as in *lemon*.
Mem	*mehm*	מ	Makes an M sound as in *mouse*.
Nun	*noon*	נ	Makes an N sound as in *no*. (And you thought only Catholics had nuns.)
Samekh	*sah*-mehḥ	ס	Makes an S sound as in *soda*.
Ayin	*ah*-yeen	ע	Makes a barely audible guttural sound in the back of the throat. (For practical purposes, as most non-native speakers can't make this sound, this letter is a silent letter. You pronounce the vowels that are placed below it, but the letter itself doesn't make a sound.)

(continued)

TABLE 1-5 *(continued)*

Name of the Letter	Pronunciation	Hebrew Character	The Sound It Makes
Pey	*pay*	פּ	Makes a P sound as in *popsicle*.
Fey	*fay*	פ	Makes an F sound as in *fish*.
Tzadi	tzah-dee	צ	Makes a hard Tz sound as in *pizza*. In this book, I represent it as tz.
Kof	*kohf*	ק	Makes a K sound as in *Kansas*.
Reish	*raysh*	ר	Makes an R sound as in *round*. This letter is actually a guttural letter. Roll it like a Spanish R and pronounce it from the back of the throat.
Shin	*sheen*	שׁ	(Not Charlie's brother or Martin's long-lost son.) When the dot is on the right side of the letter, it makes a Sh sound. as in *show*. In this book, I represent it as sh.
Sin	*seen*	שׂ	When the dot is on the left side of the letter, it makes an S sound as in *Sam*.
Tav	*tahv*	ת	Makes a T sound as in *toe*.

Those dots and dashes they call vowels

Originally, Hebrew had no vowels. Vowels, in the form of dots and lines below the consonants, were added to Hebrew writing in the seventh century CE. Before then, people read without vowels. Even today, most books, magazines, and newspapers in Modern Hebrew — not to mention the Torah scroll — are written without vowels.

Modern Hebrew has both long and short vowels. As a general rule, a long vowel can make up one syllable, but a short vowel needs either another vowel or a שְׁוָא (shuh-*vah*; *two vertical dots below a consonant*) to form a syllable. For more on the שְׁוָא, see "Introducing the Shvah" later in this chapter.

As I mentioned earlier, vowels are divided into long and short vowels. This categorization doesn't have to do with their pronunciation but with the fact that long vowels are usually in open syllables — syllables that end with a vowel — and short vowels are usually in closed syllables — syllables that end with a consonant. The long vowel חִירִיק מָלֵא (Chirik Maleh), however, holds its sound longer than the corresponding short vowel חִרִיק חַסֵר (hirek haser). Table 1-6 shows the long vowels.

TABLE 1-6 **The Long Vowels**

Name of the Vowel	Pronunciation	In Hebrew	The Sound It Makes
Hirik Maleh	ḥee-*reek* mah-*leh*	אִי	Makes an Ee sound as in *see*
Holam	ḥoh-*lahm*	א	Makes an O sound as in *more*
Kamatz Gadol	kah-*mahtz*	אָ	Makes an Ah sound as in *saw*
Shuruk	shoo-*rook*	אוּ	Makes an Oo sound as in *mood*
Tzere	tzay-*reh*	אֵ	Makes an A sound as in *cape*
Vav Cholam	vahv ḥoh-*lahm*	אוֹ	Makes an O sound as in *snow*

Note: In this table, I used the letter א (*aleph*) so you could see how the vowels look when they're attached to a consanant. (The vowels are the little squiggles and dots around the א.) Unlike in English, Hebrew vowels can never be written alone; they're always attached to a consonant.

Table 1–7 shows the short vowels.

TABLE 1-7 **The Short Vowels**

Name of the Vowel	Pronunciation	In Hebrew	The Sound It Makes
Herik Haser	ḥee-*reek* ḥah-*sehr*	אִ	Makes an Ee sound as in *see*
Kamatz Katan	kah-*mahtz* kah-*tahn*	אָ	Makes an O sound as in *more*
Kubutz	koo-*bootz*	אֻ	Makes an Oo sound as in *mood*
Patach	pah-*tahḥ*	אַ	Makes an Ah sound as in *saw*
Segol	seh-*gohl*	אֶ	Makes an Eh sound as in *end*

Note: In this table, I used the letter א (*aleph*) so you could see how the vowels look when they're attached to a consanant. (The vowels are the little squiggles and dots around the א.)

Sometimes, the Kamatz Patah, Kamatz Katan, or the Segol is paired with a Shvah. This pairing doesn't change the pronunciation.

TIP

The Kamatz Katan looks identical to the Kamatz. If you see something that looks like a Kamatz at the beginning of a word followed by a Shvah or between two Shvah, it's probably a Kamatz Katan and should be pronounced O.

Introducing the Shvah

TECHNICAL STUFF

The *Shvah* looks like a colon (:), and you find it below letters. Hebrew actually has three types of Shvahs (but they all look the same):

>> Shvah Na (sh*vah nah*), which opens a syllable

>> Shvah Nach (sh*vah nah*ḥ), which closes a syllable

>> Shvah Merahef (sh*vah* mehr-rah-*ḥehf*), known as the *flying shvah*, which results from two Shvah Nas being next to each other in a word

The Shvahs don't make their own sound but are essentially placeholders for the consonant above them. The Shvah Naḥ, however, holds the sound a little bit longer. You can tell a Shvah Naḥ because it usually comes in the middle or at the end of a word. A Shvah Na is at the beginning of a word or syllable

Doing it with a Dagesh

The little dot that you see in the middle of letters is called a *Dagesh.* Most of the time, this dot doesn't change the pronunciation of the consonant except for three letters. I discuss this point later in this section.

Hebrew has two types of D'geshim (duh–*gehsh*-eem; *the plural form of Dagesh*):

>> Dagesh Kal (dah-*gehsh kahl*): Appears at the beginning of all words and at the beginning of all syllables in the following letters: ב (Bet), ג (Gimmel), ד (Dalet), כ (Kaf), פ (Pey), and ת (Tav).

>> Dagesh ḥazak (*dah*-gehsh *ḥah-zahk*): Appears after the word *the*, which in Hebrew is a prefix consisting of the letter Hey and the vowel Patach below it.

Don't get too hung up on this distinction, because all D'geshim look the same!

TECHNICAL STUFF

Sometimes in Hebrew, a letter acts like a weak letter, such as a ה (Hey) or a נ (Nun), and disappears in the course of verb conjugation. (By "weak letter," I mean that it sometimes drops out during conjugation.) When a weak letter disappears, a Dagesh Chazak appears in the letter that comes after the dropped letter. Also, certain word patterns called Mishkalim (meesh-*kah*-leem), in which all the words belong to a certain category (such as professions, colors, and physical challenges), have a Dagesh in one of the letters. Words that describe physical challenges, such as *blindness* and *deafness*, for example, always take a Dagesh ḥazak in the middle letter of the word.

HEBREW AS THE HOLY TONGUE — DON'T BITE IT

Judaism has always regarded Hebrew as a sacred language. Hebrew is often referred to as לְשׁוֹן הַקֹּדֶשׁ (le-*shohn* hah-*koh*-desh; *the Holy Tongue*), and even the Hebrew word for *letter*, אוֹת (*oht*), means "sign" or "wonder." In fact, during the period of Hebrew's revival as a spoken language, some people objected, saying that Hebrew was simply too sacred for saying things like "Take out the garbage."

Also, all Hebrew letters have numeric value. A particular form of Jewish numerology called גְּמַטְרִיָּה (gee-*meht*-ree-yah) plays on the words' numeric values. Both the Hebrew word for *wine* (יַיִן; *yah*-yeen) and *secret* (סוֹד; *sohd*) have the same numerical value. The Talmud has a saying, "When the wine goes in, secrets come out!" Other Jewish sacred writings claim that the Hebrew letters are the manifestation of divine energy patterns and even that the universe's DNA is composed of Hebrew letters.

A 13th-century mystic, Rabbi Abraham Abulafia, created a form of Jewish meditation, similar to yoga, based on the Hebraic forms. And a 16th-century mystic, Rabbi Isaac Luria, developed another form of meditation based on visualizing the Hebrew letters.

Are you totally confused yet? What difference does adding a Dagesh make? In the Sephardic pronunciation that Israelis and most Hebrew speakers today use, adding a Dagesh almost never makes a difference in pronunciation. But in a few cases, when a Dagesh is placed within a letter (always a consonant), it changes the way you pronounce that consonant. When you add a Dagesh to the letter ו (Vet), for example, the V sound becomes a B sound, and you pronounce the letter like *bet.* When you pair a Dagesh with the letter ḥaf, the *ḥ* sound becomes a K sound, so the sound of that letter becomes *kaf.* Finally, the letter פ (Fey) with a Dagesh becomes a פ (Peh).

Reading and writing from right to left

Hebrew, like other ancient Semitic languages (such as Acadian, Samarian, Uga-ritic, and Arabic), is written from right to left. Why? Is there a preponderance of lefties in the region? No!

Maybe you've read the Bible, in particular the part where Moses comes down from the mountain with the Ten Commandments in hand. And if you haven't read the Bible, perhaps you've seen the Mel Brooks film version in *History of the World: Part 1.* When Moses came down from the mountain, what was he holding? A copy of an email from the Almighty? A scroll of papyrus? No. He was holding two stone tablets! You may ask, "Well, how did the Ten Commandments get on the stone tablets? Did Moses have a special pen or something?"

When ancient Hebrew emerged, it was written by chiseling it in stone. If the writer was a rightie, they would have used their dominant hand — their right hand — to pound the mallet onto the stylus they held with their left hand. And because ancient Hebrew society (like all societies) favored righties, its language was written from right to left. The Phoenicians and then the Greeks followed suit. Then, for a while, the Greeks wrote in both directions, switching when they got to the end of the tablet or page. That practice makes sense, if you think about it; why press the Return key on your electric typewriter to go all the way back to start a new line when you can just keep going where you are in the backward direction! Then the Greeks decided that left to right would be their standard, but Hebrew scribes kept on writing right to left. Tradition! (OK, folks today are just as likely to have an electric typewriter as the ancient Greeks, but that's neither here nor there.)

TIP

If you want some practice reading, check out `https://www.easylearnhebrew.com`, an online course in Hebrew. The site can help you read Hebrew in no time!

FUN & GAMES

Write the sound that each of the following Hebrew characters makes:

ב (B) _____   ג (G) _____   ל (L)_____   ב (V) _____

ד (D) _____   ה (H) _____   ר (R)_____   א (° silent) _____

You can find the answers in Appendix C.

Chapter **2**

The Nitty-Gritty: Basic Hebrew Grammar

By birth, Hebrew is part of the Semitic family, along with Arabic, Aramaic, and some other Middle Eastern languages. To this day, Hebrew is quite similar to other Semitic languages in terms of the way words — especially verbs — are formed. Hebrew nouns and verbs are marked for gender (feminine or masculine, no neuter), just like their Semitic cousins.

Today, Hebrew, like many world languages, is grappling with inclusivity of nonbinary gender identities and the ways that language can acknowledge and accommodate them. In Israel, nonbinary people often speaking in alternating gender conjugations and there is no "singular they" as "they" is gendered in Hebrew. In the Diaspora, the Nonbinary Hebrew project has proposed a way for Hebrew to accommodate nonbinary gender identities, though their proposal has not (yet?) caught on in Israel or worldwide. For a chart of nonbinary Hebrew grammar and systematics, check out the Nonbinary Hebrew Project at www.nonbinaryhebrew. com/grammar-systematics.

The people who revived Hebrew as a modern language in the 19th and 20th centuries spoke and thought mostly in Yiddish, Russian, German, and other European languages. Those languages became the "adoptive parents" of Hebrew today. You notice their influence most strongly in the pronunciation of modern Hebrew and in the word order within sentences (syntax).

Making Sense of Hebrew Syntax

The *syntax* (the arrangement of words to make sentences), or תַּחְבִּיר (tahch–*beer*), of a Hebrew sentence is quite different from that of English. In this section, I run you through the basics of word order — what syntax looks like in English and how Hebrew is different. I also cover how to say *there is* and *there isn't*, because if you can use this simple sentence construction, you can say a lot. Just plug in the noun of your choice, and you'll be speaking Hebrew!

Putting your sentences in order

When you read or hear Modern Hebrew sentences, you may think that they're oddly constructed compared with sentences in English or any other European language. In English, so much depends on word order. Hebrew, on the other hand, is more flexible about word order. In Hebrew, for example, you could say either of the following:

>> מֶמְשָׁלָה חֲדָשָׁה קָמָה (mehm-*shah*-la**h** ah-dah-*shah* kah-*mah; literally:* A government new arises.)

>> קָמָה מֶמְשָׁלָה חֲדָשָׁה (kah-*mah* mehm-*shah*-la**h** hah-dah-*shah; literally:* Arises government new.)

Both phrases mean the same thing: A new government rises. The order of the words doesn't affect the meaning.

Look at another example in English. "Mollie kissed Fred" isn't the same as "Fred kissed Mollie," is it? It certainly isn't to Mollie — or, for that matter, to Fred.

In Hebrew, sometimes a verb, especially one without an object, comes before its subject — not after it, as in English. Under certain conditions, you can identify the *direct object* (the person or thing acted on, as opposed to person or thing doing the acting) because the word אֶת (*eht*) precedes the direct object. You know that it was Mollie who did the kissing whether I say

➤➤ מוֹלִי נִשְׁקָה אֶת פְרֶאד (moh-lee neesh-kah eht fred; literally: Mollie kissed Fred.)

➤➤ מוֹלִי אֶת פְרֶאד נִשְׁקָה (moh-lee eht fred neesh-kah; literally: Mollie Fred kissed.)

➤➤ אֶת פְרֶאד נִשְׁקָה מוֹלִי (eht fred neesh-kah moh-lee; Fred [is] kissed [by] Mollie.)

All these sentences, despite their different word order, mean essentially the same thing: Mollie kissed Fred.

TIP

To say *there is* or *there are,* use the word יֵשׁ (yehsh) before the noun you want to talk about. To say *there isn't* or *there aren't,* use the word אֵין (ayn) before the noun. For example:

➤➤ יֵשׁ בָּנָנוֹת (yehsh bah-nah-noht; There are bananas.)

➤➤ אֵין בָּנָנוֹת (ayn bah-nah-noht; There aren't any bananas.)

Now, you can find any noun in this book, put a יֵשׁ or an אֵין in front of it, and you'll be speaking Hebrew!

Questioning

When you make a question, you don't change the order of the words, as in English. You can ask a question in a few ways. The first way is by simply taking a statement and putting a question mark in your voice (by raising your voice at the end of the sentence). Thus, when asked with the proper intonation, this statement can be a question: ? יֵשׁ חָלָב בַּמְּקָרֵר (yesh hah-lahv bah-mahk-rehr?; There's milk in the refrigerator?).

Another way to turn this statement into a question is to add the word נָכוֹן (nah-chohn; correct) to the end of the statement. In grammarspeak, this word is called a *tag.* For example:

➤➤ ? יֵשׁ חָלָב בַּמְּקָרֵר נָכוֹן (yesh chah-lahv bah-mahk-rehr, nah-chohn?; There's milk in the refrigerator, correct?)

Yet another way to turn a statement into a question is to add the question word, הַאִים (hah-eem), in front of the sentence — for example ? הַאִים יֵשׁ חָלָב בַּמְּקָרֵר (hah-eem yehsh chah-lahv bah-mahk-rehr; Is there milk in the refrigerator?). This last option is the most formal option, so you won't hear it often.

Although Hebrew differs from English in that you don't need to flip the order in a statement to turn it into a question, the word-order flexibility of Hebrew allows the speaker to stress a particular part of the sentence by putting it at the beginning.

If someone just said there are no strawberries in the fridge, for example, you might ask ? יֵשׁ בָּנָנוֹת (*yesh* bah-nah-*noht*; *literally*: Bananas?; But are there bananas?). Or you might ask ? אֵין בְּנֶנּוּ (*ehn* bah-nah-*noht*?; *literally*: Bananas there aren't?; Aren't there bananas?).

Recognizing Parts of Speech

In Hebrew, you can recognize the different parts of speech — such as nouns, verbs, and adjectives — by their distinct patterns. Sometimes, however, a word is *both* a verb and a noun, and adjectives and adverbs can take on many forms, so I can't offer any easy clues for distinguishing the various parts of speech. You just need to memorize the vocabulary; then you'll know.

Naming nouns

In Hebrew, all nouns are either masculine or feminine. They're conjugated according to number (singular and plural). The noun *book* (a masculine noun), for example, can be conjugated two ways:

סֵפֶר (*seh*-fehr; book)

סְפָרִים (sfah-*reem*; books)

Look at this example of a feminine noun:

מַזְלֵג (mahz-*lehg*; fork)

מַזְלְגוֹת (mahz-leh-*goht*; forks)

REMEMBER

When masculine nouns are conjugated in the plural, they usually have an יֹם (*eem*) ending, and when feminine nouns are conjugated in the plural, they usually have an וֹת (*oht*) ending. The Nonbinary Hebrew Project proposes adding ה *to* the suffixes of most words to create a third, nonbinary gender category: מִגְדָּר רָחָב (*migdar rahav*).

Check out Table 2-1 for some common Hebrew nouns.

TABLE 2-1

Identifying Some Common Nouns

Hebrew	Pronunciation	Translation
בַּיִת	*bah*-yeet	house
דֶּרֶךְ	*deh*-rech	way, road
אִישׁ	eesh	man
אִשָׁה	ee-*shah*	woman
כֶּסֶף	*keh*-sehf	money
מַפְתֵּחַ	mahf-*teh*-ach	key
מַגֶּבֶת	mah-*geh*-veht	towel
מְקָרֵר	mahk-*rehr*	refrigerator
מַזְגָן	mahz-*gahn*	air conditioner
מַזְלֵג	mahz-*lehg*	fork
מְכוֹנִית	meh-*hoh*-neet	car
מִטְבָּח	meet-*bahch*	kitchen
מִבְרֶשֶׁת	meev-*reh*-sheht	brush
אֹכֶל	oh-**ḥ**ehl	food
סֵפֶר	*seh*-fehr	book
שֶׁמֶשׁ	*sheh*-mehsh	sun

Directing your objects

In English, when we speak of a direct object, we mean a noun that is acted on by the verb. In the sentence "He ate a cookie," for example, the word *cookie* is a direct object. In Hebrew, you say this sentence like this:

הוא אָכַל עוּגִיָה (hoo ah-*hahl* oo-gee-*yah; literally:* He ate cookie.)

Notice that Hebrew doesn't have a word for *a* in this example. The *a* is simply implied.

You can always spot an indirect object in Hebrew because it's always preceded by a preposition. If you want to say "He gave a boy a cookie," the word *boy* is an indirect object. He is being *given* something, but he isn't directly acted on. Another test for an indirect object: It can have *to* before it ("He gave a cookie *to* a boy"). In Hebrew, you say that phrase this way: הוּא נָתַן לַיֶּלֶד עוּגִיָה (hoo nah-*tahn* lah-*yeh*-lehd oo-*gee*-ah; *literally:* He gave to boy cookie.).

Defining definite objects

In Hebrew, you can tell when a noun is being used as a definite object (*the* hat as opposed to *a* hat) because it has the prefix ה (*hah*) attached to the word it modifies. Take the noun כּוֹבַע (*koh*-vah; hat). If you want to indicate that הַכּוֹבַע is a definite object, just add the prefix: הַכּוֹבַע (hah-*koh*-vah; the hat).

Getting help from the definite article

You can easily spot a definite object by the placement of a definite article ה (*hah*; the) in front of it. If that definite object is also a direct object, אֶת (*eht*) also precedes it. In the following sentence, when you understand that הוּא רוֹצֶה (*hoo roh-tzeh*) means *he wants*, you can figure out the meaning of the entire sentence: הוּא רוֹצֶה אֶת הַכּוֹבַע (hoo roh-*tzeh* eht hah-*koh*-vah; He wants the hat.). Notice the אֶת is in front of the הַכּוֹבַע. (**Note:** אֶת is placed only before a *definite* direct object.) אֶת is kind of like a road sign that says "D.D.O.A: Definite Direct Object Ahead."

Unfortunately, Hebrew doesn't have indefinite articles (*a* or *an*). But Hebrew sentences certainly have indirect objects! Instead, you can tell that an object is nonspecific (*a hat* as opposed to *the hat*) by the omission of אֶת (*eht*) or any other preposition. So, if you want to say "He wants a hat" in Hebrew, the sentence looks like this: הוּא רוֹצֶה כּוֹבַע (hoo roh-*tzeh koh*-vah).

Perfecting your pronouns

When you don't want to name nouns, you can always call in their pinch-hitters: the *pronouns* (words that stand in for nouns).

Clarifying this and that

Hebrew has a set of pronouns for "this" or "that" that are specialized according to masculine singular (MS), feminine singular (FS), and masculine plural for both masculine and feminine (NB). Although nonbinary pronouns are in their nascence in Hebrew, I'm including them here along with binary gendered pronouns:

זֶה (zeh; this [is]) (MS)

זֹאת (zoht; this [is]) (FS)

זֹאֶת (zeht. This is) (NB)

אֵלֶּא (ay-*leh*; these [are]) (MP/FP)

These words can function as the subject of an "is" sentence or as adjectives:

>> זֶה מַפְתֵּחַ (zeh mahf-tay-ah): This is a key.

>> הַמַּפְתֵּחַ הַזֶּה (hah -mahf-tay-ah hah-zeh)-: this key

Getting personal

Personal pronouns are nouns that apply to particular people — or, um, *persons*. In English, the personal pronouns are "I", "you," "he," "she," "we," and "they." In Hebrew, there are four forms for the personal pronoun "you": masculine singular (MS), feminine singular (FS), masculine plural (MP), and feminine plural (FP). The personal pronoun "they" has two forms: masculine and feminine (MP and FP). Table 2-2 shows *subjective case* (when the pronoun serves as the subject of the sentence) personal pronouns in Hebrew.

TABLE 2-2

Personal Pronouns Used as Subjects

Hebrew	Pronunciation	Translation
אֲנִי	ah-*nee*	I (M/F)
אַתָּה	ah-*tah*	you (MS)
אַתְּ	aht	you (FS)
הוּא	hoo	he
הִיא	hee	she
אֲנַחְנוּ	ah-*nahch*-noo	we (MP/FP)
אַתֶּם	ah-*tehm*	you (MP)
אַתֶּן	ah-*tehn*	you (FP)
הֵם	hehm	they (MP)
הֵן	hehn	they (FP)

Nonbinary Hebrew pronouns are emerging and gaining in acceptance. Suggestions from the Nonbinary Hebrew Project are as follows:

אַתֶּה	ah-*teh*	you (singular nonbinary)
אַתְּמֶן	Aht -*mehn*	you (plural nonbinary)

הֵה	heh	they (singular)
הֵהֶמֵּן	hay *mehn*	they (nonbinary plural)

Hebrew also has what English calls *objective case pronouns*, personal pronouns used as the direct object of a verb ("she saw me"). I'm talking about the English words "me," "you," "him," "her," "us," and "them." Like other Hebrew pronouns, there are four forms of "you" in the objective case: masculine singular (MS), feminine singular (FS), masculine plural (MP), and feminine plural (FP). Table 2-3 lists the objective case pronouns.

TABLE 2-3

Personal Pronouns Used as Objects

Hebrew	Pronunciation	Translation
אוֹתִי	oh-*tee*	me (M/F/NB)
אוֹתְךָ	oht-*ha*	you (MS)
אוֹתָךְ	oh-*tah*	you (FS)
אוֹתוֹ	oh-*toh*	him
אוֹתָה	oh-*tah*	her
אוֹתָנוּ	oh-*tah*-noo	us (MP/FP)
אֶתְכֶם	eht-*hem*	you (MP)
אֶתְכֶן	eht-*chen*	you (FP)
אוֹתָם	oh-*tahm*	them (MP)
אוֹתָן	oh-*tahn*	them (FP)

Showing possession

Hebrew, like English, has stand-alone possessive pronouns, such as "mine," "yours," "his," "ours," and "theirs." You'll notice a few differences, however. First, the stand-alone possessive pronoun comes after the noun and not before, as in English. In addition, if an object has possession, it has to be a definite object, so you must add the prefix הַכּוֹבַע שֶׁלִּי (hah-*koh*-vah sheh-*lee*; *literally:* the hat mine).

In addition, Hebrew differentiates between the singular and plural "your" in both the masculine and feminine forms. Check out Table 2-4 to see the differences.

TABLE 2-4

Stand-Alone Possessive Pronouns

Hebrew	Pronunciation	Translation
שֶׁלִּי	sheh-*lee*	my, mine
שֶׁלְּךָ	shel-*cha*	your, yours (MS)
שֶׁלָּךְ	sheh-*lach*	your, yours (FS)
שֶׁלּוֹ	sheh-*loh*	his
שֶׁלָּהּ	sheh-*lah*	her, hers
שֶׁלָּנוּ	she-*lah*-noo	ours
שֶׁלָּכֶם	sheh-lah-***h****em*	your, yours (MP)
שֶׁלָּכֶן	sheh-lah-*hen*	your, yours (FP)
שֶׁלָּהֶם	sheh-lah-*hem*	their, theirs (MP)
שֶׁלָּהֶן	sheh-lah-*hen*	their, theirs (FP)

Hebrew doesn't have different words for "my" and "mine." Both concepts are expressed in the Hebrew word שֶׁלִּי (sheh-*lee*; my, mine). Also, "your" and "yours" are expressed with the same word.

TECHNICAL STUFF

In English, you sometimes pair a pronoun with another noun to show possession, as in "my teacher," "your hat," "his paper," and so on. In Hebrew, you can show that a noun belongs to someone by attaching a suffix to the noun. The suffix changes according to the personal pronoun it represents and is called a *pronomial suffix*. The Nonbinary Hebrew Project has created nonbinary pronomial suffixes. The forms for male/female and nonbinary pronomial suffixes in both singular and plural form are shown in Table 2-5 and Table 2-6.

TABLE 2-5

Male and Female Pronomial Suffixes

ִי	*ee*	mine
וֹ	*oh*	his
הּ	*ah*	hers
ְךָ	*hah*	yours (MS)
ֵךְ	*ech*	yours (FS)
כֶם	*hem*	yours (MP)
כֶן	*hen*	yours (FP)
הֶם	*hem*	theirs (M)
הֶן	*hen*	theirs (F)

TABLE 2-6

Nonbinary Pronominal Suffixes

Second person singular	ךְ (heh)
Second person plural	כְמֶן (hemen)
Third person singular (single subject)	ה ֶ (eh)
Third person plural (single subject)	מֶן (men)
Third person singular (plural subject)	יהֶ ֶ (he'eh)
Third person plural (plural subject)	יהֶמֶן (hemen)

TIP

Check out this YouTube video on Hebrew pronomial suffixes: www.youtube.com/watch?v=CaLTQF39Hj4.

Applying adjectives

In Hebrew, the noun comes first, followed by the adjective, which is the opposite of English. So, for example, you say יַלְדָּה טוֹבָה (yahl-*dah* toh-*vah*; girl good), meaning "good girl." You also need to know that adjectives need to match the nouns they modify, both in gender and in number. Table 2-7 lists some common adjectives. For more on number and gender, see the section "Understanding Gender and Number" later in this chapter.

TABLE 2-7

Exploring Some Common Adjectives

Hebrew	Pronunciation	Translation
טוֹב	tohv	good (MS)
טוֹבָה	toh-*vah*	good (FS)
טוֹבִים	toh-*veem*	good (MP)
טוֹבוֹת	toh-*voht*	good (FP)
רַע	rah	bad (MS)
רָעָה	rah-*ah*	bad (FS)
רָעִים	rah-*eem*	bad (MP)
רָעוֹת	rah-*oht*	bad (FP)
גָּדוֹל	gah-*dohl*	big (MS)
גְּדוֹלָה	guh-doh-*lah*	big (FS)

Hebrew	Pronunciation	Translation
גְּדוֹלִים	guh-doh-*eem*	big (MP)
גְּדוֹלוֹת	guh-doh*loht*	big (FP)
קָטָן	kah-*tahn*	small (MS)
קְטַנָּה	kuh-tah-*nah*	small (FS)
קְטַנִּים	kuh-tah-*neem*	small (MP)
קְטַנּוֹת	kuh-tah-*noht*	small (FP)
מָהִיר	mah-*heer*	quick (MS)
מְהִירָה	muh-hee-*rah*	quick (FS)
מְהִירִים	muh-hee-*reem*	quick (MP)
רוֹת	muh-hee-*roht*	quick (FP)
אִטִּי	ee-*tee*	slow (MS)
אִטִּי	ee-*teet*	slow (FS)
אִטִּיִּים	ee- tee-*yeem*	slow (MP)
אִטִּיּוֹת	ee-tee-ee-*yoht*	slow (FP)

TIP

In addition, use this adjective pattern: Add an י (*ee*) ending to change a noun into an adjective. אָבִיב (ah-*veev*) is "spring" (the season), (ah–vee-*vee*) is "springlike," יַלְדוּת (yahl-*doot*) is "childhood," and יַלְדוּתִי (yahl–doo-*tee*) is "juvenile." Cool, huh?

Pinpointing Hebrew verbs

The Hebrew verb is an amazing animal! Verbs are conjugated in the present tense according to gender (male and female) and number (singular and plural). In the future and past tenses, verbs have gender, number, and person (first, second, or third). In the imperative (command form), you have only three forms to choose among: masculine singular (MS), feminine singular (FS), and plural (P). When you conjugate a verb, it must match the gender and number of the subject. See Appendix A for examples.

REMEMBER

Hebrew doesn't have a word for "is" or "are."

Putting verbs through their tenses

Hebrew has five verb tenses: the infinitive tense ("to" plus the verb); the past tense; the present tense; the future tense; and the imperative, which is the command form (as in "Shut the door"). In this section, I conjugate לִכְתֹּב (leech-*tohv*; to write) to show the conjugations because לִכְתֹּב is a regular verb with no exceptions.

LIVING IN THE PRESENT

In the present tense, Hebrew verbs are conjugated in four ways: masculine singular, feminine singular, masculine plural, and feminine plural. For example:

כּוֹתֵב (koh-*tehv*; write) (MS)

כּוֹתֶבֶת (koh-*teh*-veht; write) (FS)

כּוֹתְבִים (koht-*veem*; writes) (MP)

כּוֹתְבוֹת (koht-*voht*; writes) (FP)

PUTTIN' IT IN THE PAST

In the past tense, Hebrew verbs are conjugated according to number, gender, and person. You can either say the personal pronoun (I, you, he, she, we, you, they), as in אֲנִי כָּתַבְתִּי (ah-*nee* kah-*tahv*-tee; I wrote), or drop it, in which case the subject is implied: כָּתַבְתִּי (kah-*tahv*-tee; [I] wrote).

כָּתַבְתִּי (kah-*tahv*-tee; [I] wrote)

כָּתַבְתָּ (kah-*tahv*-ta; [you] wrote) (MS)

כָּתַבְתְּ (kah-*tahvt*; [you] wrote) (FS)

כָּתַב (kah-*tahv*; [he] wrote)

כָּתְבָה (kaht-*vah*; [she] wrote)

כָּתַבְנוּ (kah-*tahv*-noo; [we] wrote) (MP/FP)

כְּתַבְתֶּם (kah-*tahv*-tehm; [you] wrote) (MP)

כְּתַבְתֶּן (kah-*tahv*-tehn; [you] wrote) (FP)

כָּתְבוּ (kaht-*voo*; [they] wrote) (MP/FP)

LOOKING TO THE FUTURE

Like the past tense, the future tense has number, gender, and person, and you can either include the personal pronoun (אֲנִי אֶכְתֹּב, ah-*nee* ehḥ-*tohv*; I will write) or drop it (אֶכְתֹּב, ehḥ-*tohv*; [I] will write) because it's implied. Here are some examples:

אֶכְתֹּב (ech-*tohv*; [I] will write)

תִּכְתֹּב (tee**ḥ**-*tohv*; [you] will write) (MS)

תִּכְתְּבִי (teeh-tuh-*vee*; [you] will write) (FS)

יִכְתֹּב (yee**h**-*tohv*; [he] will write)

תִּכְתֹּב (tee**h**-*tohv*; [she] will write)

נִכְתֹּב (nee**h**-*tohv*; [we] will write)

תִּכְתְּבוּ (tee**h**-tuh-*voo*; [you] will write) (MP/FP)

יִכְתְּבוּ (yee**h**-tuh-*voo*; [they] will write) (MP/FP)

COMMAND PERFORMANCE

To make a command (the imperative mood), you can choose among three forms: "you" (MS), "you" (FS), and "you" (MP/FP). Believe it or not, many Modern Hebrew speakers consider this tense to be quite rude — like something an army commander or strict teacher would say. Generally speaking, you should avoid the command tense. Use the future tense instead, because it's perceived to be more polite. But if you really want to, you can conjugate the command form like this:

כתוב (kuh-*tohv*; [you] Write!) (MS)

כִּתְבֵי (keet-*vee*; [you] Write!) (FS)

כִּתְבוּ (keet-*voo*; [you] Write!) (MP/FP)

Looking at some common verbs

The beauty of the Hebrew verb lies in its versatility as well as its simplicity. In Table 2-8, I include some common Hebrew verbs listed in their present tense, masculine singular form.

TABLE 2-8

Some Common Present-Tense Verbs

Hebrew	Pronunciation	Translation
הוֹלֵךְ	hoh-*lehch*	goes, walks
קוֹרֵא	koh-*reh*	reads
כּוֹתֵב	koh-*tehv*	writes
מַחֲלִיט	mah**h**-*leet*	decides
מַדְלִיק	mahd-*leek*	lights

(continued)

TABLE 2-8 *(continued)*

Hebrew	Pronunciation	Translation
מַרְגִּישׁ	mahr-*geesh*	feels
מְדַבֵּר	meh-dah-*behr*	speaks
מִתְלַבֵּשׁ	meet-lah-*behsh*	gets dressed
מִצְטָרֵף	meetz-tah-*rehf*	joins in
נִכְנָס	neech-*nahs*	enters
נוֹסֵעַ	noh-*seh*-ah	travels
יוֹשֵׁב	yoh-*shehv*	sits

Detecting adverbs

Like English, most Hebrew adverbs are similar to adjectives — just with different endings. When you use an adjective as an adverb, you don't conjugate it; it stays in the masculine singular form. Here are a couple of examples:

הוּא כּוֹתֵב יָפֶה (hoo koh-*tehv* yah-*feh;* He writes nicely.)

הִיא כּוֹתֶבֶת יָפֶה (hee koh-*teh*-veht yah-*feh;* She writes nicely.)

Note that although the pronoun and the verb conjugation changes — in this case from masculine singular to feminine singular — the adverb remains unchanged.

TIP

You can also make an adverb by adding the prefix בְּ' (*buh;* in or with) to a noun. שִׂמְחָה (seem-*chah;* happiness), for example, becomes בְּשִׂמְחָה (buh-seem-*chah;* happily).

A third way to make an adverb is to take an adjective and add the suffix **ut** (*oot*) to make a noun. Then you add the prefix בְּשִׂמְחָה (*buh;* in or with) to make the adverb. עָדִין (ah-*deen;* gentle), for example, becomes עֲדִינוּת (ah-dee-*noot;* gentleness), and with a prefix בַּ, it becomes בעדינות (buh-ah-dee-*noot;* gently).

A fourth way to make an adverb is to add the word בְּאֹפֶן (buh-*oh*-fehn; in the way of) in front of an adjective. אוֹטוֹמָתִי (oh-toh-*mah*-tee; automatic), for example, becomes בְּאֹפֶן אוֹטוֹמָתִי (buh-*oh*-fehn oh-toh-*mah*-tee; automatically).

Table 2-9 lists some common adverbs.

TABLE 2-9 ## Common Adverbs

Hebrew	Pronunciation	Translation
בְּאֹפֶן סֵדֶר	buh-*oh*-fehn sah-*deer*	regularly
בְּסֵדֶר	buh-*seh*-dehr	okay
בְּשִׂמְחָה	buh-sim-*chah*	gladly
בְּסוֹדִיּוּת	buh-soh-dee-*yoot*	secretly
בִּמְהִירוּת	bim-hee-*root*	quickly, speedily
בִּבְרָכָה	beev-rah-*chah*	blessedly
דָּבְקָה	*dahv*-kah	ironically, spitefully
הֵיטֵב	heh-*tehv*	well
לְאַט	luh-*aht*	slowly
מָהִיר	mah-*hehr*	quickly
מְאֻחָר	meh-oo-**h**ar	late
מֻקְדָּם	mook-*dahm*	early
יָפֶה	yah-*feh*	nicely

Spotting prepositions

Prepositions are words that show relations among words (such as "in," "by," and "with," to name a few common English prepositions). In Hebrew, prepositions sometimes stand alone; at other times, they're attached to another word as a prefix. Table 2-10 breaks down prepositions for you.

TABLE 2-10 ## Hebrew Prepositions

Hebrew Preposition	Pronunciation	Translation	Presentation
עַל	*ahl*	on	stands alone
בְּ	*buh*	with/in	prefix
אֶל	*ehl*	to	stands alone
עִם	*eem*	with	stands alone
לְ	*luh*	to	prefix
מִן	*meen*	from	stands alone
מ	*mee*	from	prefix

In English, you combine prepositions with nouns to make *prepositional phrases*, such as "in the box," "by the river," or "with a friend." In Hebrew, if you want to add the word "the" — to form a prepositional phrase — you have to change the vowel sound of the preposition. The *uh* vowel sound becomes an *ah* sound.

So, if a definite direct object is preceded by a preposition, the preposition will include the definite article. "He helped a girl" is הוּא עָזַר לְיַלְדָּה (hoo ah-*zahr* luh-*yahl*-dah; *literally:* He helped to girl.). The preposition in this case is לְ. But if you want to say "He gave assistance to *the* girl," you say הוּא עָזַר לַיַלְדָּה (hoo ah-*zahr* lah-*yahl*-dah; *Literally:* he helped to the girl.). The preposition אֶל is combined with the definite article in this case and becomes לַ (*lah*; to the).

Understanding Gender and Number

In Hebrew, all nouns, adjectives and verbs have *gender*; they're classified as either masculine or feminine. Like many world languages, Hebrew has begun to grapple with nonbinary gender identities, and the Hebrew Nonbinary Project has created a third, nonbinary gender category. In addition, all nouns, adjectives, and verbs have *number*; they're classified as either singular or plural.

Nouns are classified as either masculine or feminine. Their classification as "masculine" or "feminine" doesn't have anything to do with the masculine or feminine nature of the objects. The classification is somewhat random. Usually, you can spot a feminine noun by its ending. A feminine noun often has an ending of ה (*ah*) or ית (*eet*). But you can find exceptions to this rule. A good Hebrew–English dictionary classifies masculine nouns with a Hebrew letter ז (zah-yeen) for זָכָר (zah-*hahr*; masculine) and with a Hebrew letter נ (noon) for נְקֵבָה (nuh-keh-*vah*; feminine). Both the masculine and the feminine forms of the nouns have plural forms.

In Hebrew, adjectives come in four forms: masculine singular, feminine singular, masculine plural, and feminine plural. Look back to the section "Applying adjectives," where I discuss adjectives in greater detail.

REMEMBER

Nouns and adjectives must match in terms of both gender and number. But when you have a group of people or things that are both masculine and feminine, you use the adjective's masculine plural form to describe the group. Thus, the masculine plural is for male-only groups and for male-female groups. The feminine plural is for female-only groups — only.

FUN & GAMES

Turn the following statements into questions:

1. Statement: הוּא רוֹצֶה אֶת הַמְכוֹנִית

He wants the car.

Question: _____

Does he want the car?

2. Statement: יֵשׁ מַגֶּבֶת

There is a towel.

Question: _____

Is there a towel?

You can find the answers in Appendix C.

Chapter **3**

Shalom, Shalom!: Meeting and Greeting

Shalom! If you know this word, which literally means "peace" and "welfare," and is derived from the same root as "wholeness" and "completeness," you're ahead of the game because in Hebrew, you use this word for both hellos and goodbyes, as well as for inquiries about someone's welfare. The many uses of שָׁלוֹם (sha-*lom*) make sense because peace is a central concept in Judaism and an important part of Jewish and Israeli culture. References and hopes for peace fill Jewish prayers, and many popular Israeli songs also express this sentiment.

You can use שָׁלוֹם to say hello, to say goodbye, and to ask ? מַה שְׁלוֹמְךָ (mah sh-lohm-ḥah), which literally means "How's your peace?" but really asks "How are you?" Hebrew features tons of ways to meet and greet people, and in this chapter, I introduce you to several.

CULTURAL WISDOM

Hebrew, like many languages, is gendered, assigning a binary gender to verbs, adjectives and even nouns! Today, the Hebrew-speaking world is reckoning with nonbinary gender identities. Although Hebrew has yet to formally make the leap to a being a completely gender-inclusive language, the Nonbinary Hebrew Project (www.nonbinaryhebrew.com), based in Boulder, Colorado, has taken a stab at it, creating a third gender category. Throughout the book, I'll be including some examples but know that if you use such conjugations in casual conversation, you can't always count on the Hebrew speaker being familiar with these relatively new conjugations.

Greeting and Saying Goodbye

Hebrew offers you many choices of ways to say "hello" and "goodbye." Here are a few things to say in greeting:

» שָׁלוֹם . (shah-*lohm;* Hello; peace.)

» מָה הָעִנְיָנִים ? (*mah* hah-in-yah-*neem;* How are things?)

» מָה נִשְׁמָע ? (*mah* neesh-*mah;* What's up?)

» מה מצב (mah *matz*-zahv What's the situation?)

» מָה שְׁלוֹמְךָ ? (mah shlohm-*ḥah;* How are you? *Literally:* How is your welfare?) (M)

» מָה שְׁלוֹמֵךְ ? (mah shlom-*mehḥ;* How are you? *Literally:* How is your welfare?) (F)

» מָה שְׁלוֹמְכֶה ? (mah shlom-*ḥeh;* How are you? *Literally:* How is your welfare?) (NB)

» מָה שְׁלוֹמְכֶם ? (mah shlohm-*ḥehm;* How are you?) (MP/)

Ah, but parting is such sweet sorrow. When you have to hit the road, use one of these phrases to say good-bye:

» שָׁלוֹם. (shah-*lohm;* Peace.)

» כָּל טוֹב . (*kohl* toov; Be well.)

» לְהִתְרָאוֹת . (leh-hee-trah-*oht;* See you soon.)

Greeting all day long

In Hebrew, as in every other language, the time of day when you greet a person often determines what you say. But Hebrew throws a bit of a twist into the standard mix: It also contains greetings that depend on whether you greet someone before or after the *Jewish Sabbath.* The Sabbath starts when the sun *begins to set* on Friday night and ends about 25 hours later, on Saturday night, when the sun *has completely set.*

In the morning, you can say בֹּקֶר טוֹב (*boh*-kehr tohv; good morning). If someone greets you in this manner, you can say בק בוקר טוב right back to them, or you can say בֹּקֶר אוֹר (*boh*-kehr ohr; morning light). In the afternoon, you can say צָהֳרַיִם טוֹבִים (tzoh-hoh-*rye*-eem toh-*veem;* good afternoon). If someone says these things to you, you can simply repeat the same words in response.

REMEMBER

The pattern of repeating the greeting as a reply holds true for all the time-sensitive greetings. The morning greeting is the only exception because you can reply with either בֹּקֶר אוֹר or בֹּקֶר טוֹב.

So, in the evening, you can say עֶרֶב טוֹב (*eh*-rehv tohv; good evening) whether you're greeting someone or responding to another person's salutation. At night, you can say לַיְלָה טוֹב (*lye*-lah tohv; good night). And if someone is headed off to bed, you can wish them חֲלוֹמוֹת פָּז (ḥa-loh-*moht* pahz; golden dreams)!

Got that? Good. Now I want to outline the Sabbath-related greetings. All day Friday and during the Sabbath, greeting people with the words that wish them a peaceful Sabbath is customary: שַׁבָּת שָׁלוֹם (shah-*baht* shah-*lohm*; have peaceful Sabbath). When the sun sets on Saturday night (and you can see three stars in the sky), the Sabbath is over. On Saturday nights and even on Sundays, it's customary to greet people with a cheery שָׁבוּעַ טוֹב (shah-*voo*-ah tohv), wishing them a *good week*.

CULTURAL WISDOM

The Book of Genesis describes each day as beginning in the evening: "There was evening; there was morning; a first day." Therefore, Shabbat and holidays on the Jewish calendar begin in the evening with the setting sun and last until the sun is completely set 25 hours later. The reason for 25 hours is just for safety. It should be exactly 24 hours, but rabbis added the extra hour so that we'll never start the Sabbath too late or end it too early.

Replying to a greeting

Knowing how to say hello and goodbye is a great start. But if you want to get past the initial hello, you need a few more phrases in your back pocket (like what to say when someone asks how you're doing). Who knows? These phrases could be the start of a beautiful friendship. Some responses to greetings include:

» שְׁלוֹמִי טוֹב . (shloh-*mee* tohv; My welfare is good.)

» אֶצְלִי בְּסֵדֶר גָּמוּר . (ehtz-*lee* buh-*seh-dehr* gah-*moohr;* With me, things are completely okay.)

» בְּסֵדֶר . (buh-*seh-d*ehr; Okay.)

» מַמָּשׁ טוֹב (mah-*mahsh* tohv; Really good.)

» לֹא כָּל-כָּךְ טוֹב . (loh kohl-*kahḥ* tohv; Not so good.)

» אַחְלָה (aḥ-*lah,* excellent)

>> סַבַּבָּה (suh-*bub*-ah; great)

>> מְעֻלֶּה (m'oo-*leh*; fantastic)

>> הַכֹּל טוֹב (ha*kol* tov; everything's good)

>> בְּסֵדֶר (buhseh-*dehr*; okay)

Talkin' the Talk

Michal and Kobi are old friends. They've just run into each other downtown, and they're both busy with errands on Friday before שַׁבָּת (shah-*baht*; Sabbath) starts. They quickly say hello and then dash off to complete their shopping.

Kobi: מִיכַל! שָׁלוֹם! מַה שְׁלוֹמֵךְ ?
mee-*ħahl!* shah-*lohm!* mah sh-loh-*mehħ?*
Michal! Hello! How are you?

Michal: שָׁלוֹם קוֹבִּי! מַה הָעִנְיָנִים ?
shah-*lohm* koh-bee! mah ha-in-yah-*neem?*
Hello, Kobi! How are things?

Kobi: אֲנִי מַמָּשׁ בְּסֵדֶר .
ah-*nee* mah-*mahsh* buhseh-*dehr.*
I am very well.

Michal: אֵיזֶה יֹפִי. אֲנִי חַיֶּבֶת לָרוּץ .
ay-*zeh* yoh-fee. ahz, ah-*nee* ħah-*yeh*-veht lah-*rootz.*
Terrific. Well, I've got to run.

Kobi: גַּם אֲנִי. לְהִתְרָאוֹת !
gahm ah-*nee.* leh-heet-rah-*oht!*
Me too. See you soon!

Michal: שַׁבָּת שָׁלוֹם. כָּל טוּב .
sha-*baht* shah-*lohm.* kohl-toov.
A peaceful Sabbath. All the best.

Kobi: שַׁבָּת שָׁלוֹם .
sha-*baht* shah-*lohm.*
A peaceful Sabbath.

בְּסֵדֶר	buh-*seh-der*	okay
כָּכָה־כָּכָה	kah-*ḥah* kah-*ḥah*	so-so
מַמָּשׁ	mah-*mahsh*	quite, really
רַע	rah	bad
טוֹב	tohv	good

Putting a name to a face

One surefire way to jump–start conversations is to ask people their names. Use these phrases to ask someone's name:

➤➤ ? מַה שְׁמֵךְ (mah sh-*mehḥ;* What's your name?) (F)

? מַה שִׁמְךָ (mah sheem-*ḥah;* What's your name?) (M)

? מַה שְׁמְכֶה (mah sheem-*heh;* What's your name?) (NB)

➤➤ ? אֵיךְ קוֹרְאִים לָךְ (ehḥ kohr--*eem* lahḥ; What do they call you?) (FS)

? אֵיךְ קוֹרְאִים לְךָ (ehḥ kohr-*eem* leh-*ḥah;* What do they call you?) (MS)

? אֵיךְ קוֹרְאִים לְכֶה (ehḥ **kohr**-eem leh-*heh;* what do they call you?) (NB)

The response is

➤➤ . . . שְׁמִי (sh-*mee;* My name is . . .)

➤➤ . . . הַשֵּׁם שֶׁלִּי (hah-*shehm* sheh-*lee;* My name is . . .)

➤➤ . . . קוֹרְאִים לִי (kohr-*eem* lee; They call me . . .)

GRAMMATICALLY SPEAKING

You may have noticed that there are two different ways of saying "My name is." The first way, שְׁמִי, (sh-*mee;* My name is . . .) is what we call in Hebrew an *inflection,* which occurs when two words (in this case, "name" and "my") are put together in one word, kind of like when "do" and "not" become one word, "don't." The second way of saying "My name is," הַשֵּׁם שֶׁלִּי (hah-*shehm* sheh-*lee;* My name is . . .) which literally means "the name mine." In Hebrew, unlike English, possessive pronouns come *after* the noun.

Talkin' the Talk

Gadi and Tzipi have just met each other at a party thrown by some friends. As they stand near the munchies, they chat briefly and get acquainted.

Gadi: שָׁלוֹם .
shah-*lohm.*
Hello.

Tzipi: . שָׁלוֹם
shah-*lohm.*
Hello.

Gadi: ? אֵיךְ קוֹרְאִים לָךְ
eh**h** kohr-*eem* lah**h**?
What do they call you?

Tzipi: קוֹרְאִים לִי צִיפִּי
kohr-*eem* lee tz*ee*-pee.
They call me Tzipi.

Gadi: . זֶה שֵׁם יָפֶה
zeh shehm yah-*feh.*
A nice name.

Tzipi: ? תּוֹדָה. מַה שְׁמְךָ
toh-*dah.* mah sheem-**h**ah?
Thanks. What's your name?

Gadi: . שְׁמִי גָּדִי
sh-*mee gah*-dee.
My name is Gadi.

Gadi: . מַמָּשׁ נֶחְמָד לְהַכִּיר אוֹתָךְ
mah-*mahsh* ne**h**-*mahd* leh-hah-*keer* oh-*tahh.*
Okay. It's a real pleasure meeting you.

Tzipi: . גַּם לִי
gahm lee.
For me as well.

Making Grand Introductions

One of the best ways to meet people socially or professionally is to have someone else introduce you. When you begin to make friends, bringing your friends together to meet one another is also nice. And if you think that two people *really* need to meet because you want to make a שִׁדּוּךְ (shee-*dooh.*; match), you *really* want to know what you're doing.

CULTURAL WISDOM

In Judaism, introducing people to their בַּאשֶׁערְט (bah-*shehrt*; intended one, in Yiddish) or in Hebrew — מְיֹעָד (meh-yoo-*ahd*) is considered to be a great act of חֶסֶד (*heh*-sehd; kindness). In fact, one Jewish adage teaches that a person who makes three such matches is assured a place in heaven.

Introducing yourself

At times, you may be at a party, a bus station, or even a cafe when you see someone you'd like to get to know. But what do you do if no one is around to introduce the two of you? Well, don't be shy! Just take the bull by the horns and introduce yourself. All you need are the words, and here they are:

» שָׁלוֹם אֲנִי . . . (shah-*lohm* ah-*nee*; Hello. I am . . .) (M/F/NB)

» אֶפְשָׁר לְהַכִּיר אוֹתְךָ (ehf-*shahr* leh-hah-*keer* oht-*hah*; Is it possible to get to know you?) (M)

אֶפְשָׁר לְהַכִּיר אוֹתָךְ ? (ehf-*shahr* leh-hah-*keer* oht-*ah*; Is it possible to get to know you?) (F)

» סְלִיחָה. אַתָּה מְאֹוד מוּכָּר לִי . (slee-*hah.* ah-*tah* meh-*ohd* moo-*kahr* lee; Excuse me. You look very familiar.) (M)

סְלִיחָה. אַתְּ מְאֹוד מוּכֶּרֶת לִי . (slee-*hah.* aht meh-*ohd* moo-*keh*-reht lee; Excuse me. You look very familiar.) (F)

Introducing others

Introducing people and getting introduced is always fun. The formal way of introducing two people in Hebrew is . . . נָא לְהַכִּיר אֶת (nah leh-hah-*keer* eht; Please be acquainted with . . .). The customary response is נָעִים מְאֹוד (nah-*eem* meh-*ohd*; very pleasant).

CULTURAL WISDOM

Israeli society is a very informal society, so if you visit Israel, you'll find yourself on a first-name basis with people right away. You use formal titles like Mr. and Mrs. only in the most formal situations, such as attending a party at the בֵּית הַנָּשִׂיא (*bayt* hah-nah-*see*; president's house).

WORDS TO KNOW

אֶפְשָׁר	ehf-*shahr*	Is it possible . . .
לְהַכִּיר	leh-hah-*keer*	to meet, to become acquainted with
נָא	nah	please
נָעִים מְאוֹד	nah-*eem* meh-*ohd*	very nice, very pleasant
סְלִיחָה	slee-*ẖah*	excuse me

REMEMBER

Hebrew is a biblical language, so certain words have . . . well, biblical connotations. In English, saying that you know someone is perfectly acceptable, and the meaning is quite innocent. But if you say that you know someone in Hebrew, people will understand the statement to mean that you *know* the person *biblically*. (And perhaps you do, but that subject isn't usually the topic of polite conversation in Hebrew or English.) So, when you're speaking Hebrew, just be sure to say that you're *acquainted with* someone: אֲנִי מַכִּיר /מַכִּירָה אוֹתוֹ / אוֹתָהּ (ah-nee meh-*keer*/mah-kee-*rah* oh-*toh*/oh-*tah*; I am acquainted with him/her.).

Talkin' the Talk

Ya'ara and Natan are mutual friends of Shulamit. They're all at a party on מוֹצָאֵי שַׁבָּת (moh-tze-*ay*-shah-*baht;* Saturday night). As everyone is mingling, Shulamit decides to introduce her two friends to each other.

Shulamit: בּוֹא נָתָן. אֲנִי רוֹצָה לְהַכִּיר לְךָ מִשֶּׁהִיא .

boh nah-*tan*. ah-nee roh-*tzah* leh-hah-*keer* leh-*ẖah* mee-sheh-hee.

Come, Natan. I want to you to meet someone.

Natan: טוֹב. תּוֹדָה.

tohv, toh-*dah*.

Okay, thank you.

Shulamit:	בּוֹאִי יַעֲרָה. יֵשׁ לִי מִישֶׁהוּא לְהַכִּיר לָךְ.
	boh-*ee* ya-ah-*rah*. yehsh lee *mee*-sheh-hoo leh-hah-*keer* la**h**.
	I have someone to introduce to you.
Ya'ara:	יֹפִי. אֲנִי בָּאָה.
	yoh-fee. ah-*nee bah*-ah.
	Fine. I am coming.
Shulamit:	נָתָן, נָא לְהַכִּיר אֶת יַעֲרָה
	nah-*tan*, nah leh-ha-*keer* eht yah-ah-*rah*.
	Natan, please get to know Ya'ara.
Natan:	נָעִים מְאֹד.
	nah-*eem* meh-*ohd*.
	Very pleasant.
Shulamit:	יַעֲרָה, זֶה נָתָן.
	yah-ah-*rah*, zeh nah-*tan*.
	Ya'ara, this is Natan.
Ya'ara:	נָעִים לְהַכִּיר אוֹתְךָ
	nah-*eem* leh-hah-*keer* oht-ḥah.
	Nice to meet you.
Natan:	נָעִים לְהַכִּיר אוֹתְךָ
	hah *oh*-nehg koo-*loh* sheh-*lee*.
	It's my pleasure.

. . . .

HOW MY FRIEND'S GRANDMOTHER INVENTED A HEBREW WORD

Hebrew is a gendered language. Saying something completely gender-neutral was almost impossible until recently, when nonbinary word forms began to emerge.

Take, for example, the word *rabbi*, the Jewish clergy. In English, you just call a rabbi "Rabbi." Whatever the gender, the title remains the same.

When my friend got married, the rabbi who officiated at her wedding was a woman. My friend's Israeli grandmother wanted to address this "woman of the cloth" in Hebrew. The Hebrew word for a male rabbi is רַב (rahv), but she realized that she didn't know the proper Hebrew word for "female rabbi." Upon returning to Israel, she did some research and found out that an official word for a woman rabbi didn't exist.

(continued)

(continued)

> So, my friend's clever grandmother took it upon herself to invent a Hebrew word for a woman rabbi. She came up with רַבָּה (rah-bah) as one possible way to feminize the word. She wrote to הָאָקֲדֶמְיָה לַלָּשׁוֹן הָעִבְרִית (hah-ah-kah-*dehm*-yah la-lah-*shohn* hah-*eev*-reet; *the Hebrew Language Academy*) and made her suggestion. And wouldn't you know it? The academy agreed with her suggestion and made רַבָּה (rah-bah) the official Hebrew word for a woman rabbi. Hebrew history in the making.

Getting Better Acquainted

After you meet someone and get past the introductions, you may want to get to know them better. But knowing where to start can be difficult because you're starting with a blank slate. In this section, I fill you in on some of the basics. I cover finding out whether someone speaks English (which you may want to avoid doing so you can *really* practice speaking Hebrew), asking where someone is from, and telling your new acquaintance how you feel. You'll be mixing and mingling and meeting and greeting in no time.

Finding out who speaks English

Sometimes, inquiring minds just gotta know, and you may want to know if some-one speaks English. Practicing your Hebrew is necessary, but at times, you may want to express something complicated or satisfy a need to hear some of your שְׂפַת עַם (s-*faht* ehm; *mother tongue*).

The following sentences can get you started:

- » הַאִם אַתָּה מְדַבֵּר אַנְגְּלִית ? (hah-*eem* ah-*tah* meh-dah-*behr* ahn-*gleet*; Do you speak English?) (M)

- הַאִם אַתְּ מְדַבֶּרֶת אַנְגְּלִית? (ha-*eem* aht meh-dah-*beh-reht* ahn-*gleet*; Do you speak English?) (F)

- הַאִםאַתה מדברה אנגלית? (ha-*eem* ah-*teh* meh-dah-*beh*-reh ahn-*gleet*; Do you speak English?) (NB)

- » אֵיזוֹ שָׂפָה אַתָּה מְדַבֵּר ? (ay-*zoh* sah-*fah* ah-*tah* meh-dah-*behr*; What language do you speak?) (M)

- אֵיזוֹ שָׂפָה אַתְּ מְדַבֶּרֶת? (ay-*zoh* sah-*fah* aht meh-dah-*beh*-reht; What language do you speak?) (F)

איזה שפה אתה מדברה (ay-*zoh* sah-fah ah-*teh* meh-dah-*beh*-reh; What language do you speak?) (NB)

» אֲנִי לֹא מְדַבֵּר עִבְרִית . (ah-*nee* loh meh-dah *veen* k -*behr* eev-*reet;* I don't speak Hebrew.) (M)

אֲנִי לֹא מְדַבֶּרֶת עִבְרִית . (ah-*nee* loh meh-dah-*behr*-et eev-*reet;* I don't speak Hebrew.) (F)

אני לא מדברה עברית (ah-*nee* loh meh-dah-*behr*-eh eev-*reet;* I don't speak Hebrew.) (NB)

» אֲנִי מֵבִין קְצָת עִבְרִית . (ah-*nee* meh- *veen*-ktzaht eev-*reet;* I understand a little Hebrew.) (M)

אֲנִי מְבִינָה קְצָת עִבְרִית . (ah-*nee* meh-vee-*nah* ktzaht eev-*reet;* I understand a little Hebrew.) (F)

.אֲנִי מְבִינֶה קְצָת עִבְרִית (ah-*nee* meh-vee-neh *ktzaht* eev-*reet;* I understand a little Hebrew.) (NB)

The following list shows you the Hebrew words for some commonly spoken languages:

» עֲרָבִית (ah-rah-*veet;* Arabic)

» רוּסִית (roo-*seet;* Russian)

» סְפָרַדִית (sfah-rah-*deet;* Spanish)

» צָרְפָתִית tzar-fah-*teet;* French)

» יְוָנִית (yeh-vah-*neet;* Greek)

WORDS TO KNOW

אַנְגְלִית	ahn-*gleet*	English
עִבְרִית	eev-*reet*	Hebrew
קְצָת	Ketzaht	a little
מְדַבֵּר	meh-dah-*behr*	speak (MS)
מְדַבֶּרֶת	meh-dah-*beh*-reht	speak (FS)

מְדַבְּרָה	meh-dah-*beh*-reh	speak (NBS)
מֵבִין	meh-*veen*	understand (MS)
מְבִינָה	meh-vee-*nah*	understand (FS)
מְבִינָה	meh-vee-*nah*	understand (NBS)
שָׂפָה	sah-*fah*	language

Talking about where you come from

Whenever I meet someone, one of the first things I want to know is where they're from. I want to know their nationality. I want to know whether they grew up in a big city or a little town. I want to know if they live in the country or a suburb. It's a great starting point for a longer conversation.

To ask people where they're from in Hebrew, you say

מֵאַיִן אַתָּה ? (meh-*ah*-yeen ah-*tah;* Where are you from?) (MS)

מֵאַיִן אַתְּ ? (meh-*ah*-yeen aht; Where are you from?) (FS)

But, if you want to know where in Israel a person is from, the customary questions are

מֵאַיִן אַתָּה בָּאָרֶץ (meh-*ah*-yeen ah-*tah* bah-*ah*-rehtz; Where are you from in the land?) (M)

מֵאַיִן אַתְּ בָּאָרֶץ ? (meh-*ah*-yeen aht bah *ah*-rehtz; Where are you from in the land?) (F)

To respond to these questions, you can just say . . . מִ אֲנִי (ah–*nee* meh; I am from . . .) and fill in the blank with some of the following phrases:

>> אַפְרִיקָה (*ahf*-ree-kah; Africa)

>> אַרְצוֹת הַבְּרִית (ahr-*tzoht* hah-*breet;* the United States)

>> אַסְיָה (*ahs*-yah; Asia)

>> אֵירוֹפָּה (Ay-*roh*-pah; Europe)

>> דְּרוֹם אָמֶרִיקָה (*drohm* ah-*meh*-ree-kah; South America)

>> חָלָל (hah-*lahl;* outer space)

Or perhaps you just want to tell people that you live in a עִיר (hah-*eer*; city) or a פַּרְוָר (pahr-*vahr*; suburb) or you might just live תִּמְהוֹנִי (teem-*hoo*-nee; in the "boonies," literally somewhere "eccentric").

When you're in Israel, and people suspect that you may not be a native, they may ask you whether you come from חוּץ לָאָרֶץ (ḥootz-lah-ah-*rehtz*; *literally:* outside the land), which means abroad or anywhere but Israel. People also use the acronym of this word, חוּל (ḥoo).

WORDS TO KNOW

חוּץ לָאָרֶץ	chootz lah-*ah*-rehtz	abroad
עִיר	eer	city
קָרוֹב	kah-*rohv*	close
מֵאַיִן	mah-*ah*-yeen	from where
פַּרְוָר	pahr-*vahr*	suburb

Chatting about how you feel

When all else fails in your attempt to strike up a conversation (and even if it doesn't), talking about how you feel and asking how another person feels can occupy a conversation for hours. To ask someone how they feel, you say

» ? אֵיךְ אַתְּ מַרְגִּישָׁה (eh aht mahr-gee-*shah*; How do you feel?) (F)

? אֵיךְ אַתָּה מַרְגִּישׁ (ehḥ ah-*tah* mahr-*geesh*; How do you feel?) (M)

אֵיךְ אַתָּה מַרְגִּישָׁה (ech ateh mar-*geesh*-eh; How do you feel?) (NB)

? אֵיךְ אַתֶּן מַרְגִּישׁוֹת (ehḥ ah-*tehn* mahr-gee-*shoht*; How do you feel?) (FP)

? אֵיךְ אַתֶּם מַרְגִּישִׁים (ehḥ ah-*tehm* mahr-gee-*sheem*; How do you feel?) (MP)

Table 3-1 presents some important words to talk about how you're feeling.

TABLE 3-1   **Words to Describe How You Feel**

English	Hebrew for a Male Speaker	Hebrew for a Female Speaker
curious	סַקְרָן (sahk-*rahn*)	סַקְרָנִית (sahk-*rah-neet*)
gets excited (v)	מִתְרַגֵּשׁ (meet-rah-*gehsh*)	מִתְרַגֶּשֶׁת (meet-rah-*geh*-shet)
happy	שָׂמֵחַ (sah-*meh*-a**h**)	שְׂמֵחָה (s-meh-**h**ah)
sad	עָצוּב (ahtz-*oov*)	עֲצוּבָה (ah-tzoo-*vah*)
scared	מְפַחָד (meh-foo-*chahd*)	מְפַחֶדֶת (meh-foo-**h**eh-det)
sick	חוֹלֶה (**h**oh-*leh*)	חוֹלָה (**h**oh-*lah*)
tired	עָיֵף (ah-*yehf*)	עֲיֵפָה (ah-yeh-*fah*)

TIP

If you're hot or cold, you don't say "I am hot" or "I am cold" in Hebrew. Instead, you say, "There is hot to me" and "There is cold to me." Because of the way the sentence is constructed, you don't have to worry about masculine and feminine ways of saying this. You just say

»   חַם לִי . (**h**ahm lee; I'm hot.)

»   קַר לִי . (kahr lee; I'm cold.)

Extending and Responding to Invitations

The Hebrew word for "to invite" is לְהַזְמִין (leh–hahz–*meen*). If you want to invite someone somewhere, you can say

»   ? אֶפְשָׁר לְהַזְמִין אוֹתְךָ (ef-*shar* leh-hahz-*meen* oht-**h**a; May I invite you?) (MS)

    ? אֶפְשָׁר לְהַזְמִין אוֹתָךְ (ef-*shar* leh-hahz-*meen* oht-a**h**; May I invite you?) (FS)

»   ? אֲנִי יְכוֹלָה לְהַזְמִין אוֹתְךָ (ahi *nee* yah-**h**ol leh-hahz-*meen* oht-*cha*; Can I invite you?) (M)

    ? אֲנִי יָכוֹל לְהַזְמִין אוֹתָךְ (ah-*nee* hyah-**h**ohl leh-hahz-*meen* oh-ta**h**; Can I invite you?) (F)

You can also use this phrase if you want to "treat" (that is pay) for someone at a restaurant, café, bar, or even an ice cream shop!

If you want to accept an invitation, you can say כֵּן אֲנִי אֶשְׂמַח לָבוֹא. תּוֹדָה (kehn ah-*nee* ehs-*mah***h** lah-*voh*. toh-*dah*; Yes, I'd be happy to come. Thanks.). But if you'd like to politely decline, you can say.

ASKING FOR A DATE

They say love is a universal language, but if you want to ask someone out on a date in Hebrew, a few words and phrases may be helpful. In Hebrew, the word for "date" is פְּגִישָׁה (puh-gee-*shah*), which literally means "meeting." Because this word also has the connotation of a business meeting, people in Israel often just use the English word "date" when it's a romantic meeting of sorts. Here are some phrases you can use to make a romantic invitation:

- אֶפְשָׁר לְהַזְמִין אוֹתָךְ לְכוֹס קָפֶה ? (ehf-*shah*r leh-hahz-*meen* oh-*tah* leh kohs kah-*feh*; Can I take you out for a cup of coffee?) (any gender to a female)

  אֶפְשָׁר לְהַזְמִין אוֹתְךָ לְכוֹס קָפֶה ? (ehf-*shah*r leh-hahz-*meen* oht-*hah* leh kohs kah-*feh*; Can I take you out for a cup of coffee?) (any gender to a male)

- אֲנִי מַכִּיר אוֹתָךְ מֵאֵיפֹה שֶׁהוּ ? (ah-*nee* mah-*keer* oh-*tahh* meh-*ay*-foh-sheh-*hoo*; Do I know you from somewhere?) (a male to a female)

  אֲנִי מַכִּיר אוֹתְךָ מֵאֵיפֹה שֶׁהוּ (ah-*nee* mah-keer-*ah* oht-*hah* meh-*ay*-foh-sheh-*hoo*; Do I know you from somewhere?) (a female to a male)

תּוֹדָה עַל הַזְמָנָה. אֲבָל אֲנִי לֹא יָכוֹל (toh-*dah* ahl hah-hahz-mah-*nah*, ah-*vahl* ah-*nee* loh yah-*hohl*; Thanks for the invitation, but I can't come.) (M)

תּוֹדָה עַל הַזְמָנָה. אֲבָל אֲנִי לֹא יְכוֹלָה לָבוֹא (toh-*dah* ahl hah-hahz-mah-*nah*, ah-*vahl* ah-*nee* loh yeh-*hohl-ah* lah-*voh*; Thanks for the invitation, but I can't come.) (F)

If someone invites you to their house, you may also want to ask what you can bring:

מָה אֲנִי יָכוֹל לְהָבִיא ? (mah ah-*nee* yah-*hol* leh-hah-*vee*; What can I bring?) (M)

מָה אֲנִי יְכוֹלָה לְהָבִיא ? (mah ah-*nee* yeh-*hoh*-lah leh-hah-*vee*; What can I bring?) (F)

Asking Questions: The Who, What, Where, When, Why, and How

An old saying is "Curiosity killed the cat, but information brought him back." Simply by reading this book, you're displaying a healthy curiosity about the world around you. And I'm guessing that you want to ask many questions about that world in Hebrew. Here are some basic question words to start you off:

» ? אֵיךְ (eh**h**; How?)

» ? אֵיפֹה (*ay*-foh; Where?)

» ? לָמָּה (*lah*-mah; Why?)

» ? מָה (mah; What?)

» ? מָתַי (mah-*tye*; When?)

» ? מִי (mee; Who?)

Asking yes or no questions

When you speak in Hebrew, you can indicate that you're asking a question by the tone of your voice. So, for example, you can say "There's pizza in the refrigerator" and mean it as a statement. Or you can put a question mark in your voice and use exactly the same words in the same order, and people will understand that you're asking a question. This concept is generally true only for questions that someone can answer with a simple yes or no.

Another way to indicate that you're asking a "yes or no" question is to start your question with the question word הָאִם (hah–*eem*). This handy word can be used to signal any "yes or no" question you can think of. All you need to do is put הָאִם (hah–*eem*) in front of a statement to turn it into a question:

» ? אַתָּה מְדַבֵּר רוּסִית הָאִם (hah-*eem* ah-*tah* meh-dah-*behr* roo-*seet*; Do you speak Russian?)

» ? הָאִם אַתְּ מִקָּלִיפוֹרְנְיָה (ha-*eem* aht mee-kah-lee-*fohr*-nee-yah; Are you from California?)

Forming negative questions

If you want to ask a negative question — questions that end with phrases such as "didn't she?" or "aren't you?" — use the Hebrew word for "no," לֹא (loh), or "there isn't," אֵין (ayn). These words aren't interchangeable because they have different meanings. Both לֹא and אֵין are placed before the object they're modifying in the sentence, as in these examples:

>> ? אֵין עוּגִיּוֹת (ayn oo-gee-yoht; No cookies?)

? הַאִם אֵין עוּגִיּוֹת (hah-eem ayn oo-gee-yoht; There aren't any cookies?)

>> ? אַתָּה לֹא מַכִּיר אוֹתָה (ah-tah loh mah-keer oh-tah; You don't know her?)

? הַאִים אַתָּה לֹא מַכִּיר אוֹתָה (hah-eem ah-tah loh mah-keer oh-tah; You don't know her?)

If you want to say the actual English equivalent of "didn't he?" or "aren't you?" (in grammarspeak, this is known as a *tag*), simply add the Hebrew word that means "correct," נָכוֹן (nah–ḥohn), at the end of the sentence:

>> ? אַתָּה שָׂמֵחַ, נָכוֹן (ah-tah sah-meh-ahḥ, nah-ḥohn; You're happy, aren't you?)

>> ? אַתְּ גָּרָה בָּעִיר, נָכוֹן (aht gah-rah bah-eer, nah-ḥohn; You live in the city, don't you?)

WORDS TO KNOW

אֵין	ayn	there isn't
אֵיךְ	ehh	how
אֵיפֹה	*ay*-foh	where
הַאִם	hah-*eem*	if
הַזְמָנָה	hahz-mah-*nah*	invitation
כֵּן	*kehn*	yes
לָמָּה	*lah*-mah	why
לְהַזְמִין	leh-hahz-*meen*	to invite
לֹא	loh	no
מָה	mah	what
מָתַי	*mah*-tye	when
מִי	mee	who
נָכוֹן	nah**ḥ**-ohn	correct
יֵשׁ	yesh	there is

FUN & GAMES

Match the Hebrew word with its correct translation:

1. אֵיךְ_____   A. how

2. אֵיפֹה_____   B. what

3. לְמָה_____   C. when

4. מָה_____   D. where

5. מָתַי_____   E. who

6. מִי_____   F. why

For the answers, see Appendix C.

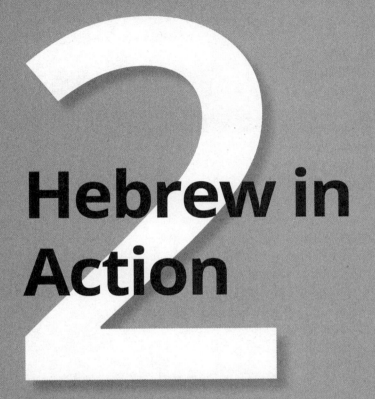

Hebrew in Action

IN THIS PART . . .

Keep the conversation going.

Discuss your favorite foods.

Make purchases.

Have fun!.

Chat on the phone.

Talk about your home and your work.

Chapter **4**

Getting to Know You: Making Small Talk

I don't know about you, but I love meeting new people. Every person is a world unto themselves, and there's so much to explore in each world. One of the most pleasant ways to get to know someone is to engage in small talk: Weather, jobs, and family all make great fodder for conversation.

Shootin' the Breeze

Casual conversation can really help pass the time. And who knows where such conversation may lead? You can use the following questions to strike up a conversation with just about anyone, just about anywhere. (For the particulars on how to construct a question, flip back to Chapter 2.)

>> ‏אַתָּה חוֹשֵׁב שֶׁיֵּרֵד גֶּשֶׁם? (ah-*tah* hoh-*shehv* sheh-yeh-*rehd geh*-shehm; Do you think it will rain?) (M)

‏אַתְּ חוֹשֶׁבֶת שֶׁיֵּרֵד גֶּשֶׁם? (aht oh-*sheh*-veht sheh-yeh-*rehd geh*-shehm; Do you think it will rain?) (F)

» ? אַתָּה נָשׂוּי (ah-*tah* nah-sooi; Are you married?) (M)

? אַתְּ נְשׂוּאָה (aht neh-soo-*ah*; Are you married?) (F)

» ? בֶּן כַּמָּה אַתָּה (ben *kah*-mah ah-*tah*; How old are you?) (M)

? בַּת כַּמָּה אַתְּ (baht *kah*-mah aht; How old are you?) (F)

? בֶּת כַּמָּה אַתֶּה (bet *kah*-mah ateh; How old are you?) (NB)

» ? אֵיפֹה אֲנִי יָכוֹל לִמְצֹא מִסְעָדָה טוֹבָה (*ay*-foh ah-*nee* yah-*chohl* leem-*tzoh* mees-ah-*dah* toh-*vah*; Where can I find a good restaurant?) (M)

? אֵיפֹה אֲנִי יְכוֹלָה לִמְצֹא מִסְעָדָה טוֹבָה (*ay*-foh ah-*nee* yeh-choh-*lah* leem-*tzoh* mees-ah-*dah* toh-*vah*; Where can I find a good restaurant?) (F)

» ? מוּסִיקָה אַתָּה אוֹהֵאֵיזוֹ (*ay*-zoh moo-zee-kah ah-*tah* oh-*hev*; What kind of music do you like?) (M)

? אֵיזוֹ מוּסִיקָה אַתְּ אוֹהֶבֶת (ay-*zeh* moo-zee-kah aht oh-*heh*-vet; What kind of music do you like?) (F)

? אֵיזוֹ מוּסִיקָה אַתֶּה אוֹהֶבֶה (ay-zoh moo-zee-kah ah-*teh* oh-*hehv*-eh; What kind of music do you like?) (NB)

» ? מֵאַיִן אַתָּה בָּאָרֶץ (meh-*ayin* ah-*tah* bah-*ah*-rehtz; Where are you from in Israel?) (M)

? מֵאַיִן אַתְּ בָּאָרֶץ (meh-*ayin* aht bah-*ah*-rehtz; Where are you from in Israel?) (F)

» ? מֵאֵיפֹה אַתָּה (meh-*ay*-foh ah-*tah*; Where are you from?) (M)

? מֵאֵיפֹה אַתְּ (meh-*ay*-foh aht; Where are you from?) (F)

» ? מְאוֹד חַם הַיּוֹם נָכוֹן (meh-*ohd* hahm hah-*yohm* nah-*chohn*; It's quite hot today, isn't it?)

» ? סְלִיחָה מָה הַשָּׁעָה (slee-*hah* mah hah-shah-*ah*; Excuse me, what is the time?)

» ? יֵשׁ לְךָ אַחִים וַאֲחָיוֹת (*yesh* leh-*ah* ah-*ḥeem* veh-ah-*ḥah*-yoht; Do you have brothers and sisters?) (MS-you)

? יֵשׁ לָךְ אַחִים וַאֲחָיוֹת (yesh la**ḥ** ach-*eem* veh-ah-chah-*yoht*; Do you have brothers and sisters?) (FS)

CULTURAL WISDOM

In the preceding list, I include the phrase for "How old are you?" Although asking someone's age may be taboo in North America, feel free to ask this question when you're in Israel. People ask you not only about your age, but also about your salary, how much you paid for your house, and other personal matters! Israelis want to know how many children you have and whether you're married. If you're not married, some folks will offer to introduce you to a nice single person. And if you're in Israel during election time, feel free to ask anyone and everyone for whom they are voting. They'll tell you. So ask away!

TIP

As you may have noticed, I also list two ways of asking someone where they're from. Use the מֵאַיִן אַתָּה בָּאָרֶץ version when you know the person is from Israel and the מֵאֵיפֹה אַתָּה version when the person could be from somewhere outside Israel.

But what if someone asks *you* one or more of the questions in the list? Keep reading; I'll tell you how you can answer.

Talking About Yourself and Your Family

Whenever I meet people, I'm always curious about their מִשְׁפָּחָה (meesh-pah-*chah*; family) and where they grew up. Where were they born? Where are their הוֹרִים (hoh-*reem*; parents) from? How many brothers and sisters do they have? People have interesting stories, and you can always uncover a lot about new acquaintances by asking some simple questions about their family. Table 4-1 gives you the Hebrew names for a bunch of family members. (Flip back to Chapter 3 to find out how to ask people where they're from.)

CULTURAL WISDOM

When you talk to Jewish people about their families, you can learn a lot about Jewish and Israeli history. Jews are a people who have wandered the globe, and every family has tales of their trials, tribulations, and joys.

TABLE 4-1

All in the Family

Hebrew	Pronunciation	Translation
אַבָּא	*ah*-bah	father
אִמָּא	*ee*-mah	mother
בֵּן	ben	son
בַּת	baht	daughter
בַּעַל	*bah*-al	husband
אִשָׁה	ee-*shah*	wife
אָח	ahch	brother
אָחוֹת	ah-*choht*	sister
יְלָדִים	yeh-lah-*deem*	children
סָבָא	*sah*-bah	grandfather
סָבְתָא	*sahv*-tah	grandmother

(continued)

TABLE 4-1 *(continued)*

Hebrew	Pronunciation	Translation
נֶכֶד	*neh-*ḥehd	grandson
נֶח נֶכְדָּה	nehḥ-*dah*	granddaughter
דּוֹד	dohd	uncle
דּוֹדָה	*doh-*dah	aunt
בֶּן דּוֹד	ben-*dohd*	cousin (M)
בַּת דּוֹדָה	baht *dohd*	cousin (F)
חַם	chahm	father-in-law
חָמָה	chah-*mah*	mother-in-law
גִּיס	gees	brother-in-law
גִּיסָה	gee-*sah*	sister-in-law

CULTURAL WISDOM

Israelis and Jews who live in the Diaspora often refer to Israel as הָאָרֶץ (hah–*ah*–rehtz), which means simply "the land."

Talkin' the Talk

Shira and Maya are sitting next to each other on a flight to Israel. The two women strike up a conversation to pass the time.

Shira:
שָׁלוֹם אֲנִי שִׁירָה אֵיךְ קוֹרְאִים לָךְ

shah-*lohm*. ah-*nee* shee-rah. eich kohr-*eem* lahch?

Hello. I'm Shira. How do they call you?

Maya:
נָעִים לְהַכִּיר אוֹתָךְ שִׁירָה קוֹרְאִים לִי מָיָה .

nah-*eem* leh-hah-*keer* oh-*tahch, shee-*rah. kohr-*eem* lee mah -*yah*.

Nice to meet you, Shira. They call me Maya.

Shira:
נָעִים מְאוֹד לָמָה אַתְּ נוֹסַעַת לְיִשְׂרָאֵל יֵשׁ לָךְ מִשְׁפָּחָה שָׁם

nah-*eem* meh-*ohd* mah-yah. *lah-*mah aht no-*sah-*aht le-yees-rah-*ehl?* yesh lahḥ meesh-pah-*chah* shahm?

Very nice [to meet you], Maya. Why are you traveling to Israel? Do you have family there?

Maya:
כֵּן הַהוֹרִים שֶׁלִי גָּרִים שָׁם שֶׁץ וְאַתְּ מֵאֵיפֹה אַתְ

ken. ha-hoh-*reem* sheh-*lee* gah-*reem* shahm. veh-aht? meh-*ay*-foh aht?

Yes. My parents live there. And you? Where are you from?

Shira: אֲנִי מִיִּשְׂרָאֵל אֲבָל הַבֵּן שֶׁלִּי גָּר בְּאַרְצוֹת הַבְּרִית .

ah-*nee* meh-yees-rah-*ehl*. ah-*vahl* hah-*ben* sheh-*lee* gahr beh-ahr-*tzoht* hah-*breet*.

I'm from Israel. But my son lives in the United States.

Maya: מֵאַיִן אַתְּ בָּאָרֶץ

meh-*ayin* aht bah-ah-*rehtz*?

Where are you from in Israel?

Shira: אֲנִי מִזִּכְרוֹן יַעֲקֹב .

ah-*nee* meh-zeech-*rohn* yah-ah-*kohv*.

I'm from Zichron Ya'akov.

• •

Chatting About the Weather

Whether it's hot and humid or cool and breezy, the מֶזֶג הָאֲוִיר (*meh*-zehg hah-ah-*veer*; weather) is always a good — and safe — topic of conversation. An interesting tidbit: The Hebrew word for weather literally means the mood of the environment! Because it affects everyone, the weather is a great way to start up a conversation. Try any of the following:

» נוֹרָא חַם הַיּוֹם נָכוֹן ? (noh-*rah* ḥahm hah-*yohm* nah-*ḥohn*; It's quite hot today, isn't it?)

» נוֹרָא קַר הַיּוֹם נָכוֹן? (noh-*rah* kahr hah-*yohm* nah-*chohn*; It's quite cold today, isn't it?)

» יוֹם יָפֶה נָכוֹן ? (yohm yah-*feh* nah-*ḥohn*; It's a nice day, isn't it?)

The easiest way to find out about weather conditions is to tune in to a תַּחֲזִית מֶזֶג הָאֲוִיר (tah-ḥah-*zeet* meh-zehg hah-ah-*veer*; weather forecast), where you're likely to hear some of these words:

» עָנָן (ah-*nahn*; cloud)

» בָּרָק (bah-*rahk*; lightning)

» גֶּשֶׁם (*geh*-shehm; rain)

» קֶשֶׁת (*keh*-sheht; rainbow)

» לַחוּת (lah-*ḥoot;* humidity)

» רַעַם (*rah*-ahm; thunder)

» רוּחַ (*roo*-a**ḥ**; wind)

» סְעָרָה (seh-ah-*rah;* storm)

» שֶׁלֶג (*sheh*-lehg; snow)

» שֶׁמֶשׁ (*sheh*-mehsh; sun)

GRAMMATICALLY SPEAKING

To say "it is" in Hebrew, just use the word זֶה (zeh; "it" or "this"). There's no "is" in Hebrew, so if you want to say something like "It is hot today," you just say זֶה חַם הַיּוֹם (zeh *ḥahm* hah–*yohm;* It's hot today.). Just follow this pattern: . . . זֶה . . . הַיּוֹם (It is . . . today). You can use the following words to fill in the blank:

» זֶה חַם הַיּוֹם (**ḥ**ahm; hot)

» קַר (kahr; cold)

» מְעֻנָּן (meh-oo-*nahn;* cloudy)

» מְעֻנָּן חֶלְקִית (meh-oo-*nahn* chel-*keet;* partly cloudy)

» יוֹרֵד גֶּשֶׁם (yoh-*rehd* geh-shehm; raining)

» יוֹרֵד שֶׁלֶג (yoh-*rehd* sheh-lehg; snowing)

RAIN, RAIN GO AWAY: FUN HEBREW EXPRESSIONS WITH THE WORD "RAIN"

Judaism is an agricultural-based religion, which explains why Hebrew has so many expressions with the word "rain." Hebrew features a special word for the first rain of the year, יוֹרֶה (yohr-*reh*) and the last rain of the season, מַלְקוֹשׁ (mahl-*kohsh*). Here are some expressions that contain the Hebrew words גֶּשֶׁם (*geh*-shehm; rain) and מָטָר (mah-*tahr;* rain shower):

- בֵּין שֶׁיָּרְדוּ גְּשָׁמִים וּבֵין שֶׁלֹּא יָרְדוּ (*bayn* sheh-yehr-*doo* geh-shah-*meem* oo-*vayn* sheh-loh yehr-*doo;* rain or shine)

- אֵינוֹ מְחַפֵּשׂ מַחֲסֶה בִּסְעָרָה (sheh-*ay*-noh meh-**ḥ**ah-*pehs* mah**ḥ**-*seh* bee-seh-ah-*rah;* not to know enough to come out of the rain)

- וַעֲרֻבּוֹת הַשָּׁמַיִם נִפְתָּחוּ (ve-ah-roo-*boht* hah-shah-*mah*-yeem neef-*tah*-choo; The sky opened up.)

To appreciate the beauty and brilliance of modern Hebrew, keep in mind that after the rain there's שְׁלוּלִית (shuh-loo-*leet*; *puddles*), after the שֶׁלֶג (sheh-leg; *snow,*) there's שְׁלוּגִית (shuh-loo-geet) which is a cross between the words for rain-puddle and snow!

Rain is so important that once a year, on the Jewish holiday of שִׁמְנִי עֲצֶרֶת (shmee-*nee* ahtz-*ehr*-reht), which falls roughly in September or October, Jews recite a special prayer for rain. שִׁמְנִי עֲצֶרֶת caps off the weeklong Jewish fall harvest holiday, סֻכּוֹת (soo-*koht*; feast of booths), with prayers for a rainy season in Israel.

There's even a Hebrew blessing to recite when you see a קֶשֶׁת (keh-sheht; rainbow) as a reminder of the Biblical promise between God and humanity never to flood the world again:

בָּרוּךְ אַתָּה יי אֱלֹקֵינוּ מֶלֶךְ הָעוֹלָם זוֹכֵר אֶת הַבְּרִית וּמַאֲמָם בִּבְרִיתוֹ וְקַיָּם בְּמַאֲמָרוֹ

bah-*rooh* ah-*tah* ah-doh-*nai* eh-loh-*hey*-noo *meh*-lehḥ hah-oh-*lahm*, zoh-*ḥehr* eht ha-*breet* veh-neh-eh-*mahn* bivree-*toh* ve-kah-*yahm* beh-mah-ah-mah-*roh*.

Praised are You the Eternal One our God, who remembers the covenant and keeps promises.

Talkin' the Talk

It's a hot day in the middle of an Israeli summer. Sivan and Tal are sitting at the beach, discussing the weather. (Track 6)

Sivan: נוֹרָא חַם הַיּוֹם נָכוֹן ?

noh-*rah* ḥahm hah-*yohm*, nah-*ḥohn?*

It's quite hot today, isn't it?

Tal: כֵּן מַמָּשׁ חַם לִי לְפָחוֹת אֵין לַחוּת בְּחוֹף הַיָּם .

kehn, mah-*mahsh* ḥahm lee. le-fah-*ḥoht* ayn lah-*ḥoot* buh-*ḥohf* hah-*yahm*.

Yes, it's quite hot. At least there's no humidity at the beach.

Sivan: כֵּן אֲנִי לֹא נֶהֱנֵת מִלַחוּת נוֹרָא לַח בָּעִיר

ken, ah-*nee* loh neh-heh-*neht* me-lah-*hoot*. noh-*rah* laḥ bah-*eer*.

Yes, I don't enjoy humidity. It's very humid in town.

Tal:	כֵּן אֲנִי יוֹדֵעַ יֵשׁ לָנוּ שָׁרָב עַכְשָׁו
	kehn, ah-*nee* yoh-*deh*-ah. yesh *lah*-new shah-*rahv* ah**ḥ**-*shahv*.
	Yes, I know. There's a heat wave now.
Sivan:	נָכוֹן אַתָּה יוֹדֵעַ מָתַי זֶה יִפָּסֵק
	nah-**ḥ**ohn. ah-*tah* yoh-*deh*-ah mah-*tye* zeh yee-pah-*sek?*
	That's true. Do you know when it will end?
Tal:	לְפִי תַּחֲזִית מֶזֶג הָאַוִּיר זֶה יִתְקָרֵר בְּעוֹד יוֹמַיִם
	le-*fee* tah-**ḥ**ah-*zeet* meh-zehg hah-ah-*veer,* zeh yeet-kah-*rehr* beh-*ohd* yoh-*mye*-eem.
	According to the weather forecast, it will get colder in two more days.
Sivan:	יוֹפִי !
	yoh-fee!
	Great!

●●

WORDS TO KNOW

עָנָן	ah-*nahn*	cloud
חַם	**ḥ**ahm	hot
גֶּשֶׁם	*geh*-shem	rain
קַר	kahr	cold
קֶשֶׁת	*keh*-sheht	rainbow
לַחוּת	lah-**ḥ**oot	humidity
מֶזֶג הָאַוִּיר	*meh*-zehg hah-ah-*veer*	weather
שֶׁלֶג	*sheh*-lehg	snow
שֶׁמֶשׁ	*sheh*-mehsh	sun

SPEAKIN' SLANG WITH THE BEST OF @'EM!

When you're speaking Hebrew and you really want to sound like a native speaker, being able to throw in some slang is handy! If you want to say that you think things are *cool,* you can say that everything is מַגְנִיב (mahg-*neev*) or סַבַּבָּה (sah-*bah*-bah). But if things aren't going your way, it's a בָּאסָה (*bah*-sah, bummer). Here's a tricky one: If you think something is really fantastic, you may declare that it's חָבָל עַל הַזְּמַן (**h**ah-*vahl* ahl haz-*mahn*), which literally means "a waste of time." (Hey, I don't make up the slang; I just report it.)

When someone or something is really great or prestigious, you can say that it's גָּדוֹל (gah-dohl) or even מַמָּשׁ גָּדוֹל (*mah*-mahsh gah-dohl) totally great. Instead of saying "obviously," Israelis will say בָּרוּר (bah-roohr). Then, for the classic "pee-your-pants funny," you can say מֵתָה פִּיפִי (metah pee-pee) חָחָ (LOL.)

If something is really terrible, you can say it's עַל הַפָּנִים (ahl hah-pah-*neem*), which literally means "on the face," as in falling flat on your face. And if you say לְהִתְקַרְנֵף (leh-heet-kahr-*nehf*), you literally mean "to act like a rhinoceros" but figuratively mean to ignore what's around you. (This particular slang expression is based on a character who dressed like a rhinoceros in an avant-garde Israeli play from many years ago.) And now for my all-time favorite. If you want to hang out on Tel Aviv's main drag, Dizengoff Street (named after the city's first mayor), there's an actual Hebrew verb for that: לְהִזְדַּנְגֵּף (le-heez-dahn-*gef;* to hang out on Dizengoff Street).

Six Days You Shall Labor: Talking About Work

You can tell a lot about someone by what they do for a living. Work takes up much of our waking hours, and people are often passionate about their chosen profession (if they're lucky). You can find out a lot about people by asking them what they do for a living. You can ask someone

>> בְּמֶה אַתָּה עוֹבֵד/ אֵת עוֹבֶדֶת? (beh-*meh* ah-*tah* oh-*vehd;* What do you do for work?) (M)

בְּמֶה אַתְּ עוֹבֶדֶת ? (beh-*meh* aht oh-vehd-*eht;* What do you do for work?) (F)

בַּמֶּה אַתֶּה עוֹבֶדֶה ? (beh-*meh* aht-eh oh-vehd-*eh;* What do you do for work?) (NB)

You can also say

» מָה הַמִּקְצוֹעַ שֶׁלְּךָ/ שֶׁלָּךְ ? (mah hah meek-*tzoh*-ah shel-*hah*; What's your profession?) (M)

מָה הַמִּקְצוֹעַ שֶׁלָּךְ ? (mah hah meek-*tzoh*-ah she-*lah* What's your profession?) (F)

מָה הַמִּקְצוֹעַ שֶׁלְּכֶה ? (mah hah meek-*tzoh*-ah shel-*he* What's your profession?) (NB)

Table 4-2 contains some occupations that either you or your conversation partner may hold. Check it out! (For additional work-related words, check out Chapter 10.)

REMEMBER

Professions are *gendered*, so they come in masculine and feminine forms.

TABLE 4-2

Calling in the Professionals

Hebrew (M/F)	Pronunciation (M/F)	Translation
אָח / אָחוֹת	ach/ah-*hoht*	nurse
חַקְלַאי / חַקְלָאִית	hahk-*lahy*/hah-klah-*eet*	farmer
רוֹאֶה חֶשְׁבּוֹן / רוֹאַת	roh-*eh* hehsh-*bon*/roh-*aht* chesh-*bon*	accountant
חַשְׁמַלַּאי / חַשְׁמַלָּאִית	hahsh-meh-*lahy*/hash-meh-lah-*eet*	electrician
עִטּוֹנַי / עִטּוֹנִית	ee-toe-*nahy*/ee-toe-nah-*eet*	journalist
מַזְכִּיר / מַזְכִּירָה	maz-*keer*/maz-kee-*rah*	secretary
מְהַנְדֵּס / מְהַנְדֶּסֶת	meh-hahn-*dehs*/meh-hahn-*deh*-set	engineer
מְנַהֵל / מְנַהֶלֶת	meh-nah-*hel*/meh-nah-*heh*-let	manager
מוֹרֶה / מוֹרָה	moh-*reh*/moh-*rah*	teacher
נַהָג / נַהֶגֶת	nah-*hag*/nah-*heh*-get	bus driver
עוֹרֵךְ דִּין / עוֹרֶכֶת דִּין	oh-reh-*deen*/oh-reh-het deen	lawyer
תִּדְבּוֹעַ יְאִאָצוֹצ דְּבוֹע /תִילְאִאָצוֹצ	oh-*vehd* sohtz-*yah*-lee/oh-*veh*-det sohtz-*yah*-leet	social worker
רַקְדָן / רַקְדָנִית	rahk-*dahn*/rahk-dah-*neet*	dancer
רוֹפֵא / רוֹפְאָה	roh-*feh*/rohf-*ah*	doctor
שׁוֹטֵר / שׁוֹטֶרֶת	shoh-*tehr*/shoh-*teh*-ret	police officer

Talkin' the Talk

 Nadav and Aviva have just met and struck up a conversation at a party. Because he wants to keep the conversation going, Nadav asks Aviva what she does for a living.

Nadav: מָה הַמִּקְצוֹעַ שֶׁלָּךְ ?

mah hah-meek-*tzoh*-ah sheh-*lah?*

What's your profession?

Aviva: אֲנִי עִתּוֹנָאִית בְּמָה אַתָּה עוֹבֵד

ah-*nee* ee-toh-nah-*eet.* beh-mah ah-*tah* oh-*vehd?*

I'm a journalist. What do you do for work?

Nadav: אֲנִי מְהַנְדֵּס .

ah-*nee* meh-hahn-*dehs.*

I'm an engineer.

Aviva: יָפֶה מְאוֹד אַתָּה נֶהֱנֶה מִזֶּה

yah-*feh* meh-*ohd.* ah-*tah* neh-heh-*neh* mee-*zeh?*

Very nice. Do you enjoy it?

Nadav: כֵּן זֶה מְאוֹד מְעַנְיֵן אֵיךְ הָעֲבוֹדָה שֶׁלָּךְ

kehn. zeh meh-*ohd* meh-ahn-*yehn.* ei**h** hah-ah-voh-*dah* sheh-*lah?*

Yes. It's very interesting. How's your work?

Aviva: אֲנִי מְאוֹד אוֹהֶבֶת אֶת זֶה אֲנִי מַמָּשׁ אוֹהֶבֶת לִכְתֹּב

ah-*nee* meh-*ohd* oh-*heh*-vet et zeh. ah-*nee* mah-*mahsh* oh-*heh*-vet lee**h**-*tohv.*

I like it very much. I really like to write.

Nadav: כָּל הַכָּבוֹד!

kohl ha-kah-*vohd!*

Good for you!

WORDS TO KNOW

עֲבוֹדָה	ah-voh-*dah*	work
כָּל הַכָּבוֹד	kohl hah-kah-*vohd*	Good for you!
מִקְצוֹעַ	meek-tsoh-*ah*	profession

Getting Addresses, Phone Numbers, Email, and Instagram/Twitter handles

Telling someone where you live and giving out your contact information — be it your cellphone number, your email address, or your Instagram handle — are often the key to continuing social contacts after you get past the nice-to-meet-you phase. You may want to carry around a כַּרְטִיס בִּקוּר (kahr-*tees* bee-*koor*; business card) to make the process a little easier, just in case. (For more information about talking on the phone, take a look at Chapter 9.)

Asking and telling where you live

To ask someone where they live, just say

>> ? אֵיפֹה אַתָּה גָּר (*ay*-foh ah-*tah* gahr; Where do you live?) (M/S)

אֵיפֹה אַתְּ גָּרָה ? (ay-foh aht gah-rah; Where do you live?) (F/S)

אֵיפֹה אַתֶּה גָּרֶה? (ay-foh ah-teh gah-reh; Where do you live?) (NB)

Any of the following phrases is an appropriate response:

>> .אֲנִי גָּר בְּ . . . (ah-*nee* gar buh; I live in . . .) (M)

אֲנִי גָּרָה בְּ . . . (ah-*nee* gah-rah buh; I live in . . .) (F)

אֲנִי גָּרֶה בְּ.. . . (ah-*nee* gah-reh buh; I live in . . .) (NB)

>> אֲנִי גָּרֶה בָּעִיר (ah-*nee* gar buh-ear; I live in the city.) (M)

אֲנִי גָּרֶה בָּעִיר (ah-*nee* gah-rah buh-ear; I live in the city.) (F)

>> אֲנִי גָּר בְּפַרְבָּר (ah-*nee* gar buh-pahr-*vahr*; I live in a suburb.) (M)

אֲנִי גָּרָה בְּפַרְבָּר (ah-*nee* gah-rah buh-pahr-*vahr*; I live in a suburb.) (F)

אֲנִי גָּרֶה בְּפַרְבָּר (ah-*nee* gah-reh buh-pahr-*vahr*; I live in a suburb.) (NB)

Depending on how well you know the person and the circumstances, someone may ask you for your כְּתֹבֶת (kuh-*toh*-vet; address). Jump to Chapter 4 to find out how to talk about your address in Hebrew.

Asking and giving a phone number, email address, or Instagram handle

If someone asks you

» מָה הַמִּסְפָּר שֶׁלָּךְ? (mah mees-*pahr* hah-*teh*-leh-fohn shel-*ḥah*/sheh-*lah*/shel-*ḥeh*; What's your telephone number?) (MS)

מָה הַמִּסְפָּר שֶׁלָּךְ? (mah mees-*pahr* hah-*teh*-leh-fohn shel-*ḥah*/sheh-*lah*/shel-*ḥeh*; What's your telephone number?) (F)

מָה הַמִּסְפָּר שֶׁלְּכֶה? (mah mees-*pahr* hah-*teh*-leh-fohn shel-*ḥah*/sheh-*lah*/shel-*ḥeh*; What's your telephone number?) (NB)

or

» אֶפְשָׁר לְבַקֵּשׁ אֶת הַמִּסְפָּר שֶׁלְּךָ? (ef-*shar* leh-vah-*kesh* eht mees-*pahr* hah-teh-leh-*fohn* shel-cha/shel-ach/; shel-*ḥ*eh; May I ask for your telephone number?) (M)

אֶפְשָׁר לְבַקֵּשׁ אֶת הַמִּסְפָּר שֶׁלָּךְ? (ef-*shar* leh-vah-*kesh* eht mees-*pahr* hah-teh-leh-*fohn* shel-cha/shel-ach/; shel-*ḥ*eh; May I ask for your telephone number?) (F)

אֶפְשָׁר לְבַקֵּשׁ אֶת הַמִּסְפָּר שֶׁלְּכֶה? (ef-*shar* leh-vah-*kesh* eht mees-*pahr* hah-teh-leh-*fohn* shel-cha/shel-ach/; shel-*ḥ*eh; May I ask for your telephone number?) (NB)

you can respond by saying

» הַמִּסְפַּר טֶלֶפוֹן שֶׁלִּי הוּא . . . (mees-*pahr* hah-teh-leh-*fohn* sheh-lee *hoo*; My telephone number is . . .)

For email, you just insert the phrase דוֹאַר אלקטרוני (doh-ahr eh-*lehk*-trah-nee), and text is אֶס אֶמ אֶס (SMS).

When you're giving out phone numbers, knowing how to count in Hebrew will probably be very useful. Refer to Chapter 1 for that information.

MINDING YOUR MANNERS

In Hebrew, there's no word for "tact"! But here are some words to use in case you want to be polite anyway:

- בְּבַקָּשָׁה (beh-vah-kah-*shah;* please *and* you're welcome.)

- הָעֹנֶג כֻּלּוֹ שֶׁלִּי (Ha-oh-*nehg* koo-*loh* sheh-*lee;* The pleasure is all mine.)

- סְלִיחָה (slee-*chah;* Excuse me.)

- תּוֹדָה (toh-*dah;* Thank you.)

- אֵין בְּעַד מָה (ein-*ba'ad-mah;* no worries)

- בְּכֵיף (b'kef; of course; *literally:* It's fun!)

FUN & GAMES

Match these family members with the Hebrew words (see below) that identify them:

(A) _____

(B) _____

(C) _____

(D) _____

(E) _____

אַבָּא

אִמָּא

אָחוֹת

אָחסְבְתָא

Chapter **5**

Eat! Eat! You're So Thin!

Jews have been called the "People of the Book." Another title that can apply is the "People of the Palate." A large part of our culture and religion revolves around food. What would שַׁבָּת (*shah*-baht; Jewish Sabbath) be without חַלָה (*ḥah*-*lah*; braided egg bread) on Friday night? What would פֶּסַח (*pay*-saḥ; Passover) be without yummy מַצָה (mah-*tzah*; unleavened bread)? And what would a good Jewish mother be without her chicken-soup recipe?

In this chapter, I provide lots of vocabulary about meals and food, including special foods eaten on Jewish holidays. With this chapter in hand, you can figure out how to place an order in a restaurant and how to shop for food at the grocery store in Hebrew. You can also uncover some terms for כַּשְׁרוּת (kahsh-*root*; Jewish dietary laws) and some basic blessings to say before you eat. בְּתֵאָבוֹן (buh-*tay-ah*-vohn; Healthy appetite!)

Jewish Love Means Never Having to Say "I'm Hungry"

A great way to find out about any culture is through its food, and Jewish culture is no different. Jewish cuisine springs from ancient traditions and bears the imprint of Jewish wanderings around the globe after the Jewish people were exiled from their homeland in the land of Israel. Within the Jewish community, distinctive foods of *Ashkenazi* (European–Jewish), *Sephardic* (Mediterranean–Jewish), and *Mizrahi* (Middle Eastern-Jewish) origin are common. These dishes often make their way from one generation to the next. Many dishes are associated with a particular holiday on the Jewish calendar. If you ask any Jewish person about their memories of Jewish holidays, I guarantee you that food will be part of the picture.

In much of Jewish culture, food is an expression of love. In Israeli culture, offering food is part of the gracious hospitality for which the warm Middle Eastern culture is known. In Israeli homes, you can usually find dishes of אֱגוֹזִים (eh-goh-*zeem*; nuts) and גַּרְעִינִים (gah-*ree*-neem; seeds) in the public gathering rooms, just waiting for guests to stop by.

Hunger and thirst pangs aren't in your future if you're in a Jewish household. The following food-related words and phrases will serve you well when you want to talk about food:

- >> אֹכֶל (oh-*hehl*; food)
- >> לֶאֱכוֹל (leh-eh-*hohl*; to eat)
- >> אוֹכֵל (oh-*hehl*; eat) (M)
  - אוֹכֶלֶת (oh-*hehl-eht*; eat) (F)
  - אוכלה (oh-*heh-leh*; eat) (NB)
  - אוֹכְלִים (o**h**-*leem*; eat) (MP)
  - אוֹכְלוֹת (oh**h**-*loht*; eat) (FP)
- >> לְהַאֲכִיל (leh-hah-ah-*heel*; to feed)
- >> מַאֲכִיל (mah-ah-*heel*; feed) (M)
  - מַאֲכִילָה (mah-ah-*hee-lah*; feed) (F)
  - מִמַאֲכִילָה (mah-ah-*hee-leh*; feed) (NB)
  - מַאֲכִילִים (mah-ah-*hee-leem*; feed) (MP)
  - מַאֲכִילוֹת (mah-ah-*hee-loht*; feed) (FP)

GRAMMATICALLY SPEAKING

In the preceding list, I note that אוֹכְלִים (oh**h**-*leem*; eat) and מַאֲכִילִים (mah-ah-*hee-leem*; feed) are masculine plural forms. But these words are also used for a group of people made up of a mix of males, females, and/or nonbinaries. In Hebrew, the masculine plural is often used for gender-neutral or inclusive language, much like the English "they." For nonbinary Hebrew speakers, they either alternate between male and female grammatical forms, or they may use the Hebrew grammar forms suggested by the Nonbinary Hebrew project (website: https://www.nonbinary-hebrew.com/). We've included some examples of nonbinary Hebrew in this book. It's important to note that the nonbinary Hebrew project is located in Colorado and while its suggestions are making inroads in the Jewish world, they haven't quite yet taken hold in Israel. It is a fluid and evolving situation.

Quieting a growling stomach

When אוֹכֶל (oh-*hehl*; food) is the subject, the first thing you need to know how to express is hunger. I just happen to have a few handy phrases:

>> אֲנִי רָעֵב. (ah-*nee* rah-*ehv*; I'm hungry.) (M)

אֲנִי רְעֵבָה. (ah-nee rah-*eh-vah*; I'm hungry.) (F)

אֲנִי רְעֵבֶה (ah-nee rah-*eh-veh*; I'm hungry.) (NB)

>> אֲנַחְנוּ רְעֵבִים. (ah-nah**h**-*noo* rah-eh-*veem*; We are hungry.) (MP)

אֲנַחְנוּ רְעֵבוֹת. (ah-nah**h**-*noo* rah-eh-*voht*; We are hungry.) (FP)

Taming a wild thirst

אַתָּה צָמֵא? (ah-*tah* tzah-*meh*; Are you thirsty? *Literally:* You must be thirsty!) After you've eaten, you probably want a שְׁתִיָּה (shuh-*tee*-ah; drink). Master the phrases in the following list, and you'll never go thirsty:

>> אֲנִי צָמֵא. (ah-*nee* tzah-*meh*; I'm thirsty.) (M)

אֲנִי צְמֵאָה. (ah-nee tz-*meh-ah*; I'm thirsty.) (F)

>> אֲנַחְנוּ צְמֵאִים. (ah-nah**h**-*noo* tz-*meh-eem*; We're thirsty.) (MP)

אֲנַחְנוּ צְמֵאוֹת. (ah-nah**h**-*noo* tz-*meh*-oht; We're thirsty.) (FP)

REMEMBER

You can easily turn the phrases I introduce here into questions. Just put a verbal question mark in your voice when you use these phrases or add the word הַאִם (hah-*eem*; if) before the phrases. Check out Chapter 3, in which I talk a little more about forming questions.

WORDS TO KNOW

אוֹכֶל	oh-*ḥehl*	food
רָעֵב	rah-*ehv*	hungry (M)
רְעֵבָה	ruh-*ehv*-ah	hungry (F)
רְעֵבֶה	ruh-*ehv*-eh	hungry (NB)
שְׁתִיָּה	shuh-*tee*-ah	drink (noun)
צָמֵא	*tzah*-mey	thirsty (M)
צְמֵאָה	tzuh-*mey*-ah	thirsty (F)
צְמֵאֶה,	tzuh-*mey*-eh	thirsty (NB)

Getting Down to Business: Food, Glorious Food!

Eating is an important part of everyone's day. Without food, your days would be numbered. But the Jewish culture (like many cultures) places a particular emphasis on food that makes it central to Jewish life — both in Israel and the *Diaspora* (the lands outside Israel where Jews have made their home). In Hebrew, the Diaspora is called הַתְּפוּצוֹת (Hah-*t'futz*-oht), which literally means "the scattering," because that's what happened to the Jewish people after the Second Temple in Jerusalem was destroyed in 70 CE.

In this section, I dish out the facts on the main meals people eat every day: breakfast, lunch, and dinner. (And you didn't think that I'd forget about snacks, did you?) I provide the lowdown on the foods that many folks commonly eat and some information on special Jewish food customs.

Starting the day with breakfast

You know what they say: Breakfast is the most important meal of the day! In Hebrew, breakfast is called בּוֹקֶר אֲרוּחַת (ah-roo-*ḥaht* boh-*kehr*; *literally:* morning meal). In the morning, lots of people can't function without a cup of קָפֶה (kah-*fay*; coffee). Or maybe your morning wouldn't be complete without a cold, refreshing glass of מִיץ תַּפּוּזִים (meetz tah-*pooz*eem; orange juice). Do you like a hearty breakfast with בֵּיצִים (bay-*tzeem*; eggs), or do you prefer simpler foods like a לַחְמָנִיָּה (lahh-mah-nee-*yah*; roll) or some יוֹגוּרְט (you know how to pronounce this one: yogurt). If you're in Israel, you may want to do as Israelis do and have a typical Israeli breakfast of עַגְבָנִיּוֹת (ahg-vah-nee-*oht*; tomatoes) and מְלָפְפוֹנִים (meh-lah-feh-foh-*neem*; cucumbers). No, I'm not kidding! The Israeli diet is akin to the much-famed (and מְמֻלָּץ moom-*lahtz*; recommended) Mediterranean diet, which means vegetables at every אֲרוּחָה (aru-*hah*; meal), including breakfast!

Here are some other common foods you might eat for breakfast:

» חָלָב (**h**ah-*lahv*; milk)

» חֲבִיתָה (hah-vee-*tah*; omelet)

» בֵּיצָה מְקֻשְׁקֶשֶׁת (beitz-*ah* muh-*koosh-kesh*-eht, scrambled egg)

» בֵּיצָה קָשָׁה (**beitz**-*ah* kah-*shah*, hard-boiled egg)

» פְּלָטַת גְּבִינוֹת (Plah-*taht* g'vee-*noht*; cheese platter)

» דַּיסָה (dye-*sah*; cereal)

» מִיץ (meetz; juice)

» מִיץ תַּפּוּזִים (meetz tah-poo-*zeem*; orange juice)

» מִיץ אֶשְׁכּוֹלִיּוֹת (meetz ehsh-kohl-*lee*-oht; grapefruit juice)

» פֵּרוֹת (pehr-*roht*; fruit)

SHAKSHUKA: AN "ALL MIXED UP" ISRAELI EGG DISH

A popular egg dish in Israel is called שַׁקְשׁוּקָה (shahk-*shoo*-kah), which is an appropriate name. The word is onomatopoeia, which is a fancy way of saying that the word sounds like exactly what it *means*. שַׁקְשׁוּקָה is literally the sound something makes when it gets all mixed up. You make the dish by taking tomatoes, garlic, tomato paste, olive oil, salt, and paprika and mixing them all up while heating them in a pan. When these ingredients are hot, you crack a few eggs and add them to the pan. The eggs cook right in the sauce. You serve the dish directly from the pan. It's quite טָעִים (*tah*-eem; delicious)!

Enjoying lunch

For many Americans, אֲרוּחַת צָהֳרַיִם (ah-roo-*haht* tzoh-hoh-rye-*eem*; lunch) is the quickest meal of the day. You can grab a כָּרִיךְ (kar-ree*h*; sandwich) and eat it on the fly. Or you can always gobble down some reheated פַּסְטָה עִם רֹטֶב (pahs-*tah* eem roh-*tehv*; pasta with sauce) at your desk. But lunch doesn't always have to be eaten at a heartburn-inducing pace. It can be a leisurely meal enjoyed with friends and family members. In Israel, lunch is eaten at a more leisurely pace and is the largest meal. On *Shabbat,* the Jewish Sabbath, lunch is the focal point of Saturday afternoon, and it often lasts for hours. Several courses are served, including מָרָק (*mah*-rahk; soup) or a special slow-cooked stew called חַמִּין (*hah*-meen). חַמִּין is prepared before the Sabbath. Then it has plenty of time — all night and the next morning — to simmer to perfection.

Here are some additional foods you might eat for lunch:

>> דָּג (dahg; fish)

>> פָלָאפֶל (fah-lah-*fehl;* fried chickpea paste in pita bread)

>> הַמְבּוּרְגֶּר (hahm-boo-*gehr;* hamburger)

>> נַקְנִיקִיָּה (nahk-nee-kee-*ah;* hot dog)

>> פִּיצָה (peetz-*ah;* pizza)

>> סָלָט (*sah*-laht; salad)

CULTURAL WISDOM

In Israel, lunch is usually the בְּשָׂרִי (b'*sah*-ree, meaty) and leisurely main אֲרֻכָּה (aroo-*hah*; meal) of the day. Chow down like an Israeli at lunch with delicacies like שְׁנִיצֶל (sh-*nitz*-el, chicken schnitzel); קְצִיצוֹת (k'*tzitz*-ee-oht; meatballs:); שְׁוַורְמָה (sh-*wahr*-mah; schwarma, roasted lamb on a spit); and the delicious מְמֻלָּאִים (meem-*lah*-eem; meat-stuffed vegetables), which are יְרָקוֹת (yeh-rah-*koht*; vegetables) stuffed with אֹרֶז (oh-*rehz*; rice) and בָּשָׂר טָחוּן (b'-sahr tah-*hoon*; fried meat). Delish!

Eating dinner

Ah, dinner! Ideally, the workday is done, and you can enjoy your meal. For Jewish families in North America — like their non-Jewish compatriots — dinner is the focal meal of the day. During dinner, you may have several courses. Perhaps מָרָק and סָלָט — familiar foods from lunch — are on the menu, followed by בָּשָׂר (bah-*sahr;* meat); עוֹף (ohf; chicken); or, if it's a special occasion, הוֹדוּ (hoh-*doo;* turkey). Usually, dinner also includes יְרָקוֹת (yeh-rah-*koht;* vegetables) and perhaps some אֹרֶז (oh-*rehz;* rice). And don't forget קִנּוּחַ (kee-noo-ah*h;* dessert)!

In Israel, Mediterranean culture predominates, and dinner is usually lighter fare because lunch serves as the main meal of the day. For dinner, Israelis usually eat a buffet of סָלָטִים (sah-*laht*-eem; salads) like חוּמוּס (*hoo-moos*; humus:), סָלָט חֲצִילִים (sah-*laht* ḥatz-*ee*-leem; baba ganoush), סָלָט קָצוּץ (salat *kagtz*-ootz; chopped "Israeli salad" with cucumbers and tomatoes), perhaps a בֵּיצָה קָשָׁה (*beitz*-ah *kah*-shah, hard-boiled egg), some פִּתָּה (*pee*-tah, pita bread), and maybe even some פַּסְטָה (*pahs*-tah, pasta).

Here are some other items you may have for אֲרֻכַּת עֶרֶב (ah-roo-*ḥah* eh-*rehvt*), which literally means "evening meal":

» אֲפוּנָה (ah-foo-*nah;* peas)

» דְּלַעַת (duh-*lah-aht;* squash)

» גֶּזֶר (*geh-zehr;* carrots)

» קִשּׁוּאִים (kee-*shoo*-eem; zucchini)

» כְּרוּבִית (kuh-roov-*eet;* cauliflower)

» עוֹף (ohf; chicken)

» עוּגָה (oo-*gah;* cake)

» תַּפּוּחַ אֲדָמָה (tah-poo-*ahḥ* ah-dah-*mah;* potatoes)

» תֶּרֶד (tay-*rahd;* spinach)

» יַיִן (*yah*-yeen; wine)

» בִּירָה (*beer*-ah; beer)

יַיִן (*yah*-yeen; wine) has long been part of Jewish and Israeli culture. It has been produced in Israel since Biblical times, and today, Israel produces more than ten million bottles of wine a year. All the major varieties are produced there, and you can even go on an Israeli wine tour! Israeli wine is highly respected by wine connoisseurs and garners international awards aplenty. And let's not forget the בִּירָה (*beer*-ah; beer)! The Israeli beer scene is . . . well, let's just say it's getting there. If you're looking for the good stuff, Tel Aviv is the place to go for suds.

Raiding the refrigerator

The irresistible snack! You can say "snack" many ways in Hebrew. You can call this indulgence an אֲרוּחָה קַלָּה, (ah-roo-*ḥah* kah-*lah;* light meal) or a חֲטִיף (*ḥah-teef; literally:* something snatched), or you can say simply that you זוֹלֵל בֵּין הָאֲרוּכוֹת (zoh-*lehl* bayn hah-ah-roo-*ḥoht;* graze between meals). Another word for snack is נֶשְׁנוּשׁ (*neesh*-noosh). The verb form for it is לְנַשְׁנֵשׁ (leh-*nahsh*-nesh; to snack).

In the present tense you say אֲנִי מְנַשְׁנֵשׁ / אֲנִי מְנַשְׁנֶשֶׁת (ah-nee meh-*nahsh*-nesh/ah-nee meh-*nahsh*-nehsh-eht; I'm snacking). But whatever you say, snacking is always fun.

Here are some foods that you might eat for a snack, including both foods that are בָּרִיא (bah-*ree*; healthy) and לֹא כָּל-כָּךְ בָּרִיא (loh kohl-*kahh* bah-*ree*; not so healthy):

» גְּלִידָה (glee-*dah;* ice cream)

» עוּגִיּוֹת (oo-gee-*oht;* cookies)

» שְׁקֵדִים (shuh-kay-*deem;* almonds)

» שׁוֹקוֹלָד (shoh-koh-*lahd;* chocolate)

» סֻכָּרִיּוֹת (soo-kahr-ee-*oht;* candy)

» תַּפּוּחַ (tah-poo-*ahh;* apple)

» צִמּוּקִים (tzee-moo-*keem;* raisins)

CULTURAL WISDOM

Ladies and gentlemen and children of all ages, may I introduce to you the all-time Israeli favorite snack food — drumroll, please — גַּרְעִינִים (gah-ree-*neem;* seeds:)! You can buy גַּרְעִינִים by the kilo at the מַכֹּלֶת (mah-*koh*-leht; little sidewalk store) in Israel. In most Israeli homes, people keep a stash to serve their friends when they pop by unexpectedly.

Going to Shabbat dinner

The main meal of the week (and a festive one at that) in Jewish households in Israel and around the world is the Friday-night dinner, אֲרֻחַת שַׁבָּת (ah-roo-*haht* shah-*baht*). The meal begins after sundown. Because אֲרֻחַת שַׁבָּת is the focal point of the week, families often set the table with a מַפָּה לְבָנָה (mah-*pah* leh-vah-*nah*; white tablecloth) and their prettiest dishes. Atop the table sits the כּוֹס לְקִדּוּשׁ (kos leh-kee-*doosh*; Kiddush cup), which is held when the blessing over the Sabbath day is said. Before the meal, Jewish people sing a song to welcome Sabbath angels and follow it with בְּרָכוֹת (brah-*choht*; blessings) over the יַיִן (yah-yeen; wine) and לֶחֶם (leh-*h*ehm bread).

CULTURAL WISDOM

In some traditional Jewish households, people ritually wash their hands before consuming bread. This act is called נְטִילַת יָדַיִם (neh-tee-*laht* yah-*dye*-eem; literally: taking up of the hands). Traditionally, Sabbath-dinner foods include עוֹף (ohf; chicken), צִמֶּיס (tzi-*mehs*; a stew made with carrots), and sometimes בָּשָׂר (bah-*sahr*; red meat). Eating דָּג (dahg; fish) on שַׁבָּת is also a traditional practice. One reason for this custom is connected to the גִּמַטְרִיָּה (geh-mah-tree-*ah*; numerology) of the fish. In numerology, each letter in a word is assigned a numerical value. It so happens that the numerical values of the letters in the Hebrew word for fish (דָּג) total seven. And שַׁבָּת is the seventh day of the week!

On a typical שֻׁלְחָן אָרוּךְ לְשַׁבָּת (shool-ḥahn ah-rooḥ leh-shah-baht; a table set for שולחן ערוך לשבת), you may also find

>> כַּפִּית כַּפִּיוֹת (kah-peet, kah-pee-oht; teaspoon, teaspoons)

>> כּוֹס כּוֹסוֹת (kohs, kohs-oht; cup, cups)

>> כּוֹס לְקִדּוּשׁ (kohs leh-kee-doosh; the Kiddush cup over which a special blessing for the Sabbath is recited)

>> מַפָּה לְבָנָה (mah-pah leh-vah-nah; white tablecloth)

>> מַפִּית מַפִּיּוֹת (mah-peet, mah-pee-oht; napkin, napkins)

>> מַזְלֵג מַזְלְגוֹת (mahz-lehg, mahz-luh-goht; fork, forks)

>> פְּרָחִים (puh-rah-ḥeem; flowers)

>> סַכִּין סַכִּינִים (sah-keen, sah-kee-neem; knife, knives)

>> צַלַּחַת צַלָּחוֹת (tzah-lah-ḥaht, tzah-lah-ḥoht; dish, dishes)

People often say הַשֻּׁלְחָן הָיָה עָמוּס בְּאֹכֶל (hah-shool-ḥahn hah-yah ah-moos beh-oh-chehl; The table was loaded with food!) on Friday nights because of the sheer amount of food present.

Chefing it up at home

It's fun to chef it up! Gather all your רְכִיבִים (reh-heev-eem; ingredients), your סִירִים וּמַחֲבַתּוֹת (seer-eem oo-mahh-bah-toht; pots and pans) and hit the מִטְבָּח (meet-bahh; kitchen)! You'll need to have some things handy, such as a קְעָרָה לְעִרְבּוּב (keeh-ah-rah lee-eehr-boov; mixing bowl), כּוֹסוֹת וְכַפִּיוֹת מְדִידָה (koh-soht u'hahf-ee-oht muh-dee-dah; measuring cups and spoons), and perhaps a מָרִית (mah-reet; spatula) or מַצֶּקֶת (mah-kehf-feht; ladle) if you're making מָרָק (mah-rahk, soup). For מַתְכּוֹנִים (meet-koh-neem; recipes), you can consult the Internet or a סֵפֶר בִּשּׁוּל (seh-fehr bee-shool; cookbook).

WORDS TO KNOW		
אֲרוּחָה	ah-roo-ḥah	meal
אֲרֶךְ אֲרוּחָת בֹּקֶר	ah-roo-ḥaht boh-kehr	breakfast
א אֲרוּחַת צָהֳרַיִם	ah-roo-ḥaht tzoh-hoh-rye-eem	lunch

אֲרוּחַת עֶרֶב	ah-roo-*haht* eh-*rehv*	dinner
אֲרוּחָה קַלָּה א	ah-roo-*haht* kah-*lah*	light meal
קִנּוּחַ	kee-noo-*ahh*	dessert

Matching Adjectives and Nouns

In Hebrew, the adjective comes *after* the noun, unlike the noun–adjective pattern in English, in which the adjective usually comes before the noun. As if that little twist doesn't make things challenging enough, the noun and adjective must match in gender (masculine or feminine) and number (plural or singular). For example:

» מַפָּה (mah-*pah;* tablecloth) (FS)

» לְבָנָה (leh-*vah*-nah; white) (FS)

» מַפָּה לְבָנָה (mah-*pah* leh-*vah*-nah; white tablecloth) (FS)

» מַפּוֹת (mah-*poht;* tablecloths) (FP)

» לְבָנוֹת (leh-*vah*-nah; white) (FP)

» מַפּוֹת לְבָנוֹת (mah-*pah* leh-*vah*-nah; white tablecloths) (FP)

» פֶּרַח (*peh*-rah**h***; flower) (MS)

» יָפֶה (yah-*feh;* pretty) (MS)

» פֶּרַח יָפֶה (*peh*-rah**h** yah-*feh;* pretty flower) (MS)

» פְּרָחִים יָפִים (prah-*heem* yah-*feem;* pretty flowers) (MP)

GRAMMATICALLY SPEAKING

All nouns are either masculine or feminine. Many nouns and adjectives ending with an *ah* or *it* sound are feminine, and most other words are masculine. But notice that I said *most,* not *all.* You just have to know whether a word is masculine or feminine, and the only way to know for sure is to memorize every word. (Sorry.) Hebrew–English dictionaries use the Hebrew letter ז (*zayin*) for masculine and the Hebrew letter נ (*nun*) for feminine to note a word's gender. English translations usually have m. for masculine and f. for feminine. (In this book, I use M and F for the same purpose.) In Colorado, The Nonbinary Hebrew Project (https://www.nonbinaryhebrew.com/) has suggested adding an *eh* at the end of verbs and nouns to signal nonbinary gender. This hasn't caught on in Israel. There, nonbinary people generally switch between masculine and feminine pronouns and verbs. In this book I use NB to indicate nonbinary. To find out more about this fascinating subject and other Hebrew grammar tidbits, take a look at Chapter 2.

Adjectives can be conjugated to be masculine singular, masculine plural, feminine singular, or feminine plural. Nouns and adjectives in the singular form are made feminine singular by adding a *ah* sound, masculine plural by adding a *im* sound, and feminine plural by adding a *ot* sound. As awareness has been raised about people with nonbinary gender identities, the Hebrew-speaking community has begun to grapple with language inclusivity. Although the official Hebrew Academy has yet to offer a solution, a Hebrew professor in Boulder, Colorado, has developed a system for nonbinary Hebrew. Basically, by adding the sound *eh* to the end of adjectives and verbs, a third, nonbinary gender category was created! For example:

» גָּדוֹל (*gah*-dohl; big) (MS)

גְּדוֹלָה (guh-*dohl*-ah; big) (FS)

גְּדוֹלֶה (guh-*dohl*-eh; big) (NB)

גְּדוֹלִים (guh-*dohl*-eem; big) (MP)

גְּדוֹלוֹת (guh-*dohl*-oht; big) (FS)

» קָטָן (kah-*tahn*; small) (MS)

קְטַנָּה (kuh-*tah*-nah; small) (FS)

קְטַנֶּה (kuh-*tah*-neh; small) (NB)

קְטַנִּים (kuh-*tah*-neem; small) (MP)

קְטַנּוֹת (kuh-*tah*-noht; small) (FP)

Talkin' the Talk

 Yaniv and Maya are a married couple. They've invited their friend, Hilah, over for Friday-night Shabbat dinner. She has just arrived.

Hilah: שַׁבָּת שָׁלוֹם !

shah-*baht* shah-*lohm!*

Good Sabbath!

Yaniv and Maya: שַׁבָּת שָׁלוֹם !

shah-*baht* shah-*lohm!*

Good Sabbath!

Maya: בּוֹאִי נֵשֵׁב

boh-*ee,* nay-*shev.*

Come, let us sit down.

Hilah: הַמַּפָּה הַלְּבָנָה כָּל כָּךְ יָפָה

hah-mah-*pah* hah-leh-vah-*nah* kohl-*kahch* yah-*fah.*

The white tablecloth is so pretty.

Maya: תּוֹדָה רַבָּה אֶפְשָׁר לָתֵת לָךְ מַשֶּׁהוּ, הִלָה

toh-*dah* rah-*bah!* ehf-*shahr* lah-*teht* lahch mah-sheh-*hoo,* hee-*lah?*

Thank you very much! Can I give you something, Hilah?

Hilah: כֵּן תְּנִי לִי דָּג עוֹף אֶרֶז וְתֶרֶד

kehn, tni *lee* dahg, ohf, oh-*rehz,* veh-teh-*rehd.*

Yes, give me fish, chicken, rice, and spinach.

Maya: אַתָּה רוֹצֶה יַיִן אָדֹם יָנִיב

Aht-ah roh-*tzeh* yah-yeen ah-*dohm,* yah-*neev?*

Would you like some red wine, Yaniv?

Yaniv: כֵּן תּוֹדָה רַבָּה

kehn, toh-*dah* rah-*bah.*

Yes, thanks very much.

Maya: בְּתֵאָבוֹן לְכוּלָם !

beh-tay-*ah-vohn* leh-choo-*lahm!*

Good appetite, everyone!

Yaniv & Hilah: בְּתֵאָבוֹן !

beh-tay-*ah-vohn!*

Good appetite!

●●

**GRAMMATICALLY
SPEAKING**

The Hebrew verb לָתֵת (lah–*teht;* to give) is an irregular verb. It has three Hebrew letters in the root: נ (*nun*), ת (*tav*), ת (*tav*). In the infinitive, future, and command forms, however, the נ (*nun*) disappears. The following table shows the conjugation of the verb לָתֵת in infinitive, present, future, and imperative tenses.

Verb Tense	Hebrew	Pronunciation	English
	לָתֵת	lah-*teht*	to give
Present	נוֹתֵן (MS)	no-*tehn*	give
	נוֹתֶנֶת (FS)	no-tehn-*eht*	give
	נוֹתְנִים (MP)	not-*neem*	give
	נוֹתְנוֹת (FP)	not-*noht*	give
Future	תִּתֵּן (MS)	not-*noht*	will give
	תִּתְּנִי (FS)	teet-*nee*	will give
	תִּתְּנוּ MP	teet-*noo*	will give
Imperative	תֵּן (MS)	tehn	Give!
	תְּנִי (FS)	t'*nee*	Give!
	תְּנוּ (MP/FP)	t'*noo*	Give!

BASIC BLESSINGS

The phrase וַאֲכַלְתָּ וְשָׂבַעְתָּ וּבֵרַכְתָּ (ah-*hahl*-tah, veh-sah-vah-*tah*, oo-vah-rahh-*tah*; You shall eat, and you shall be satisfied, and you shall bless) comes from the Book of Deuteronomy. From this verse comes the Jewish obligation to recite a blessing after eating.

Bread has special status in Judaism. On the Jewish New Year, people throw bread-crumbs from their pockets; Passover features an eight-day bread fast; and a special ritual is conducted before and after eating bread. When folks sit down to a meal that features לֶחֶם (leh-*hehm*; bread), afterward, they recite a lengthy prayer called בִּרְכַּת הַמָּזוֹן (beer kaht-hah-mah-*zohn*; *literally:* blessing over the food). When they don't eat bread, at the end of the meal they traditionally recite another prayer called בְּרָכָה אַחֲרוֹנָה (brah-*hah* ahh-roh-*nah*; last blessing).

As Judaism developed, rabbis decided that if people were required to say a blessing *after* a meal, they should recite a blessing *before* they eat as well. Here are a few basic blessings you say before eating:

- **Over bread:** בָּרוּךְ אַתָּה יְיָ אֱלֹקֵינוּ מֶלֶךְ הָעוֹלָם הַמּוֹצִיא לֶחֶם מִן הָאָרֶץ (bah-*rooh* ah-*tah* ah-doh-*noi* eh-loh-hay-*noo* meh-lehh hah-oh-lahm, hah-*moh*-tzee *leh*-hehm meen hah-*ah*-rehtz; Praised are You, the Eternal One our God, Ruler of the Cosmos, who brings forth bread from the earth.)

- **Over wine:** בָּרוּךְ אַתָּה יְיָ אֱלֹקֵינוּ מֶלֶךְ הָעוֹלָם בּוֹרֵא פְּרִי הַגָּפֶן. (bah-*rooh* ah-*tah* ah-doh-*noi* eh-loh-hay-*noo* meh-lehh hah-oh-lahm, boh-*ray* puh-*ree* hah-*gah*-fehn; Praised are You, the Eternal One our God, Ruler of the Cosmos, Creator of the fruit of the wine.)

- **Over fruit:** הָעֵץבָּרוּךְ אַתָּה יְיָ אֱלֹקֵינוּ מֶלֶךְ הָעוֹלָם בּוֹרֵא פְּרִי (bah-*rooh* ah-*tah* ah-doh-*noi* eh-loh-hay-*noo* meh-lehh hah-oh-*lahm*, boh-*ray* puh-*ree* hah-*aytz*; Praised are You, the Eternal One our God, Ruler of the Cosmos, Creator of the fruit of the tree.)

- **Over vegetables:** בָּרוּךְ אַתָּה יְיָ אֱלֹקֵינוּ מֶלֶךְ הָעוֹלָם בּוֹרֵא פְּרִי הָאֲדָמָה (bah-*rooh* ah-*tah* ah-doh-*noi* eh-loh-hay-*noo* meh-lehh hah-oh-lahm, boh-*ray* puh-*ree* hah-ah-dah-*mah*; Praised are You, the Eternal One our God, Ruler of the Cosmos, Creator of the fruit of the earth.)

Note: The prayer over the bread is a sort of a mega-blessing. If you have a meal at which bread is served, you can bless just the bread and consider everything else to be blessed.

Interesting note: Judaism considers bananas to be part of the vegetable blessing because they technically grow on a plant, not a tree!

Taking Your Grocery List to the Market

Because the main festive meal of the week takes place on Friday night, grocery shopping in Israel and in traditional Jewish households around the world often takes place on Thursdays or Friday mornings.

To buy your weekly קְנִיּוֹת (kuh-nee-*oht*; groceries), you can go to any of the following places:

>> הַסֻּפֶּר (hah-soo-*pehr*; supermarket)
>> מַכֹּלֶת (mah-*koh*-leht; little neighborhood grocery store)
>> שׁוּק (shook; open-air market)

You may also want to swing by a מַאֲפִיָּה (mah-ah-fee-*ah*; bakery) for these items:

>> לֶחֶם (leh-**h**ehm; bread)
>> עוּגִיּוֹת (oo-*gee*-oht; cookies)
>> עוּגוֹת (oo-*goht*; cakes)

And no grocery shopping errand would be complete without a trip to the שׁוֹחֵט (shoh-**h**eht; butcher) for kosher meat (unless you are צִמְחוֹנִי (tzim-**h**oh-nee; vegetarian) or טִבְעוֹנִי (tee-*voh*-nee; vegan):

>> בָּשָׂר (bah-*sahr*; meat; beef)
>> בָּשָׂר טָלֶה (bah-*sahr* tah-*leh*; lamb)
>> דָּג (dahg; fish)
>> עוֹף (ohf; chicken)

When you get to the הַסֻּפֶּר, you may have some of these items on your shopping list:

>> יְרָקוֹת (yeh-*rah*-koht; vegetables)
- עַגְבָנִיָּה (ahg-*vah-nee*-ah; tomato)
- בָּצָל (*bah*-tzahl; onion)
- חַסָּה (**h**ah-*sah*; lettuce)
- חֲצִילִים (**h**ahtz-ee-*leem*; eggplant)
- גֶּזֶר (geh-*zehr*; carrot)

- מְלָפְפוֹן (meh-*lah*-feh-*fohn;* cucumber)
- תַּפּוּחֵי אֲדָמָה (tah-poo-*hey* ah-*dah*-mah; potatoes)
- תִּירָס (*tee*-rahs; corn)
- תֶּרֶד (*tey*-rehd; spinach)

» פֵּרוֹת (*pey*-roht; fruit)

- אֲפַרְסֵק (ah-*fahr*-sehk; peach)
- אַגָּס (ah-*gahs;* pear)
- אֲנָנָס (ah-*nah*-nahs; pineapple)
- בְּנָנָה (bah-*nah-nah;* banana)
- מִשְׁמֵשׁ (*meesh*-maesh; apricot)
- אֻכְמָנִיּוֹת (oohh-*mahn*-ee-oht; blueberries)
- פֶּטֶל (peh-*tehl;* raspberry)
- שְׁזִיף (sheh-*zeef;* plum)
- תַּפּוּחַ (tah-poo-*ahh;* apple)
- תַּפּוּז (tah-*pooz;* orange)
- תּוּת שָׂדֶה (toot *sah*-deh; strawberry)

» מוּצְרֵי חָלָב (*mohtz*-ray **h**ah-lahv; dairy products)

- בֵּיצִים (*baytz*-eem; eggs)
- חָלָב (**h**ah-*lahv;* milk)
- חֶמְאָה (**h**ehm-*ah;* butter)
- גְּבִינָה (g'vee-*nah;* cheese)
- שַׁמֶּנֶת (shah-*mehn*-eht; sour cream)
- שׁוֹקוֹ (shoh-*koh;* chocolate milk)
- יוֹגוּרְט (yoh-*gurt;* yogurt)

Talkin' the Talk

The following conversation takes place in a bustling שׁוּק (shook; open-air market) on יוֹם שִׁישִׁי (yohm shee-*shee;* Friday) as everyone is busy buying food for Shabbat. Sivan is shopping for vegetables for her Shabbat dinner and approaches a מוֹכֵר (moh-**h**ehr; seller).

Sivan: הַאִם הַיְרָקוֹת טְרִיִּים. שָׁלוֹם. אֲנִי רוֹצָה לִקְנוֹתכַּמָּה יְרָקוֹת ?

shah-*lohm.* ah-*nee* roh-*tzah* leek-*noht* kah-*mah* yeh-rah-*kot.* hah-*eem* hah-yeh-rah-*koht* tree-*eem?*

Hello. I want to buy some vegetables. Are the vegetables fresh?

Mocher: בְּבַקָּשָׁה גְּבֶרֶת הַיְּרָקוֹת מְאוֹד טְרִיִּים ט רַק הִגִּיעוּ הַיּוֹם מִן הַקִבּוּץ מ מָה אַתְּ רוֹצָה

beh-vah-kah-*shah,* geh-vehr-*eht.* Hah-yeh-rah-*kot* meh-*ohd* tree-*eem* rahk hee-gee-*oo* hah-*yohm* meen hah-kee-*bootz!* Mah aht rohtz-*ah?*

Please, miss. The vegetables are very fresh. They just arrived today from the Kibbutz! What would you like?

Sivan: אֲנִי רוֹצָה שְׁנֵי קִילוֹ א עַגְבָנִיּוֹת שְׁנֵי קִילוֹ גֶּזֶר וְשְׁלֹשָׁה קִילוֹ מְלָפְפוֹן

ah-*nee* rohtz-*ah* shuh-*nay* kee-*loht* ahg-vah-nee-*oht,* shuh-*nay* kee-*loht* geh-zehr, vuh-shloh-*shah* kee-*loh* meh-lah-feh-*fohn.*

I want two kilos of tomatoes, two kilos of carrots, and three kilos of cucumbers.

Mocher: הִנֵּה הַיְרָקוֹת שֶׁלָּךְ גְּבֶרֶת זֶה תֵּשַׁע וַחֲצִי שְׁקָלִים

hey-*nay* hah-yeh-rah-*koht* sheh-*lah**h*** geh-vehr-*eht.* zeh tee-*shah* vah-**h**ehtz-*ee* sheh-*kahl*-eem.

Here are your vegetables, miss. That is nine and one-half shekels.

Sivan: יְפִי תּוֹדָה שַׁבַּת שָׁלוֹם

yoh-*fee!* toh-*dah. Shah*-baht *shah-*lohm.

Great! Thanks! Good Sabbath.

Mocher: תּוֹדָה לָךְ כָּל טוּב.

toh-*dah* lah**h**, kohl *toov.*

Thank you. All the best.

WORDS TO KNOW

קְנִיּוֹת	kuh-nee-*yoht*	groceries
כָּל טוֹב	kohl *toov*	all the best
פֵּרוֹת׃	*pey*-roht	fruit
שַׁבָּת שָׁלוֹם	*shah*-baht *shah*-lohm	a peaceful Sabbath
טָרִי	*tah*-ree	fresh
יְרָקוֹת	yeh-*rah*-koht	vegetables
יוֹפִי	*yoh*-fee	great, wonderful, beautiful

Going Out for a Bite

Ah, the joy of going out to eat — one of my favorite pastimes! When you develop an allergic reaction to pots, pans, and mixing spoons, going out to a מִסְעָדָה (mee-*sah*-dah; restaurant) is always fun. One can grab a bite of מָהִיר אֹכֶל (*oh*-hel *mah*-heer; fast food), or sometimes there's שֵׁרוּת עַצְמִי (*sheh*-root *atz* — mee; self-service), and then there's getting a קָפֶה הָפוּךְ (kah-*feh* hah-*fooh*; latte) at בֵּית קָפֶה (beit-kah-*feh*; coffeehouse). But what I really love is to go out, sit down, and get served! In a מִסְעָדָה (mee-*sah*-dah; restaurant), not only do I get to order what I want off a תַּפְרִיט (tahf-*reet*; menu) from a מֶלְצַר (mehl-*tzhar*; food server) (MS), but also, someone else has to clean up and do the dishes! It's well worth the כֶּסֶף (keh-*sehf*, money). At the end of the meal, you get a חֶשְׁבּוֹן (*hesh*-bohn; bill), which isn't as bad as a pile of dirty dishes. Of course, make sure that you give the מֶלְצַר (mehl-*tzhar*; food server) (MS) or מֶלְצָרִית (mehl-*tzahr*-it; food server) (FS) a good תֶּשֶׁר (teh-*shehr*; tip). You can לְשַׁלֵם (leh-*shah*-lehm; pay) with מְזֻמָּן (meh-*zoo*-mahn; cash) or כַּרְטִיס אַשְׁרַאי (kahr-*tees ahsh*-rei; credit card), and these days, you can even pay with your טֶלֶפוֹן נַיָּד (teh-*leh*-fohn *nah*-yahd; cellphone).

Here are some phrases you can use when ordering food in a restaurant:

» ? אֶפְשָׁר תַּפְרִיטבְּבַקָּשָׁה (ehf-*shahr* tahf-*reet* beh-vah-kah-*shah*; May I have a menu, please?)

» אֲנִי רוֹצֶה לְהַזְמִין. (ah-*nee rohz*-eh leh-hahz-*meen*; I would like to order.) (M)

» אֲנִי רוֹצָה לְהַזְמִין. (ah-*nee rohtz*-ah leh-*hahz*-meen; I would like to order.) (F)

» ? הַאִים הָאֹכֶל טָרִי (hah-*eem* hah-oh-*hehl tah*-ree; Is the food fresh?)

>> מָה אַתָּה מַמְלִיץ? (mah ah-*tah* mahm-*leetz*; What do you recommend?) (M)

>> מָה אַתְּ מַמְלִיצָה? (mah aht mahm-*leetz*-ah; What do you recommend?) (F)

>> מָה אַתֶּה מַמְלִיצֶה? (mah aht-eh mahm-*leetz*-eh; What do you recommend?) (NB)

You can also ask whether the food is מְטֻגָּן (meh-too-*gahn*; fried), אָפוּי (ah-foo-*ee*; baked), צָלוּי (tzah-loo-*ee*; grilled), or מְאֻדֶּה (meh-*oo*-deh; steamed).

.... Talkin' the Talk ....

 Dining in a restaurant is great. Oren, a bachelor, hates to cook, so he often goes out to eat. Here's what he says when the food server approaches his table:

Oren: אֶפְשָׁר לְקַבֵּל תַּפְרִיט בְּבַקָּשָׁה ?

ehf-*shar* leh-kah-*behl* tahf-*reet* beh-vah-kah-*shah*?

May I have a menu, please?

Meltzarit: כֵּן אֲדוֹנִי הִנֵּה תַּפְרִיט ה

kehn ah-doh-*nee*. Hee-*nay* hah-tahf-*reet*.

Yes, sir. Here is the menu.

Oren: הַכֹּל נִרְאֶה לִי מַמָּשׁ טָעִים מְאוֹד קָשֶׁה לִבְחֹר

hah-*kohl* nehr-*eh* lee mah-*mahsh* tah-*eem*. meh-*ohd* kah *sheh* lee leev-*chohr*.

Everything looks quite delicious. It's very difficult to choose.

Meltzarit: הַדָּג שֶׁלָּנוּ מַמָּשׁ מְצֻיָּן זֶה בָּא עִם גֶּזֶר עִם אֹרֶז

hah-*dahg* sheh-lah-*noo* hah-*yohm* mah-*mahsh* meh-tzoo-*yahn*. zeh bah eem geh-*zehr* veh-oh-*rehz*.

Our fish today is quite excellent. It comes with carrots and rice.

Oren: הַדָּג מְטֻגָּן הָאִם ?

hah-*eem* hah-*dahg* meh-*too*-gahn?

Is the fish fried?

(continued)

(continued)

Meltzarit:	כֵּן זֶה מְאוֹד טָעִים
	kehn, veh-zeh meh-*ohd* tah-*eem*.
	Yes, and it's very tasty.

Oren:	יָפִי זֶה נִשְׁמָע לִי מְצֻיָּן אֲנִי רוֹצֶה לְהַזְמִין דָּג עִם גֶּזֶר וְאֹרֶז
	yoh-*fee!* zeh neesh-*mah* lee meh-tzoo-*yahn*. ah-*nee* roh-*tzeh* leh-hahz-*meen* dahg, eem geh-*zehr* veh-oh-*rehz*.
	Great! That sounds excellent. I want to order fish with carrots and rice.

Meltzarit:	אֲנִי מִיָּד מְבִיאָה לְךָ אֲדוֹנִי
	ah-*nee* meh-*yahd* meh-vee-*ah* leh-*chah*, ah-doh-*nee*.
	I'll bring it to you right away, sir.

• •

WORDS TO KNOW

בְּהֶחְלֵט	beh-**h**ehch-*leht*	absolutely
עִם	eem	with
מַמָּשׁ	mah-*mahsh*	quite
מֶלְצַר	mehl-*tzahr*	waiter
מֶלְצָרִית	mehl-tzahr–*eet*	waitress
מְאוֹד	meh-*ohd*	very
מְצֻיָּן	meh-tzoo-*yahn*	excellent
מִסְעָדָה	mee-sah-*dah*	restaurant
תַּפְרִיט	tahf-*reet*	menu
טָעִים	tah-*eem*	tasty, delicious

KEEPING THINGS KOSHER

Some Jewish people in both in יִשְׂרָאֵל (yees-*rah*-ehl; Israel) and הַתְּפוּצוֹת (Hah-tfoo-*tzoht*; the Jewish Diaspora) keep כָּשֵׁר (*koh*-sher; kosher), which means that certain things don't go together. You may have heard someone say that they "keep kosher." In Hebrew, that person would say אֲנִי שׁוֹמֵר/שׁוֹמֶרֶת (ah-*nee* shoh-*mehr*/shoh-mehr-*eht* ahl kahsh-*root*; I keep kosher.). This declaration means that the person observes the Jewish dietary laws written in the Torah, which rabbis later interpreted and extrapolated. Specifically, בְּשָׂרִי (*buh*-sari; meat) and חֲלָבִי (hah-*lah*-vee; dairy) foods don't mix! That's good to know so that you don't bring גְּלִידָה (*glee*-dah; ice cream) for קִנּוּחַ (kee-*noo*-ahh; dessert) after a meat meal. If a food is neither meat nor dairy, it's called פַּרְוֶה (par-eh-*veh*; pareve). Some מִשְׁפָּחוֹת (meesh-*pah*-hoht; families) may keep separate sets of צַלָּחוֹת (tzah-lah-hot; dishes) for אֲרוּחוֹת חֲלָבִיּוֹת וַאֲרוּחוֹת בְּשָׂרִיּוֹת (ah-*roo*-hoht hah-*lahv*-ee-oth vah-ah-*roo*-hoht bee-*sahr*-ee-oht; meals. And some foods are absolutely off limits, such as pork and certain kinds of shellfish and seafoods, which Israelis refer to with the catch-all phrase טְרֵיף (*traif*; not kosher).

CULTURAL WISDOM

In Israel, as in many North American and European cities, meeting friends in cafés is a popular pastime. When the weather is good, many cafés have outdoor seating where you can watch the people go by as you enjoy some coffee and dessert. Speaking of coffee, an Israeli תַּפְרִיט (tahf-*reet*; menu) usually contains several kinds of coffee:

» קָפֶה פִילְטֶר (kah-*fay* fil-*tehr*; filtered coffee). The filter is placed on top of the cup and brought to your table while it's brewing.

» קָפֶה הָפוּךְ (kah-*fay* hah-*fooch*; café latte)

» קָפֶה קַר (kah-*fay* kahr; iced coffee)

» קָפֶה נֶמֶס (kah-*fay* neh-*mehs*; instant coffee)

You can also order coffee עִם קָפֵאִין (kahf-*een*; with caffeine) or נְטוּל קָפֵאִין (n'*tool* kahf-*een*; without caffeine).

TIP

When asking someone whether they like their food, it's common in Israel to ask ? טָעִים לְךָ (M) (tah-*eem* leh-*hah*; literally: Is it tasty to you?) or ? טָעִים לָךְ (F) (tah-*eem* lahh). The answer (if you like the food) is כֵּן זֶה טָעִים לִי (kehn zeh tah-*eem* lee; Yes, it is tasty to me.).

Talkin' the Talk

Dor and Yael have met for coffee at a popular cafe. They're finishing their coffee and dessert, and they ask the מֶלְצָר (mehl-*tzahr;* waiter) for their חֶשְׁבּוֹן (ḥesh-*bohn;* bill).

Yael: הָאֹכֶל הָיָה טָעִים לְךָ ?

hah-oh-*chehl* hah-*yah* tah-*eem* leh-*chah?*

Did your food taste good?

Dor: כֵּן זֶה הָיָה מַמָּשׁ טָעִים לִי. נֶהֱנֵת מֵהַגְּלִידָה שֶׁלָּךְ ?

kehn, zeh hah-*yah* mah-*mahsh* tah-*eem* lee. Neh-neh-*neht* meh hah-glee-*dah* sheh-*lahch?*

Yes, it was delicious. Did you enjoy your ice cream?

Yael: כֵּן הַגְּלִידָה הָיְתָה מַמָּשׁ טוֹבָה

kehn, hah-glee-*dah* hah-yee-*tah* mah-*mahsh* toh-*vah.*

Yes, the ice cream was quite good.

Dor: טוֹב מֶלְצָר הַחֶשְׁבּוֹן בְּבַקָּשָׁה !

tohv! mehl-*tzahr!* hah-*ḥehsh*-bohn beh-vah-kah-*shah!*

Good! Waiter! The bill, please!

Meltzar: הִנֵּה הַחֶשְׁבּוֹן אֲדוֹנִי

hee-*nay* hah-*ḥesh*-bohn, ah-doh-*nee.*

Here is the bill, sir.

Dor: תּוֹדָה יָעֵל אֲנִי מַזְמִין .

toh-*dah.* yah-*ehl,* ah-*nee* mahz-*meen.*

Thanks. Yael, my treat.

Yael: תּוֹדָה רַבָּה לְךָ

toh-*dah* rah-*bah* leh-*chah.*

Thank you very much.

Meltzar: אַתָּה צָרִיךְ עֹדֶף ?

ah-*tah* tzah-*reech* oh-*dehf?*

Do you need change?

Dor: לֹא זֶה בִּשְׁבִילְךָ .

loh, zeh beesh-veel-*chah.*

No, that's for you.

Meltzar: תּוֹדָה אֲדוֹנִי .

toh-*dah,* ah-doh-*nee.*

Thanks, sir.

• •

WORDS TO KNOW

אֲנִי מַזְמִין	ah-*nee* mahz-*meen*	my treat (M)
אֲנִי מַזְמִינָה	ah-*nee* mahz-*mee-nah*	my treat (F)
גְּלִידָה	guh-lee-*dah*	ice cream
חֶשְׁבּוֹן	**h**ehsh-*bohn*	bill
טָעִים לִי	tah-*eem lee*	This is delicious.

FUN & GAMES

Here's a table all set for dinner. Using the following words, can you identify all the things in the picture?

כַּפִּית	מָרָק	סַכִּין
מַפָּה	מַזְלֵג	יַיִן
מַפִּית	עוֹף	

Chapter **6**

Going Shopping

ow many times has this happened to you? You have a closet full of clothes but nothing to wear. You only have one solution to this malady: Hit the stores! In this chapter, I talk about all the places where you can buy clothes and all the words you need to know so you can dress yourself. You've heard the saying "Clothes make the man (or woman)." Dress for success!

Exploring Places to Shop

Now that you want to buy some clothes, the question becomes where to get them. You can go to a

» קַנְיוֹן (kan-*yohn; shopping mall*)

» מֶרְכַּז קְנִיּוֹת (mehr-*kahz* kuh-nee-*yoht; shopping center*)

» מִדְרָכוֹב (meed-reh-ḥohv; *outdoor shopping mall,* usually lined with cafes and cute little shops)

» שׁוּק הַפִּישְׁפִּישִׁים (shook hah-peesh-peh-*sheem; flea market*)

One of my favorite places to shop in Israel is the שוק הַפִּשְׁפְּשִׁים (shook hah-peesh-peh-sheem; flea market) in Old Jaffa. You can find it by walking down the main road of Old Jaffa, Tel Aviv-Jaffa Way, and looking for the signs. There, you find cavernous alleys with sellers offering everything from fine leather to cheap T-shirts to pots and pans. You have לְהִתְמַקֵּחַ (leh-heet-mah-kah-ah; to bargain), and it's great fun! I've found some great bargains there. The dresses I bought there never fail to bring in מַחְמָאוֹת (mah-mah-oht; compliments).

Selecting the Perfect Outfit

The word to dress oneself in Hebrew is לְהִתְלַבֵּשׁ (le-heet-lah-behsh). In general, you לוֹבֵשׁ (loh-vehsh; wear) בְּגָדִים (beh-gah-deem; clothes). In Hebrew, however, you use specific verbs when you wear a כּוֹבַע (koh-vah; hat), נַעֲלַיִם (nah-ah-lye-eem; shoes), גַּרְבַּיִם (gahr-bye-eem; socks), שָׁעוֹן (shah-ohn; a watch), חֲגוֹרָה (hah-go-rah; a belt), מִשְׁקָפַיִם (meesh-kah-fah-eem; glasses), עֲנִיבָה (ah-nee-vah; a necktie), or תַּכְשִׁיטִים (tah-shee-teem; jewelry).

The verb you use to talk about wearing a hat, for example, is לַחֲבֹשׁ (lah-hah-vosh; to wear a hat). For words like חֻלְצָה (hool-tzah; shirt), מִכְנָסַיִם (meeh-nah-sah-eem; pants), שִׂמְלָה (seem-lah; dress); חֲצָאִית (hah-tzah-eet; skirt), תַּחְתּוֹנִים (tahh-toh-neem; underwear); and חֲזִיָּה (hah-zee-yah; bra), you use the same verb, לוֹבֵשׁ (loh-vehsh; wear)

>> הוּא חוֹבֵשׁ כּוֹבַע (hoo hoh-vehsh koh-vah; He wears a hat.)

>> כּוֹבַע הִיא חוֹבֶשֶׁת (hee hoh-veh-shet koh-vah; She wears a hat.)

>> חוֹבֶשֶׁת כּוֹבַע הֵא (heh hoh-veh-sheh koh-vah; They (s.) wear a hat.) (NBS)

הֵם חוֹבְשִׁים כּוֹבַע (hem hohv-sheem koh-vah; They wear a hat.) (MP)

הֵן חוֹבְשׁוֹת כּוֹבַע (hen hohv-shot koh-vah; They wear a hat.) (FP)

When you want to talk about wearing shoes, use the verb לִנְעֹל (lin-ohl; to wear shoes):

>> הוּא נוֹעֵל נַעֲלַיִם (hoo noh-el nah-ah-lye-eem; He wears shoes.)

>> הִיא נוֹעֶלֶת נַעֲלַיִם (hee noh-eh-let nah-ah-lye-eem; She wears shoes.)

>> הֵא נוֹעֶלָה נַעֲלַיִם (hee noh-eh-leʸ nah-ah-lye-eem; They (s.) wear shoes.) (NBS)

הֵם נוֹעֲלִים נַעֲלַיִם (hem noh-ah-leem nah-ah-lye-eem; They wear shoes.) (MP)

הֵן נוֹעֲלוֹת נַעֲלַיִם (hen noh-ah-lot nah-ah-lye-eem; They wear shoes.) (FP)

To talk about wearing socks, use the verb גּוֹרֵב: (goh–rehv)

» הוּא גּוֹרֵב גַּרְבַּיִם (hoo goh-*rehv* gahr-*bye*-eem; *He wears socks.*)

» הִיא גּוֹרֶבֶת גַּרְבַּיִם (hee goh-*rehv-et* gahr-*bye*-eem; *She wears socks.*)

» הֵא גּוֹרְבה גַּרְבַּיִם (heh goh-*rehv*-eh gahr-bye-eem; *They* (s.) *wear socks.*) (NBS)

הֵם גּוֹרְבִים גַּרְבַּיִם (hen gohrv-*eem* gahr-*bye*-eem; *They wear socks.*) (MP)

הֵן גַּרְבַּיִם גוֹרְבוֹת הֵן גּוֹרְבוֹת גַּרְבַּיִם (hen gohrv-*oht* gahr-bye-*eem*; *They wear socks.*) (FP)

To talk about wearing glasses, use the verb לְהַרְכִּיב (leh–har–*keev*; *to wear glasses*):

» הוּא מַרְכִּיב מִשְׁקָפַיִם (hoo mar-*keev* meesh-kah-*fye*-eem; *He wears glasses.*)

» הִיא מַרְכִּיבָה מִשְׁקָפַיִם (hee mahr-kee-*vah* meesh-kah-*fye*-eem; *She wears glasses.*)

» הֵא מַרְכִּיבָה מִשְׁקָפַיסהָא (heh mahr-kee-*veh* meesh-kah-*fye*-eem; *They* (s.) *wear glasses.*) (NBS)

הֵם מַרְכִּיבִים מִשְׁקָפַיִם (hem mahr-kee-*veem* meesh-kah-*fye*-eem; *They wear glasses.*) (MP)

הֵן מַרְכִּיבוֹת מִשְׁקָפַיִם (hen mahr-kee-*voht* meesh-kah-*fye*-eem; *They wear glasses.*) (FP)

To talk about wearing a belt, use the verb לַחְגֹּר (lah–*gohr*; *to wear a belt*):

» הוּא חוֹגֵר חֲגוֹרָה (hooḥoh-*gair* ḥah-go-*rah*; *He wears a belt.*)

» הִיא חוֹגֶרֶת חֲגוֹרָה (hee ḥohg-*gair*-et ḥah-go-*rah*; *She wears a belt.*)

» הֵא חוֹגֶרֶה חֲגוֹרָהֵא (heh ḥohg-*gair*-et ḥah-go-*reah*; *They* (s.) *wear a belt.*) (NBS)

הֵם חוֹגְרִים חֲגוֹרָה (hem ḥohg-*reem* ḥah-go-*rah*; *They wear a belt.*) (MP)

הֵן חוֹגְרוֹת חֲגוֹרָה (hen ḥohg-*roht* ḥah-go-*rah*; *They wear a belt.*) (FP)

To talk about wearing a watch or jewelry, use the verb לַעֲנֹד (lah–ah–*nohd*; *to wear jewelry*):

» הוּא עוֹנֵד שָׁעוֹן (hoo oh-*nehd* shah-*ohn*; *He wears a watch.*)

» הִיא עוֹנֶדֶת שָׁעוֹן (hee oh-*neh*-deht shah-*ohn*; *She wears a watch.*)

» הֵא עוֹנֶדֶה שָׁעוֹן (heh oh-*neh*-deh shah-*ohn*; *They* (s.) *wear a watch.*) (NBS)

הֵם עוֹנְדִים שָׁעוֹן (hem ohn-*deem* shah-*ohn*; *They wear a watch.*) (MP)

הֵן עוֹנְדוֹת שָׁעוֹן (hen ohnd-*doht* shah-*ohn*; *They wear a watch.*) (FP)

WORDS TO KNOW

עֲנִיבָה	ah-nee-*vah*	tie
חֲגוֹרָה	ẖah-gor-*ah*	belt
חֲלִיפָה	ẖah-lee-*fah*	suit
חֲצָאִית	ẖah-tzah-*eet*	skirt
חֲזִיָּה	ẖah-zee-*yah*	bra
חֻלְצָה	ẖool-*tzah*	shirt
גַּרְבַּיִם	gahr-bye-*eem*	socks
כּוֹבַע	*koh-vah*	hat
מִכְנָסַיִים	miẖ-nah-*sah-yeem*	pants
מִשְׁקָפַיִם	meesh-kah-*fey-eem*	eyeglasses
נוֹעַל	nah-ah-*lye-eem*	shoes
שָׁעוֹן	shah-*ohn*	watch
שִׂמְלָה	seem-*lah*	dress
תַּחְתּוֹנִים	taẖ-toh-*neem*	underwear

TIP

Be very careful not to confuse the word for pants, מִכְנָסַיִים (mich-nah-*sah*-yeem), with the word for eyeglasses מִשְׁקָפַיִם, (meesh-kah-*fahy*-eem)! I know someone who did this once — with very embarrassing results. He forgot his glasses on the bus, so he went to the central bus station's information desk to ask for help. He carefully explained to the clerk how he had forgotten his glasses — how he'd taken them off while he was on the bus, folded them, and placed them beside him. But he didn't say מִשְׁקָפַיִם (meesh-kah-*fey*-yeem; *glasses*); he said ממכנסיים (miẖ-nah-*sah*-yeem; *pants*)! The clerk thought he was very strange indeed!

CULTURAL WISDOM

Judaism has a blessing for everything, even clothes! The traditional blessing for wearing new clothes the first time is

בָּרוּךְ אַתָּה יְ-יָ אֱלֹקֵינוּ מֶלֶךְ הָעוֹלָם הַמַּלְבִּישׁ עֲרוּמִים

bah-*rooẖ* ah-*tah* ah-doh-*nai* eh-loh-*hey*-nu *meh*-leẖ hah-oh-*lam*, mal-*beesh* ah-roo-*meem*

Praised are You the Eternal One our God who clothes the naked.

Talkin' the Talk

 Orit is shopping for new clothes in the כָּל-בּוֹ (kohl-*boh*; *depart*ment store). A saleswoman named Maya offers to help her.

Maya: שָׁלוֹם גְּבֶרֶת אֶפְשָׁר לַעֲזֹר לָךְ?

(shah-*lohm* ge-*vai*-ret. ef-*shahr* lah-ah-*zor lah*?)

Hello, miss. May I help you?

Orit: כֵּן תּוֹדָה אֲנִי מְחַפֶּשֶׂת בְּגָדִים אֲנִי רוֹצָה חֻלְצָה מִכְנָסַיִים שִׂמְלָה וַחֲצָאִית

(Kehn, toh-*dah* ah-nee meh-ḥah-*peh*-set beh-gah-*deem* ah-nee roh-*tzah* meeḥ-nah-*sye*-eem seem-*lah* veh-chah-tzah-*eet.*)

Yes, thank you. I am looking for clothes. I want a shirt, pants, a dress, and a skirt.

Maya: יֹפִי אֵיזֶה צְבָעִים אַתְּ אוֹהֶבֶת

(? *yoh*-fee *ay*-zeh tz-vah-*eem* aht oh-*heh*-vet.)

Great. What colors do you like?

Orit: אֲנִי אוֹהֶבֶת חוּם שָׁחֹר וְלָבָן

(ah-*nee* oh-*heh*-vet ḥoom shah-*ḥohr* veh-lah-*vahn*.)

I like brown, black, and white.

Maya: מָה מִדָּה שֶׁלָּךְ?

(mah hah-*mee*-dah sheh-*laḥ*?)

What is your size?

Orit: מִדָּה שֶׁלִּי שְׁלוֹשִׁים וְשֵׁשׁ

(*mee*-dah sheh-*lee* shloh-*sheem* veh-*shehsh*.)

I'm a size 36.

Maya: טוֹב אֲנִי מִיָּד אָבִיא לָךְ אֶת הַבְּגָדִים שֶׁלָּךְ לַחֶדֶר הַחֲלַבְשָׁה

(Tohv. ah-*nee* meh-*yahd* ah-*vee* eht hah-beh-gah-*deem* she-*laḥ* leh-ḥeh-*dahr* hah-hal-bah-*shah*.)

Good. I'll bring the clothes to the dressing room right away.

Some people love to shop; others hate it. But if you want to be well dressed, shopping is a task that you just must do. You know the routine: Go to a חֲנוּת (hah-*noot*; *store*) and grab a bunch of בְּגָדִים (beh-gah-*deem*; *clothes*) that you like. Get your correct מִדָּה (mee-dah; *size*) And take a look at the מְחִיר (meh-*heer*; *price*). You don't want anything too יָקָר (yah-*kahr*; *expensive*)!

Maybe a sale is going on, and the מְחִיר (meh-*heer*; *price*) is really זוֹל (zohl; *inexpensive*). You need to find a חֲדַר הַחַלְבָּשָׁה (hah-*dahr* hal-bah-*shah*; *dressing room*) לִמְדֹד (leem-*dohd*; *to try on*) all your בְּגָדִים (beh-gah-*deem*; *clothes*). You don't want בְּגָדִים (beh-gah-*deem*; *clothes*) that are too רְפוּיִים (reh-foo-*eem*; *loose*) or too צְמוּדִים (tzhmoo-*deem*; *tight*).

When you've made your choice, find a קֻפָּה (koo-*pah*; *cash register*) so that you can pay for your purchases.

תִּתְחַדְּשׁוּ! /תְחַדְּשָׁה תִּתְחַדֵּשׁ/תִּתְחַדְּשִׁי

(teet-*hahd*-*desh*/teet-*hahd*-*shee*/teet-*hahd*-*sheh*/ teet-*hahd*-*shoo*; May you be renewed by your new purchase!) (M/F/NB/MFP)

WORDS TO KNOW

בְּגָדִים	beh-gah-*deem*	clothes
חֲדַר הַחַלְבָּשָׁה	ha-*dar* hal-bah-*shah*	dressing room
מִדָּה	*mee*-dah	size
קֻפָּה	koo-*pah*	cash register
לִמְדֹד	leehm-*dohd*	to try on
מְחִיר	meh-*heer*	price
עוֹדֶף	oh-def	change
רְפוּיִ	ruh-*foo-ee*	loose
צָמוּד	tzah-*mood*	tight
יָקָר	yah-*kahr*	expensive
זוֹל	*zohl*	inexpensive

CULTURAL WISDOM

When someone buys something new, particularly clothing, you customarily say to them ! תִּתְחַדֵּשׁ (teet-ḥah-*desh*), if you're speaking to a man), ! תִּתְחַדְּשִׁי (teet-ḥahd-*shee*) if you're speaking to a woman, תִּתְחַדְּשֶׁה (teed-ḥahd-sheh) (if you're speaking to a nonbinary), or ! תִּתְחַדְּשׁוּ (teet-ḥahd-*shoo*) if you're speaking to more than one person. Basically, you're saying "May you be refreshed and renewed by your purchase!"

Styling Your Clothes around the Seasons

When you buy clothes, of course, you want to dress for the season. Whether you're wearing בְּגָדִים יוֹמְיוֹמִים (beh-gah-*deem* yoh-mee-*eem; casual clothes*), לְבוּשׁ חֲגִיגִי (leh-voosh ḥah-gee-*gee; dressy clothes*), or even your בִּגְדֵי שַׁבָּת (beeg-*day* shah-*baht; Sabbath clothes,* the Hebrew equivalent of "Sunday best"), or if you live in a climate with four seasons, you want to have all kinds of clothes handy for different weather.

Fall fashion

Ah, fall, when the air is crisp, and the leaves are colorful! On the Jewish calendar, fall is the time of the High Holidays, including Rosh Hashanah and Yom Kippur — the Jewish New Year and the Day of Atonement. And in Israel, the weather in fall is still hot! But I digress. Fall is a time for new beginnings. It's also a great time to get some new clothes. The following Hebrew words are a few fall items you may want to have on hand:

>> אֲפֻדָּה (ah-foo-*dah; vest*)

>> מְעִיל קָצָר (meh-*eel* kah-*tzar; jacket* or *short coat*)

>> מְעִיל גֶּשֶׁם (meh-*eel* geh-shem; *raincoat*)

The winter look

Winter! What a magical time of year. If your home area receives snow, this time can be especially fun — and cold! Thus, you need to bundle up. I include some special winter clothing you'll want to take out of storage when the temperatures start hovering around freezing:

>> כְּפָפוֹת (k-*fah*-foht; *gloves*)

>> כּוֹבַע (koh-vah; *hat*)

>> מַגָּפַיִם (mah-gah-*fye*-eem; *boots*)

» מְעִיל (meh-*eel; coat*)

» צָעִיף (tzah-*eef; scarf*)

CULTURAL WISDOM

Israel — the land of sand and sun — has one, and only one, ski resort; it's up in the north on הַר חֶרְמוֹן (ḥahr hehr-mohn; *Mount Hermon*). If you go, you'll need special בִּגְדֵי סְקִי (beeg-*day* skee; *ski clothing*) such as a חֲלִיפַת שֶׁלֶג (ḥah-*lee*-fah sheh-lehg; *snowsuit*), מִשְׁקְפֵי שֶׁלֶג (meesh-*kah*-fay sheh-lehg; *snow goggles*), תַּחְתּוֹנִים תֶּרְמִיִּים (tahḥ-*too*-neem trah-*meem; thermal underwear*), and maybe even some קְלִיפִּים אֶמְצָעִיִּים (klee-*peem* ehm-*tzah*-eem; *mitten clips*). Stay warm and have fun!

Talkin' the Talk

Dani and Orit are about to play in the שֶׁלֶג (sheh-leg; *snow*). Before they go, they make sure that they have everything they need.

Dani: אוֹ–קֵי אֲנַחְנוּ הוֹלְכִים לְיוֹם שֶׁלֶג אֶת מוּכָנָה ?

(oh-*kay*. Ah-nach-*noo* hol-*ḥeem* leh-*yohm sheh*-leg. Aht moo-ḥah-*nah*?)

Are you ready for a day in the snow?

Orit: כֵּן אֲנִי מוּכָנָה אֲנִי גּוֹרֶבֶת גַּרְבַּיִם מִצֶּמֶר אֲנִי נוֹעֶלֶת מַגָּפַיִם וַאֲנִי לוֹבֶשֶׁת מְעִיל חַם

(Kehn. Ah-*nee* moo-ḥah-*nah*. Ah-*nee* goh-reh-vet garh-*bah*-yeem mee-*tze-mer*, ah-*nee* noh-*eh*-let mah-gah-fye-*eem*, ah-*nee* loh-*veh*-shet meh-*eel* ḥahm.)

Yes, I am wearing wool socks, boots, and a warm coat.

Dani. יֹּפִי יֵשׁ לִי צָעִיף וּכְפָפוֹת אַל תִּשְׁכְּחִי אֶת הַכּוֹבַע שֶׁלָּךְ !

(Yoh-fee. Yaysh-*lee* tzah-*eef*, ook-fah-*foat*. Al teesh-keh-*ḥee* eht hah *koh*-vah sheh-*lahch*!)

Great. I have a scarf and gloves. Don't forget your hat!

Orit: טוֹב שֶׁהִזְכַּרְתָּ לִי!

(tohv sheh-heez-kahr-*tah* lee!)

Good that you reminded me!

Spring attire

Spring is wonderful! The days grow longer and warmer. Trees and flowers begin to bloom. And we can finally stop wearing those wool gloves and toss off that heavy coat in favor of a lighter jacket. Be sure to dress in שְׁכָבוֹת (shuh–ḥah–voht; layers). Now we can wear

>> חֻלְצָה עִם שַׁרְווּלִים קְצָרִים (ḥool-tzah eem shahr-voo-leem *keh-tzah*-reem; a short-sleeved shirt)

>> גְ׳קֶט (**jay-keht; jacket**)

And for those Spring Showers you might want to carry . . .

>> מִטְרִיָּה (mee-tree-*yah*; *umbrella*)

Summer wear

The dog days of summer bring long sunny days, ice cream cones, and clothes you can wear only on the hottest days of the year:

>> בֶּגֶד יָם (*beh*-gehd yahm; *bathing suit*)

>> מִכְנָסַיִם קְצָרִים (mee**ḥ**-nah-*sah*-yeem ktzah-*reem; shorts*)

>> מִשְׁקְפֵי שֶׁמֶשׁ (meesh-kah-*fay Sheh*-mesh; *sunglasses*)

>> סַנְדָּלִים (sahn-dah-*leem; sandals*)

>> כּוֹבַע קַשׁ (koh-*vah* kahsh; *straw hat*)

>> גּוּפִיָּה (goof-ee-*ah*; *sleeveless shirt*)

Sweatin' it out in the summer

In the summers in Israel, you bake under the Mediterranean sun, and it's hot, hot, hot! People tend to stay indoors between the hours of 10 a.m. to 4 p.m., and when they do venture out, they're wearing קרם הגנה (hah-gah-*nah; sunscreen),* מִשְׁקְפֵי שֶׁמֶשׁ (meesh-kah-*fay sheh*-mesh; *sunglasses*), and pop on a כּוֹבַע קַשׁ (koh-vah-kahsh; *straw hat*). גּוּפִיּוֹת (goof- ee-*oht; sleeveless shirts*) and שְׂמָלוֹת (suh-mahl-*oht; dresses*) are popular during the summer months, as are a special kind of breezy Middle Eastern pants called שרוואלים (shahr-*vahl*-eehm).

HEADS, SHOULDERS, KNEES, AND TOES: MODESTY RULES

If you're going to an Orthodox synagogue or neighborhood, you want to take note of the dress code and dress appropriately. Many shades of orthodoxy exist, of course, from the ultra-Orthodox who observe Jewish law stringently and are somewhat suspicious of the modern world to the modern Orthodox who are dedicated to both Jewish law and being part of the modern world. In general, in Orthodox settings, women should wear a dress or skirt that covers their knees and sleeves that cover their shoulders or elbows. Men should cover their head. In the ultra-Orthodox neighborhood of Mea She'arim in Jerusalem, signs request that all who enter the neighborhood abide by the dress code. And if you visit the הַכֹּתֶל, (hah-*koh*-tel; the Western Wall) in the Old City of Jerusalem, men are given head coverings and women skirts before they approach Judaism's holiest site.

GRAMMATICALLY SPEAKING

When you put two nouns together to form one word, you have a dependent relationship or a compound noun. In Hebrew, you call this compound a שְׁמִיכוּת (smee-*ḥoot*). A good example in English is the word *fireplace*. In Hebrew, when both nouns are singular, putting them together in a שְׁמִיכוּת (smee-*ḥoot*) is easy. The word for *swimsuit* in Hebrew, for example, is בֶּגֶד יָם (beh-gehd *yahm*), which means "sea suit." *Note:* In Hebrew, the order is the opposite of what you see in English. In the previous example, בֶּגֶד means "clothes" or "suit," and יָם means "sea." So literally, the Hebrew term means "clothing of the sea." Furthermore, if the nouns have only one syllable, their pronunciation remains the same. The one exception is the word for room חֶדֶר (*ḥeh*-dair). In שְׁמִיכוּת, חֶדֶר (smee-*hoot*, cheh-*dair*) becomes חֲדַר (*ḥah*-dar). Hence, the Hebrew word for *dressing room* is חֲדַר הַחלָהֶש (*ḥ*ah-dar hahl-bah-*shah*). If the first word in שְׁמִיכוּת (smee-*ḥoot*) is masculine plural, the final ם (*mem*, a Hebrew letter; see Chapter 1 for more about Hebrew letters) drops off. *Sunglasses*, for example, is מִשְׁקְפֵי שֶׁמֶשׁ (meesh-kah-*fey sheh*-mesh). One more tidbit: If you want to add the word הַ (hah; *the*) to a שְׁמִיכוּת s (smee-*ḥoot*), put it in front of the second noun, as in these examples:

» בֶּגֶד הַיָם (beh-*gehd* hah-*yahm*; *the bathing suit*)

» חֲדַר הַחלָהֶשָׁה (*ḥ*ah-*dar* hah-hahl-bah-*shah*; *the dressing room*)

» מִשְׁקְפֵי הַשֶׁמֶשׁ (meesh-kah-*fey* hah-*sheh*-mesh; *the sunglasses*)

Talkin' the Talk

Dani and Orit are getting ready to go to the beach on a hot summer day. Before they go, they make sure that they have everything. (Track 12)

Dani: נוֹרָא חַם הַיּוֹם טוֹב שֶׁאֲנִי לוֹבֵשׁ מִכְנָסִים קְצָרִים .

(noh-*rah* ḥahm hah-*yohm*! tohv sheh-ah-*nee* loh-vehsh-*eht* miḥ-nah-*sye-eem* k-tzahr-*eem*.)

It's hot today! I'm glad I'm wearing shorts.

Orit: כֵּן הַשִּׂמְלָה בְּלִי הַשַּׁרְווּלִים וְהַסַּנְדָּלִים מַתְאִימִים לְשֶׁמֶשׁ הַחַמָּה .

(kehn. hah-seem-*lah* buh-*lee* shahr-voo *leem* veh-hah-san-dah-*leem* mah-teem-*meem*-lah-*sheh*-mehsh hah-*ḥah*-mah.)

Yeah. My sleeveless dress and sandals feel good in the hot sun.

Dani: יֵשׁ לָךְ אֶת מִשְׁקְפֵי הַשֶּׁמֶשׁ שֶׁלָּנוּ ?

(yehsh lahḥ eht meesh-kah-*fay*-hah-*sheh*-mesh sheh-*lah*-noo.)

Do you have our sunglasses?

Orit: כֵּן יֵשׁ לְךָ אֶת הַמַּגָּבוֹת וְהַקְרֵם נֶגֶד שִׁזּוּף?

(kehn. yehsh leh-*chah* hah-mah-geh-*voht* ve-hah-kreme *neh*-gehd shee-*zoof*?)

Yes. Do you have the towels and the sunblock?

Dani: כֵּן יֵשׁ לִי וְגַם יֵשׁ לִי אֶת בִּגְדֵי הַיָּם אֲנִי גַּם חוֹבֵשׁ כּוֹבַע .

(Kehn. yehsh *lee*. veh-*gahm* yehsh-*lee* eht beeg-*day* hah-*yahm*. ah-*nee* gahm ḥoh-*vehsh koh-vah*.)

Yes. I have them. I have the swimsuits too. And I'm also wearing a hat.

Orit: טוֹב שֶׁהִזְכַּרְתָּ לִי אֲנִי גַּם רוֹצֶה לַחֲבשׁ כּוֹבַע .

(tohv sheh-heez-*kahr*-tah *lee*! ah-*nee* gahm roh-*tzah* lach-*vohsh koh*-vah.)

It's good that you reminded me! I also want to wear a hat.

WORDS TO KNOW

בֶּגֶד יָם	*beh*–gehd yahm	swimsuit
כְּפָפוֹת	kfah-*foht*	gloves
כּוֹבַע	*koh*–vah	hat
מְעִיל	meh-*eel*	coat
מִטְרִיָּה	mee-tree-*yah*	umbrella
מִשְׁקְפֵי שֶׁמֶשׁ	meesh-kah-*fay sheh*-mehsh	sunglasses
צָעִיף	tzah-*eef*	scarf

GRAMMATICALLY SPEAKING

When you use a sentence in which the definite direct object follows a verb, you must precede the object with the word אֶת (*eht*), as in אֲנִי רוֹצֶה לִרְאוֹת אֶת הַכּוֹבַע (ah-*nee* roh-*tzah* leer-*ot* eht hah-*koh*-vah; *I want to see the hat*).

The word אֶת (*eht*) has no direct equivalent in English, so I won't offer a translation. Think of it as a tiny signpost pointing out the fact that the noun that follows is the direct object of the verb.

CULTURAL WISDOM

GARBING YOURSELF FOR GOD

Jews wear several ritual garments. In Orthodox circles, only men wear these garments. But increasingly in non-Orthodox settings and even in some liberal Orthodox communities, you also find women wearing them. Observant Jews wear a prayer shawl, or a טַלִּית (ta-*leet*), during morning prayers and on Yom Kippur, the Day of Atonement. The טַלִּית (ta-*leet*) is a rectangular garment with צִיצִית (tzee-*tzeet; fringes*) on its four corners. The fringes are tied in such a way that they're symbolic of the 613 מִצְווֹת (meetz-*voht; commandments*) that Jews are obligated to observe.

Jews cover their heads as a sign of respect. Hence, men and some women cover their heads with a skullcap, or כִּפָּה (kee-*pah*). Some observant Jews wear a טַלִּית קָטָן (tah-*leet kah*-tahn), which is a four-cornered garment under the shirt. Each corner of the garment also has צִיצִית (tzee-*tzeet; fringes*). Some people tuck their טַלִּית קָטָן (tah-*leet* kah-*tahn*) in their clothes, and others leave them hanging out so they're able to see them and remember their Jewish obligations.

CULTURAL WISDOM

THE GREEN MAN

To hear Hebrew colors in action, listen to Yonatan Gefen's recording of הָאִישׁ הַיָּרוֹק (hah-*eesh* hah-*yah*-rohk; "The Green Men") on his CD הַכֶּבֶשׂ הַשִּׁשָּׁה עָשָׂר (Hah-keh-vees hah-*shee-sah*-ehsahr; *The Thirteenth Lamb*). You can find a version at https://youtu.be/jE6BkZdNPwA.

Color Me Beautiful

When you buy בְּגָדִים (beh-gah-*deem*), look for the צְבָעִים (tzvah-*eem*; *colors*) that look best on you. Some people like צְבָעִים מַבְרִיקִים (tzvah-*eem* mahv-ree-*keem*; *bright colors*), and others don't. Here are the colors:

» אָדֹם (ah-*dohm*; *red*)

» כָּתֹם (kah-*tohm*; *orange*)

» כָּחֹל (kah-**h**ohl; *blue*)

» לָבָן (lah-*vahn*; *white*)

» סָגוֹל (seh-*gohl*; *purple*)

» שָׁחוֹר (shah-*chor*; *black*)

» צָהֹוב (tzah-*hohv*; *yellow*)

» וָרֹד (vah-*rohd*; *pink*)

» יָרֹק (yah-*rohk*; *green*)

TIP

If you want to tell someone that you like their hat, shirt, or shoes, use a Biblical phrase and say that the object finds favor in your eyes. Here's an example: הַכּוֹבַע שֶׁלְּךָ מוֹצֵא חֵן בְּעֵינַי! (hah-*koh*-vah sheh-*lah* moh-*tzay* chen buh-ay-*nye*; *I like your hat!*, which literally means *Your hat finds favor in my eyes*).

The Israeli Fashion Scene

CULTURAL WISDOM

The Israeli אָפְנָה (*ohf*-nah; *fashion scene*) has a flair all its own. That's been true from the state's early days, when brands like Gottex, Meskit, and Beged-Or were all the rage, to today's scene, which produced מִשְׁקְפֵי שֶׁמֶשׁ תְּלַת מֵמַד (meesh *kah*-fey *sheh*-mesh tah-*laht* mei-*mahd*; *3D sunglasses*) — a collaboration between an Israeli jeweler and an Israeli drag queen!

Fashion Week takes place in Tel Aviv in the early spring. Israeli fashion tends to be צִבְעוֹנִי (tzee-*vohn*-ee; *colorful*), יְצִירָתִי (yeh-*tzeer-ah*-tee; *creative*), יוֹמְיוֹמִים (yohm-*yohm-ee*-eem; *casual*), and even שִׁמּוּשִׁים (shee-*moosh*-ee-eem; *utilitarian*). עֲנִיבוֹת (ah-*nee*-voht; *neckties*) are rarities. True story: The late Israeli Prime Minister Yitzhak Rabin arrived in Washington, D.C., for the signing of the Oslo peace accords with preknotted ties and needed help from none other than President Bill Clinton himself to straighten his ties.

Getting More (and Less) Than You Bargained For

Remember when Sally in *Harry Met Sally* went to a restaurant? She wanted a little more of this, less of that, the least of that other thing, and so on. You can be fussy in Hebrew, if only you know the right words. In this section, I tell you how to say words like *more than*, *less than*, *the most*, and *the least*. That way, you can tell people exactly what you want!

Making comparisons

If you want to say that something is bigger, taller, more beautiful, and so on, use the word יוֹתֵר (yoh-*tehr*) before or after the adjective, as follows:

Adjective	Comparative
טוֹב (*tohv*; *good*)	יוֹתֵר טוֹב (yoh-*tair* tohv; *better*)
גָּדוֹל (gah-*dohl*; *big*)	גָּדוֹל יוֹתֵר (gah-*dohl* yoh-*tair*; bigger)

If you want to say that something is less in some way, use the Hebrew word פָּחוֹת (*pahchoht*) in front of the adjective:

Adjective	Comparative
טוֹב (*tohv*; *good*)	פָּחוֹת טוֹב (pah-*hoht* tohv; *not as good*)
גָּדוֹל (gah-*dohl*; *big*)	פָּחוֹת גָּדוֹל (pah-*hoht* gah-*dohl*; *not as big*)

If you want to say that something is more than or less than something else, use the Hebrew word מ (*mee*) to make the comparison. If a יֶלֶד (*yeh*-lehd; *boy*) is bigger than a יַלְדָּה (yahl-*dah*; *girl*), for example, say so in either of these ways:

הַיֶּלֶד גָּדוֹל יוֹתֵר מֵהַיַּלְדָּה (hah-*yeh*-led yoh-*tair* gah-*dohl* mee-hah-yahl-*dah*; *The boy is bigger than the girl.*)

פָּחוֹת גְּדוֹלָה מֵהַיֶּלֶד (hah-yahl-*dah* pah-ḥ oht g-doh-*lah* mee-hah-yeh-lehd; *The girl is not as big as the boy*.)

Speaking in hyperbole

If you want to say that something is the most, the biggest, the most expensive, the prettiest, and so on, use the Hebrew word הֲכִי (*ha- ḥee*) in front of the adjective, as in these examples:

הַחֻלְצָה הֲכִי יָפָה בַּחֲנוּת (hah-**ḥ**ool-*tzah* hah-chee yah-*fah* bah-**ḥ**ah-*noot*; *the prettiest shirt in the store*)

הַמִּכְמָסַיִם הֲכִי יְקָרִים בַּחֲנוּת (*Hah*-mee**ḥ**-nah-*sah*-eem hah-*hee* Yeh-kah-*reem* bah-**ḥ**ah-*noot*; *the most expensive pants in the store*)

CULTURAL WISDOM

If you want to hear הֲכִי (ha-*hee*) in action, you definitely want to listen to that famous (and classic) Israeli song הַיַּלְדָּה הֲכִי יָפָה בַּגַּן (hah-*yahl*-dah ha**h**ee *yah*-fah beh-*gahn*; "The Prettiest Girl in Kindergarten"). Check it out at https://www.youtube.com/watch?v=FouJ0-ePBm4.

MEASURING UP

Finding your size can be tough any time you go shopping. But if you're shopping in Israel, the problem is compounded because clothing sizes aren't the same as in the United States. Israel uses the European system. When you're in Israel, use the following charts to help you find your size.

Use these approximate equivalents for women's clothing:

United States	4	6	8	10	12	14	16	18	20
Israel	34	36	38	40	42	44	46	48	50

For men's jackets and suits, use these rough conversions:

United States	38	40	42	44	46	48	50
Israel	48	50	52	54	56	58	60

If you want to ask how big something is or inquire about its size, ask מַה הַמִּדָּה? (*mah-hah-mee-*dah; *What's the size?*).
For more information on numbers, see Chapter 1.

FUN & GAMES

These four people are dressed in fall, winter, spring, and summer clothes. Can you match the correct Hebrew word with the correct article of clothing? Using the vocabulary in the word bank, write the correct words in the space provided.

חֲלִצָה, שִׂמְלָה, כּוֹבַע, מִשְׁקְפֵי שֶׁמֶשׁ , מְעִיל קָצָר, צָעִיף, כְּפָפוֹת, מִטְרִיָּה , חֲגוֹרָה, מִכְנָסִים, גַּרְבַּיִם, נַעֲלַיִם, מַגָּפַיִם , סַנְדָּלִים, בֶּגֶד יָם

A. _____   F. _____   K. _____

B. _____   G. _____   L. _____

C. _____   H. _____   M. _____

D. _____   I. _____   N. _____

E. _____   J. _____   O. _____

Chapter 7

Having Fun Hebrew Style

This chapter is about having fun. Whether you want to go to the movies, check out a museum, or see the animals at the zoo, you can do it using Hebrew!

Before you dash out to have a day of fun or a night on the town, you need to figure out some basics, including how to tell time and how to say the days of the week in Hebrew. After all, you need to know when the fun begins.

Counting the Hours and Minutes

Whether you're chronically early, always late, or right on time, you want to know the time of day. If you don't have a watch, you can ask a passerby "סְלִיחָה מָה הַשָּׁעָה?" (slee-*ḥah* mah hah-shah-*ah*?; *Excuse me, what is the time?*). If you want to know the time of a specific event, you can ask "הַ שָׁעָה הַ . . ." (shah-*ah hah* . . .; *At what time does such-and-such occur?*).

Telling time like an American

Hebrew speakers use two different systems for telling time. One system is similar to the one used in the United States, which is based on the numbers on a standard clock (1 to 12). Israelis commonly use the 24-hour clock, often referred to as *military time.* For more on the 24-hour system, see the sidebar "Using the 24-hour clock" later in this chapter.

On the hour

Saying the time at the top of the hour is easy. You just say: הַשָּׁעָה . . . (hah-shah-ah; *The hour is . . .*), followed by the number of the correct hour. Use the feminine form of numbers when telling time. (See Chapter 1 for more details about numbers and counting.)

On the half hour

If you want to say half past the hour, the hour comes first and then the expression וָחֵצִי (vah-*heh*-tzee). An example is 3:30, which is שָׁלוֹשׁ וָחֵצִי (shah-*lohsh*-vah-*heh*-tzee; *three and a half*).

You may also hear וּשְׁלוֹשִׁים (oo-shlo-*sheem*). שָׁלוֹשׁ וּשְׁלוֹשִׁים (shah-*lohsh* oo-shlo-*sheem*) is an alternative to שָׁלוֹשׁ וָחֵצִי (shah-*lohsh*-vah-*heh*-tzee; *three and a half*) as an expression for 3:30, meaning *3 and 30*.

On the quarter hour

If you want to say that the time is either 15 minutes before or after the hour, you need these expressions:

>> רֶבַע ל . . . (reh-*vah* luh; *It's a quarter to . . .*)

>> וָרֶבַע (vah-*reh*-vah; *and a quarter . . .*)

When you say, "a quarter to," the hour comes after the expression. If you want to say "a quarter after," however, you state the hour first and then the expression, as in these examples:

>> For 2:45, you say רֶבַע לְשָׁלוֹשׁ (reh-*vah* leh-shah-*lohsh*; *a quarter to three*).

>> For 3:15, you say שָׁלוֹשׁ וָרֶבַע (shah-*lohsh* vah-*reh*-vah; *three and a quarter*).

A few minutes before or after the hour

Sometimes, time doesn't neatly divide itself into half and quarter hours. In such cases, you can use the same preceding patterns, substituting the times in terms of minutes before or after the hour. Here are a couple of examples:

>> For 2:50, you say עֲשָׂרָה לְשָׁלוֹשׁ (ah-sah-*rah* leh-shah-*lohsh*; *ten to three*).

>> For 3:10, you say שָׁלוֹשׁ וַעֲשָׂרָה (shah-*lohsh* veh-ah-sah-*rah*; *ten after three*).

USING THE 24-HOUR CLOCK

To avoid any misunderstanding, Israelis often use the 24-hour system of telling time, which means you don't have to bother with "AM" or "PM" or specify "morning" or "night," since each time of day occurs only once a day using a 24-hour clock. You'll notice this style of telling time on any timetable, such as when a movie starts, when a bus arrives or leaves, or when a bank or business remains open.

In this system, after you reach 12, you just keep adding to it. So 1 p.m. in this system is 13, 2 p.m. is 14, 3 p.m. is 15, and so on. In the 24-hour system, you don't say "a quarter to" or "ten minutes to." T, as in these examples:

- הַשָּׁעָה עֲרָבָה עֶשְׂרָה וַעֲשָׂרָה (hah-shah-*ah* ar-bah-es-*reh* vuh-ah-sah-*rah*; *The hour is 14 and ten minutes*). This time corresponds to 2:10 p.m.

- הַשָּׁעָה עֶשְׂרִים וְאַחַת וָחֵצִי (hah-shah-*ah* es-*reem* ve-ah-*ḥaht* vah-*ḥeh-tzee*; *The hour is 21 and a half*). This time corresponds to 9:30 p.m.

- הַשָּׁעָה שֵׁשׁ שֵׁשׁ-עֶשְׂרָה וַחֲמִשִּׁים (hah-shah-*ah* shaysh-es-*reh* ve-chah-mee-*sheem*; *The hour is 16 and 50*). This time corresponds to 4:50 p.m.

Knowing the time of day

No matter what time of day it is, you need to know the correct Hebrew words for it. Use the following terms to say what time of day it is:

» אַחַר הַצָּהֳרַיִם (ah-ḥar-*ray-ha*-tzoh-hoh-*rah*-yeem; *afternoon*)

» לִפְנוֹת בֹּקֶר (leef-*noht boh*-kehr; in the middle of the night, literally "turning into morning")

» בֹּקֶר (*boh*-kehr; *morning*)

» עֶרֶב (*er*-rehv; *evening*)

» לַיְלָה (*lye*-lah; *night*)

» צָהֳרַיִם (tzoh-hoh-*rah*-yeem; *noon*)

Relating time to the past, present, and future

Sometimes when you're talking about time, you don't speak of events in terms of their exact תַּאֲרִיךְ (tah–ah–*reeḥ*; *date*) or point in time. Instead, you speak of time relative to the present. Hence, you speak of אֶתְמוֹל (eht-*mohl*; *yesterday*), שִׁלְשׁוֹם (shil-*shohm*; *the day before yesterday*), אֶמֶשׁ (*eh*-mehsh; *last night*), מָחָר (mah-*ḥar*; *tomorrow*), and מָחֳרָתַיִם (maḥ-*ḥar*-ta-*yeem*; *the day after tomorrow*). In you want to indicate you will get something done within some certain future time-frame you can say בְּעוֹד (beh-*ohd*; *within*, literally: *in-yet*) as in בְּעוֹד שָׁבוּעַ (beh-*ohd* shah-*voo*-ah; *next week*), בְּעוֹד חוֹדֶשׁ (beh-*ohd* ḥo -dehsh; *next month*), or even בְּעוֹד שָׁנָה (beh-*ohd* shah-*nah*; *in a year*).

You can also talk about הַשָּׁבוּעַ שֶׁעָבַר (ha-shah-*voo*-ah sheh-ah-*vahr*; *last week*) and הַשָּׁבוּעַ הַבָּא (ha-shah-*voo*-ah ha-*bah*; *next week*). When you tell a story about the past, and you want to say, "the next day" (in the past) you use this handy world לְמָחֳרָת (leh-mah *ḥahr*-aht). And if you're feeling particularly nostalgic, you can talk about הַשָּׁנָה שֶׁעָבְרָה (ha-shah-*nah* sheh-av-*rah*; *last year*). And, of course, you always haveהַשָּׁנָה הַבָּאָה (ha-shah-*nah* hah-bah-*ah*; *next year*)!

CULTURAL WISDOM

L'Shana Haba'ah B'Yerushalayim (Hebrew: לְשָׁנָה הַבָּאָה בִּירוּשָׁלַיִם), lit. "Next year in Jerusalem," is a phrase that is often sung at the end of the Passover Seder and at the end of the נְעִילָה, (neh-ee-*lah*; locking as in "the locking of the gates") service on Yom Kippur, which is the day's last service. This saying reflects the centrality of Israel and Jerusalem to Judaism and also to Jews throughout the millennia no matter where they have fled to or have roamed.

GRAMMATICALLY SPEAKING

The Hebrew infinitive for "to be" is לִהְיוֹת (le-hee-*yoht*). Check out Table 7-1 to see how to conjugate this important verb in the past and future tenses. לִהְיוֹת doesn't have a present tense, however; the tense is implied in the pronoun. So, when you want to say "I am" in Hebrew, all you need to say is אֲנִי (ah-*nee*; *I*).

TIP

One helpful phrase when talking about time in Hebrew is בְּעֵרֶךְ (buh-ehr-*ehh*; *approximately*), which you can use when you are flexible about timing and giving an approximate time. When you want to communicate the need to be exactly on time, use the phrase בְּדִיּוּק (beh-dee-*yook*; *exactly*) which is what Israelis use for the American expression "sharp" as in "ten o'clock sharp."

Here are a couple of other tidbits about the infinitive לִהְיוֹת:

>> Two popular Israeli expressions that use this verb are יִהְיֶה טוֹב (yeh-hee-*yeh* tohv; *Things will get better*), and מָה יִהְיֶה? (mah yeh-hee-*yeh*, *What will be?* or *What's going to happen?*).

>> The Hebrew equivalent of "Once upon a time" uses this verb. The expression is הָיֹה הָיָה (hah-*yoh* ha-*yah*).

TABLE 7-1 Conjugating לִהְיוֹת (le-hee-*yoht*; *to be*)

English Verb	Hebrew Verb	Pronunciation	Gender
Past Tense			
I was	הָיִיתִי	hah-*yee*-tee	MS/FS
you were	הָיִיתָ	hah-*yee*-tah	MS
you were	הָיִית	hah-*yeet*	FS
he was	הָיָה	hah-*yah*	MS
she was	הָיְתָה	hei-*tah*	*FS*
we were	הָיִינוּ	hah-*yee*-noo	MP/FP
you were	הֱיִיתֶם	hah-*yee*-tehm	MP
you were	הֱיִיתֶן	hah-*yee*-tehn	FP
they were	הָיוּ	hah-*yoo*	MP/FP
Future Tense			
I will be	אֶהְיֶה	eh-heh-*yeh*	MS/FS
you will be	תִּהְיֶה	teh-he-*yeh*	MS
you will be	תִּהְיִי	tee-hee-*yee*	FS
he will be	יִהְיֶה	yee-hee-*yeh*	(MS)
she will be	תִּהְיֶה	tee-he-*yeh*	(FS)
we will be	נִהְיֶה	nee-he-*yeh*	MP/FP
you will be	תִּהְיוּ	te-hee-*yoo*	MP/FP
they will be	יִהְיוּ	yee-hee-*yoo*	MP/FP

WORDS TO KNOW

בֹּקֶר	boh-*kehr*	morning
חֲצִי שָׁעָה	ḥah-*tzee* shah-*ah*	half an hour
דַּקָּה	dah-*kah*	minute
אֶמֶשׁ	eh-mehsh	last night
עֶרֶב	eh-rehv	evening
אֶתְמוֹל	eht-*mohl*	yesterday

לַיְלָה	*lai*-lah	night
מָחָר	mah-*chahr*	tomorrow
מָחֳרָתַיִם	ma**h**-rah-*tah*-eem	day after tomorrow
רֶגַע	*reh*-gah	moment
שְׁנִיָּה	sh-nee-*yah*	second
שָׁעָה	shah-*ah*	hour
שָׁבוּעַ	shah-*voo*-ah	week
שִׁלְשׁוֹם	shil-*shohm*	day before yesterday
תַּאֲרִיךְ	tah-ah-*reeh*	date
צָהֳרַיִם	tzoh-hoh-*rah*-yeem	noon
זְמַן	z-*mahn*	time

CULTURAL WISDOM

Israelis are excellent multitaskers. When an Israeli is in the middle of something but wants to indicate to you that they'll pay attention to you in a moment and you should wait a bit, they may cup the fingers of their hand and shake it at you. When you see this gesture, it means רַק רֶגַע (*rahk reh-*gah; *just one moment*) or maybe דַּקָּה (dah-*kah*; one minute) or שְׁנִיָּה (*shnee*-ah; just a second). Whatever it is, just shush up and hang tight!

Talkin' the Talk

Natan is waiting for the bus on a Sunday morning. He forgot to wear his watch today and left his cellphone at home, so he asks the man standing next to him for the time.

Natan: סְלִיחָה אֲדוֹנִי מָה הַשָּׁעָה ?

(slee-**h**ah ah-doh-*nee*. Mah-hah-shah-*ah*?)

Excuse me, sir, what's the time?

Man: הַשָּׁעָה שְׁמוֹנָה וָחֵצִי.

(hah-shah-*ah* shh-*moh*-neh vah- **h**eh-tzee)

The time is eight-thirty.

Natan: . תּוֹדָה רַבָּה לְךָ אֲדוֹנִי

(toh-*dah* rah-*bah* leh-*chah* ah-doh-*nee*)

Thank you very much, sir.

Man: . בְּבַקָשָׁה

(beh-*vah*-kah-*shah*)

You're welcome.

Natan: ? בְּאֵיזוֹ שָׁעָה הָאָטוֹבּוּס אָמוּר לְהַגִּיעַ

(beh-ay-*zoh* shah-*ah* hah-oh-toh-*boos* ah-*moor* leh-hah-*gee*-ah?)

When is the bus supposed to come?

Man: . עוֹד חָמֵשׁ דַקוֹת

(ohd **h**ah-*mesh* dah-*koht*)

In five more minutes.

• •

**CULTURAL
WISDOM**

All day on יוֹם שִׁשִׁי (*yohm* shee-*shee*; *Friday*) and also on יוֹם שַׁבָּת (*yohm* shah-*baht*; *Saturday*), the customary greeting is שַׁבָּת שָׁלוֹם (shah-*baht* shah-*lohm*; *a peaceful Sabbath*). When שַׁבָּת (shah-*baht*; *the Sabbath*) is over on מוֹצָאֵי שַׁבָּת (moh-*tza-ay* shah-*baht*; *Saturday night*), you should wish people a שָׁבוּעַ טוֹב (shah-*voo*-ah *tohv*; *a good week*).

HAVING FUN WITH ISRAELI SLANG

Hebrew has several ways to express having a good time. The word for "fun" in Hebrew is כֵּיף (*kehf*). If something is really fun, you may want to comment that it's כֵּיף לֹא נוֹרְמָלִי (kehf loh nor-*mal*-ee; *fun beyond the norm*). Or you may want to say עָף עַל זֶה (*ahf-ahl zeh*; *flying on it*) or חֲבָל עַל הַזְמַן (**h**ah-*vah*l al hah-*zman*; *a waste of time,* but it means the opposite, *a great time*). Then there's סוֹף הַדֶּרֶךְ (*sohf* hah-*dehr*-re**h**; *end of the road*). If you want to say, "to have fun," you can say לְכַיֵּף (leh-kah-*yehf*), or you can tell someone לַעֲשׂוֹת חַיִּים (lah-ah-*soht* **h**ah-*yeem*; literally: *to do/make life*). If you want to tell someone to have a good time, the expression is בִּלּוּי נָעִים ! (bee-looy nah-*eem*).

Discovering the Days in a Week

In Hebrew, the only day that has an official name is the Sabbath, which falls on the seventh day of the week: Saturday. That day is called שַׁבָּת (shah-*baht*). Friday afternoon is called עֶרֶב שַׁבָּת (*eh*-rehv shah-*baht*; *Shabbat afternoon*), and Friday evening is לֵיל שַׁבָּת (*layl* shah-*baht*; *Shabbat evening*). Take a look at Chapter 1, where I cover all this numbers. The rest of the days of the week are numbered as follows:

» יוֹם רִאשׁוֹן (*yohm* ree-*shohn*; *the first day, Sunday*)

» יוֹם שֵׁנִי (*yohm* shay-*nee*; *the second day, Monday*)

» יוֹם שְׁלִישִׁי (*yohm* sh-lee-*shee*; *the third day, Tuesday*)

» יוֹם רְבִיעִי (*yohm* reh-*vee-ee*; *the fourth day, Wednesday*)

» יוֹם חֲמִישִׁי (*yohm* ḥah-mee-*shee*; *the fifth day, Thursday*)

» יוֹם שִׁשִּׁי (*yohm* shee-*shee*; *the sixth day, Friday*)

In traditional Jewish households around the world, יוֹם שִׁשִּׁי (*Friday*) is often a hectic day of preparing for שַׁבָּת (*Sabbath*). Everyone is out buying the items they need for the day of rest. People often buy פְּרָחִים (prah-*cheem*; *flowers*) to adorn the dinner table to help emphasize the festive nature of the day.

According to the Hebrew calendar, days begin in the evening, so the Jewish Sabbath starts at sunset on Friday. The time, of course, varies during the year. In the winter, שַׁבָּת can start as early as 3 p.m., and in the summer, שַׁבָּת may not start until as late as 8 p.m. שַׁבָּת lasts a total of 25 hours from the time the sun begins to set on עֶרֶב שַׁבָּת until it has completely set on מוֹצָאֵי שַׁבָּת (moh-*tzay* shah-*baht*; *Saturday night*) and you can see three stars in the sky.

The workweek in Israel runs from Sunday to Friday. Friday is a half day, however, and more and more companies in Israel are converting to a five-day workweek, with Friday considered to be part of the weekend. School in Israel is still in session six days a week, though, likely to the chagrin of schoolchildren and the joy of parents (who can get a half day off from work and parenting responsibilities).

Catching Some Culture

So, you want to go out for a good time. What do you want to do? Opportunities abound! How about a movie? Perhaps you'd like to hear live music or take in some live theater. Or maybe you want to nurture your aesthetic side and spend some time strolling through a museum. All you have to do is choose. If you want to name your choice in Hebrew, keep reading; I'll show you how.

Visiting museums and art galleries

If you want to go somewhere to nurture your נְשָׁמָה (neh-shah-mah; soul), a מוּזֵאוֹן (moo-zeh-ohn; museum) is a wonderful place to go. Wandering the quiet מִסְדְּרוֹנוֹת (mees-de-roh-noht; halls) and examining the works of אָמָנוּת (oh-mah-noot; art) or artifacts of אַרְכֵיאוֹלוֹגְיָה (ar-che-oh-log-yah; archaeology) are always inspiring. I love to catch the latest תְּצוּגָה (tetz-oo-gah; exhibition) and stroll through the גָּלֶרְיַת אָמָנוּת (gah-lehr-yaht oh-mah-noot; art gallery), and even take some סִיּוּרִים מֻדְרָכִים (see-yoor-eem mood-rah-cheem; guided tours) if they're offered. But before you go, check out שְׁעוֹת מוּזֵאוֹן (sheh-oht hah-moo-zeh-ohn; the museum hours), because you don't want to arrive to closed doors!

WORDS TO KNOW		
גָּלֶרְיַת אָמָנוּת	gah-lair-yaht oh-mah-noot	art gallery
מוּזֵאוֹן	moo-zeh-ohn	museum
שְׁעוֹת פְּתִיחַת הַמּוּזֵאוֹן	sh-oht puh-tee-ḥaht hah-moo-zeh-ohn	museum hours
סִיּוּרִים מֻדְרָכִים	see-your-eem moo-drah-ḥeem	guided tours
תְּצוּגָה	teh-tzoo-gah	exhibition

Going to the movies

I like all kinds of סְרָטִים (srah-teem; movies). I'm happy to see a סֶרֶט דְּרָמָה (seh-reht drah-mah; a dramatic film) or a סֶרֶט קוֹמֶדְיָה (seh-reht koh-meh-dee-ah; a comedy). Believe it or not, I love a good סֶרֶט פְּעֻלָּה (seh-reht pe-oo-lah; action film), and if it's not too scary, I'm even up for a סֶרֶט מֶתַח (seh-reht meh-taḥ; thriller).

Some people choose movies if they like the בַּמַּאי (bah-mai; director) or the מֵפִיק (meh-feek; producer); others like to go see their favorite שַׂחְקָן (tzahḥ-kahn; actor) or שַׂחְקָנִית (saḥ-kah-neet; actress). If one of the actors is particularly מְפֻרְסָם (meh-foor-sahm; famous), they often have a big draw at the box office.

When you go to a קוֹל נוֹעַ (kohl noh-ah; movie theater), you need to buy a כַּרְטִיס (kahr-tees; ticket) at the קֻפָּה (koo-pah; box office). In Israel, sometimes you have מ מְקוֹמוֹת שְׁמוּרִים (meh-koh-moht shohm-reem; assigned seats). Also, in Israel, movies have פִּרְסוֹמוֹת (peer-soh-*moht; commercials*) before the show and a הַפְסָקָה (hahf-sah-*kah; intermission*)! So, if you forget to go to the שֵׁרוּתִים (sheh-roo-*teem; bathroom*) before the show, you can go during the intermission.

WORDS TO KNOW

בַּמַּאי	bah-*mai*	director
הַפְסָקָה	hahf-*sah*-kah	intermission
כַּרְטִיס	kahr-*tees*	ticket
קוֹל נוֹעַ	kohl-*noh*-ah	movie theater
קֻפָּה	koo-*pah*	box office
מְפֻרְסָם	meh-four-*sahm*	famous
מֵפִיק	meh-*feek*	producer
צ שַׂחְקָן	tzah**h**-*kahn*	actor
שַׂחְקָנִית	tzah**h**-kah-*neet*	actress
סֶרֶט	seh-reht	movie
שֵׁרוּתִים	sheh-roo-*teem*	restrooms

TIP

To sound like a native, use slang. Israeli slang uses expressions that include the Hebrew word for "film," סֶרֶט (seh-reht) in totally different contexts. You use אֵיזֶה סֶרֶט (ay-*zeh ser*-eht), which literally means "what a movie," when you want to say that something is really great. כְּבָר הָיִיתִי בַּסֶרֶט הַזֶּה (kvahr hah-*yee*-tee ba-*seh-reht* hah-*zeh; I've already been in this movie*) is the Hebrew equivalent of "Been there, done that."

Enjoying live entertainment: Music and theater

If you want a real treat, you might spend an evening taking in ט תֵּאַטְרוֹן (ta-*aht-rohn; live theatre*). Israel has its own national theater company, הַבִּימָה (hah-bee-*mah; The Stage*). Theater is an incredible art form. In Israel, a country whose national anthem, הַתִּקְוָה (hah-teek-*vah*), means "the hope," theater plays an important role in continuing to shape and define the country's national identity and chronicling its hopes and dreams for the future.

WATCHING ISRAELI FILMS AND TV SHOWS ON NETFLIX AND MORE!

Israeli television and movies have come of age. They used to be pretty בֵּינוֹנִי וּמַטָה (bay-no-nee oo-*mah*-tah; mediocre), but now, they're sooooo good. There have been lots of crossover hits, many of them easily accessible on various streaming services. I heartily recommend checking them out, because watching great Israeli movies is fun, entertaining, and a great way to practice your Hebrew. Start slow by watching Israeli films and television shows with the English subtitles turned on. That way, you can accustom your ear to an authentic Israeli accent, pick up a bunch of new words, and discover a little about Israeli culture, all while being thoroughly entertained. What do you have to lose? I recommend the following flicks and television series:

- הַקַיִץ שֶׁל אֲבִיָּה (Ha-kah-*yeetz* shehl ah-*vee*-yah; *Aviya's Summer*): This classic film, winner of the Silver Bear Award from the Berlin International Film Festival, is about a widow and her young daughter who have made their way to Israel after surviving the Holocaust. Based on Gila Almagor's autobiographical novel of the same name, the story presents a touching picture of life in Israel's early years of independence and a period known as תְּקוּפַת הַצֶּנַע (t'kufat; *The Period of Austerity*). Then the young state implemented austerity measures such as food rations to cope with the severe financial challenges in its early years The film is presented through the eyes of the novel's author when she was a little girl. The real author of the novel plays the part of her mother in the movie. The movie doesn't seem to be streaming anywhere these days, but you can get the DVD on Amazon if you still have a DVD player that works. It's definitely worth the trouble to find.

- בְּלוּז לַחֹפֶשׁ הַגָּדוֹל (blooz lah-*choh*-fehsh hah-gah-*dohl*; *Late Summer Blues*): Nearly four decades after this film was released, it still paints a touching portrait of Israeli youth coming of age amid the tensions of war. This powerful film, set in 1970 during the Arab-Israeli War of Attrition (1967–70), chronicles the lives of seven Israeli teenagers during the summer following their high-school graduation and before their compulsory army service.

- סִפּוּר אַהֲבָה וְחֹשֶׁךְ (see-*poor* ah-hah-*vah* ve-**h**oh-she**h**, *A Tale of Love and Darkness*): Set during the British Mandate period (1918–48), before Israel achieved Independence, the film stars (and is directed by) Natalie Portman (yes, *that* Natalie Portman), who was born in Israel and speaks fluent Hebrew! Based on Amos Oz's autobiography of the same name, it tells the story of a Jewish family in the years leading up to Israel's independence.

(continued)

(continued)

- פאודה (*Fauda*; Chaos (Arabic)): This hit Israeli TV show found fans all over the world when Netflix picked it up. Based on the lived experiences of Israeli writers Lior Raz and Avi Issacharoff, both of whom served in צְהַ״ל (*Tzah*-hahl; *the Israeli Defense Forces*) in a specialized unit called מִסְתַּעַרְבִים (mees-*tah*-ah-*rahv*-eem; *undercover*), the show follows them as they go undercover in counterterrorism, intelligence, and search and rescue efforts. The show is full of suspense, drama, and Hebrew and Arabic dialogue.

- שְׁטִיסֶל (*stheh*-sehl; *Shtisel*): This three-season series set in the Geula neighborhood of Jerusalem tells the stories of the loves and losses of the Shtisels, an ultra-Orthodox Jewish family. You'll laugh, you'll cry, and you'll get to hear not only Hebrew, but also another Jewish language, Yiddish. You'll also get to hear a special dialect of Hebrew known as לשון הקודש (lah-*shohn* hah-*koh*-dehsh; *holy language*) in which Hebrew words used to describe Jewish sacred texts or religious obligations is spoken with an Ashkenazi (Eastern European Jewish) accent, instead of the Mizrahi (Middle Eastern) accent used today by most Israelis. The series is streaming on Netflix.

- חֲטוּפִים (ḥah-*too*-feem, *Hostages*): If you loved *Homeland,* you don't want to miss the Israeli series on which the American show was based. This two-season Israeli show follows the lives of two soldiers who return home to Israel after 17 years in captivity. The series is an emotional journey through their personal lives, the Israeli intelligence apparatus, and war and terror in the Middle East. Streaming on Hulu.

- מַלְכַּת הַיֹּפִי שֶׁל יְרוּשָׁלַיִם (*mahl*-kaht hah *yoh*-fee shehl yeh-*roo-shah-lah*-yeem; *The Beauty Queen of Jerusalem*): This epic television series brings to life the years from 1917, when the future state of Israel was under Ottoman rule, through 1948 and Israel's war for independence, viewing that period through the eyes of the Ermosas, a Sephardic Jewish family in Jerusalem. The period drama features some of Israel's best actors, retelling history that's still relevant today, and presenting the tragic times and loves of one family. You'll hear not only Hebrew, but also Turkish, Arabic, and even Ladino — another Jewish language. Produced by YES studios in Israel, it will be streaming worldwide soon. Watch for it.

Wherever you are, you get a thrill watching the צַחְקָנִים (saḥ-kah-neem; *actors*) perform on a בִּימָה (bee-*mah*; *stage*) and joining in the thunderous מְחִיאַתכַּפַּיִם (meh-chee-*aht* kah-*pah*-eem; *applause*) as the פַּרְגּוֹד (pahr-*gohd*; *stage curtain*) falls.

I love מוּזִיקָה (moo-*zee*-kah; *music*). One of my favorite things to do is go to a מוֹעֲדוֹן (moh-ah-*dohn*; *nightclub*) to hear a הוֹפָעָה חַיָּה (hoh-fah-*ah* ḥai-*yah*; *live show*). Even if I've never heard of the לַהֲקָה (leh-hah-*kah*; *band*), I'm happy to soak up the atmosphere.

I love to hear זַמָּרִים (zah-mah-*reem*; *singers*) who have written the מִלִּים (mee-*leem*; *words*) and לַחַן (*lah-ḥan*; *melody*) to their own שִׁירִים (shee-*reem*; *songs*). And if the music is אָקוּסְטִי (ah-*koos*-tee; *acoustic*), all the better.

When you're in Israel, be sure to take in some live tunes. Listening to songs is a great way to accustom your ears to the lilting sounds of Hebrew while mixing with the locals and having a great time. In Jerusalem, check out הַתַּחֲנָה הָרִאשׁוֹנָה (ha-tah-hah-*nah*- hah-ree-*shohn*-nah; *The First Station*) formerly the site of an old railroad station and now a shopping and cultural center or head out to הַצּוֹלֶלֶת הַצְּהֻבָּה (hah-tzoh-*lehl*-leht ḥah-tzoo-*hoo*-bah; *The Yellow Submarine*), the latter of which is a not-for-profit venue that donates proceeds to organizations working for דּוּ קִיּוּמִיּוֹת (doo-koo-*mee*-ooot; *coexistence*) between Arab and Jewish citizens of Israel. For a truly magnificent experience in a larger venue, soak up the sounds and vibes at an ancient archaeological site and musical venue all in one at בריכת הסלטן (bray-*ḥaht* sool-tahn; *Sultan's Pool*), once a water basin built on the western slope of Jerusalem's Mount Zion in the early Ottoman years by Suleiman the Magnificent.

For more info on the First Station, check out: www.touristisrael.com/jerusalem-first-station/28141/.

At a הוֹפָעָה חַיָּה (hoh-*fah*-ah hai-*yah*, *live performance*), you may hear several נַגָּנִים (nah-gah-*neem*; *musicians*) who like לְנַגֵּן בְּ (leh-nah-*gehn* buh; *to play [an instrument]*) many types of כְּלִי נְגִינָה (klai-neh-*gee*-nah, *instruments*).

Instruments may include

- » חָלִיל (ḥah-*leel*; *flute*)
- » חֵמֶת חָלִיל (ḥeh-*maeht* ḥa-lee-*leem*; *bagpipes*)
- » גִּיטָרָה (gee-*tah*-rah; *guitar*)
- » כְּלֵי הַקָּשָׁה (klee hah-kah-*shah*; *percussion*)
- » כִּנּוֹר (kee-*nohr*; *violin*)
- » קְלִידִים (klee-*deem*; *keyboards*)
- » תֻּפִּים (too-*peem*; *drums*)

WORDS TO KNOW

בִּימָה	bee-*mah*	stage
הוֹפָעָה חַיָה	hoh-fah-*ah* cha-*yah*	live show
כְּלֵי נְגִינָה	klee neh-gee-*nah*	instrument
לְנַגֵּן	leh-nah-*gehn*	to play [an instrument]
לַהֲקָה	leh-hah-*kah*	band
מוֹעֲדוֹן	moh-ah-*dohn*	club
מוּזִיקָה	*moo-zee-kah*	music

Talkin' the Talk

Shulie and Nomi are שֻׁתָּפוֹת (shoo-tah-*foht*; *roommates*). They're sitting around their דִּירָה (dee-*rah*; *apartment*) one evening, trying to decide what to do. Shulie suggests that they go to a מוֹעֲדוֹן (moh-ah-*dohn*; *club*) to hear a cool band called אֶסְטָה (ehs-*tah*; *Esta*).

Nomi: מָה אַתְּ רוֹצָה לַעֲשׂוֹת הָעֶרֶב ?

(mah *aht* roh-*tzah* lah-ah-*soht* hah-eh-*rehv?*)

What do you want to do this evening?

Shulie: בָּא לִי לִשְׁמֹעַ מוּזִיקָה .

(*bah lee leesh-moh-ah moo*-zee-kah.)

I feel like listening to music.

Nomi: מִי מוֹפִיעָה בַּמּוֹעֲדוֹן בַּשְׁכוּנָה ?

(mee moh-*fee*-ah bah-moh-ah-*dohn* bah-shuh-choo-*nah*.)

Who is playing at the neighborhood club?

Shulie: יֵשׁ לַהֲקָה מְצֻיֶּנֶת בְּשֵׁם אֶסְטָה .

(yesh leh-hah-*kah* meh-tzoo-*yeh*-net be-*shehm* ehs-*tah*.)

There's an excellent band called Esta.

Nomi: יֹפִי! שָׁמַעְתִּי שֶׁהֵם חֲבָל עַל הַזְּמַן !

(*yoh*-fee. Shah-mah-*tee* sheh-*hem* chah-*vahl* ahl hah-*zmahn*.)

Great! I heard they're amazing!

Shulie: נָכוֹן יֵשׁ לָהֶם תֻּפִּים חָלִיל גִּיטָרָה קְלִידִים וַאֲפִילֵי חֲמֶת חֲלִילִים.

(nah-*chohn*. Yesh lah-*hem* too-*peem* chah-*leel*, gee-*tah*-rah, klee-*deem* kee-*nor*, ve-ah-fee-*loo cheh*-meht chah-lee-*leem*.)

That's right. They have drums, a flute, a guitar, keyboards, a violin, and even bagpipes.

Nomi: בּוֹא נֵלֵךְ !

(boh neh-*lech*)

Let's go!

• •

CULTURAL WISDOM

Esta is a real Israeli band, and the group is excellent. The musicians are a world-fusion band that bring together the sounds from many musical traditions. They're worth checking out! Also, I can't imagine a better way to learn some Hebrew. You can find out more about this incredible band at www.estamusic.com or www.israel-music.com. You can also check out Esta's CDs, along with plenty of other awesome Israeli music.

The Israeli Music Scene

Jews are a people who have wandered the globe, scattering from their ancestral homeland in the first century, seeking refuge in many host countries until their return home to Israel in the 19th and 20th centuries. The wanderings and wonderings of the Jewish people have made their way into Israeli music, creating a fusion sound all its own. It's an incredible sound and listening to it is a great way to learn Hebrew. Some of my faves include Ishay Ribo, a Modern Orthodox Israeli singer who brings new sounds to ancient texts; Ivri Lider, who is somewhere on the seam between folk and rock; Ofra Haza, the Yemenite Israeli singer whose Yemenite melodies crossed over into the mainstream; Netta, who won the Eurovision Song Contest in 2018 with her hit feminist song "I'm Not Your Toy"; Rami Kleinshtein, who's kind of an Israeli Billy Joel; David Broza, who sings in Hebrew, English, and Spanish, and plays an incredible Spanish guitar; and hip-hop group HaDag Nahash, led by Koby Oz, a lifelong Jerusalemite, peace activist, and bar owner who sends his children to a joint Arab-Jewish school. Worth a mention is

Mira Awad, a Christian Palestinian with Israeli citizenship who teamed up with Ahinoam Nini, a fifth-generation צַבָּרִית (tzah-*bahr*-eet, *native-born Israeli*) of Jewish–Yemenite descent, to represent Israel in the 2009 Eurovision contest, singing "There Must Be Another Way." (Check them out at https://www.youtube.com/watch?v=RN8B1xvCxI0.)

As for my ultimate favorite, that has to be the Idan Raichel Project. With his breakout hit בּוֹאִי (*Boh*-ee; "Come"), Raichel brought Ethiopian voices and melodies to a mass audience in Israel. Their next hit, the haunting מִמַּעֲמַקִּים (Mee-mahm-*mah*-ah-keem; "*Out of the Depths*"), based on biblical psalms, fuses ancient text and the cultural diversity of Israel in a sound that blends East and West. This YouTube page provides an English translation of the lyrics: https://www.youtube.com/watch?v=aQSJVsphUnY.

This list wouldn't be complete without mentioning the Jerusalem Choir, an Israeli and Palestinian youth choir that practices in Jerusalem's YMCA. Their rendition of אֲנִי יוֹדֵעַ שֶׁהַכֹּל יִהְיֶה בְּסֵדֶר (ah-nee yoh-*day*-ah sheh hah-*kohl* yee-*hee*-yeh beh-seh-dehr; "*I Know Everything Will Be Okay*") gives hope that things just might work out. Check out their video of the song at https://www.youtube.com/watch?v=11H0VwhYf9A.

TIP

You can learn more about this remarkable group of young people at https://jerusalemyouthchorus.org/.

The Animals Went on the Ark Two by Two: Visiting the Zoo!

The גַּן חַיּוֹת (*gahn* chah-*yoht*; *zoo*) is a wonderful place to spend the afternoon with family members or friends. Table 7-2 lists some of the animals you might see at the zoo.

And although you might not see these animals at the zoo, you may have a חָתוּל (chah-*tool*; *cat*) or a כֶּלֶב (*keh*-lehv; *dog*) as a pet! And if you're visiting a farm, you may see a פָּרָה (pah-*rah*; *cow*), a סוּס (soos; *horse*), a חֲזִיר (chah-*zeer*; *pig*), and maybe even a תַּרְנְגוֹל (tahr-neh-*gohl*; *rooster*).

TABLE 7-2

Animals You May See at a Zoo

Hebrew	Pronunciation	English Translation
אַרְיֵה	ahr-*ee*-yeh	lion
דָּג	*dahg*	fish
דֹב	*dohv*	bear
גִּירָפָה	*jeerah*-fah	giraffe
קַרְנַף	*kahr*-nahf	rhinoceros
קִפּוֹד	*kee*-pohd	porcupine
קוֹף	*kohf*	monkey
פִּיל	*peel*	elephant
סוּס הַיְאוֹר	*soos* hah-*yeh*-ohr	hippopotamus
צָב	*tzahv*	turtle
צִפּוֹר	*tzee*-pohr	bird

Spicing Up Your Sentences with Adverbs

Hebrew doesn't have a single formula for changing *adjectives* (words that describe a noun) into *adverbs* (words that describe a verb). In English, for example, *slow* becomes *slowly*, *hungry* becomes *hungrily*, and *angry* becomes *angrily*. In Hebrew, you just put the phrase בְּאֹפֶן (buh–*oh*–fehn; literally: *in the manner of*) in front of the adjective to change it to an adverb. Here are a few examples:

» קָבוּעַ (kah-*voo*-ah; *permanent*) becomes קָבוּעַ בְּאֹפֶן (buh-*oh*-fehn kah-*voo*-ah; *permanently*).

» מָהִיר (mah-*hair*; *quick*) becomes מָהִיר בְּאֹפֶן (buh-*oh*-fen mah-*heir*; *quickly*).

You can also convert an adjective to an adverb by preceding the noun with ב (*with*) and adding the suffix וּת (*oot*) at the end:

» עָדִין (*ah*-deen; *gentle*) becomes עֲדִינוּת (buh ah-dee-*noot*; literally: *with gentleness*; *gently*).

» מָהִיר (*mah*-hair; *quick*) becomes בִּמְהִירוּת (bim-hee-*root*; literally: *with quickness*; *quickly*).

Some adverbs are adjectives used in their masculine singular form. You may see some adjectives used in the following way:

>> חָזָק (chah-*zahk*; *strong*)

>> קָשֶׁה (kah-*sheh*; *difficult*)

>> מְצֻיָּן (meh-tzoo-*yahn*; *excellent*)

>> נוֹרָא (noh-*rah*; *terrible*)

>> רַע (*rah*; *bad, badly*)

>> טוֹב (*tohv*; *good* and *well*)

>> יָפֶה (yah-*feh*; *pretty*)

>> יָשָׁר (yah-*shar*; *straight*)

For more on making masculine and feminine adjectives, take a look at Chapter 2.

FUN & GAMES

See the pictures of different בַּעֲלֵי חַיִּים (bah-ah-*lei* ḥah-*yeem; animals*). Using the word list, write the correct name of the animal below its picture.

אַרְיֵה, חָתוּל, דָּג, כֶּלֶב, פָּרָה, פִּיל, סוּס, סוּס הַיְאוֹר, תַּרְנְגוֹל, צִפּוֹר

Chapter **8**

Enjoying Your Free Time: Hobbies, Sports, and Other Fun Activities

ll work and no play can make you a very dull child. The antidote, of course, is to have a good time! Sports, hobbies, and interests are all great ways not only to have fun, but also to meet people and restore energy. I believe that everyone should play at least one instrument and one sport and pursue at least one other interest. Leisure activities make you well rounded.

In this chapter, you discover how to talk about your recreational passions: the sports you love, the hobbies you adore, and the myriad activities you like to do whenever you find the time. בְּלוּי נָעִים! (bee-looy e nah-eem; Have fun!).

Chatting About Your Hobbies

Our hobbies and interests make great fodder for conversation. In this section, I tell you what words you need to know to gab away with your friends and family members about what you enjoy!

Amassing an amazing collection

Some people like to collect anything and everything. If you stuff items into a box or under your bed, we call you a pack rat. But if you take the items you collect and put them on display, we call that activity a תַּחְבִּיב (tahch–*beev; hobby*), a שַׁעֲשׁוּעַ (shah–ah–*shoo*–ah; *amusement*), or even a שִׁגָּעוֹן (shee–gah–*ohn; madness*). Truth be told, collecting is an enjoyable activity; you're always searching for the next great find to add to your mix. You can tell people what you like to collect by saying the following:

>> אֲנִי אֹסֵף. . . (ah-*nee* oh-*sehf; I collect . . .*) (M)

אֲנִי אוֹסֶפֶת. . . (ah-*nee* oh-*seh*-feht; *I collect . . .*) (F)

אֲנִי אוֹסֶפֶה. . . (ah-*nee* oh-*seh*-feh; *I collect . . .*) (NB)

If you want to say you are interested in something you would say:

>> אֲנִי מִתְעוּנֵּין. . . (ah-*nee* meh-oon-*yahn* beh; I am interested in . . .) (M)

אֲנִי מְעֻנְיֶנֶת ב. . . (ah-nee meet-*oon-yeh*-neht beh; *I am interested in . . .*) (F)

אֲנִי מִתְעוּנְיֶנֶה ב. . . (ah-*nee* meht-oon-*yeh*-neh beh; *I am interested in . . .*) (NB)

At the end of the phrases, you can name the item you like to collect, such as any of the following:

>> עַתִּיקוֹת (ah-tee-*koht; antiques*)

>> בֻּבּוֹת (boo-*boht; dolls*)

>> בּוּלִים (boo-*leem; stamps*)

>> מַטְבְּעוֹת (mat-be-*oht; coins*)

Creating things with your hands

Making things with your hands isn't only fun, but also satisfying. Gazing upon some item you created with your own hands is very rewarding. So, you're probably not surprised that many hobbies revolve around different types of handicrafts. In Hebrew, you can tell someone about your favorite hobby by using one of the following phrases:

» תַּחְבִּיב שֶׁלִּי . . . (hah-tach-*beev* sheh-*lee*; *My hobby is* . . .)

» תַּחְבִּיבִי . . . (tach-bee-*vee*; *My hobby is* . . .)

However, this is a rather formal way of speaking. In Israel, people are more likely to say אֲנִי מִתְעַנְיֶנֶת [ah-nee *meet*-ahn-yehn-*eht*; I am interested in (FS)] or אֲנִי מִתְעַנְיֵן [ah-nee *meet*-ahn-*yehn*; I am interested in (MS)]. Another way to talk about your hobby is to say "I enjoy *plus an infinitive*" for example: אֲנִי נֶהֱנֶה/נֶהֱנֵית לְבַשֵּׁל which means "I enjoy cooking." These days Israelis are less likely to say the word "hobby" and are more likely to just say "I enjoy . . ." At the end of the phrase, you tack on the name of the thing you like to do, such as

» עֲבוֹדוֹת בְּעֵץ (ohv-*doht* buh-*ehtz*; *woodworking*)

» בִּשּׁוּל (bee-*shool*; *cooking*)

» גִּנּוּן (gee -*noon*; *gardening*)

» אִסּוּף (ee-*soof*; *collecting*)

» צִיּוּר (tzee-*yoor*; *painting*)

» אָמָנוּת (oo-mah-*noot*; *craft*)

GRAMMATICALLY
SPEAKING

In Hebrew, you can show possession and indicate that something belongs to someone by attaching a particle to the end of the object. In grammarspeak, this particle is known as a *personal-possessive suffix*. The suffixes are as follows:

י (ee; *my, mine*)

ךָ (*ḥ*ah; *you, yours*) (MS)

ךְ (eh*ḥ*; *you, yours*) (FS)

כֶה (*ḥ*eh; *you, yours*) (NB)

ו (oh; *his*)

ה (ah; *her, hers*)

נוּ (noo; *our, ours*)

כֶם (chehm; *your, yours*) (MP)

כֶן (chehn; *your, yours*) (FP)

ם (ahm; *theirs*) (M)

ן (ahn, *theirs*) (F)

After you attach the preceding suffixes to words, they look like the following list (in which I use the word for "hobby"):

תַּחְבִּיבִי (tah**h**-bee-*vee*; *my hobby*)

תַּחְבִּיבְךָ (tah**h**-beev-*hah*; *your hobby*) (MS)

תַּחְבִּיבֵךְ (tah**h**-bee-*vehh*; *your hobby*) (FS)

תַּחְבִּיבְכֶה (tahch-beev-*heh*; *your hobby*) (NB)

תַּחְבִּיבוֹ (tah**h**-bee-*voh*; *his hobby*)

תַּחְבִּיבָהּ (tah**h**-bee-*vah*; *her hobby*)

תַּחְבִּיבֵנוּ (tahch-bee-*vei*-noo; *our hobby*)

תַּחְבִּיבְכֶם (tah**h**-beev-*hem*; *your hobby*) (MP)

תַּחְבִּיבְכֶן (tah**h**-beev-*hen*; *your hobby*) (FP)

תַּחְבִּיבָם (tah**h**-bee-*vam*; *their hobby*) (M)

תַּחְבִּיבָן (tah**h**-bee-*van*; *their hobby*) (F)

Another way to show possession is to state the object followed by the *ownership phrase*, such as *mine, yours,* or *ours.* You can use the personal suffix or the ownership phrase for all nouns, as in תַּחְבִּיב שֶׁלִּי (tach–*beev* sheh–*lee*; *my hobby*).

TECHNICAL STUFF

If you're speaking about more than one person who possesses the certain object, or if you're talking about more than one object, the *word stem* changes a wee bit. If the object ends with the letter ה (*hey*), the ה (*hey*) disappears and is replaced by a ת (*tahv*).

Talkin' the Talk

 Ziv and Hod are discussing their hobbies as they wait for the bus. (Track 15)

Ziv: מֶה אַתָּה אוֹהֵב לַעֲשׂוֹת בַּזְּמַן הַפְּנוּי שֶׁלְּךָ ?

(mah ah-*tah* oh-*hev* lah-ah-*soht* bah-z'*mahn* hah-pah-noo*y* shel-*ḥah*?)

What do you like to do in your free time?

Hod: אֲנִי אֹסֵף בּוּלִים וַאֲנִי גַּם עוֹסֵק בַּעֲבוֹדַת עֵץ כְּתַחְבִּיב .

(ah-*nee* oh-*sef* boo-*leem*. veh ah-*nee* gahm oh-*sehk* buh-ah-voh-*daht* ehtz kuh-tach-*beev*.)

I collect stamps. And I also do woodworking as a hobby.

Ziv: אֵיזֶה קֶטַע גַּם אֲנִי אֹסֵף בַּיְלֶם תַּחְבִּיבִי בְּשׁוּל .

(ay-*zeh keh*-tah! Gahm ah-*nee* oh-*sef* boo-*leem*. Tach-*bee-vee* Bee-*shool*.)

Wow! I also collect stamps. Cooking's my hobby.

Hod: שִׁגָּעוֹן

shi-gah-*ohn*.

Awesome.

WORDS TO KNOW

אַתִּיקוֹת	ah-tee-*koht*	antiques
בִּשׁוּל	bee-*shool*	cooking
בֻּבּוֹת	boo-*boht*	dolls
בּוּלִים	boo-*leem*	stamps
גַּנָּנוּת	gah-nah-*noot*	gardening
מַטְבְּעוֹת	maht-beh-*oht*	coins
תַּחְבִּיב	tahch-*beev*	hobby
צִיאָר	tzee-*oor*	painting

Playing and Watching Sports

Whether you're a spectator or a participant, sports are a great way to let off some steam. In this section, I share some key sports words and equip you with the lingo for chatting about your favorite sports.

Kickin' to score in soccer

In many parts of the world, you find many אוֹהֲדִים (oh-hah-*deem; fans*) of כַּדּוּרֶרֶגֶל (kah-*dur* reh-gel; *soccer*). The World Cup final is practically a national holiday in some countries, with the workplaces clearing out for soccer-loving fans to cheer on their favorite קְבוּצָה (kvoo-*tzah; team*). Many international soccer matches have the יְצִיעִים (yeh-tzih-*eem; stands*) packed as people root for and cheer on their favorite שַׂחְקָן (sa**h**-*kahn; player*), yelling הוּא גָּדוֹל הוּא גָּדוֹל הוּא גָּדוֹל (hoo gah-*dohl*, hoo gah-*dohl*, hoo gah-*dohl; He's great, he's great, he's great*).

TIP

The literal translation of soccer, כַּדּוּר רֶגֶל, is *football*, which is what the sport is called everywhere but North America. If you want to talk about the popular American game of football, you have to specify כַּדּוּר רֶגֶל אָמֶרִיקָנִי (kah-*dur* reh-gehl ah-mer-ee-*kah*-nee), which literally means *American football*. Check out Table 8-1 for terms you use on a soccer field.

TABLE 8-1   ## Common Soccer Terms

Hebrew	Pronunciation	Translation
בְּעִיטָה חָפְשִׁית	beh-ee-*tah* chof-*sheet*	free kick
בְּעִיטָה עֳנָשִׁין	beh-ee-*taht* ohn-*sheen*	penalty kick
חָלוּץ	**h**a-*lootz*	forward (M)
חֲלוּצָה	**h**a-loo-*tzah*	forward (F)
אִצְטַדְיוֹן	itz-tahd-*yohn*	stadium
כַּדּוּר	kah-*dur*	ball
קָשָׁר	kah-*shar*	midfielder (M)
קָשֶׁרֶת	kah-*she*-reht	midfielder (F)
בְּעִיטַת קֶרֶן	bay-*taht keh*-ren	corner kick
לְהַבְקִיעַ שַׁעַר	leh-hav-*kee*-ah *sha*h-ahr	to score a goal
מָגֵן	mah-*gehn*	defender (M)

Hebrew	Pronunciation	Translation
מַגֵנָּה	mah-gee-*nah*	defender (F)
נִבְדָּל	neev-*dahl*	offsides
שׁוֹעֵר	shoh-*air*	goalkeeper (M)
שׁוֹעֶרֶת	shoh-*eh*-reht	goalkeeper (F)
שׁוֹפֵט	*Shoh*-feht	referee
מִגְרָשׁ	Meeg-*rahsh*	Soccer field
שַׁעַר	Shah-*ahr*	goal

Shooting for three in basketball

כַּדּוּרסַל (kah-*dur* sahl; *basketball*) is a great game to play and watch. If you're a שַׂחְקָן גָּבוֹהַּ (sach-*kahn* gah-voh-*hah*; *tall player*), you have a distinct advantage over a שַׂחְקָן נָמוּךְ (sach-*kahn* nah-*mooch*; *short player*). But height doesn't make much of a difference if you're a שַׂחְקָן גָּרוּעַ (sach-*kahn* gah-roo-*ah*; *terrible player*)! See Table 8-2 for some common basketball terms.

TABLE 8-2

Common Basketball Terms

Hebrew	Pronunciation	Translation
עֲבֵרָה	ah-vee-*rah*	foul
כַּדּוּר חוֹזֵר	kah-*dur* ḥoh-*zair*	rebound
לְכַדְרֵר	leh-kah-*drair*	to dribble
מִגְרָשׁ כַּדּוּרסַל	meeg-*rahsh*	Court
פֶּסֶק זְמַן	*peh*-sehk z-*mahn*	time-out
סַל	sahl	basket
צְעָדִים	tzeh-ah-*deem*	traveling
זְרִיקַת עוֹנְשִׁין	zeh-ri-*kaht* ohn-*sheen*	free throw

Swinging away at baseball

Ah! כַּדּוּר בָּסִיס (kah-*dur* bah-*sees*; *baseball*)! That great American pastime! At baseball games, you can sit in the יַצֵאַם (yeh-tzee-*eem*; *stands*), get some בָּטְנִים

(boht-*neem*; *peanuts*) or (בְּיְגָּלֶה bay-geh-*leh*; *pretzels*), a nice cold בִּירָה (bee-rah; *beer*) or סוֹדָה (soh-dah; *soda*), and cheer on your favorite קְבוּצָה (kvoo-*tzah*; *team*). Table 8-3 provides some terms you use on a baseball diamond.

TABLE 8-3

Common Baseball Terms

Hebrew	Pronunciation	Translation
בָּסִיס	*bah*-sees	base
גְּלִישָׁה	*glee*-shah	slide
כַּדּוּר גָּבוֹהַ	*kah*-dur *gah-voh*-hah	fly ball
כַּדּוּר קַרְקַע	*kah*-dur *kahr*-kah	ground ball
קַשָּׁר	kah-*shahr*	shortstop
כְּפָפַת חוֹבֵט	k-*fah*-faht **h**oh-veht	batting glove
קְבוּצַת הַבַּיִת	*kvoo-tzaht hah-bye*-eet	home team
מַחְבֵּט	mach-*beht*	baseball bat
מַגִּישׁ	mah-*geesh*	pitcher
סַפְסָל	sahf-*sahl*	bench
שׁוֹפֵט	shoh-*feht*	umpire
תְּנוּפָה	tnoo-*fah*	swing

GOING FOR JEWISH GOLD

Who says Jews can't jump? Believe it or not, the Jewish people have their own Olympics of sorts. Called the מַכַּבִּיָּה (mah-kah-bee-*yah*) after the hero of the חֲנֻכָּה (**h**ah-noo-*kah*; Hanukkah) story, Judah the Maccabee, this worldwide Jewish sporting event was founded in 1895. Since 1957, the מַכַּבִּיָּה has been held every four years in Israel, bringing together Jewish athletes from all over the world to celebrate their shared culture, history, and values and to compete in the sports that they love. The 21st Maccabia games, scheduled to take place in Tel Aviv in 2021, were postponed to 2022 due to the COVID-19 pandemic. In 2017, more than 10,000 athletes competed in this event, which is considered to be the third-largest sporting event in the world! Among the famous alumni of this illustrious Jewish sporting extravaganza are gymnast Aly Raisman; swimmer Garrett Webber-Gale; judoka Felipe Kitadai; karateka Adam Kovacs; swimmer Mark Spitz; gymnast Mitch Gaylord; National Basketball Association stars Ernie Grunfeld, Dolph Schayes, and Danny Schayes; golfer Bruce Fleisher; tennis pros Brad Gilbert and Dick Savitt; and World Cup soccer star Jeff Agoos.

ISRAEL AND THE OLYMPICS

Israel began competing in the Olympic Games in 1952 — just four years after its founding, which was quite a feat, given that the country was recovering from war while also being flooded with Jewish refugees from around the globe. Small but mighty, the Israeli team persisted, eventually winning its first Olympic מֶדַלְיָה (meh-*dahl*-lee-ah; *medal)* after 10 Olympic Games. In 1992, Judoka Yael Arad brought home the silver in women's ג'וּדוֹ (*joo*-doh; *judo*). It wasn't until 2004 that Israel won its first gold, when Gal Friedman won in men's גְּלִישַׁת רוּחַ (guh-lee-*shaht* roo-*ah*; *windsurfing*). Israel has fared better in the Paralympic Games, winning a total 375 medals.

Sadly, the team has also known tragedy. During the 1972 Games in Munich, 11 Israeli athletes were murdered by terrorists. These athletes were memorialized in 2021 during the opening ceremonies of the postponed 2020 Olympic Games. זִכְרוֹנָם לִבְרָכָה (zee*h*-roo-nahm leev-rah-*h*ah; *May their memories be a blessing*).

Taking a dip in the pool

I love לִשְׂחוֹת (lees-*h*oht; *to swim*). Swimming is the best הִתְעַמְלוּת (heet-ahm-*loot*; *exercise*) because it's a great workout for your גּוּף (goof; *body*). What more could you want? Also, it's fun! In the קַיִץ (kah-yeetz; *summer*), I love to swim בַּחוּץ (bah-*chootz*; *outdoors*) in an אֲגַם (ah-*gahm*; *lake*). When the weather turns cooler, it's the בְּרֵכַת שְׂחִיָּה (brei-*chaht*-schee-*yah*; *swimming pool*) for me — preferably one that's indoors, though admittedly in California, I'm swimming outside year-round because the weather never gets thaaaaat cold.

When you're swimming, you may want to try these strokes:

» מִשְׂחֶה חָזֶה (mees-*h*eh *h*ah-*zeh*; *breaststroke*)

» מִשְׂחֶה חָפְשִׁי (mees-*h*eh *h*ohf-*shee*; *freestyle*)

» מִשְׂחֶה גַּב (mees-*h*eh gahv; *backstroke*)

» מִשְׂחֶה פַּרְפַּר (mees-*h*eh pahr-*pahr*; *butterfly*)

Working up a sweat playing other sports

The list of sports I mention in this chapter is by no means exhaustive, of course. Sports are great because something is available for everyone. If you don't like תַּחֲרוּת (tah-chah-*root*; *competition*), plenty of sports allow you to go solo. And of course, you can play plenty of sports just for fun. Table 8-4 lists some other popular sports.

TABLE 8-4

Other Popular Sports

Hebrew	Pronunciation	Translation
גַּלְגִּלִּיּוֹת	gahl-gee-*lee-yoht*	inline skating
גַּלְשָׁן	gahl-*shahn*	surfboarding
גְּלִישָׁה בְּשֶׁלֶג	guh-lee-*shah* buh-*sheh*-lehg	skiing
גּוֹלְף	*gohlf*	golf
חֲלָקַת עַל הַקֶּרַח	hach-lah-*kaht* ahl hah-*kai*-rahch	ice skating
כַּדּוּר עָף	kah-dur-*ahf*	volleyball
כַּדֹּרֶת	kah-*doh*--reht	bowling
רְכִיבָה עַל הָעוֹפַנַּיִם	reh-*chiva* ahl oh-fah-*nah*-yeem	bicycling
רִיצָה	ree-*tzah*	running
סִירַת פֶּדָלִים	⁧teer-*aht* pah-dahl-*eem*	paddleboarding

TAKE ME OUT TO THE BALL GAME . . . IN ISRAEL!

Ah, כַּדּוּר בָּסִיס (kah-*doohr* bah-*sees; baseball* — that great American pastime. In fits and starts, כַּדּוּר בָּסִיס has slowly begun taking root in Israel — many thanks to Jewish–American עוֹלִים (Oh-*leem; immigrants*) who brought their love of baseball with them, hoping to hit some home runs in their homeland. הָאֲגֻדָּה הַלֹּאֻמִית לְבַיְס-בָּל (hah-ah-*goo*-dah hah-loo-*mee*-eet luh-bays-*bahl*; The Israeli Association of Baseball) is the organizing body for leagues from youth to seniors. On the international scene, Israeli baseball was the underdog for many years, jokingly referred to as the Jamaican bobsled team of the baseball world. But scrappy Israel kept getting back in the batter's box, qualifying for the World Baseball Classic in 2013 and again in 2017. In 2021, the Israeli baseball team — comprised mostly of American Jews and four native-born Israelis — made it to round two before losing out to the Dominican Republic. In 16 cities in Israel, both Jewish and Arab youngsters meet on the baseball diamond as teammates in 80 teams and 5 leagues. For more info, check out https://www.baseball.org.il.

WORDS TO KNOW

הִתְעַמְּלוּת	heet-ahm-*loot*	exercise
אִצְטַדְיוֹן	itz-tahd--*yohn*	stadium
כַּדּוּר	kah-*door*	ball
כַּדּוּרֶגֶל	kah-*dur reh*-gehl	soccer
כַּדּוּרסַל	kah-dur *sahl*	basketball
קְבוּצָה	kuh-*voo*-tzah	team
מִגְרָשׁ	meeg-*rahsh*	court
אוֹהֲדִים	oh-hahd-*eem*	fans
רִיצָה	ree-*tzah*	running
סַל	sahl	basket
שְׂחִיָּה	s'chee-*yah*	swimming

Talkin' the Talk

 Gal and Sivan are waiting for the bus. While they're waiting, they talk about sports.

Gal: לְאָן אַתְּ נוֹסַעַת ?

(Leh-*ahn* aht noh-*sah*-aht?)

Where are you going?

Sivan: אֲנִי נוֹסַעַת לַמִּגְרָשׁ בָּעִיר לְשַׂחֵק כַּדּוּרסַל .

(Ah-*nee* noh-*sah*-aht lah-meeg-*rahsh* bah-*ear* leh-sah-*chek* kah-*dur sahl*.)

I'm going to a court in the city to play basketball.

Gal: כָּל הַכָּבוֹד אֲנִי נוֹסַעַת לְשַׂחֵק כַּדּוּרֶגֶל .

(Kohl hah-kah-*vohd* ah-*nee* noh-*sah*-aht leh-sah-*chek* kah-*dur* reh-*gehl*.)

Good for you! I'm going to play soccer.

Sivan: ? אֵיזֶה תַּפְקִיד אַתְּ

(Ay-*zeh* tahf-*keed* aht?)

What position do you play?

Gal: . אֲנִי שׁוֹעֶרֶת

(Ah-*nee* shoh-*eh*-reht.)

I'm a goalie.

Venturing Outdoors for Some Fun

The outdoors is a wonderful place for recreation. Getting outdoors is not only a great way to get some fresh air, but also a wonderful way to renew your soul. Some useful words for talking about nature include

» עֵמֶק (*eh*-mehk; *valley*)

» עֵץ (etz; *tree*)

» הַר (hahr; *mountain*)

» מִדְבָּר (meed-*bahr*; *desert*)

» נָהָר (nah-*har*; *river*)

» סֶלַע (seh-lah; *rock*)

» יָם (yahm; *sea*)

A wise rabbi, Rabbi Nachman of Bratslav, advised his disciples that they should make it their practice to spend time in nature every day. Table 8-5 refers to some outdoor activities.

CULTURAL WISDOM

If Israel has a national sport, it just might be מַטְקוֹת (*maht*-koht; *beach paddle tennis*). Played on Israel's sunny beaches with a wooden paddle and a ping-pong-size ball, players stake out territory in the sand (no defined space is necessary) and thwack the little plastic ball back and forth as loudly as possible. The goal is to keep the rally going rather than beat your opponent. No rules, no points — that's it. The sport has been popular in Israel since the days of the British Mandate.

There's even a painting by famed Israeli artist Nahum Guttman of children playing the sport on the beach. If Israel has a sound of summer, it's the unmistakable sound of a small plastic ball hitting wood amid the sound of crashing Mediterranean waves. Check out his link for a video where you can see this sport in action: https://youtu.be/sxwZGzVfvjE

TABLE 8-5 **Popular Outdoor Activities**

Hebrew	Pronunciation	Translation
דַּיִג	*dah-yeeg*	fishing
קִיר טִפּוּס	keer-tee-*poos*	Rappelling
סְקִי מַיִם	skee *mah*-yeem	water skiing
הַפְלָגָה	haf-lah-*gah*	boating
קֶמְפִּינג	mach-*nah*-oot	camping
טִפּוּס חוֹפְשִׁי	tee-*poos* chohf-*shee*	free climbing
טִפּוּס מְצוּקִים	tee-*poos* meh-tzoo-*keem*	rock climbing
הֲלִיכָה	hah-lee-ḥah	walking

Boogieing Till You Drop

Do you like לִרְקֹד (leer-*kohd; to dance*)? I love to dance, and I also love to watch it. I love לִרְקֹד at a מוֹעֲדוֹן (moh-ah-*dohn; club*) all night!

I also enjoy going to a הוֹפָעָה (hoh-fah-*ah; show*) to see a לַהֲקַת מָחוֹל (lah-hah-*kaht* mah-*chohl; dance group*). I like everything from רִקּוּד בָּלֶט (ree-*kood* bah-*let; ballet*) to מָחוֹל עַכְשָׁוִי (mah-ḥohl ahch-shah-*vee; modern dance*). I enjoy watching the רַקְדָנִים (rahk-dah-*neem; dancers*) move in time to the קֶצֶב (keh-tzehv; *rhythm*) of the music.

CULTURAL WISDOM

מָחוֹל (mah-*hohl*), the Hebrew word for a kind of rhythmic dancing in which the body moves joyously in concert with a specific musical rhythm, shares the same root with the Hebrew word for "forgiveness": מְחִילָה (meh-ḥee-*lah*). At first glance, these two concepts — dancing and forgiveness — seem to be disparate. But both acts require a certain giving over of the self, a moving in harmony with an outside force.

TAKING A SPIN AROUND THE DANCE FLOOR: FOLK DANCING ISRAELI-STYLE

Dance has always been an integral part of Jewish culture. Dance was the response of the ancient Israelites after crossing the Sea of Reeds. And who hasn't been to a Jewish wedding and danced all night?

Today, רִקּוּדֵי עַם (ree-koo--day ahm; folk dancing) is a quintessential Israeli art form bearing the imprint of the Jewish people and their wanderings across the globe. A cross section of the Israeli population participates in more than 300 Israeli folk-dance circles around the country. The dance steps include the Yemenite (which depicts the way one would move barefoot on hot sand); the Tcherkessia (from Russia); the Debka (an Arabic step); and moving in circle aform reflective of the Hora, a closed-circle dance with origins in Romania.

Israeli folk dancing spans 37 countries, with sessions taking place in cities as far apart as Tokyo, New York City, Amsterdam, and Los Angeles. An annual international folk-dance festival held each summer in the Galilee development town of Karmiel draws more than 250,000 devotees from all over the world. Workshops and performances are held during the day. When the sun goes down, the outdoor dancing begins and continues until the sun begins to rise the next morning. Then the dancers warily climb Karmiel's hills back to their rented rooms to catch some sleep before the revelry resumes.

Keeping up with the latest dances is an art in itself. Those who miss a chunk of sessions find themselves watching on the sidelines, leaving no middle ground in Israeli dancing. Outside beginner circles, you're either in or you're out. In Israel, folk-dance sessions draw close to 1,000 people, and clubs in cities such as Los Angeles and New York City draw crowds in the hundreds.

Shoulder-to-shoulder dancers twist and turn, moving in time to popular Israeli music as they represent a unique and authentic Israeli cultural phenomenon, a true קִבּוּץ גָּלֻיּוֹת (kee-bootz gahl-oo-yoht; gathering of the exiles), creating an art form that is both ancient and timeless — a reflection of the land and modern state that Jews the world over call home.

FUN & GAMES

Using the word list, identify the activities in the picture. בִּלּוּי נָעִים (bee-*looy* nah-*eem; Have fun!*) לִכְתֹּב סֵפֶר, לִרְקֹד בָּלֶט, לָגֶר, הַחֲלָקָה, טַיֵל.

Chapter **9**

Talking on the Phone

Gone are the days when there was a phone in every room and on every street corner. These days, you are mostly likely to find your phone in your back pocket. Telephones — landlines and cellular — are a part of life, so figuring out how to speak on one is an important part of picking up any new language. In this chapter, I give you the essential phrases that you need to have a שִׂיחַת טֶלֶפוֹן (see-*chat* teh-leh-*fohn*; *telephone conversation*) in Hebrew.

CULTURAL WISDOM

The word that people commonly use in Hebrew for the English word *telephone*, טֶלֶפוֹן (teh-leh-*fohn*), wasn't the word that the Academy for Hebrew Language created. (The Academy for Hebrew Language happens to be the supreme institute for the Hebrew language that makes decisions about modern Hebrew grammar and coins new Hebrew words as the need arises.) No, telephones didn't always exist, so someone had to create a Hebrew word for the concept. The academy created a Hebrew word for *telephone* — שָׂח רָחוֹק (sach-rah-*hohk*), which literally means *long-distance conversation*. Clever, right? That term didn't stick with the Hebrew-speaking public, however, so טֶלֶפוֹן it is.

Dialing Up the Basics

Having a conversation on the phone in Hebrew is great, but you need to start at the beginning. In this case, the beginning is simply nailing down the various Hebrew words associated with the actual telephone equipment:

>> טֶלֶפוֹן (teh-leh-*fohn; telephone*)

>> טֶלֶפוֹן צִבּוּרִי (teh-leh-*fohn* tzee-boo-*ree; public telephone*)

>> פֶּלֶאפוֹן or טֶלֶפוֹן סֶלוּלָרִי (peh-leh-*fohn* or teh-leh-*fohn* seh-loo-lah-*ree; cellphone*)

>> אָזְנִית (ohz-*neet; headphone or ear bud*)

>> קַו הַטֶּלֶפוֹן (kahv hah-teh-leh-*fohn; telephone line*)

Finding someone's number

In the United States, if you want to find out someone's מִסְפַּר טֶלֶפוֹן (mees-*pahr* teh-leh-*fohn; phone number*), you dial 411. In Israel, you dial 144. When you reach the מֶרְכָּזָן (M)/מֶרְכָּזָנִית (F) (mehr-*kah*-zahn/mehr-*kah*-zah-nit; *operator*), they'll generally ask you for the person's שֵׁם מִשְׁפָּחָה (shem meesh-*pah*-ah; *family name*), שֵׁם פְּרָטִי (shem prah-*tee; first* or *private name*), and perhaps the עִיר (ear; *city*) in which the person lives. You can also try the מַדְרִיךְ טֶלֶפוֹן (mah-*dreech* teh-leh-*fohn; phone book*), or if you're looking for a particular business or service, the דַּפֵּי זָהָב (dah-*pay* za-*hahv; yellow pages*) may be helpful, though these days you can pretty find anything on the אִינְטֶרְנֶט (*Internet*).

Telling someone to call you

CULTURAL WISDOM

You can always find someone's phone number, but sometimes, simply asking them to call you is easier. In Hebrew, you have several options when you want to ask someone to give you a call:

>> תָּרִים טֶלֶפוֹן (tah-*reem* teh-leh-*fohn;* literally: *pick up the phone*) (M)

   תָּרִימִי טֶלֶפוֹן (tah-ree-*mee* teh-leh-*fohn;* literally: *pick up the phone*) (F)

   תָּרִימֶה טֶלֶפוֹן (tah-*ree*-meh teh-leh-*fohn;* literally: *pick up the phone*) (NB)

>> תֵּן לִי צִלְצוּל (tehn *lee* tzil-*tzool; give me a ring*) (M)

   תְּנִי לִי צִצּוּל (tnee *lee* tzil-*tzool; give me a ring*) (F)

   תְּנֶה לִי צִלְצוּל (tneh *lee* tzi-ltzool; *give me a ring*) (NB)

>> טִלְפֵּן אֵלַי (til-*fehn* eh-*lie; phone me*) (M)

טַלְפְנִי אֵלַי (tahl-*feh-nee* eh-*lie*; phone me) (F)

טִלְפְנֶה אֵלַי (tihl-*feh-neh* eh-*lie*; phone me) (NB)

➤➤ צַלְצֵל אֵלַי (tzil-*tzehl* eh-*lie*; ring me) (M)

צַלְצְלִי אֵלַי (tzahl-tzhel eh-*lie*; ring me) (F)

Talkin' the Talk

Shira and Nomi have just met for lunch. After lunch, Shira asks Nomi to call her.

Shira: צַלְצְלִי אֵלַי.

(tzahl-tzeh-*lee* eh-lah-*y*.)

Give me a ring.

Nomi: טוֹב אֲנִי אֲטַלְפֵּן אֵלַיִךְ

(tohv. ah-*nee* ah-tahl-*fehn* eh-*lay*-eech.)

Good. I'll phone you.

Shira: מִסְפַּר הַטֶּלֶפוֹן שֶׁלִּי שֵׁשׁ אֶחָד שֵׁשׁ שֶׁבַע שֶׁבַע שֶׁבַע .

(-mees-*hah-pahr* teh-leh-*fohn* sheh-*lee* shaysh, eh-*chahd*, shaysh, *sheh*-vah, *sheh*-vah, *sheh*-vah.)

My telephone number is six, one, six, seven, seven, seven.

Socializing in fake time (also known as social media)

These days, who talks on the phone unless they're a Boomer? Communication is all about רֶשֶׁת חֶבְרָתִית (reh-*sheht* ḥehv-rah-teet; *social media*). If you don't get on the right קְבוּצַת וַטְסְאָפּ (k'voo-*tzaht whatz*-ahp; *WhatsApp group*), you might as well be on the moon. Gone are the days when people said תֵּן לִי צִלְצוּל (nteh-lee-*tzil*-tzool; *give me a ring*). Now it's just לִשְׁלֹחַ אֶס אֶם אֶס (leesh-*loh*-ah ehs ehm ehs; *send a text*). And instead of people talking to themselves, or to the hand, they talk to their פֶּלֶאפוֹן (peh-*leh*-fohn; *cellphone*), מַקְלִיט (mahk-leet; *record*) themselves, and מְפַרְסֵם (meh-*fahr*-sehm; *post*) it! Ideally, they'll get a תְּגוּבָה (tuh-*goo*-vah; *reaction*, also known as a "like"); maybe they'll even הוֹפֵךְ וִירָאלִי (hah-fe**ẖ** vee-*rah*-lee; *go viral*) and נִצְפֶּה מִלּוֹן פַּעַם (neetz-*peh* mil-*yohn* pahm; *get a million views*)! Woohoo! This is living!

WORDS TO KNOW

דַּפֵּי זָהָב	dah-*pay* zah-*hahv*	yellow pages
קַו הַטֶּלֶפוֹן	kahv hah-*teh*-leh-fohn	telephone line
מַדְרִיךְ טֶלֶפוֹן	mahd-*reech* teh-leh-*fohn*	phone book
פֶּלֶאפוֹן	peh-*leh*-fohn	cellphone
טֶלֶאפוֹן	*teh*-leh-fohn	telephone
טֶלֶאפוֹן צִבּוּרִי	*teh*-leh-fohn tzee-*bohr*-ee	public telephone
לִשְׁלֹח אֶס אֶם אֶס	leesh–*loh*-a**ẖ** ehs ehm ehs	to send a text
הָפוּךְ וִרָאלִי	hah-*foẖ* vir-*ah*-lee	went viral
תְּגוּבָה	tuh-*goo*-vah	reaction (a "like" in social media)
לְתַיֵּג	leh-*tah*-yehg	to tag
לְשַׁתֵּף	leh-*shah*-tehf	to share
רֶשֶׁת	*reh*-sheht	Internet

Asking for People and Getting the Message

In this section, I provide vocabulary and useful expressions that you can use when you want to speak to someone on the phone or leave a message. When you call someone on the טֶלֶאפוֹן (teh–leh-fohn; *telephone*), the person on the other end of the קַו הַטֶּלֶפוֹן (kahv hah-teh-leh-*fohn*; *telephone line*) generally says either הָלוֹ (which is basically hello, but the "h" sound is so soft it sounds like "ah-loh" to English speakers) or שָׁלוֹם (shah-*lohm; peace*).

Talkin' the Talk

Chaim and Michal are beginning a שִׂיחַת טֶלֶפוֹן (see-*ḥaht teh*-leh-fohn; *phone conversation*).

Chaim: שָׁלוֹם.

(shah-*lohm.*)

Hello.

Michal: שָׁלוֹם מְדַבֶּרֶת מִיכַל אֶפְשָׁר לְדַבֵּר עִם חַיִּים?

(shah-*lohm.* meh-dah-*beh*-reht mee-*chah*l. ef-shahr le'dah-*ber* eem chah-*eem?*)

Hello. This is Michal speaking. May I speak to Chaim?

Chaim: מְדַבֵּר.

(meh-dah-*ber.*)

Speaking.

Leaving a message

Sometimes, the person with whom you want to speak isn't answering the phone. When that happens, you can leave a הוֹדָעָה (hoh–dah–*ah*; *message*).

Talkin' the Talk

Michal is calling her boyfriend, Haim. He's not home, so she leaves a message with his sister, Shira.

Shira: שָׁלוֹם.

(shah-*lohm.*)

Hello.

Michal: שָׁלוֹם הַאִם חַיִּים נִמְצָא?

(shah-*lohm.* hah-*eem* chah-*yeem* neem-*tzah*)

Hello. Is Chaim there?

Shira:	הוּא אֵינוֹ נִמְצָא כָּרֶגַע .
	(hoo ay-*no* neem-*tzah* kah-*reh*-gah.)
	He's not here right now.
Michal:	אֶפְשָׁר לְהַשְׁאִיר הוֹדָעָה ?
	(ef-*shahr* le-hahsh-*eer* hoh-dah-*ah*?)
	May I leave a message?
Shira:	בְּוַדַאי .
	(beh-vah-*dai*.)
	Certainly.
Michal:	תּוֹדָה תַּגִּיד לוֹ שֶׁמִּכָל הִתְקַשְּׁרָה .
	(Toh-*dah*. Tah-*geed* loh sheh mee-*chahl* heet-kahsh-*rah*.)
	Thanks. Tell him Michal called.
Shira:	טוֹב אֲנִי אֶמְסֹר לוֹ .
	(tohv. ah-*nee* em-*sor* loh.)
	Good. I'll tell him.
Michal:	תּוֹדָה רַבָּה לָךְ .
	(toh-*dah* rah-*bah* lach.)
	Thank you very much.
Shira:	אֵין בְּעַד מָה .
	(ayn be'*ahd* mah.)
	It's nothing.

● ●

WORDS TO KNOW

בְּוַדַאי	beh-vah-*dai*	certainly
הוֹדָעָה	hoh-*dah*-ah	message
כָּעֵת	kah-*eht*	right now
תָּפוּס	*tah*-foos	busy
אֶס אֶם אֶשׁ	ehs-ehm-es	text

Dealing with voicemail and other annoyances

Technology! It's a part of life. This section goes over how to deal with the wonders of telephone technology.

The dreaded voice mail-argh!

In this technology-driven society, it's amazing that we actually speak to one another at all. These days, we just שׁוֹלְחִים אֶס אֶמ אֶס (shloh-*ḥeem* es-em-es; *send a text*), and occasionally, we leave a message on someone's voicemail. Here's an example of an outgoing message you might hear on someone's voicemail:

שָׁלוֹם הִגַּעְתֶּם לְמִסְפָּר שֵׁשׁ אֶחָד שֶׁבַע שֵׁשׁ אֶחָד חָמֵשׁ שֶׁבַע אָרִי וְשַׁלְוִי אֵינָם נִמְצָאִים כְּעֵט נָא לְהַשְׁאִיר הוֹדָעָה אַחֲרֵי הַצִּפְצוּף

(shah-*lohm*. hee-*gah*-tem le-mees-*pahr* shaysh eh-*chad* sheh-*vah*, shaysh eh-*chad* sheh-vah chah-*mehsh*. ah-ree veh-shahl-vee ay-*nahm* neem-tzah-*eem* kah-*eht*. Nah le-hahsh-*eer* hoh-dah-*ah* ah-chah-*ray* hah-tzeef-*tzoof*.)

Hello. You have reached (telephone) number 617-6175. Ari and Shalvi aren't here right now. Please leave a message after the beep.

Dealing with voicemail

If you fail to reach a real live person when you place a call, you may find yourself wading through a barrage of תָּא קוֹלִי (tah koh-*lee*; *voicemail*) instructions asking you to choose an option from a תַּפְרִיט (tahf-*reet*; *menu*) of options. When this happens, I generally press אֶפֶס (eh-*fehs*; *zero*) in the hope of reaching the מַזְכִּירָן (M)/מַזְכִּירָנִית (F) (mehr-kah-*zahn*/mehr-kah-zah-*neet*; *operator*). Here's an example of an automated message you might hear in Hebrew:

זוֹהִי הוֹדָעָה מֻקְלֶטֶת אִם בִּרְצוֹנְךָ לְהַגִּעַה לְמַחְלֶקֶת הַבְּגָדִים הַקַּשׁ אֶחָד לְמַחְלֶקֶת הָאֹכֶל הַקַּשׁ שְׁתַּיִם .

zo hee hoh-dah-*ah* mook-*leh*-teht. eem beer-tzohn-*ḥa* leh-hah-gee-*ah* le-maḥ-*leh*-ket hah-bah-*deem* hah-*kehsh* eh-chahd. le-maḥ-*leh*-ket hah-*oh*-hel hah-*kehsh* sh-*tah*-yeem-j.

This is a recorded message. If you want to reach the clothing department, press one. For the food department, press two.

Dumping the dreaded telemarketer

To me, no phone frustrations are worse than the מְשַׁוֵּק בְּטֶלֶפוֹן (meh-shah-*vek* buh-teh-leh-*fohn*; *telemarketer*) who disturbs you at home by trying to sell you some wonderful product or service like siding for your house or a fifth mortgage. חֲצֻפָּה

(ẖootz–*pah*; such nerve)! Here's an example of something you might hear in Hebrew when you pick up the phone and a telemarketer is on the line:

שָׁלוֹם רָצִינוּ לְעַנְיֵן אוֹתְךָ בְּחֹפֶשׁ בְּחִנָּם **(M)**

(shah-*lohm*. rah-tzee-*noo* leh-ahn-*yehn* oht-*ẖah* buh-*ẖoh*-fesh buh-*ẖee*-nahm.)

Hello. We wanted to interest you in a free vacation.

If you want to be polite, you can answer in the following fashion:

אֵין לִי זְמַן לְדַבֵּר עַכְשָׁו אַתָּה יָכוֹל לִשְׁלֹחַ לִי מָשֶׁהוּא בַּדֹּאַר ?

(ayn lee ze-*mahn* leh-dah-*bear* ach-*shahv*. ah-*tah* yah-*chohl* leesh-loh-*ach* lee *mah*-sheh-hoo buh-*doh*-ahr?)

I don't have time to speak right now. Can you send me something in the mail?

Or if you're feeling less polite, you can לִטְרֹק אֶת הַטֶּלֶפוֹן (lit–*rohk* eht hah–*teh*–leh–fohn; *slam down the phone*) or לְנַתֵּק אֶת הַשִּׂיחָה (le–nah–*tek* eht hah–see–*ẖa*; *hang up*). If you're feeling particularly silly, you can answer with the line my uncle always uses when these folks call:

הוּא אֵינוֹ נִמְצָא כָּאן יוֹתֵר הוּא עָבַר לְסִין אַתָּה רוֹצֶה אֶת מִסְפַּר הַטֶּלֶפוֹן שָׁם ?

(hoo ay-*noh* neem-*tzah* kahn yoh-*tair*. hoo ah-*vahr* leh-*seen*. ah-tah roh-*tzeh* et mees-*pahr* hah-*teh*-leh-fohn sheh-*loh* sham?)

He doesn't live here anymore. He moved to China. Would you like his phone number there?

WORDS TO KNOW

הַקֵּשׁ	hah-*kehsh*	to press (or to dial)
הוֹדָעָה מֻקְלֶדֶת	hoh-dah-*ah* mook-*leht*	recorded message
כָּאן	kahn	here
מְשַׁבֵּק בַּטֶּלֶפוֹן	meh-shah-*vek* buh-*teh*-leh-fohn	telemarketer
נָא	na	please
שָׁם	shahm	there
תָּא קוֹלִי	tah koh-*lee*	voicemail
צְפְצוּף	tzeef-*tzoof*	beep

Making Arrangements over the Phone

The phone is a useful instrument for conducting your social life, but you use it for other purposes as well: discussing business, calling the doctor to make an appointment, calling a hotel to make a reservation, and so on. But dealing with businesses on the phone requires some specific language. Check it out.

Using the טֶלֶפוֹן (teh-leh-*fohn*; *telephone*) to make a הַזְמָנָה (hahz-*mah*-nah; *reservation*) at a מִסְעָדָה (mees-ah-*dah*; *restaurant*) or a מָלוֹן (mah-*lohn*; *hotel*) is easy. And, if you're not feeling well, you may want to make a תּוֹר אֵצֶל רוֹפֵא (tor *eh*-tzel hah-roh-*feh*; *appointment at the doctor*). Here are some words you can use in these situations.

>> לְהַזְמִין מָקוֹם (leh-hahz-*meen mah*-kohm; *to make a reservation*)

>> לְהַזְמִין תּוֹר (leh-hahz-*meen* tor; *to make an appointment*)

Check out Chapter 7 for more on talking about and telling the time — two useful concepts for making reservations or appointments. And look at Chapter 10 for more stuff on work life, Chapter 5 for information on eating in a restaurant, and Chapter 16 for dealing with illnesses and other emergencies. No matter what kind of arrangement you need to make over the phone, I have you covered.

Talkin' the Talk

Hod is calling Elephant Solutions, a קִנְזֶח תרבֶח (hehv-raht *hehz*-nek; *startup company*) in Jerusalem. He reaches a קִנְזֶח תרבֶח (mahz-kee-*rah*; *secretary*). Hod asks her to transfer him to the correct וֹפַלֶט תחוֹלש (shloo-*haht* teh-leh-fohn; *extension number*).

Mazkirah:	שָׁלוֹם חֶבְרַת פִּיל אֶפְשָׁר לְהַמְתִּין רֶגַע ?
	(shah-*lohm.* *h*eh-*vraht* peel. ehf-*shahr* leh-hahm-*teen* reh-*gah?*)
	Hello. Elephant Solutions. Can you wait a moment?
Hod:	כֵּן .
	(kehn.)
	Yes.
Mazkirah:	סְלִיחָה עַל הַהַמְתָּנָה
	(suh-lee-*hah* ahl hah ham-*tahn*-ah.)
	Sorry about the wait.

Hod:	אֶפְשָׁר לְדַבֵּר עִם אָדוֹן הֶלְמָן מִסְפַּר הַשְּׁלוּחָה שֶׁלּוֹ אֶפֶס אֶפֶס חָמֵשׁ .

(ehf-*shahr* le-dah-*bear* eem ah-*dohn* helman? mees-pahr hah-shloo-*chah* sheh-*loh* eh-fes, *eh*-fes, chah-*mehsh*.)

May I speak with Mr. Hellman? His extension number is zero, zero, five.

Mazkirah:	אֲנִי מִיָּד מַעֲבִירָה אוֹתְךָ לַשְּׁלוּחָה שֶׁלּוֹ .

(ah-nee mee-*yahd* mah-ah-veer-*rah* oht-*ḥah* lah-sh-loo-*chah* sheh-*loh*.)

I'll transfer you right now to his extension.

Hod:	תּוֹדָה רַבָּה לָךְ .

(toh-*dah* rah-*bah* lahch.)

Thank you very much.

●●

WORDS TO KNOW

הַזְמָנָה	hahz-*mah*-nah	reservation
שְׁלוּחָה	mees-*pahr* sh-loo-*ḥah*	extension number
שְׁלוּחַת טֶלֶפוֹן	shuh-loo-*ḥaht teh*-leh-fohn	telephone extension
תּוֹר	tohr	appointment

Talking About the Past: How Was Your Shabbat?

During a conversation, most people often talk about the past. With all the everyday hustle and bustle, folks often need to catch one another up on what's been going on in their lives. Calling a friend on the phone is an easy way to catch up. When you talk about what has already happened to you, you speak in the past tense. In Hebrew, the past tense is created by attaching a *suffix* — or ending — to the root of the verb. Check out Table 9-1 for a list of verb suffixes. (*Note:* There's no suffix for *he*.) For more information on all this grammar stuff, take a look at Chapter 2.

TABLE 9-1

Verb Suffixes

Suffix	Pronunciation	English Translation
תִי	tee	I
תָ	tah	you (M)
תְ	t	you (F)
ה	ah	she
נוּ	noo	we
תֶם	tehm	you (MP)
תֶן	tehn	you (FP)
וּ	oo	they

Here's an example of a past-tense verb conjugation using the Hebrew infinitive לְטַלְפֵּן (leh-tahl-*fehn*; *to phone*). (An *infinitive* is the form of the verb that expresses action — to do something — without referring to a person. *To phone, to walk,* and *to sleep* are infinitives.)

Hebrew	Pronunciation	Translation (Gender)
טִלְפַּנְתִי	til-*fahn*-tee	I phoned
טִלְפַּנְתָ	til-*fahn*-tah	you phoned (M)
טִלְפַּנְתְ	til-*fahnt*	you phoned (F)
טִלְפֵּן	til-*fehn*	he phoned
טִלְפְּנָה	til-feh-*nah*	she phoned
טִלְפֵּנוּ	til-feh-*noo*	we phoned
טִלְפַּנְתֶם	til-*fahn*-tehm	you phoned (MP)
טִלְפַּנְתֶן	til-*fahn*-tehn	you phoned (FP)
טִלְפְּנוּ	til-*feh*-noo	they phoned

When you speak in the past tense in Hebrew, you often don't need to use the words *I* or *you* when speaking in the first or second person because the pronoun is understood within the context of the conversation, as in these examples:

>> ? מָתַי טִלְפַּנְתְּ (mah-*tye* til-*fahn*-tah; *When did [you] call?*)

>> .טִלְפַּנְתִּי בַּבֹּקֶר (til-*fahn*-tee bah-*boh*-kehr; *[I] called in the morning.*)

REMEMBER

The Hebrew past tense is the equivalent of four different past-tense forms in English: simple past, immediate past, past perfect, and past progressive. Pretty cool, huh? You have to figure out only one set of rules instead of four, which makes things easier when you're trying to learn Hebrew. So אֲנִי טִלְפַּנְתִּי (ah-*nee* til-*fahn*-tee; *I called*) can mean all of the following:

>> I called.

>> I just called.

>> I have called.

>> I was calling.

FUN & GAMES

Here are some questions that are commonly asked on the phone. Match them up with the correct responses.

שְׁאֵלוֹת (sheh-eh-*loht*; *questions*)

1. ? אֶפְשָׁר לְדַבֵּר עִם חַיִּים (ehf-*shahr* leh-*dah*-behr eem hah-*yeem*: May I speak to Chaim?)

2. ? אֶפְשָׁר לְהַשְׁאִיר הוֹדָעָה (ehf-*shahr* leh-hee-*shah*-ehr hoh-*dah*-ah; May I leave a message?)

3. ? הַאִם ה חַיִּים נִמְצָא (hah-*eem* hah-*yeem* neem *tzah*; Is Chaim there?)

תְּשׁוּבוֹת (tshoo-*voht*; *possible answers*)

A. הוּא אֵינוֹ נִמְצָא כָּעֵת (hoo *ayn*-noh neem *tzah* kuh-*eht*; he's not here right now)

B. בְּוַדַּאי. (beh-vah-*dah*-ee; certainly)

C. מְדַבֵּר. (meh-*dah*-beher; speaking)

Chapter **10**

At the Office and Around the House

The Torah says, "Six days you shall labor and do *any* kind of work." Why, you may ask, does the text say *any* kind of work? Because *any* kind of work — even busywork — is preferable to idleness. As my mother says, "Hard work is good for you!" Ideally, עֲבוֹדָה (ah-voh-*dah*; *work*) should be more than something that just takes up our time; it also provides our livelihood. For many people, our work is a calling — a way of contributing to the world.

In this chapter, I fill you in about all the good "work" words you need to know. I also talk about the little sanctuary you create when you aren't working: your home.

Finding Your Way Around Your Job

If you work מִשְׂרָה מְלֵאָה (mees-*rah* meh-leh-*ah*; *full-time*), your מִשְׂרָד (mees-*rahd*; *office*) is almost a second home. So why not personalize your מְקוֹם עֲבוֹדָה (m שh-*kohm* ah-voh-*dah*; *workspace*) so that the place just screams you? I like to put up תְּמוּנוֹת (te-moo-*noht*; *pictures*), decorate my מַחְשֵׁב (mach-*shehv*; *computer*) with מַדְבֵּקוֹת (mahd-bay-*koht*; *stickers*), and place on my שֻׁלְחַן עֲבוֹדָה (shool-*chahn* ah-voh-*dah*; *desk*) קִשּׁוּט (kee-*shoot*; *trinket*) or two. You also need to have all the צִיּוּד (tzee-*yood*; *supplies*) you need to get your job done.

Supplying your office

When you're setting up a work area, whether at home or at an office, have these items close at hand:

» מַדְפֶּסֶת (mahd-*peh*-set; *printer*)

» טֶלֶפוֹן (te-leh-*fohn*; *telephone*)

Aside from the machinery, I keep my desk stocked with the following supplies:

» אטב (ah-*tehv*; *bulldog clip*)

» דַּפְדְּפָן (dahf-deh-*fahn*; *notepad*)

» דֶּבֶק (*deh*-vehk; *glue*)

» עֵט (eht; *pen*)

» עִפָּרוֹן (ee-pahr-*rohn*; *pencil*)

» מְחַק (*mah*-**h**ahk; *eraser*)

» מְהַדֵּק (meh-hah-*dehk*; *paper clip*)

» סֶרֶט דָּבִיק (*seh*-reht dah-*veek*; *tape*)

» שַׁדְכָן (shahd-*hahn*; *stapler*)

» דִיסְק אוֹן קִי (*deesk* ohn *key*, *flashdrive*)

If you've run out of paper) or misplaced your עֵט (*eht*; *pen*) for the umpteenth time, you can always ask your colleagues whether they have one you can use. You might ask

יֵשׁ לְךָ עֵט? (*yesh* le-**h**ah eht; *Do you have a pen?*) (M)

יֵשׁ לָךְ עֵט? (*yesh* la**h** eht; *Do you have a pen?*) (F)

יֵשׁ לְכֶה עֵט? (yesh leh-**h**eh eht; *Do you have pen?*) (NB)

Talkin' the Talk

Shulamit is working at the office. She has misplaced all her pens again and is about to go into a meeting where she must take notes. So he asks an התימע (ah-mee-*tah*; *colleague*) whether she can borrow a pen from her.

Shulamit: סְלִיחָה אֶפְשָׁר לְהַשְׁאִיל לִי עֵט ?

(slee-*hah*, ehf-*shahr* leh-hahsh-*eel lee eht?*)

Excuse me, can you loan me a pen? (literally: *Is it possible to loan to me a pen?*)

Colleague: כֵּן הִנֵּה .

(*kehn*. hee-*nay*.)

Yes. Here it is.

Shulamit: וְגַם יֵשׁ לָךְ דַּפְדְּפָן ?

(ve'*gahm yesh lahh* dahf-deh-*fahn?*)

And do you also have a notepad?

Colleague: בְּוַדַּאי קְחִי .

(beh-vah-*dye*. k*chee.*)

Certainly. Take it.

WORDS TO KNOW

עֲבוֹדָה	ah-voh-*dah*	work
עָמִית	ah-*meet*	colleague (M)
עֲמִיתָה	ah-mee-*tah*	colleague (F)
עֵט	eht	pen
עִפָּרוֹן	ee-pahr-*ohn*	pencil
מָחַק	*mah*-chahk	eraser
מַחְשֵׁב	mahch-*shev*	computer

מִשְׂרָד	mees-*rahd*	office
מִלְאָה מִשְׂרָה	mees-*rah* meh- lay-*ah*	full-time position
שַׁדְכָן	shahd-*chahn*	stapler
שֻׁלְחַן עֲבוֹדָהhh	shool-*chahn* ah-voh-*dah*	desk

Searching for the perfect job

Searching for the perfect עֲבוֹדָה (ah-voh-*dah*; *work*) can be a full-time job in and of itself. It can also be fun. Job searching is exciting. You get to see all the available possibilities. Also, you can get away with הִתְהַלְּלוּת (heet-hah-leh-*loot*; *bragging*)!

When you go in for your רֵאָיוֹן (reh-ah-*yohn*; *interview*), be prepared to talk about your נִסָּיוֹן (ne-sah-*yohn*; *experience*) and have a copy of your קוֹרוֹתחַיִּים (koh-*roht* chah-*yeem*; *résumé*). Before you accept any job, make sure that you check out the מַשְׂכֹּרֶת (mahs-*koh*-reht; *salary*) and the הֲטָבוֹת (hah-tah-*vot*; *benefits*)!

Some of the particulars you want to hear about are

» בִּטּוּחַ בְּרִיאוּת בְּ (bee-*too*-ach bree-*ooht*; *health insurance*)

» חֻפְשָׁה (choohf-*shah*; *vacation*)

» מַס הַכְנָסָה (mahs hach-nah-*sah*; *income tax*)

» מַשְׂכֹּרֶת (mahs-*koh*-reht; *salary*)

GOOFING OFF AT WORK

You're at a מִשְׂרָה (mees-*rah*; *job*) מִתֵּשַׁע עַד חָמֵשׁ (mee-*tay*-shah *ahd* chah-*mesh*; *from nine to five*), and during your weekly 40 hours you run out of tasks to do. אוֹי וַאֲבוֹי (oye-vah-ah-*voye*; *Oh no*). What are you to do? Look busy? You can לִגְלֹשׁ בָּרֶשֶׁת (leeg-*lohsh* buh-reh-*sheht*; *surf the web*). Or maybe you want לְדַבֵּר בַּטֶּלֶפוֹן (leh-dah-*bear* bah-*teh*-leh-fohn; *to speak on the phone*). You can always try אֶת שֻׁלְחַן הָעֲבוֹדָה (leh-sah-*dair* eht shool-*chahn* hah-ah-voh-*dah*; *to straighten up your desk*). Or maybe you want לְפַלְרְטֵט (leh-flahr-*teht*; *to flirt*) with that cute עָמִית (M)/עֲמִיתָה (F) (ah-*meet*/ah-mee-*tah*; *co-worker*). And then you can choose that favorite Israeli (and American) pastime: קָפֶה (leesh-*toht* ca-*faeh*; *drinking coffee*). In Hebrew, this scenario is called תֵּשַׁע-חָמֵשׁ-אֶפֶס (*tay*-shah-chah-*mesh*-eh-fehs; *nine-five-zero*). You work 9 to 5 but accomplish nothing.

» פֶּנְסְיָה (pens-yah; pension)

» שָׁעוֹת נוֹסָפוֹת (shah-oht noh-sah-foht; overtime)

» תַּשְׁלוּם שָׁעוֹת נוֹסָפוֹת (tahsh-loom shah-oht noh-sah-foht; overtime pay)

Whatever your מִקְצוֹעַ (meek-tsoh-ah; profession), ideally, you're a חָרוּץ (ḥah-rootz; hard worker) (M) or חֲרוּצָה (ḥah-roo-tzah; hard worker) (F), and you won't lose your job. You don't want to contribute to the growing problem of אַבְטָלָה (ahv-tah-lah; unemployment). But if you do lose your job — and it happens to the best of us — don't be a עַצְלָן (ahtz-lahn; lazy person) (M) or a עַצְלָנִית (ahtz-lah-neet; lazy person) (F). Get out there and look for work!

Talkin' the Talk

Nurit and Ya'ir are meeting at a coffee shop, and their conversation turns to their work.

Ya'ir (M):   אֵיךְ הוֹלֵךְ לָךְ בַּעֲבוֹדָה ?

(Ehḥ hoh-lech lahḥ buh-ah-voh-dah?)

How's it going with you at work?

Nurit (F):   לֹא כָּל-כָּךְ טוֹב .

(Loh kohl-kahḥ tohv.)

Not so good.

Yair: לָמָה ?

Lah-mah?

Why?

Nurit: הָעֲבוֹדָה עַצְמָהּ הִיא בְּסֶדֶר אֲבָל אֲנִי לֹא אוֹהֶבֶת אֶת הַמְּנַהֵל שֶׁלִּי

(Hah-ah-voh-dah ahtz-mah hee beh-sed-der, ah-vahl ah-nee loh oh-hev-veht eht hah-meh-nah-hel sheh-lee.)

The work itself is okay, but I don't like my boss.

Yair: בְּאַסָּה מָה תַּעֲשִׂי ?

(Bah-sah mah tah-ah-see?)

Bummer! What are you going to do?

Nurit: הָאֱמֶת, אֲנִי מְחַפֶּשֶׂת. אַתָּה מַכִּיר מַשֶּׁהוּ שֶׁמַּתְאִים לִי?

(Hah-eh-*meht,* ah-nee beh-chee-*poos.* Ah-*tah* yoh-*deh-ah* *mah*-sheh-hoo sheh-maht-*eem lee?*)

Truth to tell, I'm looking. Do you know of something suitable for me?

. . . .

WORDS TO KNOW

עַצְלָן	ahtz-*lahn*	lazy person (M)
עַצְלָנִית	ahtz-lah-*neet*	lazy person (F)
אַבְטָלָה	ahv-tah-*lah*	unemployment
הַטָּבוֹת	hah-tah-*voht*	benefits
קוֹרוֹת חַיִּים	koh-*roht* ḥah-*yeem*	résumé
נִסָּיוֹן	nee-sah-*yohn*	experience
מַשְׂכֹּרֶת	mahs-*koh*-reht	salary
מְנַהֵל	meh-nah-*hel*	manager (M)
מְנַהֶלֶת	meh-nah-*heh*-leht	manager (F)
מִקְצוֹעַ	meek-tzoh-*ah*	profession
רַאָיוֹן	reh-ah-*yohn*	interview

GRAMMATICALLY SPEAKING

The word את (eht) means *with.* (**Note:** This word is different from the Hebrew word for *pen,* eht, which is spelled with an *ayin* and a *tet,* whereas the word for *with* is spelled with an *aleph* and a *tav.*) When you combine את (eht) with a personal pronoun such as me, you, him, her, us, or they (in Hebrew grammarspeak, this is called *inflecting*), it takes on the forms in the following list:

>> אִתִּי (ee-*tee; with me*)

>> אִתְּךָ (eet-*ḥah; with you*) (MS)

>> אִתָּךְ (ee-*tahch; with you*) (FS)

- אִתּוֹ (ee-*toh*; *with him*) (MS)

- אִתָּה (ee-*tah*; *with her*) (FS)

- אִתָּנוּ (ee-*tah*-noo; *with us*) (any gender)

- אִתְּכֶם (eet-ḥehm; *with you*, used when talking to lots of people, males or a mixed group)

- אֶתְכֶן (eet-ḥen; *with you*) (FP)

- אִתָּם (e-*tahm*; *with them*) (MP)

- אִתֶּן (ee-*tahn*; *with them*) (FP)

You can also use את in combination with suffixes that indicate different pronouns to mean "to me," "to you," and so on. It's inflected as follows:

- אוֹתִי (oh-*tee*; *me*)

- אוֹתְךָ (oht-*hah*; *you*) (MS)

- אוֹתָךְ (oh-*tach*; *you*) (FS)

- אוֹתוֹ (oh-*toh*; *him*) (MS)

- אוֹתָהּ (oh-*tah*; *her*) (FS)

- אוֹתָן (oh-*tah*-noo; *us*)

- אֶתְכֶם (eht-*chem*); *you*) (MP, but also used for a mixed bunch of people)

- אֶתְכֶן (eht-*chen*; *you*) (FP)

- אוֹתָם (oh-*tahm*; *them*) (MP, but also used for a mixed bunch of people)

- אוֹתָן (oh-*tahn*; *them*) (FP)

You can also use את (which can be modified to be MS, FS, MP, or FP) when you want to indicate that something is the same. In Hebrew, of course, this word must match gender and number:

- אוֹתוֹ הַיֶּלֶד (oh-*toh* hah-*yeh*-lehd; *the same boy*)

- אוֹתָהּ הַיַּלְדָּה (oh-*tah* hah-yahl-*dah*; *the same girl*)

- אוֹתָם הַיְלָדִים (oh-*tahm* hah-yeh-lah-*deem*; *the same boys*)

- אוֹתָן הַיְלָדוֹת (oh-*tahn* hah-yeh-lah-*doht*; *the same girls*)

LOOKING FOR JOBS IN ALL THE RIGHT PLACES

A good way to look for a job is to search the עִתּוֹן (ee-tohn; newspaper) or the Internet for מוֹדָעוֹת דְּרוּשִׁים (moh-dah-oht droo-sheem want ads). The ads generally start with the word דָּרוּשׁ (dah-roosh (M); wanted) or דְּרוּשָׁה (duh-roo-shah (F); wanted). The ad may also specify כִּשּׁוּרִים (kee-shoo-reem; qualifications), דְּרִישׁוֹת (duh-ree-shoht; requirements), and הַכְשָׁרָה (hah-shah-rah; training). Other phrases you may see are נָא לִפְנוֹת לְ . . . (nah leef-noht le; please respond to . . .) and נָא לִשְׁלֹחַ אֶת קוֹרוֹת הַחַיִּים לְ . . . (nah leesh-loh-ah eht koh-roht heh-chah-yeem le; please send your résumé to . . .).

WORDS TO KNOW

דְּרִישׁוֹת	dree-shoht	requirements
הַכְשָׁרָה	hahh-shah-rah	training
עִתּוֹן	ee-tohn	newspaper
כִּשּׁוּרִים	kee-shoo-reem	qualifications
מוֹאֲדוֹת מוּדְעוֹת דְּרוּשִׁים	moh-dah-oht droo-sheem	want ads
קוֹרוֹת חַיִּים	Koh-roht hah-yeem	résumé

Working from Home

The world has changed post-COVID. Now, for many of us, לַעֲבֹד מֵהַבַּיִת (lah-ah-vohd mee-hah-bah-yeet; working from home) is the norm. Some people call it עֲבוֹדָה מֵרָחוֹק (ah-voh-dah meh-rah-hohk; remote work), and some call it סִגְנוֹן הִיבְּרִידִי (seeg-nohn hey-bree-dee; hybrid work), in which you work some days at the מִשְׂרָד (mees-rahd; office) and some days בַּבַּיִת (bah-bah-yeet; at home). But whatever you call it, this way of work means working in your PJs, keeping your כֶּלֶב (keh-lehv; dog) or other חַיּוֹת מַחְמָד (hah-yoht mah-mahd, pets) company and sometimes even להפעיל מכונת כביסה (leh-hahf-eel meh-hoh-naht kuv-vee-sah; throwing in a load of laundry) between work calls and meetings.

When you work from home, you need to be careful about איזון בין עבודה וחיי משפחה (eez-*zoon* beyn hei-*yay* ah-*voh*-dah veh hei-*yay* meesh-pah-ḥah; *work–life balance*) and setting גבולות (guh-*voo*-loht; *boundaries*) between your חיים מקצועיים (hah-yeem meek-*soh*-ee-ee; *professional life*) and your חיים אישיים (hah-*yeem* ee-shee-*eem*; *personal life*). You'll also need a מקוםעבודה מגדר (mah-kohm ah-*voh*-dah *moog*-dahr; *dedicated workspace*), the right תאורה (teh-*ohr*-rah; *lighting*), and the ability to use all kinds of nifty טכנולוגיה (tehḥ-noo-*lohg*-gee-ah; *technology*). You'll need to know how להשתיק (leh-*hahsh*-teek; *to mute*) and לבטל את ההשתקה (leh-*vah*-tehl eht hah-hahsh-*tah*-kah; *unmute*) yourself on video calls, how לשתף (leh-shah-*tehf*; *to share*) your מסך (mah-*sahḥ*; *screen*), and how להעביר קבצים (leh-hah-*ah*-veehr; *to drop a file*) or a קשור (keeh-shohr; *link*) into the chat, for starters. You might want to have some fun virtual backgrounds and use a filter so that you'll look your best.

Knowing your way around סביבת עבודה של גוגל (suh-*vee-vaht* ah-*voh*-dah shehl goo-*gehl*; *Google Suite*) is de rigueur. You'll need to know how ליצר (lee-*tzohr*; *to create*) a תיק (teehk; *folder*) in Google Drive, how לשתף (leh-*shah*-tehf; *to share*) מסמכים (mees-*mah*-ḥeem; *documents*), and how להכניס (leh-*hahḥ*-nees; *to insert*) a video or image into Google Slides.

WORDS TO KNOW

עֲבוֹדָה מֵרָחוֹק	ah-voh-*dah* meh-*rah*-ḥohk	remote work
לַעֲבֹד מֵהַבַּיִת	lah-ah-*vohd* mee-hah-*bah*-yeet	working from home
סִגְנוֹן הִיבְּרִידִי	seeg-*nohn* hey-*bree*-dee	hybrid work
איזון בין עבודה וחיי משפחה	eez-*zoon* beyn hei-*yay* ah-*voh*-dah veh hei-yay meesh-pah-ḥah	work–life balance
גבולות	guh-*voo*-loht	boundaries
תְּאוּרָה	teh-*ohr*-rah	lighting
טֶכְנוֹלוֹגְיָה	tehḥ-noo-*lohg*-gee-ah	technology
לְהַשְׁתִּיק	leh-*hahsh*-teek	to mute
לְבַטֵּל אֶת הַהַשְׁתָּקָה	leh-*vah*-tehl eht hah-hahsh-*tah*-kah	unmute
לְשַׁתֵּף	leh-*shah*-tehf	to share
קֳבָצִים	kuh-*vahtz*-eem	electronic files

קִשּׁוּר	*kee*-shohr	link
סְבִיבַת עֲבוֹדָה שֶׁל גּוּגֶל	suh-*vee-vaht* ah-*voh-* dah shehl goo-*gehl*	Google Suite
לִיצֹר	lee-*tzohr*	to create
תִּיק	*teek*	folder
לְהַכְנִיס	leh-*hahḥ*-nees	to insert

Hanging Out at Home

Home is your refuge from the hustle and bustle of the outside world. In Jewish tradition, every home has the potential of being a מִקְדָּשׁ מְעַט (meek-*dash* meh-*aht*; *mini sanctuary*). The Jewish value of שְׁלוֹם בַּיִת (sh-*lohm* bah-*yeet*; *peace within the home*) is an important concept. Thus, the items we bring into our homes and the ways we behave within those walls have the potential to bring the sacred into our everyday lives. In this section, I tell you about all the stuff you need — both sacred and everyday — to make your house a home.

Looking through the rooms

How many חֲדָרִים (ḥah-dahr-*eem*; *rooms*) does your דִּירָה (dee-*rah*; *apartment*) or בַּיִת (bah-*yeet*; *house*) have? Do you have plenty of space where you live? Or do you want some more elbow room? Whether you live in an apartment or house, your dwelling probably has the following:

>> אַמְבַּטְיָה (ahm-*baht*-yah; *bathroom*)

>> אָרוֹן (ah-*rohn*; *closet*)

>> חֲדַר שֵׁנָה (ḥah-*dar* shay-*nah*; *bedroom*)

>> מִטְבָּח (meet-*bach*; *kitchen*)

>> פִּנַּת אֹכֶל (pee-*naht* oh-chel; *place to eat*)

>> פְּרוֹזְדוֹר (prohz-*dohr*; *hallway*)

>> סָלוֹן (sah-*lohn*; *living room*)

And if you're fortunate, your property may have some of these features as well:

» גֶּדֶר (gah-*dair*; *fence*)

» גִּנָּה (gee-*nah*; *yard*)

» מִרְפֶּסֶת (meer-*peh*-seht; *balcony*)

» מוּסָךְ (moo-*sach*; *garage*)

CULTURAL WISDOM

At the entrance of a traditional Jewish home, you may find a small amulet called a מְזוּזָה (meh-zoo-*zah*) containing a very important Jewish prayer. Around the entrance, you may also find a בִּרְכַּת הַבַּיִת (beer-*kaht* hah-*bah*-yeet; *blessing for the home*). On the eastern wall, you may find a מִזְרָח (meez-*rach*), which literally means "east" and is usually a decorative picture. Jews place this item on the eastern wall because that's the direction of Judaism's holy city, Jerusalem, and the direction in which Jews face during prayer. If you live in Israel, however, you place the מִזְרָח on the wall facing Jerusalem, so if you live 5 kilometers north of Jerusalem, you place it on the southern wall.

WORDS TO KNOW

אַמְבַּטְיָה	ahm-*baht*-yah	bathroom
בַּיִת	bah-yeet	house
חֲדַר שֵׁנָה	ḥah-*dahr* shay-*nah*	bedroom
מִרְפֶּסֶת	meer-*peh*-seht	balcony
מִטְבָּח	meet-*bahch*	kitchen
סָלוֹן	sah-*lohn*	living room

Furnishing your humble abode

After you move into your home, you need רָהוּט (reeh-*hoot*; *furniture*). You can buy it new, troll the yard sales, or see what you can bum off family and friends. I'm always surprised to see what people have sitting around in their מַרְטֵף (mahr-*tehf*; *basement*) or עֲלִיַּת גַּג (ah-lee-*yaht* gahg; *attic*) that they're happy to give away. What do you need?

» כִּסֵּא נוֹחַ (kee-seh *noh*-aḥ; *easy chair*)

» כִּסֵּא (kee-*seh*; *chair*)

- » מַדָּף סְפָרִים (mah-*dahf* sfah-*reem*; *bookshelf*)
- » מִטָּה (mee-*tah*; *bed*)
- » סַפָּה (sah-*pah*; *couch*)
- » שֻׁלְחָן (shool-**ḥ**ahn; *table*)

Then, of course, you have all the electrical conveniences that are part of modern-day living. How did we ever get along without them?

- » כִּירַיִם (kee-*rah*-yeem; *stove*)
- » מְקָרֵר (meh-kah-*rair*; *refrigerator*)
- » מַזְגָן (mahz-*gahn*; *air conditioner*)
- » מְכוֹנַת כְּבִיסָה (meh-choh-*naht* kvee-*sah*; *washing machine*)
- » מִקְרוֹגָל (meek-roh-*gahl*; *microwave*)
- » תַּנּוּר (tah-*noor*; *oven*)
- » טוֹסְטֶראוֹן (tah-nooh-*rohn*; *toaster oven*)
- » טֶלֶוִיזְיָה (teh-leh-*viz*-yah; *television*)

DOING THE SPONJAH: HOUSECLEANING THE ISRAELI WAY!

When I got my first apartment in Israel, an Israeli friend came over to help me לְסַדֵּר אֶת הַמָּקוֹם (lee-sah-*der* eht hah-mah-*kohm*; *to straighten up the place*). He found me trying to wash the floor, pushing a damp סְמַרְטוּט (smahr-*toot*; *rag*) about the רִצְפָּה (reetz-*pah*; *floor*) with a מַגָּב (mah-*gahv*; *squeegee*). He scolded me, saying that I didn't know how to clean house properly, promptly grabbed a דְּלִי (*dlee*; *bucket*), and filled it with hot soapy water. Then he dumped all the hot soapy water on the floor! Expertly, he wrapped the סְמַרְטוּט (smahr-*toot*; *rag*) around the מַגָּב (mah-*gahv*; *squeegee*) and whisked the soapy water down the פֶּתַח נִקּוּז (peh-ta**ḥ**neeh-*kooz*; *drain opening*) in the middle of the floor.

Believe it or not, most Israeli houses are built this way, and Israelis wash their floors in this manner. This method is called לַעֲשׂוֹת סְפוֹנְגָה (lah-ah-soht spon-jah; *to do the sponjah*). It's actually quite effective. Israelis wonder how we חוּלְנִיקִים (**ḥ**ool-nee-keem; *foreigners*) ever manage to get our floors clean. If you inspect the wooden feet of furniture in Israeli homes, you notice that they're often a bit swollen, which is what happens to wood from sitting in all that hot soapy water. But if you don't want to go through all this hassle every time you want the floor clean, you can always use your מַטְאַטֵא (mah-tah-*teh*; *broom*)!

כִּירַיִם	kee-*rah*-yeem	stove
כִּסֵּא	kee-*seh*	chair
מִקְרֹגַל	*meek*-roh-gahl	microwave
מִטָּה	mee-*tah*	bed
סַפָּה	sah-*pah*	couch
שֻׁלְחָן	shool-*chahn*	table
תַּנּוּר	tah-*noor*	oven

Residing in an Apartment

Wherever you live, if in the עִיר (*eer*; *city*) or a פַּרְבָּר (pahr-*vahr*; *suburb*), or if you're new to town, you may need to find a new דִּירָה (dee-*rah*; *apartment*) — unless, of course, you're a student and you live in the מְעוֹנוֹת (meh-oh-*noht*; *dorms*). Do you want to live לְבַד (leh-*vahd*; *alone*) or with שֻׁתָּפִים (shoo-tah-*feem*; *roommates*)? Do you have a מְכוֹנִית חֲנָיָה (meh-choh-*neet*; *car*) and thus need a מְקוֹם חֲנָיָה (meh-*kohm* chah-nah-*yah*; *parking spot*)? Or are you car-free and prefer to live near תַּחְבּוּרָה צִבּוּרִית (tach-boo-*rah* tzee-boo-*reet*; *public transportation*)?

Hunting for your very own flat

When you're מְחַפֵּשׂ (M)/ מְחַפֶּשֶׂת (F) (meh-chah-*pes*/meh-chah-*peh*-set; *looking for an apartment*), you first want to decide in which שְׁכוּנָה (shhoo-*nah*; *neighborhood*) you want to live. You want to know whether the דִּירָה is on קוֹמָה רִאשׁוֹנָה (koh-*mah* ree-shoh-*nah*; *the first floor*) or קוֹמָה עֶלְיוֹנָה (koh-*mah* ehl-yoh-*nah*; *an upper floor*).

CULTURAL WISDOM

What Americans call the first floor is the קוֹמַת קַרְקַע (koh-*maht kahr*-kah; *ground floor*) in Israel. Furthermore, when Israelis say the קוֹמָה רִאשׁוֹנָה (koh-*mah* ree-shoh-*nah*; *first floor*), they mean what Americans call the second floor.

If the בִּנְיָן (been-*yahn*; *building*) has many קוֹמוֹת (koh-*moht*; *floors*), you may want to inquire about a מַעֲלִית (mah-ah-*leet*; *elevator*). You also need to ask how much the שְׂכַר הַדִּירָה (s'*ḥahr* hah-dee-*rah*; *apartment rent*) is, of course. When you sign the חוֹזֶה שְׂכִירוּת (ḥoh-*zeh* s'chee-*root*; *rental contract*), you need to provide a לְפִקָּדוֹן תַּיֶּק (check pee-kah-*dohn*; *deposit check*) and a document called a שְׁטַר עַרְבוּת (sh'*tahr* ahr-reh-*voot*; *guarantee*), which guarantees that you have the ability to pay rent month after month.

CULTURAL WISDOM

In Israel, a two-room house means a חֶדַר שֵׁנָה (chah-*dar* shay-*nah; bedroom*) and a סָלוֹן (sah-*lohn; living room*), whereas in the United States, two rooms often refers just to the bedrooms. For more on the names of rooms in dwelling places, check out "Looking through the rooms" earlier in this chapter.

Talkin' the Talk

Rina is looking for an apartment. She and her real estate agent are discussing what type of apartment she wants.

Realtor:	כַּמָה חֲדָרִים אַתְּ רוֹצָה ?
	(kah-*mah* chah-dah-*reem* aht- roh-*tzah*?)
	How many rooms do you want?
Rina:	אֲנִי רוֹצָה שְׁנֵי חֲדָרִים .
	(ah-nee roh-*tzah* sh-*nay* chah-dah-*reem*.)
	I want two rooms.
Realtor:	אִכְפַּת לָךְ אִם זֶה בְּקוֹמָה עֶלְיוֹנָה בְּלִי מַעֲלִית ?
	(eech-*paht lach* eem zeh beh-koh-*mah* ehl-yoh-*nah* vuh-*ayn* mah-ah-*leet*?)
	Does it matter to you if it's on an upper floor and there's no elevator?
Rina:	לֹא זֶה לֹא אִכְפַּת לִי אֲנִי צְעִירָה גַם זֶה בָּרִיא לְטַפֵּס בְּמַדְרֵגוֹת .
	(loh. zeh loh eech-*paht lee*. ah-*nee* tze-ee-*rah* vuh-*gahm* zeh bah-*ree* le-tah-*pehs* buh-mahd-reh-*goht*.)
	No, that doesn't matter to me. I'm young, and it's also healthy to climb stairs.

GRAMMATICALLY SPEAKING

If you want to ask someone whether something matters to them, you use the Hebrew phrase אִכְפַּת (eeh-*paht*), and you inflect the personal pronoun with a לְ (lamed; *to*). *Inflecting* means combining the words, as in these examples:

» אִכְפַּת לִי (eeh-*paht lee; it matters to me*)

» אִכְפַּת לְךָ (eech-*paht* leh-*hah; it matters to you*) (MS)

>> אִכְפַּת לָךְ (eech-*paht* lach; *it matters to you*) (FS)

>> אִכְפַּת לְכֶה (eeḥ-*paht* leh-ḥeh; *it matters to you*) (NB)

>> אִכְפַּת לוֹ (eeḥ-*paht* loh; *it matters to him*) (MS)

>> אִכְפַּת לָה (eeḥ-*paht* lah; *it matters to her*) (FS)

>> אִכְפַּת לָנוּ (eeḥ-*paht* lah-noo; *it matters to us*)

>> אִכְפַּת לָכֶם (eech-*paht* lah-*ḥehm*; *it matters to you*) (MP or for a group of people)

>> אִכְפַּת לָכֶן (eech-*paht* lah-*chen*; *it matters to you*) (FP)

>> אִכְפַּת לָהֶם (eech-*paht* lah-*hem*; *it matters to them*) (MP or mixed plural)

>> אִכְפַּת לָהֶן (eech-*paht* lah-*hen*; *it matters to them*) (FP)

Giving your apartment some flair

After you settle into your new דִּירָה (*dee*-rah; *apartment*), you probably want to spruce it up! Colorful שְׁטִיחִים (shtee-ḥeem; *rugs*) always help brighten the place, and צְמָחִים (tzmah-ḥeem; *plants*) can make the place seem like home. Even some דָּגִים (dah-*geem*; *fish*) in a little אָקוַרְיוּם (ahk-*vahr*-yoom; *aquarium*) add a nice touch. Hanging some אָמָנוּת (oh-mah-*noot*; *art*) on the קִירוֹת (keer-*oht*; *walls*), including פּוֹסְטֶרִים (*pohs*-ter-eem; *posters*), can be pleasant and homey. Don't forget תְּמוּנוֹת (tmoo-*noht*; *pictures*) of your family members and friends and get plenty of funky מַגְנֶטִים (mag-*neh*-teem; *magnets*) for the מְקָרֵר (mahk-ah-*rair*; *refrigerator*). Speaking of which, Hebrew magnetic poetry is a really good idea!

Keeping your apartment safe

You don't want to have a בַּיִת שָׂרוּף (*bah*-yeet sah-*roof*; *burned-down house*), and you don't want a גַּנָּב (*gah*-nahv; *thief*) or רוֹצֵחַ (roh-*tzeh*-aḥ; *murderer*) to break in! חַס חָלִילָה (ḥahs-veh-ḥah-*lee*-lah; *heaven forbid*)! And you don't want to waste energy either. So, you need to take some precautions. You need to take the following steps when leaving the house:

>> לְכַבּוֹת ל אֶת הָאוֹר (leh-*ḥah*-boht eht hah-*ohr*; *to turn off the light*)

>> אֶת הָאוֹר (leen-*ohl* eht hah-*deh*-leht; *to lock the door*)

>> לִסְגֹר אֶת הַחַלּוֹן (lees-*gohr* eht hah-ḥah-*lohn*; *to close the window*)

>> לִסְגֹר אֶת הַגַּז (lees-*gor* eht hah-*gahz*; *to close the gas valve*)

DANGER ON THE ROOF!

One year when I was living in Israel, the דִּירָה (dee-*rah; apartment*) I was sharing with two שֻׁתָּפִים (shoo-tuh-*feem; roommates*) שֻׁתָּפוֹת (Shutafot) is the word to use for female roommates, but in this case, I was living with a man and a woman, so I use the form that works for either male plural or mixed gender. We had the kind of heating system that required ordering a vat of גַּז (*gahz; fuel*) from the local gas company: פָּז גַּז (*pahz gahz*), which literally means "golden gas." The gas man came out and installed this large tank of גַּז (*gahz; fuel*) right on top of our גַּג (*gahg; roof*)! I was a little disconcerted, to say the least. "What happens," I sensibly asked my שֻׁתָּפָה (shoo-tah-*fah; roommate* [F]), "if בָּרָק (bah-*rahk; lightning*) strikes the גַּז (*gahz; fuel*) while we're all in the דִּירָה (dee-*rah; apartment*)? "Well," my שֻׁתָּפָה (shoo-tah-*fah; roommate* [F]), replied, "We'll just try not to think about it while it's happening."

WORDS TO KNOW

בִּנְיָן	been-*yahn*	building
חֶדֶר	ḥeh-dair	room
חֲדָרִים	ḥah-dahr-*eem*	rooms
חַלּוֹן	ḥah-*lohn*	window
דִּירָה	dee-*rah*	apartment
מַעֲלִית	mah-ah-*leet*	elevator
מְקָרֵר	meh-kah-*rair*	refrigerator
מְקוֹם חֲנָיָה	meh-*kohm* ḥah-na-*yah*	parking spot
שָׁטִיחַ	sha-*tee*-ach	rug
שֻׁתָּף	shoo-*tahf*	roommate (M)
שֻׁתָּפָה	shoo-tah-*fah*	roommate (F)
צֶמַח	tzeh-*maḥ*	plant

Commanding People: Do As I Say

Hebrew uses a special verb tense to make commands called צִבּוּי (tzee-*vooy*). Unfortunately, you'll probably hear this verb tense a lot around the office, and if you're *really* unlucky, around the house as well. This special verb tense is like the future tense, but the prefix is dropped. The following mini-table shows some examples.

Tense	Hebrew	Pronunciation	Translation	Gender
Future tense	תִּשְׁמַע	teesh-*mah*	You will hear	(MS)
Command tense	שְׁמַע!	sh*mah*	Hear!	(MS)
Future tense	תִּשְׁמְעִי	teesh-meh-*ee*	You will hear	(FS)
Command tense	שִׁמְעִי	sheem-*ee*	Hear!	(FS)

In the command tense in the feminine singular and masculine plural, the vowels change just a bit. You can tell someone to finish something in the following ways:

>> גְּמֹר! (*gmohr*; *Finish up!*) (MS)

גִּמְרִי! (geem-*ree*; *Finish up!*) (FS)

גִּמְרוּ! (geem-*roo*; *Finish up!*) (for a group of people, male, female, and mixed gender)

Here's how you tell someone to sit:

>> שֵׁב! (sh*ehv*; *Sit!*) (MS)

שְׁבִי! (sh-*vee*; *Sit!*) (FS)

שְׁבוּ! (sh-*voo*; *Sit!*) (for a group of people, male, female, or mixed gender)

If you want to tell someone *not* to do something, you use the word אַל (*ahl*) in combination with the future tense, as in these examples:

>> אַל תִּכְתֹּב (*ahl* teech-*tohv*; *Don't write*) (MS)

אַל תִּכְתְּבִי (*ahl* teech-te-*vee*; *Don't write*) (FS)

תִּכְתְּבוּ (*ahl* teech-te-*voo*; *Don't write*) (for a group of people, male, female, or mixed gender)

FUN & GAMES

Use the following word list to identify the pictured rooms. Check Appendix C for the answers.

אַמְבַּטְיָה, אָרוֹן, חֲדַר שֵׁנָה, מִטְבָּח, מוֹסָךְ, סָלוֹן

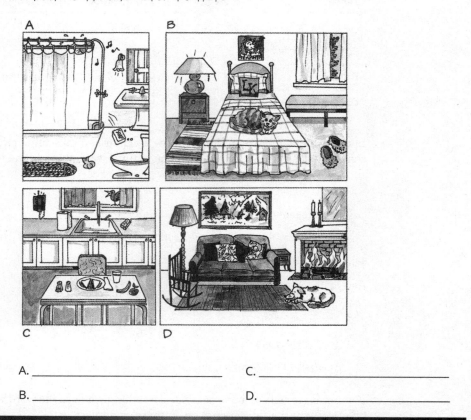

A. _____   C. _____

B. _____   D. _____

3

Hebrew on the Go

Chapter **11**

Planning and Taking a Trip

You want to take a trip, but you don't know where to go. In this chapter, I give you some key Hebrew words and phrases that can help you decide where to visit and how to plan your trip.

As for me, I think I'll take a חֹפֶשׁ (*oh*-fehsh; *vacation*) when I'm done writing this book. The places I want to go! So many countries I want to see; so many things I want to do. I want to hike in Costa Rica, sail down the canals in Italy, sunbathe in Greece, dip in the thermal pools in Iceland, and go on a safari in Africa. And oh, yeah, I really want to go have tapas in Spain, see the museums in France, and gawk at all the tall blonde people in the Scandinavian countries. And I really want to visit Estonia. I'm game for just about anything. Did I mention India? נְסִיעָה טוֹבָה (neh-see-*ah* toh-*vah*; *Happy traveling!*)

Choosing Your Final Destination (And When You Want to Go)

Figuring out when you're going to take your trip is as important as choosing your destination. You won't be happy if you visit some place during the worst weather all year. Then again, maybe you want to visit then because everything will be cheap! No matter when you go, a little planning is good. Table 11-1 shows the months when you might plan a vacation:

TABLE 11-1

Rattling Off the Months

Hebrew	Pronunciation	Translation
יָנוּאָר	*yan*-oo-ahr	January
פֶבְּרוּאָר	*feh*-broo-ahr	February
מֶרְץ	*mehrtz*	March
אַפְּרִיל	a-*preel*	April
מַאי	*mahye*	May
יוּנִי	*yoo*-nee	June
יוּלִי	*yoo*-lee	July
אוֹגוּסְט	owe-*goost*	August
סֶפְּטֶמְבֶּר	sehp-*tehm*-bear	September
אוֹקְטוֹבֶּר	ohct-*oh*-bear	October
נוֹבֶמְבֶּר	noh-*vehm*-bear	November
דֶּצֶמְבֶּר	deh-*tzehm*-bear	December

Whittling down your choices — so many places you can go!

Then, of course, there are many אֲרָצוֹת (ah-rah-tz-*oht*; *countries*) you can choose to visit. When I travel, I'm less interested in the אֲתָרֵי תַּיָּרוּת (ah-tah-*rey* tah-yah-*root*; *tourist sites*) and more interested in the תּוֹפְעוֹת טֶבַע (toh-fah-*oht* teh-vah; *natural phenomena*) and the חַיֵּי הַיוֹם (ẖah-*yey* hah-*yohm daily life*) of the people who live there. Also, I always find it interesting to visit עִיר הַבִּירָה (eer hah-beer-*ah*; *the capital city*). Of the following countries in Table 11-2, where would you like to go?

TABLE 11-2

Names of Countries

Hebrew	Pronunciation	Translation
אַנְגְּלִיָּה	*ahng*-lee-*yah*	England
אַרְצוֹת הַבְּרִית	ahrtz-*oht* hah-*breet*	United States
אָמֶרִיקָה	drohm ah-*meh*--ree-kah	South America
גֶּרְמַנְיָה	gayr-*mah*-nee-yah	Germany
הֹדּוּ	*hoh*-doo	India
אִיטַלְיָה	ee-*tahl*-yah	Italy
מֶקְסִיקוֹ	*mehks*-ee-koh	Mexico
מִצְרַיִּים	meetz-*rah*-yeem	Egypt
פּוֹלִין	poh-*leen*	Poland
רוּסְיָה	roo-see-*yah*	Russia
שְׁוַיִץ	sh-*vaitz*	Switzerland
סְפָרַד	sfahr-*ahd*	Spain
שְׁוֶדְיָה	shuh-*vehd*-ee-*yah*	Sweden
סִין	*seen*	China
טוּרְקִיָה	*toor*-kee-*yah*	Turkey
צָרְפַת	tzar-*faht*	France
יַפָּן	yah-*pahn*	Japan
יַרְדֵּן	yahr-*dehn*	Jordan
יָוָן	yah-*vahn*	Greece

CULTURAL WISDOM

The literal meaning of the Hebrew word for the United States — אַרְצוֹת הַבְּרִית (ahrtz-*oht* hah-*breet*) — is "the lands of the covenant." A *covenant* is an unbreakable agreement between parties. In the case of the United States of America, the covenant is the Constitution.

Talkin' the Talk

Orli and Yoni are planning to travel. Orli wants to go to South America, but Yoni wants to go to India.

Yoni: טוֹב לְאָן נוֹסְעִים ?

(*tohv*, leh-*ahn* noh-s-*eem*?)

Good. Where are we traveling?

Orli: אֲנִי הָיִיתִי רוֹצָה לִנְסֹעַ לִדְרוֹם אָמֶרִיקָה .

(ah-*nee* hah-*yee*-tee roh-*tzah* leen-soh-*ah* leh-drohm ah-*mehr*-ee-kah.)

I want to travel to South America.

Yoni: דַּוְקָא אֲנִי הָיִיתִי רוֹצֶה לִנְסֹעַ לְהֹדוּ .

(dahv-*kah* ah-*nee* hah-*yee*-tee roh-*tzah* leen-soh-*ah* leh-*hoh*-doo.)

But I really want to travel to India.

Orli: בּוֹא נִתְפַּשֵּׁר וְנִסַּע לִשְׁתֵּיהֶן .

(boh neet-pah-*shehr* vuh-nee-*sah* luhsh-tay-*hehn*.)

Let's compromise and travel to both.

Finding your way around

GRAMMATICALLY SPEAKING

In Hebrew, when you want to indicate direction, you add the sound *ah* to the end of certain common words, stressing the syllable before that ending. So instead of saying: אֲנִי רוֹצָה לַחֲזֹר לַבַּיִת (ah-*nee* roh-*tzah* lah-*zohr* lah-*bah*-yeet; literally: *I want to return to-the-house*), you can just say אֲנִי רוֹצָה לַחֲזֹר הַבַּיְתָה (ah-*nee* roh-*tzah* lach-*zohr* hah-*bahy*-tah; which is something more like "I want to go houseward").

Use these words when you're trying to find your way around:

Noun of place	Directional
אָחוֹר (shah **h**oh; *back*)	אֲחוֹרָה (ah-ah-*hohr*-rah; *backward*)
אֶרֶץ (*ahr*-ehtz; *Land of Israel*)	אַרְצָה (*ahrtz*-ah; *to the Land of Israel*)
דָרוֹם (Dah-*rohm*; *south*)	דְרוֹמָה (dah-*roh*-mah; *southward*)

Noun of place	Directional
הַחוּץ (Ha-**ḥ**ootz; *outside*)	הַחוּצָה (ha-*chootz*-ah; *[to] outside*)
הָעִיר (hah-*eer*; *the town*)	הָעִירָה (hah-*eer*-ah; *to town*)
קֶדֶם (*keh*-dehm; *front*)	קָדִימָה (kah-*dee*-mah; *forward*)
נֶגֶב (*neh*-gehv; *the Negev, south*)	נֶגְבָּה (*nehg*-bah; *southward*)
פְּנִים (p'*neem*; *inside*)	פְּנִימָה (p-*nee*-mah; *to the inside*)
שְׂמֹאל (smohl; *left*)	שְׂמֹאלָה (*smoh*-lah; *leftward*)
צָפוֹן (tzah-*fohn*; *north*)	צָפוֹנָה (tzah-*foh*-nah; *northward*)
יָמִין (yah-meen; *right*)	יָמִינָה (yah-*mee*-nah; *rightward*)

Packing

I love לִנְסֹעַ (leen-soh-*ah*; *to travel*), but I hate לֶאֱרֹז (leh-eh-*rohz*; *to pack*)! I often wait until the last minute לֶאֱרֹז (*to pack*) just before I'm ready לַעֲזֹב (lah-ah-*zov*; *to leave*) my house for my טִיוּל (tee-*yool*; *trip*). A bad הֶרְגֵּל (hehr-*gehl*; *habit*) I know. I want to share a tip my aunt taught me: Instead of לְקַפֵּל (leh-kah-*pehl*; *folding* [literally: *to fold*]) your בְּגָדִים (beh-gah-*deem*; *clothes*), לְגַלְגֵּל (leh-gah-*gehl*; *roll*) them instead. It really does save space in your מִזְוָדָה (meez-vah-*dah*; *suitcase*)!

MAKING YOUR WAY TO MACHTESH RAMON

One of the most amazing תוֹפָעוֹת טֶבַע (toh-fah-*oht* teh-*vah*; *natural phenomena*) in Israel is the Machtesh Ramon, the largest crater in the world. When I first heard about this place and heard that it was a crater, I immediately thought of the moon. The Machtesh Ramon isn't like the moon's craters, however; rather, it's a cave drained by a single וָאדִי (ah-dee; *riverbed*). You can find the Machtesh Ramon in the Negev Desert in Israel, a few hours south of the southern city of Beersheva. The Machtesh Ramon is home to many beautiful trees, shrubs, and flowers, such as חַנֲנִיוֹת (chee-noh-nee-*oht*; *daisies*) and צִבְעוֹנִים (tzeev-oh-*neem*; *tulips*). Many animals live there, including the יָעֵל (yah-*ehel*; *ibex*), נָמֵר (nah-*mehr*; *leopard*), צָבוֹעַ (tzah-*vooh*-ah; *hyena*), שׁוּעָל (shoo-*ahl*; fox), and צְבִי (tzuh-vee; *deer*). Rock formations, fossils, and volcanic phenomenon — some as old as 220 million years — fill the place. The site also has an amazing museum. And if you like to hike, the Machtesh Ramon has some great trails. If you really want to rough it, consider camping. At night, you can enjoy some incredible צְפִיָּה בַּכּוֹכָבִים (tzee-*pee*-yah bah-koh-chahv-*eem*; *stargazing*) as the area has few artificial lights, and the air is crisp and clear.

WORDS TO KNOW

חוֹפֶשׁ	ḥoh-*fehsh*	vacation
לֶאֱרוֹז	leh-eh-*rohz*	to pack
לַעֲזֹב	lah-ah-*zohv*	to leave
לִנְסֹעַ	leen-soh-*ah*	to travel
מִזְוָדָה	meez-vah-*dah*	suitcase
טִיּוּל	tee-*yool*	trip

Booking a trip

When you're ready to arrange your travel and your lodging, you may want to consider using a סוֹכְנוּת נְסִיעוֹת (sohḥ-*noot* neh-see-*oht*; *travel agency*). These professionals can arrange everything for you — your plane tickets, your hotel reservation, your car rental (if you need one), and even deals on complete tour packages. They're worth checking out. They can book you on a הַפְלָגָה בַּיָּם (hahf-lah-*gah* buh-*yahm*; *cruise*) or on a טִיּוּל מְאֻרְגָּן (tee-*ool* meh-oor-*gahn*; *organized tour*). Maybe they can even get you a הֲנָחָה (hah-nah-*chah*; *discount*).

Traveling internationally

If you're traveling abroad, you have a host of additional things to consider. Make sure that your דַּרְכּוֹן (dahr-*kohn*; *passport*) is current and you've checked with the קוֹנסוּלְיָה (kon-*soo*-lee-ah; *consulate*) or the שַׁגְרִירוּת (shahg-ree-*root*; *embassy*) to see whether you need a visa. When you cross the border of a country, you may have to go through מֶכֶס (meh-chehs; *customs*) and declare what you're bringing with you. See Chapter 12 for more words you can use when traveling.

CULTURAL
WISDOM

RECITING THE TRAVELERS' PRAYER

You find a תְּפִלַּת הַדֶּרֶךְ (tuh-fee-*laht* hah-*dair*-re**h**; *travelers' prayer*) in many Jewish סִדּוּרִים (see-dur-*eem*; *prayer books*) that Jews traditionally say any time they leave their own city. You also find this prayer on the backs of keychains or on little cards you can stick in your wallet. In Israel, taxi drivers often hand out cards with this prayer on it, with the other side of the card serving as a business card. Jews even recite a special תְּפִלַּת הַדֶּרֶךְ (*travel-er's prayer*) for traveling on an airplane! The prayer beseeches God שֶׁתּוֹלִיכֵנוּ לְשָׁלוֹם (sheh-toh-lee-*hay*-noo leh-shah-*lohm*; *that we will be guided in peace*) and שֶׁתַּחֲזִירֵנוּ לְבֵיתֵנוּ בְּשָׁלוֹם (sheh-ta**h**-zear-*aye*-noo le'veit-*ay*-noo beh-shah-*lohm*; *that we will return home in peace*).

WORDS TO KNOW

קוֹנסוּלִיָּה	kon-*soo*-lee-ah	consulate
דַּרְכּוֹן	dahr-*kohn*	passport
הַפְלָגָה בַּיָּם	hahf-lah-*gah* buh-*yahm*	cruise
עִיר בִּירָה	eer beer-*ah*	capital city
מֶכֶס	*meh*-chehs	customs
שַׁגְרִירוּת	shahg-*ree*-root	embassy
טִיּוּל מְאֻרְגָּן	tee-*yool* meh-oohr-*gahn*	organized tour

Coming and Going: Knowing Where You Are

You can announce your arrival in several ways. You can say אֲנִי בָּא (M) or אֲנִי בָּאָה (F) (ah-*nee* bah or ah-*nee* bah-*ah*; *I'm coming*). You can also use the expression אֲנִי מַגִּיעַ (M) or אֲנִי מַגִּיעָה (F) (ah-*nee* mah-*gee*-ah or ah-*nee* mah-gee-*ah*; *I'm arriving*). When you're traveling in a group, after you've arrived somewhere, say הִגַּעְנוּ (hee-*gah*-noo; *We have arrived*).

When you leave, you can say any of the following:

» אֲנִי עוֹזֵב (ah-*nee* oh-*zehv*; *I'm leaving.*) (M)

אֲנִי עוֹזֶבֶת (ah-*nee* oh-*zehv-et*; *I'm leaving.*) (F)

» אֲנִי הוֹלֵךְ (ah-*nee* hoh-*lech*; *I'm going.*) (M)

אֲנִי הוֹלֶכֶת (ah-*nee* hoh-*lech-eht*; *I'm going.*) (F)

» אֲנִי זָז (ah-*nee* zahz; *I'm moving.*) (M)

אֲנִי זָזָה (ah-*nee* zahz-ah; *I'm moving.*) (F)

Then, of course, you can use that favorite, often-used Israeli expression יַאלְלָה בַּיי (*yah*-lah *bye*; *Let's go. Bye!*). You may also want to say לְהִתְרָאוֹת (leh-hee-trah-*oht*; *See you soon!*).

Talkin' the Talk

Jill has spent the past month visiting her cousin in Israel. Her cousin, Polly, has agreed to drive her to the airport. They're discussing when the plane will leave and what time they need to leave the apartment to arrive at the airport on time.

Polly: מָתַי הַטִּיסָה שֶׁלָּךְ ?

(mah-*tye* hah-tee-*sah* sheh-*lach*)

When is your flight?

Jill: הַמָּטוֹס מַמְרִיא בְּתֵשַׁע

(hah-mah-*tohs* mahm-*ree* buh-*tay*-shah)

The plane takes off at nine.

Polly: יֵשׁ לָךְ אֶת כַּרְטִיס הַטִּיסָה וְאֶת הַדַּרְכּוֹן שֶׁלָּךְ ?

(yaysh lach eht kahr-*tees* hah-tee-*sah* veh-*eht* hah-dahr-*kohn* sheh-*lach*)

Do you have your plane ticket and your passport?

Jill: כֵּן יֵשׁ לִי .

(kehn *yesh*-lee)

Yes, I have them.

Polly:	טוֹב אֲנִי אַקְפִּיץ אוֹתָךְ עוֹד מְעַט לִנְמַל הַתְּעוּפָה אֲנִי לֹא רוֹצֶה שֶׁתְּאַחֲרִי . וּתְפַסְפְסִי אֶת הַטִּיסָה שֶׁלָךְ

(tohv ah-*nee* ak-*peetz* oh-*tach* ohd meh-*aht* leh-neh-*mahl* hah-teh-oo-*fah* ah-*nee* loh-roh-*tzah* sheh-teh-*ach-ree* ve-teh-fahs-feh-*see* eht hah-tee-*sah* sheh-*lach*)

Good. I'll drop you by the airport soon. I don't want you to be late and miss your flight.

• •

WORDS TO KNOW

בַּזְמַן	buhz-*mahn*	on time
כַּרְטִיס טִיסָה	kahr-*tees* ti-*sah*	airline ticket
לְהַמְרִיא	leh-hahm-*ree*	to take off
לִנְחוֹת	lin-*chot*	to land
מָטוֹס	mah-*tohs*	airplane
מְאַחָר	meh-oo-*chahr*	late
נְמַל הַתְּעוּפָה	neh-*mahl* hah-tuh-oo-*fah*	airport
טִיסָה	tee-*sah*	flight

Discussing the Future: Verb Forms and Popular Expressions

GRAMMATICALLY SPEAKING

When you want to say something in the future tense, for most Hebrew verbs, you add prefixes to the שֹׁרֶשׁ (shoh-resh; *verb root*), and in some cases, you add suffixes. In the future tense, you add the following prefixes and suffixes to the root:

I	אֶ	eh
You (MS)	תִ	tee
You (FS)	תִ‎ee	
+ the suffix	י	ee

He	יְ	*yee*
She	תְ	*tee*
We	נְ	*nee*
You (MP/FP)	תְ	*tee*
+ the suffix	וּ	*oo*
They	יְ	*yee*
+ the suffix	וּ	*oo*

Conjugate the word לִכְתֹב (leeh–*tohv*; *to write*) in the future tense like this:

» אֲנִי אֶכְתֹב (ah-*nee* e**ḥ**-*tohv*; *I will write.*)

» אַתָּה תִּכְתֹב (ah-*tah* tee**ḥ**-*tohv*; *You will write.*) (M)

  אַתְּ תִּכְתְּבִי (aht teech-teh-*vee*; *You will write.*) (F)

» הוּא יִכְתֹב (hoo yee**ḥ**-*tohv*; *He will write.*) (SM)

» הִיא תִּכְתֹב (hee tee**ḥ**-*tohv*; *She will write.*) (SF)

» אֲנַחְנוּ נִכְתֹב (ah-na**ḥ**-*noo* neech-*tohv*; *We will write.*)

» אַתֶּם (MP)/אַתֶּן תִּכְתְּבוּ (FP) (ah-*tem*/ah-*ten* tee**ḥ**-teh-*voo*; *You* [plural, whether it means a bunch of guys, a bunch of gals, or some combination]; *You will write.*)

» הֵן יִכְתְּבוּ (FP)/ הֵם יִכְתְּבוּ (MP) (hem/hen yee**ḥ**-teh-*voo*; *They will write.*)

Finding the Hotel That's Right for You

Everyone likes to have a warm, comfy place to rest their head at night whenever traveling. In this section, I help you with the Hebrew vocabulary and phrases you need to find a hotel, make reservations, inquire about your hotel's facilities, and check in and out so you can have a restful night of sleep.

If you're looking for לִינָה (lee–*nah*; *lodging*), you may want to pick up a travel guide or hit the Internet to find out about accommodations. If you're feeling adventurous, you can wait until you get to your desired destination and take your chances. But if you're traveling during tourist season, be prepared to find a lot of "no vacancy" signs. A good way to find a hotel is to ask people you know whether they can recommend a reliable place to stay. You can ask

>> אַתָּה יָכוֹל לְהַמְלִיץ עַל מְקוֹם לִינָה בָּאֵזוֹר ? (ah-*tah* yah-chohl leh-hahm-*leets* ahl *mah*-kohm lee-*nah* bah-eh-*zohr*; *Can you recommend lodging in the area?*) (M)

>> אַתְּ יְכוֹלָה לְהַמְלִיץ עַל מְקוֹם לִינָה בָּאֵזוֹר ? (aht yeh-chohl-*lah* leh-hahm-*leets* ahl *mah*-kohm lee-*nah* bah-eh-*zohr*; *Can you recommend lodging in the area?*) (F)

>> אַתָּה מַכִּיר מָלוֹן טוֹב ? (ah-*tah* mah-*keer* mah-*lohn* tohv; *Do you know of a good hotel?*) (M)

>> אַתְּ מַכִּירָה מָלוֹן טוֹב ? (aht mah-*keer*-ah mah-*lohn* tohv; *Do you know of a good hotel?*) (F)

You may also want to specify the דֵּרוּג (deh-*roog*; *rating*) you want. Will only חֲמִשָּׁה כּוֹכָבִים (chah-mee-*shah* koh-chah-*veem*; *five stars*) suffice, or can you make do with something a little less מְפֹאָר (meh-foh-*ahr*; *luxurious*)?

You can choose among all sorts of מְלוֹנוֹת (meh-lohn-*oht*; *hotels*) with different kinds of נְעִימוֹת (neh-eem-*oht*; *amenities*). In addition to the מָלוֹן (mah-*lohn*; *hotel option*), you might consider staying at

>> אַכְסַנְיָה (ach-sahn-ee-*ah*; *a hostel*)

>> לִינָה כַּפְרִית (lee-*nah* kuhfr-*reet*; *a village inn*)

>> צִימֶר (tsee-mer; *a bed-and-breakfast inn*)

Making your reservations

If you're a planner, you probably want to book your room reservation in advance. But if you're a free spirit, you'll probably have better luck finding an empty חֶדֶר (cheh-*dair*; *room*) in מְלוֹנוֹת or אַכְסַנְיוֹת (ahch-sah-nee-*oht*; *hostels*) outside מֶרְכַּז הָעִיר (mehr-*kahz* hah-*eer*; *the city center*).

These days, you'll probably be making your הַזְמָנָה (hahz-*mah*-nah; *reservation*) over the Internet, where you can use English. But just in case you make your הַזְמָנָה (hahz-*mah*-nah; *reservation*) in person or over the phone, here's the lingo: אֶפְשָׁר ? לְהַזְמִין חֶדֶר (ehf-*shahr* leh-hahz-*meen* cheh-*dair*?; *May I reserve a room?*).

If you want to reserve more than one room, insert the proper number: שְׁנֵי חֲדָרִים (shuh-*nay* chah-dahr-*eem*; *two rooms*), שְׁלוֹשָׁה חֲדָרִים (shuh-loh-*shah* chah-dahr-*eem*; *three rooms*), אַרְבָּעָה חֲדָרִים (ahr-bah-*ah* chah-dahr-*eem*; *four rooms*), and so on.

You also want to know, of course, whether the מָלוֹן (mah-*lohn*; *hotel*) has a חֶדֶר פָּנוּי (cheh-dair pah-noo-ee; *vacant room*) and whether the room has one מִטָּה (mee-*tah*; *bed*) or two מִטּוֹת (mee-*toht*; *beds*). And you want to inquire about the תַּעֲרִיף (tah-ah-*reef*; *rate*) for each night.

TIP

Before you call to make your reservation, you may want to read Chapter 9 to brush up on your phone-conversation skills and also the sections on telling time and the days of the week in Chapter 7.

WORDS TO KNOW

חֶדֶר	ẖeh-*dair*	room
הַזְמָנָה	hahz-mah-*nah*	reservation
נְעִימוֹת	neh-eem-oht	amenities
מָלוֹן	mah-*lohn*	hotel
מִטָּה	mee-*tah*	bed
תַּעֲרִיף	tah-ah-*reef*	rate

Here's a list of handy-dandy phrases you might want to keep on hand when asking about the נְעִימוֹת (neh-eem-*oht*; *amenities*) and שֵׁרוּתִים (sheh-root-*eem*; *services*) that come with the hotel room. Start by asking הַאִם יֵשׁ (hah-*eem* yehsh . . .; *Is there . . .*) and then plug in any of the vocabulary words in Table 11-3.

TABLE 11-3   **Common Hotel Amenities**

Hebrew	Pronunciation	English Translation
בְּרֵכַת שִׂיחָה	bray-*ẖaht* chee-*yah*	swimming pool
חֲדַר כֹּשֶׁר	chah-*dahr* koh-*sher*	weight room
גַ'קוּזִי מְקוֹרָה	jah-*koo*-zee meh-kohr-ah	indoor Jacuzzi
כַּסֶּפֶת	kah-*sehf*-eht	a safe
לוּל לְתִינוֹק	lool leh-tee-*nohk*	a baby's playpen
מִזּוּג אֲוִיר מֶרְכָּזִי	mee-*zoog* ah-*veer* mehr-kahz-*ee*	central air conditioning
מִגְרָשׁ טֶנִיס	meeg-*rahsh teh*-nees	tennis court
מִרְפֶּסֶת	meer-*pehs*-eht	a balcony
הַפְעָלוֹת בְּדוּר לִילָדִים	peh-ee-*luht* bee-*door* leh-yeh-lah-*deem*	children's activities
שֵׁרוּת כְּבִיסָה	sheh-*root* kvee-*sah*	laundry service
טֶלֵוִיזְיָה	the-leh-*veez*-ee-ah	television

RISE AND SHINE: BREAKFASTS AT ISRAELI HOTELS

If you've never had breakfast in an Israeli hotel, you're in for a real treat! Most hotels in Israel serve a buffet breakfast as part of the service. At the buffet, you find an incredible spread of vegetables (yes, Israelis eat raw vegetables for breakfast — a healthy and delicious habit); fruits of all kinds; and a wonderful display of Israeli milk products, including yogurt and לְבֶּנֶה (la-*bah*-neh) a delicious milk product not found in North America but common in the Middle East. You also can eat all sorts of breads, hard-boiled eggs, and f(or the North American palate) all kinds of cereals. But I recommend that when you're in Israel, do as the Israelis do: Fill your plate with veggies, fruit, a bit of bread, and perhaps some yogurt. I can't think of a better way to start the day! בְּתֵאָבוֹן (beh-*teh*-ah-*vohn; Good appetite!*).

Asking about the price

If you like the hotel and want to stay there, ask about the price: ? כַּמָּה עוֹלֶה הַחֶדֶר (kah-*mah* oh-*leh* hah-*cheh*-dehr?; *How much does the room cost?*).

You can also ask whether the hotel offers a הֲנָחָה (hah-nah-*hah; discount*) or מִבְצָע (meev-*tzah; special* or *sale*). Just talk to מְנַהֵל הַמָּלוֹן (meh-nah-*hehl* hah-mah-*lohn; the hotel manager*). When you're traveling off-season, sometimes you can find good deals!

WORDS TO KNOW		
חֲדַר שֵׁנָה	ḥah-*dahr* shay-*nah*	bedroom
הֲנָחָה	hah-nah-*ḥah*	discount
מְפוֹאָר	meh-foo-*ahr*	luxurious
מְנַהֵל הַמָּלוֹן ח	meh-nah-*hehl* hah-mah-*lohn*	hotel manager
מִטָּה זוּגִית	mee-*tah* zoo-*geet*	double bed
מִטַּת יָחִיד	mee-*taht* yah-*ḥ*eed	single bed
מַפְתֵּחַ	mahf-*tay*-a**ḥ**	key
נ מִתְקָנִים	meet-*kahn*-eem	amenities
שֵׁרוּתִים	sheh-roo-*teem*	services

Checking In: Names, Addresses and Room Numbers

After you arrive at your hotel, go straight to the קַבָּלָה (kah-bah-*lah*; *reception desk*) to check in. Ideally, you've reserved a room. If not, you just have to take your chances! If you're the planning-in-advance type and indeed made reservations, you have to let the receptionist know by saying אֲנִי הִזְמַנְתִּי חֶדֶר (ah-*nee* heez-*mahn*-tee *ḥeh*-dair; *I reserved a room*).

Tell the receptionist your name by saying . . . הַשֵּׁם שֶׁלִּי (hah-*shehm* sheh-*lee* . . .; *My name is* . . .).

The receptionist may ask you for your אֹפֶן הַתַּשְׁלוּם (oh-*fehn* Hah-tahsh-*loom*; *method of payment*), including מְזֻמָּן (meh-zoo-*mahn*; *cash*) or כַּרְטִיס אַשְׁרַי (kahr-*tees* ash-*rye*; *credit card*). For more information on money, be sure to read Chapter 13.

Filling out the registration form

At some מְלוֹנוֹת (muh-*lohn*-oht; *hotels*), the receptionist may ask you to provide your personal information on a טֹפֶס (*toh*-fehs; *form*) as part of the registration process. If so, the receptionist may say נָא לְמַלֵּא אֶת הַטֹּפֶס (nah leh-mah-*leht* eht hah-*toh*-fehs; *Please fill out this form*). Sometimes, the form is on paper, but most likely, it's on a tablet computer.

You may have to provide some personal information on the טֹפֶס (*toh*-fehs; *form*). Table 11-4 shows some common information you may have to provide.

TABLE 11-4   **Information to Know When You Check into a Hotel**

Hebrew	Pronunciation	English Translation
חֲתִימָה	chah-teeh-*mah*	signature
אֵזוֹר מִקּוּד	ay-*zohr* mee-*kood*	zip code
אֶרֶץ	ah-*rehtz*	country
עִיר	*eer*	city
לְאֹם	leh-*ohm*	nationality
מְקוֹם לֵדָה	meh-*kohm* lay-*dah*	birthplace
מִקְצוֹעַ	meek-*tsoh*-ah	profession

Hebrew	Pronunciation	English Translation
מִסְפַּר הַבַּיִת	mees-*pahr* hah-*bah*-yeet	house number
רְחוֹב	reh-*chohv*	street
שֵׁם מִשְׁפָּחָה	shem meesh-pah-*chah*	last name (literally: family name)
שֵׁם פְּרָטִי i	shehm prah-*tee*	first name (literally: private name)
תַּאֲרִיךְ לֵדָה	tah-ah-*reech* lay-*dah*	birthdate

Talkin' the Talk

Yaniv has arrived at a hotel for a week's vacation. He goes to the פָּקִיד (pah-keed; receptionist) to check in.

Yaniv: עֶרֶב טוֹב הַשֵּׁם שֶׁלִּי יָנִיב אֲנִי הִזְמַנְתִּי חֶדֶר .

(eh-rehv tohv! hah-*shem* sheh-*lee* yah-*neev*. ah-*nee* heez-*mahn*-tee *cheh*-dehr.)

Good evening! My name's Yaniv. I reserved a room.

Receptionist: נָכוֹן חֶדֶר עִם מִטָּה זוּגִית וְאַמְבַּטְיָה נָא לְמַלֵּא אֶת הַטֹּפֶס .

(nah-*chohn*. ẖeh-dehr ech-*ahd* eem mee-*tah* zoo-*geet* veh-ahm-*bah*-tee-*ah*. nah leh-mah-*leh* eht hah-*toh*-fehs.)

Correct. One room with a double bed and a bathroom. Please fill out the form.

Yaniv: הַאִם יֵשׁ לָכֶם בְּרֵכָב וַחֲדַר כֹּשֶׁר

(hah-*eem* yaysh lah-ẖehm bray-*chah* veh-chah-*dahr* *koh*-shehr?)

Do you have a pool and a workout room?

Receptionist: בְּוַדַּאי הִנֵּה הַמַּפְתֵּחַ שֶׁלְּךָ הַחֶדֶר שֶׁלְּךָ שָׁלוֹשׁ מֵאוֹת וְחָמֵשׁ .

(beh-vah-*dai*. hee-*nay* hah-mahf-*tay*-ach shehl-chah. hah-*cheh*-dehr shehl-*chah* shuh-*lohsh* meh-*oht* veh-chah-*maysh*.)

Certainly. Here's your key. Your room is 305.

Yaniv: תּוֹדָה רַבָּה .

(Toh-*dah* rah-*bah*.)

Thank you very much.

Settling into your room

After you check in, the receptionist will let you know your room number, saying something like this:

>> מִסְפַּר הַחֶדֶר שֶׁלְּךָ . . . (mees-*pahr* hah-**ḥ**eh-dehr shehl-**ḥ**ah; *Your room number is* . . .) (M)

מִסְפַּר הַחֶדֶר שֶׁלָךְ . . . (mees-*pahr* hah-**ḥ**eh-dehr shehl-*ach*; *Your room number is* . . .) (F)

Then, סוֹף כָּל סוֹף (-sohf kohl sohf; *finally*), you'll be led to your room. You can לָנוּחַ (lah-noo-*ahḥ*; *rest*)! Kick off your נַעֲלַיִם (nah-ah-*lah*-eem; *shoes*) and pour yourself a מַשְׁקֶה חָרִיף (mahsh-keh **ḥ**ah-*reef*; *drink*) from the minibar. Maybe you want to order שֵׁרוּת חֲדָרִים (sheh-*root* **ḥ**eh-dahr-*reem*; *room service*), לְהַדְלִיק אֶת הַטֶּלֶוִיזְיָה (leh-hahd-*leek* eht hah-the-leh-*veez*-ee-ah; *flip on the television*), or open the הַחַלּוֹן (hah-chah-*lohn*; *window*) and take in the beautiful נוֹף (nohf; *view*). שֶׁהוּת נְעִימָה (sheh-*hoot* neh-ee-*mah*; *Have a nice stay!*).

TIP

When you want to hang out in your room and don't want to be disturbed, hang the little door sign that bears the following message: נָא לֹא לְהַפְרִיעַ ! (nah loh leh-hah-*free*-ah; *Please do not disturb!*).

WORDS TO KNOW

בְּרֵכָה	bray-**ḥ**ah	pool
קַבָּלָה	kah-bah-*lah*	reception
לָנוּחַ	lah-noo-*auch*	to rest, relax
לְמַלֵּא	leh-mah-*leh*	to fill out
מַפְתֵּחַ	mahf-tay-*aḥ*	key
ל לְהַפְרִיעַ	nah loh-leh-hah-*free*-ah	Please don't disturb!
נוֹף	*nohf*	view
שֵׁרוּת חֲדָרִים	sheh-*root* **ḥ**eh-dehr-eem	room service
טֹפֶס	*teh*-fehs	form

Checking Out and Paying the Bill

You just enjoyed your stay at the hotel, and now you need to hit the road. Whether you were there for business or pleasure, I hope you used some of the שֵׁרוּתִים נְעִימוֹת (shehr–root–teem; *amenities*) and took in some of the sights. Now all you need to do is check out. Hebrew has no exact phrase that's comparable to the English term "to check out." You just say לַעֲזֹב אֶת הַחֶדֶר (lah–ah–*zov* et hah–*ḥeh*–dehr; *to leave the hotel*). If you want to ask about a specific checkout time, you can say either of the following:

» ? בְּאֵיזֶה שָׁעָה אֲנִי צָרִיךְ לָצֵאת מִן הַחֶדֶר (buh-ay-*zeh* shah-*ah* ah-*nee* tzah-*reech* lah-*tzhet* meh-hah-cheh-*dehr*; *At what time to I need to exit the room?*) (M)

בְּאֵיזֶה שָׁעָה אֲנִי צָרִיכה לָצֵאת מִן הַחֶדֶר (beh-eizeh shah-*ah* ah-*nee* tz-ree-chah lah-*tzhet* meh-hah-cheh-*dehr*; *At what time to I need to exit the room?*) (F)

» ? בבְּאֵיזֶה שָׁעָה אֲנִי צָרִיךְ לַעֲזֹב אֶת הַחֶדֶר (buh-ay-*zph* shah-*ah* ah-*nee* tzah-*reech* lah-ah-*zohv* eht hah-cheh-*dehr*; *What time do I need to leave the room?*) (M)

? בְּאֵיזֶה שָׁעָה אֲנִי צָרִיכָה לַעֲזֹב אֶת הַחֶדֶר (buh-ay-*zeh* shah-*ah* ah-*nee* tzuh-ree-chah lah-ah-*zohv* eht hah-cheh-*dehr*; *What time do I need to leave the room?*) (F)

TIP

See Chapter 13 for the vocabulary for paying a bill.

Asking for your bill

When you're ready to leave, simply approach the ב קַבָּלָה (kah-bah-*lah*; *reception desk*) and let the receptionist know your intentions by saying

» אֲנִי עוֹזֵב אֶת הַמָּלוֹן (ah-*nee* oh-*zehv* eht hah-mah-*lohn*; *I'm leaving the hotel.*) (M)

אֲנִי עוֹזֶבֶת אֶת הַמָּלוֹן (ah-*nee* oh-*zeh*-vet eht hah-mah-*lohn*; *I'm leaving the hotel.*) (F)

אֲנַחְנוּ עוֹזְבִים אֶת הַמָּלוֹן (ah-*nach*-nu ohz-*veem* eht hah-mah-*lohn*; *We're leaving the hotel.*) (MP/FP)

The פְּקִיד (M)/פְּקִידָה (F) (pah–*keed*/peh-kee-*dah*; *receptionist*) may begin preparing your חֶשְׁבּוֹן (ḥehsh-*bohn*; *bill*). But you can also request it by asking ? אֶפְשָׁר לְקַבֵּל אֶת הַחֶשְׁבּוֹן בְּבַקָּשָׁה (ehf-*shahr* leh-kah-*behl* eht-hah-*ḥehsh-bohn* beh-vah-kah-*shah*; *May I have the bill, please?*).

Asking about special charges

When you check out, you discover all those extra charges on your חֶשְׁבּוֹן (ḥehsh-bohn; bill). If you ordered שֵׁרוּת חֲדָרִים (sheh-root cheh-dehr-eem; room service) every night, eaten the minibar out of house and home, or spent a lot of time chatting on the phone in your hotel room, prepare for a little shock! You can inquire about these little (and not-so-little) charges by asking הַאִם הָיוּ עֲלוּיוֹת נוֹסָפוֹת? (hah-eem hah-yoo ah-looyoht noh-sah-foht?; Were there extra charges?).

Leaving the hotel

If you want to hang around town after you've checked out, you can usually arrange to leave your luggage in hotel storage. Just ask אֶפְשָׁר לְהַשְׁאִיר אֶת מִזְוַדוֹת שֶׁלִּי בְּאַחסוּן הַמָּלוֹן? (ehf-shahr leh-hash-ir eht hah-meez-vah-doht sheh-lee beh-eech-soohn hah-mah-lohn?; May I leave my luggage in the hotel storage?).

GRAMMATICALLY SPEAKING

In Hebrew, you can tell that something is plural if it has an ending of ים (eem) or ות (oht). ים is a masculine ending, and ות is a feminine ending. Here are a couple of examples:

>> Take the feminine singular noun הַמִזְוָדָה (meez-vah-dah; luggage): Its plural form is הַמִזְוָדוֹת (meez-vah-doht; luggage).

>> The masculine singular noun תִּיק (teek; bag) becomes תִּיקִים (teek-eem; bags) in the plural form.

When you return to the hotel to pick up your luggage, you can ask אֶפְשָׁר לְקַבֵּל אֶת הַמִזְוָדוֹת שֶׁלִּי? (ehf-shahr leh-kah-behl eht hah-meez-vah-doht sheh-lee?; May I have my luggage?).

GRAMMATICALLY SPEAKING

In Hebrew, when you want to indicate ownership of something, you use the possessive adjective שֶׁל (shehl) inflected with certain letters and vowels to indicate "mine," "ours," and so on:

Adjective	Pronunciation	Meaning
שלי	sheh-lee	mine
שלך	shehl-chah	yours (MS)

Adjective	Pronunciation	Meaning
שלך	shehl-*ach*	yours (FS)
שלו	sheh-*loh*	his
שלה	sheh-*lah*	hers
שלנו	sheh-*lah*-noo	ours
שלכם	sheh-lah-*chem*	yours (MP or FP)
שלכן	sheh-lah-*hen*	yours (FP)
שלהם	sheh-lah-*chehm*	theirs (MP or FP)
שלהן	sheh-lah-*chehn*	theirs (FP)

Because possessives are adjectives, place them *after* the noun. Also, when you place the possessive adjective *after* the noun, you need to place the ה (*hay*; the Hebrew word for *the* or the definite article) in *front* of the noun, as in these examples:

>> הַמִּזְוָדוֹת שֶׁלָּנוּ (hah-meez-vah-*doht* sheh-*lah*-noo; *our luggage*)

>> הַמִּזְוָדוֹת שֶׁלָּכֶם (hah-meez-vah-*doht* sheh-lah-*chehm*; *your [plural] luggage)*

>> הַמִּזְוָדוֹת שֶׁלָּה (hah-meez-vah-*doht* sheh-*lah*; *her luggage*)

>> הַמִּזְוָדוֹת שֶׁלִּי (hah-*seh*-fehr sheh-*lee*; *my luggage*)

After you retrieve your הַמִּזְוָדוֹת (meez–vah–*doht*; *luggage*), you can ask the פְּקִיד (M)/ פְּקִידָה (F) (pah–*keed*/peh–kee–*dah*; *receptionist*) to call a cab by saying

>> אַתָּה יָכוֹל לְהַזְמִין לִי מוֹנִית ? (ah-*tah* yah-*chohl* leh-hahz-*meen* lee moh-*neet*; *Can you call a cab for me?*) (M)

>> אַתְּ יְכוֹלָה לְהַזְמִין לִי מוֹנִית ? (aht yah-chohl-*ah* leh-hahz-*meen* lee moh-*neet*; *Can you call a cab for me?*) (F)

Talkin' the Talk

 Yael and Yaniv (a woman and a man, respectively) are checking out of their hotel after a week's stay. They go to the reception desk to check out.

Yael: בֹּקֶר טוֹב אֲנַחְנוּ עוֹזְבִים הַיּוֹם אֶפְשָׁר לְקַבֵּל אֶת הַחֶשְׁבּוֹן

(Boh-kehr tohv! Ah-nach-noo ohz-veem hah-yohm. Ehf-shahr leh-kah-behl eht hah-chehsh-bohn?)

Good morning! We're leaving today. May I have the bill?

Receptionist: בֹּקֶר טוֹב רַק רֶגַע אֲנִי מִיָּד אָבִיא לָךְ אֶת הַחֶשְׁבּוֹן .

(Boh-kehr ohr. Rahk reh-gah. Ah-nee mee-yahd ah-vee lach eht hah-chesh-bohn.)

Morning light.* One moment. I'll bring you the bill right away.

Yael: תּוֹדָה רַבָּה אֶפְשָׁר לְהַשְׁאִיר אֶת הַמִּזְוָדוֹת שֶׁלָּנוּ בְּאַחְסוּן עַד הָעֶרֶב ?

(Toh-dah rah-bah. Ehf-shahr leh-ha-sha-ir eht hah-meez-vah-doht sheh-lah-noo beh-ah**h**-soohn ahd hah-eh-rehv?)

Thank you very much. May we leave our luggage in the storage until the evening?

Receptionist: בְּוַדַּאי תַּחְתְּמִי פֹּה בְּבַקָּשָׁה נְסִיעָה טוֹבָה !

(Beh-vah-dai. Tach-teh-mee poh beh-vah-kah-shah. Neh-see-ah toh-vah!)

Certainly. Sign here, please. Have a nice trip!

*When someone says to you בֹּט רֶקֹב (boh-kehr tohv; Good morning), respond by saying רֹא רֶקֹב (boh-kehr ohr; Morning light).

חֶשְׁבּוֹן	**h**ehsh-bohn	bill
קַבָּלָה	kah-bah-lah	receipt
לַעֲזֹב	lah-ah-zohv	to leave
לָצֵאת	lah-tzeht	to exit
מַחְסָן	mach-sahn	storage
מִזְוָדָה	meez-vah-dah	luggage
נְסִיעָה טוֹבָה !	neh-see-ah toh-vah!	Have a nice trip!

WORDS TO KNOW

CULTURAL WISDOM

When you're in Israel, you'll want to fill your phone with all the right אַפְּלִיקַצְיָה (app-lee-kahtz-ee-ah; *apps*)! Yes, there's אוּבֶּר (oo-behr; *Uber*), but it works only in Tel Aviv. There's an app called מוּבִיט (moov-it; *Move-it*) for ride shares, and there's an app called גֶּט (geht; *Gett*), which is similar to Uber. If you're planning to use public transportation in Israel — as you should, because it's affordable and accessible, and goes everywhere — you'll want רַב-קַו (Rav-Kav), an app that lets you pay for all of Israel's public transportation, including buses, trains, and light rail. If you're driving a rental car, be sure to use וֵיז (Waze). If you get the munchies, there's וולט (Wolt), which is basically *Uber-eats*. And of course, because you're in the Middle East, you definitely want to install צֶבַע אָדֹם (Tzeh-vah *ah*-dohm; *Color Red*), which will alert you if missiles are headed in your general direction so you can get yourself to a מִקְלָט (*mee*-klaht *bomb shelter*) in a hot minute. Don't worry — there are plenty of shelters, and Israel also has כִּפַּת בַּרְזֶל (kee-paht-*bahrz*-ehl; *Iron Dome*, an air defense missile system with a radar that detects incoming rockets and intercepts and destroys them before they can harm innocent civilians).

Staying at an Airbnb

These days, I prefer אייר בִּי אֶנְד בִּי (Airbnb) to hotels most of the time. It's חַסְכוּנִי (hahs-hoo-nee; *economical*) or, to use another word, מוּזָל (moo-zahl; *cheap*), and I get a chance to get a taste of local flavor. You can eat your אֲרוּחַת בֹּקֶר (ah-rhoo-*haht* boh-kehr; *breakfast*) and make your קָפֶּה (kah-*feh*; *coffee*) at home each morning before setting out for a day of fun. In Hebrew, you say *Air BnB* just as you say it in English: אייר בִּי אֶנְד בִּי. But if you want to sound like a local in Israel, say it with an Israeli accent (some Jewish humor there).

So, when you want to book your next getaway, you may want לְהִסְתַּכֵּל (leh-hees-*tah*-kehl; *to browse*) the Airbnb אֲתָר (*ah*-tahr; *website*). You'll want to decide whether you're planning a שְׁהוּת קְצָרַת טְוָח (shee-*hoot* kuh-*tzah*-raht t'vahh; *short-term stay*) or a שְׁהוּת אֲרוּכַת טְוָח (shee-*root* ah-roo-*haht* t'vahh; *long-term stay*). What מְקוֹם (mee-koom; *location*) do you prefer? Maybe you want to check out some יְעָדִים פּוֹפּוּלָארִיִּים (yeh-eh-*deem* pop-poo-*lahr*-eem; *popular destinations*). Do you want to bring along Fido? Then make sure that the place is יְדִידוּתִי לַכְּלָבִים (yeh-dee-*oot* leh-k'lah-veem; *pet-friendly*). Before you make a הַזְמָנָה (hahz-mah-nah; *reservation*), find out what the אֶפְשָׁרוּת בִּטּוּל (ehf-*shar-ee*-oot leh-bee-*tool*; *cancellation options*) are and whether צֶ'ק אִין עַצְמִי (chehk-ehn ahtz-mee; *self-check-in*) is a possibility. (Check-in is always easier when that's an option, IMHO.) Then you'll want לְהַזְמִין (leh-*hahz*-meen; *to reserve*) a room, mark the date on the calendar, and pack your bags! Wah-hoo! Who doesn't like just being somewhere else for a while?

WORDS TO KNOW

אֵייר בִּי אֶנְד בִּי	ehr-*bee*-ahnd-*bee*	Airbnb
שָׁהוּת קְצָרַת טְוָח	shee-*hoot* kuh-*tzah–raht* t'vah**ẖ**	short-term stay
שָׁהוּת אֲרוּכַת טְוָח	shee-*root* ah-roo-**ẖaht** t'vah**ẖ**	long-term stay
מָקוֹם	mee-*koom*	location
יְדִידוּתִי לַכְּלָבִים	yeh-dee-*oot* leh-k'*lah*-veem	pet-friendly
הַזְמָנָה	hahz-*mah*-nah	reservation
יְעָדִים פּוֹפּוּלָארִיִּים	yee-ah-*deem* pop-oo-*lahr*-eem	popular locations
לְחַפֵּשׂ	leh-*ẖah*-pehs	to search
לְהִסְתַּכֵּל	leh-hees-*tah*-kehl	to browse
לְהַזְמִין	leh-*hahz*-meen	to reserve
צֶ׳ק אִין עַצְמִי	*chehk*-ehn *ahtz*-mee	self-check-in
אֶפְשָׁרוּת בִּטּוּל	ehf-*shar–ee*-oot leh-bee-*tool*	cancellation options
חַסְכָנִי	**ẖ**ahs-*ẖah*-nee	economical

If you get lost, don't hesitate to ask for directions! Otherwise, you may end up going in circles for hours or end up in a place you don't want to be. Speak up and ask!

Making Sure You Don't Get Lost

In this section, I give you the Hebrew words and phrases necessary for giving and asking directions. Where do you want to go? Is it רָחוֹק (rah-*chohk*; *far*) or קָרוֹב (kah-*rohv*; *near*)? Do you want to take the אוֹטוֹבּוּס (*oh*-toh-boos; *bus*), or can you לָלֶכֶת בָּרֶגֶל (lah-*leh*-cheht bah-*reh*-gehl; *walk*)? This chapter also gives you the words you need so you can navigate a map, talk about various destinations, and discuss modes of transportation.

Suppose that you want to go to הַכֹּתֶל הַמַּעֲרָבִי (hah-*koh*-tehl hah-mah-ah-rah-*vee*; *the Western Wall*). You know that it's in the הָעִיר הָעַתִּיקָה (hah-eer hah-ah-tee-*kah*; *Old City of Jerusalem*), but you're not sure how to get there, and you certainly don't want to get lost! If you're a good navigator, you may want to consult a ה (mah-pah; *map*). But I never trust my map-reading skills. I get better results if I walk up to the nearest friendly-looking stranger and לְבַקֵּשׁ עֶזְרָה (leh-vah-*kehsh* ehz-*rah*; *ask for help*).

Where in Hebrew is אֵיפֹה (*ay*-foh). Another Hebrew word, לְאָן (leh-*ahn*), means "to where," as in "Where are you going?" or "Where is this bus going?" To ask for directions, first say "סְלִיחָה (slee-*chah*; *Excuse me*)" and then ask away:

» סְלִיחָה אֵיפֹה ה... (slee-*hah ay*-foh hah . . .; *Excuse me, where is the . . .*)

» סְלִיחָה אֵיךְ אֲנִי יָכוֹל לְהַגִּיעַ לְ ... (slee-*chah*, eich ah-*nee* yah-chohl-ah le-hah-*gee*-ah leh; *Excuse me, how can I get to . . .*) (M)

סְלִיחָה אֵיךְ אֲנִי יְכוֹלָה לְהַגִּיעַ לְ... (slee-*chah*, eich ah-*nee* yeh-*choh*-lah le-hah-*gee*-ah leh . . .; *Excuse me, how can I get to . . .*) (F)

» סְלִיחָה אֵיךְ אֲנִי יָכוֹל לִמְצֹא... (slee-*chah ay*-*foh* ah-*nee* yah-*chohl* leem-*tzoh* . . .; *Excuse me, where can I find . . .*) (M)

סְלִיחָה אֵיךְ אֲנִי יְכוֹלָה לִמְצֹא ... (slee-*chah ay*-*foh* ah-*nee* yeh-choh-*lah* leem-*tzoh* . . .; *Excuse me, where can I find . . .*) (F)

Table 11-5 has several locations you may want to ask about finding.

TABLE 11-5

Looking for Locations

Hebrew	Pronunciation	Translation
בֵּית חוֹלִים	bayt *choh*-leem	hospital
בֵּית כְּנֶסֶת	bayt *kneh*-seht	synagogue
דֹּאַר	*doh*-ahr	post office
קוֹלְנוֹעַ	kohl-*noh*-ah	cinema
כְּנֵסִיָּה	kneh-see-*yah*	church
מִסְגָּד	mees-*gahd*	mosque
נְמַל הַתְּעוּפָה	neh-*mahl* hah-teh-oo-*fah*	airport
תַחֲנָה	tah-chah-*nah*	station
תֵּאַטְרוֹן	tay-aht-*rohn*	theater

If you're lost, you can use one of these phrases (and using סְלִיחָה [slee–*chah*; *excuse me*] in these cases won't hurt either):

» אֲנִי הָלַכְתִּי לְאִבּוּד (ah-*nee* hah-*lah*-tee leh-ee-*bood*; *I got lost.*)

» אֲנִי אִבַּדְתִּי אֶת הַצָּפוֹן (ah-*nee* ee-bah-de-*tee* eht hah-tzah-*fohn*; *literally: I lost the north.*)

» אֲנִי טָעִיתִי בַּדֶּרֶךְ (ah-*nee* tah-ee-*tee* bah-*deh*-reh; *I made a mistake along the way.*)

Note: All the preceding phrases are gender-neutral because they're in the past tense for "I," which is the same whether the speaker is male or female.

If you're taking an אוֹטוֹבּוּס (oh-toh–*boos*; *bus*) and want to know where it's going, you can ask ? לְאָן הָאוֹטוֹבּוּס נוֹסֵעַ (leh–*ahn* hah–*oh*–toh-boos noh–*seh*-ah; *(to) Where is this bus going?*).

If you're driving a car and want to know how to get somewhere, you can ask for directions:

» אֵיךְ אֲנִי יָכוֹל לְהַגִּיעַ . . . (ei*h* ah-*nee* yah-*hohl* leh-hah-*gee*-ah leh . . .; *How can I get to . . .*; *literally: to arrive at . . .*) (M)

אֵיךְ אֲנִי יְכוֹלָה לְהַגִּיעַ לְ . . . (eich ah-*nee* yeh-*hoh*-*lah* leh-hah-*gee*-ah leh . . .; *How can I get to . . .*; *literally: to arrive at . . .*) (F)

אֵיךְ אֲנִי יְכוֹלֶה לְהַגִּיעַ לְ . . . (eich ah-*nee* yeh-*hoh*-*leh* leh-hah-*gee*-ah leh . . .; *How can I get to . . .*; *literally: to arrive at . . .*) (NB)

If you want to ask others where they're going, the sentences are similar:

» ? לְאָן אַתָּה הוֹלֵךְ (leh-*ahn* ah-*tah* hoh-*leh*?; *Where are you going?*) (M)

? לְאָן אַתְּ הוֹלֶכֶת (leh-*ahn* aht hoh-*leh*-*h*eht?; *Where are you going?*) (F)

? לְאָן אַתֶּם הוֹלְכִים (leh-*ahn* ah-*tem* hol-*cheem*; *Where are you going?*) (MP)

? לְאָן אַתֶּן הוֹלְכוֹת (leh-*ahn* ah-*ten* hol-*hot*; *Where are you going?*) (FP)

» ? לְאָן הֵם הוֹלְכִים (leh-*ahn* hem hohl-*cheem*?; *Where are they going?*) (MP)

? לְאָן הֵן הוֹלְכוֹת (leh-*ahn* hen hohl-*choht*?; *Where are they going?*) (FP)

WORDS TO KNOW

בֵּית חוֹלִים	bayt **h**oh-*leem*	hospital
בֵּית כְּנֶסֶת	bayt -*kneh*-seht	synagogue
דֹּאַר	*doh*-ahr	post office
קוֹלְנוֹעַ	kohl *noh*-ah	movie theater
נְמָל הַתְּעוּפָה	neh-*mahl* hah-teh-oo-*fah*	airport
סְלִיחָה	slee-*chah*	excuse me

Giving and Understanding Directions For Lost Souls

I remember how excited I was after tourists started asking me for directions when I lived in Jerusalem. At first, I thought it was because I'd become so acculturated to the place people thought I was Israeli. Then I realized that tourists asked me for directions because they could tell I spoke English.

Nonetheless, I did direct an Israeli or two while I lived there. Even today, years after moving back to the United States, I can still give walking directions on the streets of Jerusalem. I know the place like the back of my hand. Table 11-6 can help you give directions (or understand likely responses whenever you need to ask directions).

TIP

In Hebrew, you don't say "on the right" or "on the left," as you do in English. To indicate that something is on the right side, you say בְּצַד יָמִין (buh–*tzahd* yah-*meen*). To indicate that something is on the left side, you say בְּצַד שְׂמֹאל (buh–*tzahd* s-*mohl*). These literally mean "on right side" or "on left side."

CULTURAL WISDOM

You can give directions in the infinitive, future, and command tenses. Using the infinitive is a more classical form of Hebrew. You hear the infinitive as well as the future and command tenses on the streets of Israel. Even though the command tense is technically correct, some people in Israel think that using the imperative is somewhat rude, like something a teacher or a military commander would use, so they speak in future tense instead.

TABLE 11-6 Giving and Understanding Directions

Hebrew	Pronunciation	Translation
עַל-יַד	ahl-*yahd*	next to
בַּחוּץ z	bah-*chootz*	outside
בֵּין	*bayn*	between
בִּפְנִים	beef-*neem*	inside
לַעֲבֹר אֶת ה	lah-ah-*vohr* eht hah	to pass the
לַחֲזוֹת אֶת הַכְּבִישׁ	lah-cha-*tzot* eht hahk-*veesh*	to cross the street
לָלֶכֶת יָשָׁר	lah-*leh*-cheht yah-*shahr*	to go straight
לְמַעְלָה	leh-*mah*-lah	up
לְמַטָּה	leh-*mah*-tah	down
לִפְנוֹת יָמִינָה בַּצֹּמֶת	leef-*noht* yah-*mee*-nah bah-*tzoh*-meht	to turn right at the junction
מִמּוּל	mee-*mool*	across from
מִתַּחַת	mee-*tah*-chaht	under
פֹּה	*poh*	here
שָׁם	*shahm*	there

When you're giving or receiving directions, you may hear or refer to various landmarks. You might tell someone that they need to turn at a רַמְזוֹר (rahm-*zohr*; *traffic light*) or at a צֹמֶת (*tzo*-meht; *intersection*). If someone is walking, you may refer to the מִדְרָכָה (meed-rah-*chah*; *sidewalk*) or the כִּכָּר (kee-*kahr*; *square*). Then again, if you're driving, someone may mention הַכְּבִישׁ הָרָאשִׁי (hah-*kveesh* hah-rah-*shee*; *the main road*) or a גֶּשֶׁר (geh-*shehr*; *bridge*).

WORDS TO KNOW

אֵיךְ	*ehḥ*	how
אֵיפֹה	ay-*foh*	where
גֶּשֶׁר	*geh*-shehr	bridge
כִּכָּר	kee-*kahr*	square

כִּוּוּן	kee-*voon*	direction
לְאָן	leh-*ahn*	to where
מַפָּה	mah-*pah*	map
מִדְרָכָה	meed-rah-*ḥah*	sidewalk
רַמְזוֹר	rahm-*zohr*	traffic light
צֹמֶת	*tzoh*-meht	junction

Talkin' the Talk

Sarah is in the Old City of Jerusalem, looking for the Western Wall. She's in the Jewish Quarter and knows that she's close, but she still can't find it. So, she asks a woman for directions.

Sarah: סְלִיחָה

(Slee-*ḥah*.)

Excuse me.

Woman: כֵּן ?

(Kehn?)

Yes?

Sarah: אֲנִי הָלַכְתִּי לְאִבּוּד אֵיפֹה אֲנִי יְכוֹלָה לִמְצֹא אֶת הַכֹּתֶל הַמַּעֲרָבִי .

(Ah-*nee* ha-*laḥ*-tee leh-ee-*bood*. Ay-*foh* ah-*nee* yeh-choh-*lah* leem-*tzoh* eht hah-*koh*-tehl hah-mah-ah-rah-*vee*?)

I'm lost. Where can I find the Western Wall?

Woman: זֶה לֹא רָחוֹק תֵּלְכִי יָשָׁר יָשָׁר יָשָׁר וְאָז תִּשְׁאֲלִי .

(Zeh loh rah-*chohk* til-*chee* yah-*shahr*, yah-*shahr*, yah-*sharhr* ve-*ahz* tee-shah-*lee*.)

It's not far. Go straight, straight, straight, and then ask.

Sarah: תּוֹדָה .

(Toh-*dah*)

Thanks.

CULTURAL WISDOM

PROVIDING DIRECTIONS THE ISRAELI WAY

Israelis are infamous for their way of giving directions. They commonly gesticulate wildly and say something like יָשָׁר יָשָׁר יָשָׁר עַד הַסּוֹף (yah-*shahr*, yah-*shahr*, yah-*shahr*, ahd hah-*sohf*; *straight, straight, straight until the end!*). As if that's helpful. Sometimes, you even hear יָשָׁר יָשָׁר יָשָׁר וְאָז תִּשְׁאַל! (yah-*shahr*, yah-*shahr*, yah-*shahr*, veh-*ahz* teesh-*ahl*; *straight, straight, straight, and then ask*). Idiomatically speaking, that phrase means "I don't know how to get there, but I'm too proud to admit it. So keep going in the direction you're going and then try asking again. Good luck."

Keeping North, South, East, and West Straight

When you're traveling, it can be helpful to know the cardinal points on the compass:

>> דָּרוֹם (dah-*rohm*; *south*)

>> מַעֲרָב (mah-ah-*rahv*; *west*)

>> מִזְרָח (meez-*rah*; *east*)

>> צָפוֹן (tzah-*fohn*; *north*)

To describe where something is by using the cardinal points, preface it with the preposition (and prefix!) בְּ . . . (*buh* . . .), which means "on" or "in." Here's an example: אֲנִי בַּמִּזְרָח (ah-*nee* bah-meez-*rach*; *I am in the East*).

GRAMMATICALLY SPEAKING

If you want to say the Hebrew equivalent of *northward*, *southward*, and so on, you indicate direction by adding the Hebrew character ה (*hey*) at the end of the word:

>> דָּרוֹמָה (dah-*roh*-mah; *southward*)

>> מַעֲרָבָה (mah-ah-*rah*-vah; *westward*)

>> מִזְרָחָה (meez-*rah*-hah; *eastward*)

>> צָפוֹנָה (tzah-*foh*-nah; *northward*)

CULTURAL WISDOM

לִבִּי בַּמִּזְרָח וְאָנֹכִי בְּסוֹף מַעֲרָב! (lee-*bee* bah-meez-*rach* veh-ah-noh-*chee* buh-*sohf* mah-ah-*rahv*!; *My heart is in the East, but I'm at the edge of the West!*). These words are by the famous Jewish poet יְהוּדָה הַלֵּוִי (yeh-hoo-*dah* hah-*leh*-vee; Yehuda HaLevi), who wrote them in 12th-century Spain. His poetry expressed the Jewish longing for Zion, the Land of Israel. *Songs of Zion* (שִׁירֵי צִיּוֹן) is among this prolific Hebrew poet's most celebrated works.

Talkin' the Talk

Michael, an American tourist in Israel, wants to go to the shopping mall and doesn't know whether he should walk or take the bus. So, he asks a man on the street.

Michael: ‏סְלִיחָה אֵיפֹה הַקַּנְיוֹן ?

(Slee-*chah*. Ay-*foh* hah-kehn-*yohn?*)

Excuse me. Where's the shopping mall?

Man: ‏זֶה מַמָּשׁ רָחוֹק מִפֹּה בְּאֵזוֹר מָלְחָה .

(Zeh mah-*mahsh* rah-**h**ohk mee-*poh* beh-ay-*zohr* mahl-**h**ah.)

It's quite far from here, in the Malcha area.

Michael: ‏אֲנִי יָכוֹל לָלֶכֶת בְּרֶגֶל ?

(ah-*nee*. Yah-**h**ohl lah-leh-**h**eht bah-*reh*-gehl?)

Can I get there by foot?

Man: ‏זֶה רָחוֹק מִדַּי צָרִיךְ לָקַחַת אוֹטוֹבּוּס .

(loh zeh rah-*chohk* mee-*dye*. Tzah-*reech* lah-*kah*-chaht *oh*-toh-boos.)

No, it's too far. You need to take a bus.

Michael: ‏אֵיזֶה אוֹטוֹבּוּס נוֹסֵעַ לְשָׁם ?

(ay-*zeh oh*-toh-boos noh-*seh*-ah leh-*shahm?*)

Which bus goes there?

Man: ‏אַתָּה יָכוֹל לָקַחַת קַו שֵׁשׁ הַתַּחֲנָה בְּדִיּוּק מִמוּל הַמַּשְׁבִּיר .

(ah-*tah* yah-*chohl* la-*kah*-chaht kahv *shehsh*. hah-tah-chah-nah bee-dee-*yook* mee-*mool* hah-mahsh-*beer*.)

You can take line six. The (bus) station is exactly across from the Mashbir (department store).

Michael: ‏תּוֹדָה רַבָּה .

(Toh-*dah* rah-*bah*.)

Thanks a lot.

FUN & GAMES

Fill in the missing words with one of the three possible answers below each sentence. Have fun! Flip to Appendix C for the answers.

1. אֲנִי רוֹצָה _____ לְאַפְרִיקָה .

I want to travel to Africa.

לְהִשְׁתַּזֵּף, לִנְסֹעַ, לְטַיֵּל

2. אֲנִי רוֹצֶה _____ בְּמַכְתֵּשׁ רָמוֹן

I want to hike in the Machtesh Ramon.

להיפגש, לטייל, לנסוע

3. אֲנַחְנוּ רוֹצִים _____ עַל הַכִּנֶּרֶת

We want to sail on the Kinneret.

לְהַפְלִיג, לְטַיֵּל, לִנְסֹעַ

4. הַמָּטוֹס _____ בְּעוֹד שָׁעָה

The plane will take off in another hour.

ימריא, ילך, יכתוב

5. יֵשׁ לְךָ אֶת ה _____ שֶׁלְּךָ ?

Do you have your passport? (FS)

דרכון, כרטיס, מטוס

Chapter **12**

Getting Around: Flying, Driving, and Riding

אוֹי וַאֲבוֹי (oye-vah-ah-*vohye; Oh, no!*). I'm probably the last person in the world who should write this chapter. I get lost everywhere I go. It's a special talent I have, though this particular talent isn't very useful. So don't depend on me for directions. And if you're traveling with me, plan on doing the navigating yourself — or plan on getting lost. But I'm good for something: I can tell you how to say everything you need to get from here to there in Hebrew.

Getting Through the Airport

Here's the scene: You're about to leave the house to take a טִיסָה בֵּן לְאֻמִּית (tee-sah behn-leh-oo-*meet; international flight*). כַּרְטִיס טִיסָה (kahr-*tees* tee-*sah; plane ticket*)? Check. דַּרְכּוֹן (dahr-kohn; *passport*)? Check. מִזְוָדָה (meez-vah-*dah; suitcase*)? Check. What else do you need? Nothing? Then you're ready to go. Traveling light is always your best bet!

Checking in

When you arrive at the נְמַל הַתְּעוּפָה (nah-*mahl* hah-teh-oo-*fah*; *airport*), you usually head for the דֶּלְפֵּק רִשׁוּם (dal-*pahk* ri-*shoom*; *check-in counter* where you check your מִזְוָדָה (meez-vah-*dah*; *luggage*). The security questioning flying in and out of Israel may be the most intense you've ever experienced. Don't be alarmed or offended. They know what they are doing, and their questioning is designed to keep us all safe by catching anyone with evil intentions before they harm someone. So, when you are flying to Israel, the friendly פָּקִיד (pah-*keed*; *clerk*) may have a few questions for you:

> ➤ לְךָ נָתַן לְךָ מַה שֶׁהוּא הַאִם מַשֶּׁהוּ לְהַעֲבִיר ? (hah-*eem* mee-sheh-hoo loh moo-*kahr* leh-*h*ah nah-*tahn* leh-*h*ah mah-sheh-hoo; *Has someone unknown to you given you anything?*) (M)

> הַאִם מַשֶּׁהוּ לְהַעֲבִיר לְךָ מַה הָאִים מִישֶׁהוּא לֹא מֻכָּר לָךְ נָתַן לָךְ מַה שֶׁהוּאשֶׁהוּא ? (hah-*eem* mee-sheh-hoo loh moo-*kahr* lach nah-*tahn* lach mah-sheh-hoo; *Has someone unknown to you given you anything?*) (F)

> ➤ הַאִם אָרַזְתָּ אֶת הַמִּזְוָדָה שֶׁלְךָ? (hah-*eem* ah-*rahz*-tah eht hah-meez-vah-*dah* shehl-chah; *Did you pack your luggage?*) (M)

> הַאִם אָרַזְתְּ אֶת הַמִּזְוָדָה שֶׁלָּךְ? (hah-*eem* ah-*rahzt* eht hah-meez-vah-*dah* shel-*ah*; *Did you pack your luggage?*) (F)

> ➤ הַמִּזְוָדוֹת הָיוּ אֶצְלְךָ מֵאָז שֶׁאָרַזְתָּ אוֹתָם הַאִם הַמִּזְוָדוֹת הָיוּ אֶצְלְךָ מֵאָז שֶׁאָרַזְתָּ אוֹתָם ? (hah-*eem* hah-meez-vah-*doht* hah-*yoo* ehtz-leh-*chah* mee-*ahz* sheh-ah-*rahz*-tah oh-*tahm*; *Has your luggage been with you since you packed?*) (M)

> הַאִם הַמִּזְוָדוֹת הָיוּ אֶצְלָךְ מֵאָז שֶׁאָרַזְתְּ אוֹתָן ? (hah-*eem* hah-meez-vah-*doht* hah-yoo ehtz-*lech* mee-*ahz* sheh-ah-*rahzt* oh-*tahn*; *Has your luggage been with you since you packed?*) (F)

After you pass this battery of questions, you walk through a מְגַלֶּה מַתָּכוֹת (meh-gah-*leh* mah-tah-*h*oht; *metal detector*) and send your תַּרְמִילִים (tar-mee-*leem*; *carry-on luggage*) through the מַכְשִׁיר רֶנְטְגֶּן (ma*h*-*sheer* rehnt-*gehn*; *X-ray machine*). After this final check, you should be ready to hop on the plane.

CULTURAL WISDOM

Israelis are famous for their pre-boarding screening. Their techniques once led them to discover that an engaged (and pregnant) Irish woman was carrying explosives and a timed triggering device onto the flight, unbeknownst to her on behalf of her terrorist finance. This is known as the Hindawi Affair, and it happened in 1986 in London prior to an El Al flight flying to Tel Aviv. The pre-boarding screening saved the lives of some 370 passengers who would have died if the plane exploded in flight as the terrorist Nezar Hindawi had planned. And that is why I always fly El Al, Israel's national airline.

REACHING FOR A BARF BAG AND OTHER EMERGENCIES

Sometimes, you just don't wanna hear some words — especially on an airplane. But — חַס וְחָלִילָה (ḥahs veh-chah-*lee*-lah; *heaven forbid*) — in the unlikely event of a עַל הַמַּיִם חֲתַת חֵרוּם (ḥee-*taht* cheh-*room* ahl hah-*mah*-yeem; *emergency water landing*), you need to know what to do. Pay attention to the הוֹרָאוֹת בְּטִיחוּת (hoh-rah-*oht* beet-*ḥoh*- nee-*yoht*; *safety instructions*) and locate the nearest פֶּתַח חֵרוּם (peh-*tach* ḥe-*room*; *emergency exit*). The חֲגוֹרַת הַצָּלָה (hah-gohr-*aht* ha-tza-*lah*; *life jackets*) can usually be found under your כִּסֵּא (key-*seh*; *seat*). The מַסֵּכוֹת חַמְצָן (mah-seh-*choht* cham-*tzahn*; *oxygen mask*) usually comes down בְּאֹפֶן אוֹטוֹמָטִי (beh-*oh*-fehn ah-toh-*mah*-tee; *automatically*) from a compartment above.

Ideally, you and a large body of water won't meet during your flight, and the worst event you'll be subjected to is a little מֶזֶג אֲוִיר בִּלְתִּי יַצִּיב (meh-*zehg* ah-*veer* bil-*tee* yah-*tzeev*; *unstable weather conditions*) and perhaps a bit of מְעַרְבּוֹלוֹת (mah-ahr-boh-*loht*; *turbulence*). Fasten your חֲגוֹרַת בְּטָחוֹן (ḥah-goh-*raht* beet-ah-*ḥohn*; *seat belt*) and try not to get too sick. But if your stomach starts doing back flips, grab the שַׂקִּית הֲקָאָה (sah-*keet* hah-kah-*ah*; *barf bag*) in the seat pocket in front of you. טִיסָה נְעִימָה (tee-*sah* neh-ee-*mah*; *Have a nice flight*)!

Suffering through the flight

Are you a bit of a קְוֵרֶץ (k-*vehch*; *whiner*) when you have to fly? If so, you may need all sorts of צִיּוּד (tzee-*yood*; *supplies*) to see you through your journey. You may need מַסְטִיק (mahs-*teek*; *chewing gum*) and אַטְמֵי אָזְנַיִם (oht-*may* ohz-*nye*-eem; *earplugs*) to help you deal with the pressure in your ears and perhaps some טִפּוֹת אָזְנַיִם (tee-poht leh-aye-*nah*-eem; *eyedrops*) to combat all that dry cabin air. You can ask the דַּיָּל (M) or דַּיֶּלֶת (F) (dah-*yahl* or dah-*yeh*-leht; *flight attendant*) for a כָּרִית (kah-*reet*; *pillow*) and שְׂמִיכָה (s-mee-*chah*; *blanket*). I always bring my סִדּוּר (see-*door*; *prayer book*) and say a little תְּפִלָּה (tfee-*lah*; *prayer*) before the מָטוֹס (mah-*tohs*; *plane*) מַמְרִיא (mahm-*ree*; *takes off*).

Getting your feet back on the ground

בְּעֶזְרַת הַשֵּׁם (beh-ehz-*raht* hah-*shem*; *with God's help*), the plane will land safely. Then you can head off to your next destination. Gather all your belongings (please don't drop your briefcase on the little old lady's head as you remove it from the overhead bin), and you're ready לָרֶדֶת מֵהַמָּטוֹס (lah-*reh*-deht meh-hah-mah-*tohs*; *to get off the plane*). But not so fast! You're not out of the woods yet. You have to go through מֶכֶס (meh-chehs; *customs*) when you take an international flight. Someone will stamp your דַּרְכּוֹן (dahr-kohn; *passport*). Then you can collect your מִזְוָדָה (meez-vah-*dah*; *luggage*) and find ground transportation.

	WORDS TO KNOW	
בִּטָּחוֹן	beeh-tah-**hohn**	security
דַּרְכּוֹן	dahr-*kohn*	passport
דַּיָּל	dah-*yahl*	flight attendant (M)
דַּיֶּלֶת	dah-*yeh-leht*	flight attendant (F)
כַּרְטִיס	kahr-*tees*	ticket
לַעֲזֹב	lah-ah-*zohv*	to leave
לְהַמְרִיא	leh-ham-*ree*	to take off
לְהַגִּיעַ	leh-hah-*gee*-ah	to arrive
לִנְחוֹת	leen-*hoht*	to land
מָטוֹס	mah-*tohs*	airplane
מִזְוָדָה	meez-vah-*dah*	luggage
נְמַל הַתְּעוּפָה	neh-mahl teh-oo-*fah*	airport
טַיָּס	tah-*yahs*	pilot (M)
טַיֶּסֶת	tah-*yeh*-seht	pilot (F)

Renting a Vehicle and a Phone to Go with It

When you visit a different town, state, province, or country, the most convenient transportation option often is לִשְׂכֹּר רֶכֶב (lees-*kor* reh-*hehv*; *to rent*) a vehicle. Most folks usually rent a מְכוֹנִית (meh-choh-*neet*; *car*), but in Israel, you can also rent an אוֹפַנּוֹעַ (ohf-ah-*noh*-ah; *motorcycle*). To rent any vehicle, you need to present a valid רִשְׁיוֹן נְהִיגָה (ree-shah-*yohn* neh-hee-*gah*; *driver's license*) and כַּרְטִיס אַשְׁרַאי (kahr-tees ahsh-*rye*; *credit card*). The clerk at the rental counter usually asks whether you want to purchase בִּטּוּחַ (bee-*too*-aḥ; *insurance*) and informs you that you must accept liability if you decline it. And, if you put the pedal to the metal one time too many and get דּוֹחוֹת (doh-*choht*; *tickets*), you're responsible for paying that bill as well. So סַע בִּזְהִירוּת (sah beez-hee-*root*; *drive carefully*).

When you drive around town, make sure that you stay in the same נָתִיב (nah-*teev*; *lane*), and don't weave through traffic. Pay attention to all the תַּמְרוּרִים (tahm-roo-*reem*; *traffic signs*) and obey the רַמְזוֹר (rahm-*zohr*; *traffic signal*). Look both ways when you stop at a צֹמֶת (tzoh-*meht*; *junction*) and stop for all pedestrians; they have the זְכוּת קְדִימָה (z-*choot* kdee-*mah*; *right-of-way*), you know. Before you drive down any רְחוֹב (reh-*chohv*; *street*), make sure that it isn't a רְחוֹב חַד סִטְרִי (reh-*ḥohv* ḥahd-seet-*ree*; *one-way street*). You don't want to drive in the wrong כִּוּוּן (kee-*voon*; *direction*). And if you need to cover some major ground, forget taking a רְחוֹב (reh-*chohv*; *street*); hop on a כְּבִישׁ מָהִיר (*kveesh* mah-*heer*; *expressway*).And yes — Phew — Israelis drive on the right side of the road just like Americans. No British customs here!

Renting a car

If you decide to rent a car, you need to find a חֶבְרַת הַשְׂכָּרַת רֶכֶב (chehv-*raht* hahs-kar-*aht* reh-*chehv*; *car-rental agency*). You can often find these businesses right at the נְמַל הַתְּעוּפָה (neh-*mahl* hah-teh-oo-*fah*; *airport*). Step right up, and an attendant greets you and asks you what kind of car you want to rent. They may say something like אֵיזֶה סוּג רֶכֶב אַתָּה רוֹצֶה ? (M) *or* אֵיזֶה סוּג רֶכֶב אַתְּ רוֹצָה ? (F) (aye-*zeh* soog reh-*ḥehv* ah-*tah*/aht roh-*tzeh*/roh-*tzah*; *What kind of vehicle would you like?*). You can respond with any of the following:

» מְכוֹנִית (meh-choh-*neet*; *car*)

» מִסְחָרִית (mees-chah-*reet*; *van*)

» אוֹפַנּוֹעַ (ohf-*noh*-ah; *motorcycle*)

» גִּיר אוֹטוֹמָטִי (geer oh-toh-mah-tee; *automatic transmission*)

» מוֹט הִלּוּכִים (mot hee-loo-*cheem*; *stick shift*)

GRAMMATICALLY SPEAKING

Ideally, you know your own mind. The only thing you need is some Hebrew vocabulary so you can express it. If you want to rent a blue motorcycle, or if you're wondering whether you can get a car with a CD player, all you need to do is ask. Here are some handy-dandy phrases you may want to use:

» אֲנִי רוֹצֶה . . . (ah-*nee* roh-*tzeh*; *I want* . . .) (M)

אֲנִי רוֹצָה . . . (ah-*nee* roh-*tzah*; *I want* . . .) (F)

» אֶפְשָׁר r . . . (ehf-*shahr*; *Is it possible* . . . or *May I* . . .)

» ‏. . . אֶפְשָׁר לְקַבֵּל‏ (ehf-shahr leh-kah-behl; May I have . . .)

» ‏. . . הַאִים יֵשׁ‏ (hah-eem yesh; Is there . . .)

» ‏. . . תֵּן לִי‏ (tehn lee; Give me . . .) (M)

   ‏. . . תְּנִי לִי‏ (tnee lee; Give me . . .) (F)

Understanding the rental contract

The clerk may also ask you about the terms of your rental contract. Expect to hear any of the following:

» ‏? לְכַמָּה זְמַן אַתָּה רוֹצֶה לִשְׂכֹּר אֶת הָרֶכֶב‏ (leh-kah-mah z-mahn ah-tah roh-tzeh lees-kor eht hah-reh-ḥehv; How long do you want to rent the vehicle?) (M)

   ‏? לְכַמָּה זְמַן אַתְּ רוֹצָה לִשְׂכֹּר אֶת הָרֶכֶב‏ (leh-kah-mah z-mahn aht roh-tzah lees-kor eht hah-reh-ḥehv; How long do you want to rent the vehicle?) (F)

» ‏? מָתַי אַתָּה רוֹצֶה לִשְׂכֹּר אֶת הָרֶכֶב מָתַי אַתָּה הָרָחָב‏ (mah-tye ah-tah roh-tzeh lees-kor eht hah-reh-ḥehv; When do you want to rent the vehicle?) (M)

   ‏? מָתַי אַתְּ רוֹצָה לִשְׂכֹּר אֶת הָרֶכֶב‏ (mah-tye aht roh-tzah lees-kor eht hah-reh-ḥehv; When do you want to rent the vehicle?) (F)

» ‏? אֵיפֹה אַתָּה רוֹצֶה לְהַחֲזִיר אֶת הָרֶכֶב‏ (aye-foh ah-tah roh-tzeh le-hach-zeer eht hah-reh-chehv; Where do you want to return the vehicle?) (M)

   ‏? אֵיפֹה אַתְּ רוֹצָה לְהַחֲזִיר אֶת הָרֶכֶב‏ (aye-foh aht roh-tzah le-hach-zeer eht hah-reh-ḥehv; Where do you want to return the vehicle?) (F)

To which you can reply

» ‏. . . אֲנִי רוֹצֶה לִשְׂכֹּר אֶת הָרֶכֶב לְ‏ (ah-nee roh-tzeh lees-kor eht hah-reh-ḥehv leh; I want to rent the vehicle for . . .) (M)

   ‏. . . אֲנִי רוֹצָה לִשְׂכֹּר אֶת הָרֶכֶב לְ‏ (ah-nee roh-tzah lees-koor eht hah-reh-ḥehv leh; I want to rent the vehicle for . . .) (F)

» ‏. . . אֲנִי רוֹצֶה לִשְׂכֹּר אֶת הָרֶכֶב בְּ‏ (ah-nee roh-tzeh lees-kor eht hah-reh-ḥehv beh; I want to rent the vehicle on . . .) (M)

   ‏. . . אֲנִי רוֹצָה לִשְׂכֹּר אֶת הָרֶכֶב בְּ‏ (ah-nee roh-tzah lees-kor eht hah-reh-ḥehv beh; I want to rent the vehicle on . . .) (F)

» ‏. . . אֲנִי רוֹצֶה לְהַחֲזִיר אֶת הָרֶכֶב בְּבִיר‏ (ah-nee roh-tzeh lehach-zeer eht hah-reh-ḥehv beh; I want to return the vehicle at . . .) (M)

   ‏. . . אֲנִי רוֹצָה לְהחזיר אֶת הָרֶכֶב בְּ‏ (ah-nee roh-tzah lehach-zeer eht hah-reh-chehv beh; I want to return the vehicle at . . .) (F)

You're going to need some additional Hebrew vocabulary with these expressions. Start with the days of the week in Chapter 7.

Talkin' the Talk

Alon has just arrived in Tel Aviv. After going through customs, he stops by a car-rental agency and talks to an employee, a lovely woman named Sivan.

Alon: בֹּקֶר טוֹב אֲנִי רוֹצֶה לִשְׂכֹּר רֶכֶב.

(boh-*kair tohv.* ah-*nee* roh-*tzah* lees-*kor* reh-*chehv.*)

Good morning. I would like to rent a car.

Sivan: אֵיזֶה סוּג רֶכֶב אַתָּה רוֹצֶה ?

(aye-*zeh* soog *reh*-chehv ah-*tah* roh-*tzeh?*)

What kind of vehicle would you like?

Alon: אֲנִי רוֹצֶה רֶכֶב בִּמְחִיר הֲכִי זוֹל שֶׁיֵּשׁ .

(ah-*nee* roh-*tzeh* meh-choh-*neet.* hah-*chee zoh-la* sheh-*yaysh.*)

I would like a car. The least expensive one that you have.

Sivan: אַתָּה רוֹצֶה רֶכֶב עִם הִלוּכִים אוֹ גִּיר אוֹטוֹמָט ?

(ah-*tah* roh-*tzeh reh-ḥehv* eem hee-loo-*ḥeem* oh geer oh-toh-*mah*-tee.)

Would you like a stick shift or an automatic tranmission?

Alon: עִם הִלוּכִים - בְּוַדַּאי !

(eem hee-loo-*cheem,* beh-vah-*dai!*)

A stick shift, of course!

Sivan: לְכַמָּה זְמַן אַתָּה רוֹצֶה לִשְׂכֹּר אֶת הָרֶכֶב ?

(leh-kah-*mah* z'mahn ah-*tah* roh-*tzeh* lees-*kor* eht hah-*reh*-chehv?)

For how long would you like to rent the car?

Alon: לִשְׁבוּעַיִם .

(leh-sh-voo-ah-*yeem.*)

For two weeks.

CULTURAL WISDOM

DRIVING LIKE AN ISRAELI

Israelis are infamous for their driving habits. So, if you drive in Israel, watch out for Israeli drivers who are known לִצְעֹק (leetz-*ohk; to yell*) and לְקַלֵּל (leh-kah-*lehl; to swear*) out the חַלּוֹן (chah-*lohn; window*) run through the אוֹר אָדֹם (ohr ah-*dohm; red light*), and make plenty of illegal פְּנִיּוֹת פַּרְסָה (p-nee-*yoht* pahr-*sah; U-turns*). Be careful, because it's common practice to ignore all the תַּמְרוּרִים (tahm-roo-*reem; traffic signs*), go faster than the מְהִירוּת מַקְסִימָלִית מֻתֶּרֶת (meh-hee-root mahks-ee-*mah*-leet moo-*teh*-reht; *speed limit*), and לַעֲקֹף (lah-ah-*kohf; pass*) other cars whenever possible. Here's some good news — Israelis drive on the right side of the road, just like Americans.

WORDS TO KNOW

חַד סִטְרִי	chahd-seet-*ree*	one way
כְּבִישׁ מָהִיר	k-*veesh* mah-*heer*	expressway
מְכוֹנִית	meh-choh-*neet*	car
נָתִיב	nah-*teev*	lane
אוֹפַנּוֹעַ	oh-ah-noh-ah	motorcycle
רַמְזוֹר	rahm-*zohr*	traffic signal
רְחוֹב	reh-*hohv*	street
צֹמֶת	*tzoh*-meht	intersection
זְכוּת קְדִימָה	z-*hoot* k-dee-*mah*	right-of-way

Navigating Public Transportation

Whether you're traveling or simply getting around your hometown, using תַּחְבּוּרָה צִבּוּרִית (taḥ-boo-*rah* tzee-booh-*reet; public transportation*) is often an inexpensive and environmentally friendly way to go. Letting someone else do the driving is also a lot less stressful. A great app to use is רַב-קַו אוֹנְלַיְן (*rahv*-kahv *ohn*-line; *Rav-Kav Online*), where you can buy tickets for the public buses, light rail, or the Metronit (a rapid bus system in Israel).

Traveling by taxi

When you leave the נְמַל הַתְּעוּפָה (nah-*mahl* hah-teh-oo-*fah*; *airport*), you may decide to take a cab to your next destination. If you travel in Israel, you have the option of a שֵׁרוּת (sheh-*root*; *shared taxi*) or a מוֹנִית סְפֶּשְׁל (moh-*neet* speh-shl; *special* or *private taxi*). A שֵׁרוּת (sheh-*root*; *shared taxi*) is a great big taxi, often with two or three back seats, and five to ten people can share them. They operate out of the airport and between central bus stations of major cities. Either way, the נֶהָג (nah-*hahg*; *driver*) happily takes your מִזְוָדָה (meez-vah-*dah*; *luggage*) and helps you to your seat. They may ask you לְאָן אַתָּה נוֹסֵעַ ? (M) or לְאָן אַתְּ נוֹסַעַת ? (F) (leh-*ahn* ah-*tah*/aht noh-seh-ah/noh-sah-aht; *Where are you traveling?*). You can respond by saying אֲנִי נוֹסֵעַ לְ (M) or נוֹסַעַת לְ (F) (ah-*nee* noh-seh-ah/noh-sah-aht luh; *I'm traveling to . . .*).

מוֹנִיּוֹת (moh-nee-*yoht*; *taxis*) are great and convenient ways to get around. In Israel, if you want to flag one down, just point your index finger toward the ground. A מוֹנִית (moh-*neet*; *taxi*) will pull right over. The נֶהָג (nah-*hahg*; *driver*) may ask you whether you want a קָבוּעַ מְהִיר (meh-*chear*; *flat fee*) or מוֹנֶה (moh-*neh*; *meter*). Responding הִשְׁתַּמֵּשׁ מוֹנֶה (heesh-tah-*mehsh* bah-moh-*neh*; *Use the meter*) is usually your best option. And when you arrive at your destination, be sure to ask for a קַבָּלָה (kah-bah-*lah*; *receipt*).

Uber works only in Tel Aviv, which is fine when you arrive in Israel, because that's where the airport is. Other transportation apps include גֶּט (geht; Gett), יַנְגוֹ (*yahng*-oh; Yango), and מוּבִּיט (*Moov*-it; Moovit).

CULTURAL WISDOM

Cabbies in Israel are notoriously friendly and often freely spout their opinions on anything, such as religion, politics, and the state of world peace. Talking to them is a great way to learn about the country and take the pulse of the people living there. Also, remember that tipping the driver isn't customary. So, when they quote you a price, you can give them exact change or expect עֹדֶף (*oh*-dehf; *change*) in return. Check out Chapter 14 for the scoop on money matters.

Watching the wheels on the bus go round and round

Riding on an אוֹטוֹבּוּס (*oh*-toh-boos; *bus*) in Israel is a cultural experience. Buses go everywhere. If you're a frequent traveler on the bus system, you may want to get a כַּרְטִיסִיָּה (kahr-tee-see-*yah*; *bus ticket*) that contains places where the נֶהָג (nah-*hahg*; *driver*) punches a hole every time you board. Different כַּרְטִיסִיּוֹת (kahr-tee-see-*yoht*; *bus tickets*) are available for children, youths (ages 12 to 18), adults, and senior citizens. You also may want to consider a חָפְשִׁי חָדְשִׁי (chohd-*shee* chohf-shee; *monthly bus pass*) that you can flash at the driver upon boarding. Or if you're an occasional bus traveler, you can forget the tickets and passes altogether and simply pay the fare in cash.

CULTURAL
WISDOM

GETTING SPECIFIC ABOUT THE ISRAELI BUS SYSTEM

Although the Israeli bus system serves a population slightly larger than 6 million, it operates 4,000 buses on thousands of scheduled routes and is the second-largest bus system in the world, just after London Transport. Most of the buses in the country are run by a cooperative called אֶגֶד (*Egged,*) which literally means *linked together,* but דָּן (*Dan*) serves the population in the greater Tel Aviv area. National poet Haim Nachman Bialik proposed the name אֶגֶד (*Egged*) to epitomize the cooperative nature of the Jewish state. In the cooperative, members perform all duties to run the company, own a share of the company, and collectively make management decisions.

The cooperative was founded in 1933 as a merger of four bus cooperatives. Then, during the times of the British Mandate before Israel's independence in 1948, the bus lines ran scheduled routes to Lebanon, Syria, Iraq, Trans-Jordan, and Egypt. Today, אֶגֶד (*Egged*) is still a cooperative with 3,250 members and 4,550 salaried employees, serving 1 million domestic passengers a day.

In Israel, you place the fare in the bus driver's hand, and they make עֹדֶף (*oh-*dehf; change) for you. Sometimes, if a lot of people are waiting at the תַּחֲנַת הָאוֹטוֹבּוּס (tah-chah-*naht* hah-*oh*-toh-boos; *bus stop*), the נְהַג הָאוֹטוֹבּוּס (neh-*hahg* hah-oh-toh-*boos; bus driver*) opens the back door of the bus. People in the back pass their fare or their כַּרְטִיסָיה (kahr-tee-see-*yoht; bus tickets*) to the front of the אוֹטוֹבּוּס (*oh-*toh-boos; *bus*). Miraculously, the correct change and the correct bus ticket always come back to their rightful owners. It's an honor system, and it really works!

CULTURAL
WISDOM

Folks in Israel tell a joke about a rabbi and an Israeli bus driver who, after living long and full lives, arrive in heaven. The rabbi is chagrined to discover that the bus driver received a higher place in heaven than they did. So, the rabbi marches right up to God to register a complaint. "God," the rabbi says, "how can this be? I've devoted my entire life to you, yet a bus driver earns a higher place in heaven than I?" God looks at the rabbi and responds, "Look. It's this way. Whenever you started teaching, your congregants started sleeping. But whenever the bus driver started driving, their passengers started praying!"

Traveling on trains and the light rail

The first ת (rah-*kehv*-eht; *railroad*) in אֶרֶץ יִשְׂרָאֵל (eh-rehtz yees-rah-*ehl; the Land of Israel*) was established in 1892. Then and throughout the years of Ottoman rule and the British Mandate, the פַּסִּים (pah-*seem; tracks*) reached all the way to מִצְרַיִם (meetz-rah-*eem; Egypt*), סוּרְיָה (*soor-*yah; *Syria*), and לְבָנוֹן (leh-vah-*nohn; Leba-*non). Today in Israel, the רַכֶּבֶת (rah-*kehv*-eht; *train*) is a popular and expanding form of תַּחְבּוּרָה (tach-booh-*rah*; *transportation*), with קַוִּים (kah-*veem*; *lines*) running regularly between Haifa and Tel Aviv, Tel Aviv and Jerusalem, Tel Aviv and Rechovot, and Haifa and Netanya, from Tel Aviv to Beer-Sheva, Modi'in and both Jerusalem and Tel Aviv and more.

רַכֶּבֶת יִשְׂרָאֵל (rah-*keh*-veht yees-rah-*ehl*; *Israeli Railways*) has approximately 50 רַכָּבוֹת (rah-kah-*voht*; *trains*), 70 רַכָּבוֹת נוֹסְעִים (rah-kah-*voht* noh-s-*eem*; *passenger cars*), and 1,300 רַכָּבוֹת מִטְעָן (rah-kah-*voht* meet-*ahn*; *freight cars*). You can find a לוּחַ זְמַנִּים (loo-ach z-mah-*neem*; *schedule*) at https://www.rail.co.il/en, where you can also find מוֹדיעין (moh-dee-*een*; *information*) about רַכָּבוֹת נוֹסְעִים. (rah-kah-*voht* noh-s-*eem*; *passenger trains*). The site features a מַפַּת קַוֵּי נוֹסְעִים (mah-*paht* kah-vay nohs-*eem*; *map of passenger lines*) and תַּחֲנַת נוֹסְעִים (tah-chah-*noht* noh-*seem*; *passenger stations*). These maps are sorted by תַאֲרִיך (tah-ah-*reech*; *date*), תַּחֲנַת מוֹצָא (tah-chah-*naht* moh-*tzah*; *departure station*), and תַּחֲנָה סוֹפִית (tah-chah-*nah* soh-*feet*; *final station*).

There's a children's song in Hebrew about a רַכֶּבֶת. Just keep repeating these three lines:

> hee-*nay* rah-*kehv*-eht!
>
> hee mees-toh-*veh*-veht!
>
> ahl gahl-gah-*leem,* ahl gahl-gah-*leem* ahl gahl-gah-*leem,* too, too!

> Here is a train!
>
> It goes around!
>
> On wheels, on wheels, on wheels, toot, toot!

Jerusalem has its very own light rail! הָרַכֶּבֶת הַקַּלָּה בִּירוּשָׁלַיִם (Hah-rah-*kehv*-eht hah-kah-lah Bee-*yeh*-roo-shah-lye-eem; *The Jerusalem Light Rail*) began skimming the surfaces of the town in 2011, after ten years of disruptive construction. Better late than never, as they say. הָרַכֶּבֶת הַקַּלָּה (Hah rah-*keh*-vet Hah-kah-lah; *The Light Rail*) runs from the חֵיל הָאֲוִיר (hah-*yeel* hah-*ah*-veer; *Air Force Pilot*) Station in the Pisgat Ze'ev neighborhood in the north all the way to הַר הֶרְצְל (hahr hehrtz ehl Hertzl; *Mount Herzl*) in the west end of the city, with many stops along the way. Electronic boards tell you when the train is about to arrive. You can use your רַב-קַו (rahv-kahv; Rav-Kav), or you can purchase כַּרְטִיסִיּוֹת (kahr-*tee-see*-oht; *tickets*) from the ticket machines that are always at the light-rail stop. You can find more information about the Jerusalem Light Tail at www.citypass.co.il.

After many years of work and proposals (dating back to the Ottoman era — no, I'm not kidding!), the first test drive of Tel Aviv's light rail happened in October 2021, with the first line set to start running in early 2023. בְּלִי עַיִן הָרַע (bli-*ayin*-hah-rah; *let's not temp the evil eye*), as they say! If all goes as planned, there will be four light-rail lines operating in the Tel Aviv–Jaffa metropolitan area in 2023.

Haifa doesn't have a רַכֶּבֶת קַלָּה (rah-keh-veht kah-lah; light rail), but it does have a מַטְרוֹנִית (maht-troh-neet; rapid bus system), a כַּרְמְלִית (kahr-meh-leet; subway) and also the much-beloved רַכֶּבֶל (Rah-kehv-behl; cable car) and even the רַכְּבָלִית (Rah-kah-bahl-eet; commuter cable car). In Israel they really know how to get around!

Reading maps and schedules

If you need to read a מַפָּה (mah-pah; map) or a לוּחַ זְמַנִּים (loo-ahḥ z-mah-neem; schedule), you may encounter some of these words:

>> קַו (kahv; line)

>> שָׁעָה (shah-ah; hour)

>> תַּאֲרִיךְ (tah-ah-reech; date)

>> יוֹם (yohm; day)

>> זְמַן (zmahn; time)

>> צָפוֹן (tzah-fohn; north)

>> דָּרוֹם (dah-rohm; south)

>> מַעֲרָב (mah-ah-rahv; west)

>> מִזְרָח (meez-rahḥ; east)

You'll need to tell time interpret train schedules, so check out Chapter 7. And for more info on directions, take a look at Chapter 15.

WORDS TO KNOW

אוֹטוֹבּוּס	oh-toh-boos	bus
לוּחַ זְמַנִּים	loo-ahḥ z-mahn-eem	schedule
מַפָּה	mah-pah	map
מוֹנִית	moh-neet	taxi
נוֹסֵעַ	noh-say-ah	travel (M)
נוֹסַעַת	noh-sah-aht	travel (F)
נֶהָג	neh-hahg	driver (M)

עֹדֶף	*oh*-dehf	change
רַכֶּבֶת	rah-*kehv*-eht	train
שֵׁרוּת	sheh-*root*	shared taxi

Being Early or Late

Everyone seems to have their own internal clock. Some people are always מֻקְדָּם (mook-*dahm; early*); some people are always מְאֻחָר (meh-oo-*chahr; late*); others are always בְּדִיוּק בַּזְּמַן (bee-dee-*yook* bahz-*mahn; exactly on time*). But if you're a person who is always late, and you have to catch a plane, train, or bus, you may want to consider changing your habits, if only for a day.

You can use some of the following phrases when you want to discuss such timely issues:

>> אֲנִי הָיִיתִי בְּדִיוּק בַּזְּמַן . (ah-*nee* hah-*yee*-tee bee-dee-yook bahz-*mahn; I was exactly on time.*)

>> אֲנִי הִקְדַּמְתִּי . (ah-*nee* heek-*dahm*-tee; *I was early.*)

>> אֲנִי הִקְדַּמְתִּי אוֹתְךָ . (ah-*nee* heek-*dahm*-tee oht-*ḥah; I beat you* or *I was before you.*) (M)

>> אֲנִי הִקְדַּמְתִּי אוֹתָךְ . (ah-*nee* heek-*dahm*-tee oh-*tch; I beat you* or *I was before you.*) (F)

>> אֲנִי אִחַרְתִּי . (ah-*nee* ee-*ḥahr*-tee; *I was late.*)

>> סְלִיחָה עַל הָאִחוּר . (slee-*chah* ahl-hah-ee-*choor; Excuse the lateness.*)

>> סְלִיחָה עַל הָעִכּוּב . (slee-*chah* ahl hah-ee-*koov; Excuse the delay.*)

YESTERDAY, THE DAY BEFORE YESTERDAY, AND LAST NIGHT

I'd like to introduce you to three fantastic time-oriented Hebrew words that don't exist in English, but I wish they did! One is שִׁלְשׁוֹם (shil-*shohm; the day before yesterday*); the others are אֶמֶשׁ (eh-*mehsh; last night*) and מָחֳרָתַיִם (mah-*ḥahr*-tah-yeem; *two days from now*). Fantastic! We don't have such words in English, but at least now you can say them in Hebrew.

FUN & GAMES

Find the perfect match. I've given you the questions in Hebrew and English, but the possible answers are only in Hebrew. Watch out! I've given you one too many answers. You can find the solutions in Appendix C.

Questions:

1. ‏אֵיזֶה סוּג רֶכֶב אַתָּה רוֹצֶה ? (ay-*zeh* soog reh-*chehv* ah-*tah* roh-*tzeh; What kind of vehicle do you want?*)

2. ‏מָתַי הַמָּטוֹס מַמְרִיא ? (mah-*tye* hah-mah-*tohs* mahm-*ree; When does the plane take off?*)

3. ‏הַאִם יֵשׁ לוּחוֹת זְמַנִּים שֶׁל רַכֶּבֶת הָאֵם ? (hah-*eem* yaysh loo-*ḥoht* z-mah-*neem* shehl hah-rah-keh-*veht; Is there a train schedule?*)

4. ‏אֵיפֹה תַּחֲנַת הָאוֹטוֹבּוּס ? (ay-*foh* tah-*ḥah-naht* hah-oh-toh-*boos; Where is the bus station?*)

5. ‏לְאָן אַתָּה רוֹצֶה לִנְסֹעַ ? (leh-*ahn* ah-*tah* roh-*tzeh* leen-soh-*ah; Where do you want to travel?*)

(A) ‏יֵשׁ לָנוּ לוּחוֹת זְמַנִּים .

(B) ‏יֵשׁ לָנוּ לוּחוֹת זְמַנִּים .

(C) ‏הָאוֹטוֹבּוּס נוֹסֵעַ מָהִיר .

(D) ‏אֲנִי רוֹצֶה לִנְסֹעַ לִירוּשָׁלַיִם .

(E) ‏תַּחֲנַת הָאוֹטוֹבּוּס בַּמֶּרְכָּז הָעִיר .

(F) ‏הַמָּטוֹס מַמְרִיא בְּשָׁעָה שְׁמוֹנָה בַּבֹּקֶר .

Chapter **13**

Money, Money, Money

S ome folks say that money makes the world go 'round. Other people say that it's the root of all evil. But whatever it is, money is certainly part of everyone's lives in the 21st-century world. In this chapter, I show you how to talk about the stuff that's been likened to the staff of life: bread and dough.

Going to the Bank

Ah, a trip to the בַּנְק (bahnk; bank). Some people love it; others dread it. But however you feel about visiting your bank, the task is unavoidable at times. Maybe you need to go to your local סְנִיף (sneef; branch) only to cash or deposit a הַמְחָאָה (hahm-hah-ah; check). Ideally, the סְכוּם (s-hoom; amount) you לְהַפְקִיד (leh-haf-keed; to deposit) is larger than the amount you לִמְשׁךְ (leem-shohch; to withdraw)! But often, you have to go to a larger bank to take care of big monetary matters, such as taking out a הַלְוָאָה (hal vah-ah; loan) or — gasp — applying for a מַשְׁכַּנְתָּא (mash-kahn-tah; mortgage). In this section, I give you some terms to help you with your banking communications.

Talking to tellers

So, what do you need to do? Do you need to לְהַפְקִיד כֶּסֶף (leh-haf-keed keh-sehf; deposit money) in your חֶשְׁבּוֹן (hesh-bohn; account) or לִמְשׁךְ (leem-shohch; withdraw) it? Are you there to לְהַגִּישׁ בְּבַקָּשָׁה (leh-hah-*geesh* bah-kah-*shah*; *apply for*) a הַלְוָאָה (hal vah-*ah*; *loan*) or a מַשְׁכַּנְתָּא (mash-kahn-*tah*; *mortgage*)? Maybe you need to make a תַּשְׁלוּם (tash-*loom*; *payment*). Just tell the כַּסְפָּרה/כַּסְפָּר (kahs-*pahr*/ kahs-*pahr*-ah; *teller*) what you need, and they'll be happy to help you.

Here are some helpful phrases:

» אֲנִי רוֹצֶה לִפְתּוֹחַ חֶשְׁבּוֹן . (ah-*nee* roh-*tzeh* leef-*toh*-ach chehsh-*bohn*; *I want to open an account.*) (M)

אֲנִי רוֹצָה לִפְתּוֹחַ חֶשְׁבּוֹן . (ah-*nee* roh-*tzah* leef-*toh*-ach chehsh-*bohn*; *I want to open an account.)* (F)

» אֲנִי רוֹצֶה לְהַגִּישׁ בַּקָּשָׁה לְהַלְוָאָה . (ah-*nee* roh-*tzeh* leh-hah-*geesh* bah-kah-*shah* leh-hal-vah-*ah*; *I want to apply for a loan.*) (M)

אֲנִי רוֹצָה לְהַגִּישׁבַּקָּשָׁה לְהַלְוָאָה . (ah-*nee* roh-*tzah* leh-hah-*geesh* bah-kah-*shah* leh-hal-vah-*ah; I want to apply for a loan.*) (F)

» אֲנִי רוֹצֶה לְהַעֲבִיר כֶּסֶף (ah-*nee* roh-*tzeh* leh-hah-ah-*veer* keh-sehf; literally: *I want to transfer money* or *I want to wire money.*) (M)

אֲנִי רוֹצָה לְהַעֲבִיר כֶּסֶף (ah-*nee* roh-*tzah* leh-hah-ah-*veer keh*-sehf; literally: *I want to transfer money* or *I want to wire money.*) (F)

» מַה הָרִבִּית ? (mah hah-ree-*beet*; *What's the interest rate?*)

» אֶפְשָׁר לַחְתּוֹם עַל הַהַמְחָאָה ? (ehf-*shahr* lach-*tohm* ahl hah-hahm-chah-*ah*; *Can you sign this check?*)

» מָתַי אַתָּה יָכוֹל לְשַׁלֵּם (mah-*tye* ah-*tah* yah-*chohl* leh-shah-*lehm*; *When can you make a payment?*) (M)

מָתַי אַתְּ יְכוֹלָה לְשַׁלֵּם ? (mah-*tye* aht yeh-choh-*lah* leh-shah-*lehm*; *When can you make a payment?*) (F)

Instead of schlepping all the way to the bank, you can use an ATM machine, which is called a כַּסְפּוֹמַט (kahs-poh-*maht*) in Hebrew. I always get a big kick out of seeing Hebrew on the ATM screen. Here's this ancient biblical language, and it's at home in the modern world.

Counting your change

The שֶׁקֶל (*sheh*-kehl) is the currency of Israel. The Israeli currency system is based on the שֶׁקֶל חָדָשׁ (*sheh*-kehl chah-*dahsh*; *New Israeli Shekel* [NIS]), which has been in circulation since 1985. The שֶׁקֶל חָדָשׁ (NIS) is made up of 100 *אֲגוֹרוֹת* (ah-goh-*roht*, which is the equivalent of $\frac{1}{100}$ of the currency, like a penny to the dollar; this is the plural form). Israel no longer mints the one אֲגוֹרָה (ah-goh-*rah*; *coin*), so most of the time, עֹדֶף (oh-*dehf*; *change*) also referred to as כֶּסֶף קָטָן (keh-sehf kah-*than*; *literally: "small money"*) is rounded to the nearest five אֲגוֹרוֹת (ah-goh-*roht*). If the change is two אֲגוֹרוֹת or less, the sum is rounded down. If the change is three אֲגוֹרוֹת or more, the change is rounded up.

TIP

In Hebrew, people refer to the word שֶׁקֶל חָדָשׁ (sheh-kehl chah-*dash*; *new shekel*) with the term שַׁ"ח (shaḥ) for short. This form is generally used for talking about money in an official way, such as at the bank, or when people are discussing the economy.

Shekels come in denominations of ½-, one-, five-, and ten-shekel coins. שְׁטָרוֹת (sh-tah-*roht*; *bills*) come in denominations of 10, 20, 50, 100, and 200 shekels.

SOMETHING OLD, SOMETHING NEW: ISRAELI COINS

Israeli מַטְבְּעוֹת (maht-beh-*oht*; *coins*) offer an amazing tour of ancient Israelite history. Many of today's coins are imprints of ancient Israelite coins dating back to the first century CE or even earlier.

The five-אֲגוֹרוֹת (ah-goh-*roht*) coin is a replica of a coin from the fourth year of the war between the Jews and Rome, and it depicts symbols from the Jewish harvest holiday of סֻכּוֹת (soo-*koht*; *Sukkot*). The ten-אֲגוֹרוֹת coin bears the imprint of a coin issued by the Israelite empire between BCE 40 and 37, depicting the seven-branched candelabrum that once stood in the Jewish Temple in Jerusalem.

The חֲצִי-שֶׁקֶל depicts a harp of an ancient Israelite seal, and the שֶׁקֶל (sheh-kehl; *one-shekel coin*) has an image of a lily and ancient Hebrew letters from a Judean coin from the Persian period (sixth to fourth centuries BCE).

The five-שֶׁקֶל coin shows a column typical of buildings in the ancient Israelite period between the tenth and seventh centuries BCE. The ten-שֶׁקֶל coin (the most gorgeous, in my opinion), a nickel and copper coin depicting a palm tree with seven leaves and two baskets with dates, originates from a coin minted in 69 CE, the fourth year of the Jewish–Roman war, one year before the destruction of the Second Temple in Jerusalem.

To learn more about Israeli coins check out this website: https://www.travelin-gisrael.com/tour-israeli-wallet/ or watch this video: https://youtu.be/p1z0hrniMbE

Talkin' the Talk

 Tamir goes to the bank to open an account. He talks with a bank employee who gets him started with a checking account and a credit card.

Tamir: בֹּקֶר טוֹב .

(*boh*-kehr *tohv*.)

Good morning.

Clerk: בֹּקֶר אוֹר אֶפְשָׁר לַעֲזֹר לְךָ ?

(*boh*-kehr *ohr.* ehf-*shahr* lah-ah-*zohr* leh-*chah?*)

Morning light. May I help you?

Tamir: כֵּן אֲנִי רוֹצֶה לִפְתֹּחַ חֶשְׁבּוֹן עוֹבֵר וָשָׁב וְגַם לְהַזְמִין כַּרְטִיס אַשְׁרַאי .

(kehn. ah-*nee* roh-*tzeh* leef-*toh*-ach chehsh-*bohn* hehsh-bohn oh-vehr vah-shav veh-*gahm* leh-hahz-*meen* kahr-*tees* ash-*rye*.)

Yes. I would like to open a checking account and also order a credit card.

Clerk: בְּוַדַאי נָא לְמַלֵּא אֶת הַטֹּפֶס הַזֶּה .

(beh-vah-*dai.* nah leh-mah-*leh* eht hah-*toh*-fehs hah-*zeh*.)

Certainly. Please fill out this form.

Tamir: תּוֹדָה הִנֵּה אֲנִי מִלֵּאתִי אֶת הַטֹּפֶס .

(toh-*dah.* hee-*nay.* ah-*nee* mee-*leh*-tee eht hah *toh*-fehs.)

Thanks. Here it is. I filled out the form.

Clerk: תּוֹדָה רַבָּה לְךָ אַתָּה יָכוֹל לְצַפּוֹת לְהַמְחָאוֹת וְכַרְטִיס אַשְׁרַאי בְּעוֹד שְׁלוֹשָׁה שָׁבוּעוֹת

(toh-*dah* rah-*bah* leh-*chah.* ah-*tah* yah-*chohl* leh-tzah-*poht* lah-hamcha-*oht* veh-kar-*tees* hah-ash-*rahy* buh-*ohd* sh-loh-shah shah-voo-*oht*.)

Thank you very much. You can expect your checks and your credit card in the mail in three weeks.

Tamir: יֹפִי תּוֹדָה רַבָּה .

(*yoh*-fee. toh-*dah* rah-*bah*.)

Great. Thanks a lot.

WORDS TO KNOW

בַּנְק	*bahnk*	bank
כֶּסֶף	*keh*-sehf	money
הַלְוָאָה	hal-vah-*ah*	loan
לְהַפְקִיד	leh-hahf-*keed*	to deposit
לְהַשְׁקִיעַ	leh-hahsh-*kee*-ah	to invest
לִמְשֹׁךְ	leem-*shohch*	to withdraw
מַשְׁכַּנְתָּא	mahsh-kahn-*tah*	mortgage
מַטְבֵּעַ	maht-*beh*-ah	coin
עֹדֶף	*oh*-dehf	change
סְכוּם	s-*hoom*	amount
סְנִיף	*sneef*	branch
חֶשְׁבּוֹן עוֹבֵר וָשָׁב	ḥehsh-bohn oh-vehr vah-*shav*	checking account
תַּשְׁלוּם	tahsh-*loom*	payment

CULTURAL WISDOM

Jewish villages in Eastern Europe used to participate in a רֹאשׁ הַשָּׁנָה (rohsh hah-shah-*nah; New Year's*) custom: One person would go door to door with a sack. Folks who could afford to put money in the sack did so, and people who needed money took it from the sack. The entire process was all completely anonymous. No one knew who gave money to or who took money from the sack. Everyone got what they needed, and no one was embarrassed. In this way, everyone in the קְהִלָּה (keh-hee-*lah; community*) helped one another.

CULTURAL WISDOM

CONSIDERING WEALTH IN JEWISH THOUGHT

When considering wealth, Judaism takes the middle road, advocating neither asceticism nor excessive materialism. In a book of Jewish wisdom literature, פִּרְקֵי אָבוֹת *Pirke Avot* (*peer*-kay *ah*-voht; *sayings of the ancestors*), the ancient rabbis asked, "Who is rich?" Their answer: those who find contentment in their lot. The rabbis also taught that where there is no flour, there is no Torah. This statement recognizes that physical needs and other practical matters must be met before spirituality is possible.

Changing Money

Whenever you travel — whether for business or pleasure — you usually have to exchange your money for the local currency. Most בַּנְקִים (bahn-keem; banks) will accept dollars in return for the local currency in cash. You can usually spot a board with the שַׁעַר חֲלִיפִין (shah-ahr ha-ḥa-lee-feen; exchange rate). Just go straight up to the window and say

>> • אֲנִי רוֹצֶה לְהָמִיר כֶּסֶף (ah-nee rohtz-eh leh-hah-meer keh-sehf; I want to exchange money.) (M)

אֲנִי רוֹצָה לְהָמִיר כֶּסֶף (ah-nee rohtz-ah leh-hah-meer keh-sehf; I want to exchange money.) (F)

Here are some additional phrases that may come in handy:

>> • אֲנִי רוֹצֶה לְהָמִיר דוֹלָרִים לִשְׁקָלִים (ah-nee roh-tzeh leh-hah-meer doh-lahr-eem leh-sh-kahl-eem; I want to exchange dollars for shekels.) (M)

>> • אֲנִי רוֹצָה לְהָמִיר דוֹלָרִים לִשְׁקָלִים (ah-nee roh-tzah leh-hah-meer doh-lahr-eem lehsh-kahl-eem; I want to exchange dollars for shekels.) (F)

>> מָה שַׁעַר חֲלִיפִין ? (mah shah-ahr hah-chah-lee-feen; What's the exchange rate?)

>> כַּמָה הָעֲמְלוֹת ? (kah-mah hah-ahm-loht; What are the fees?)

REMEMBER

When you exchange money, you may be asked for your ID, so have your דַּרְכּוֹן (dahr-kohn; passport) or some other form of תְּעוּדַת זֶהוּת (teh-oo-daht zeh-hoot; identification) ready. The כַּסְפָּרה/כַּסְפָּר (kahs-pahr/ kahs-pahr-ah; teller) will ask you

>> הָאִים יֵשׁ לְךָ תְּעוּדַת זֶהוּת ? (hah-eem yehsh leh-chah teh-oo-daht zeh-hoot; Do you have an identity card?) (M)

הָאִים יֵשׁ לָךְ תְּעוּדַת זֶהוּת ? (hah-eem yesh lach teh-oo-daht zeh-hoot; Do you have an identity card?) (F)

TIP

If you want to ask someone to make change or break a large bill for you, the phrase you use is? אֶפְשָׁר לִפְרֹט לִי (ehf-shahr leef-roht lee; Can you break this for me?).

TIP

If you have a כְּרָאִיס אַשְׁרַאי (kahr-tees ash-rye; credit card), you can get cash at any כַּסְפּוֹמַט (kahs-poh-maht; ATM) but watch out for the עֲמְלָה (ahm-lah; fee)!

Talkin' the Talk

 Eric, an American tourist in Israel, heads to the bank to change money.

Eric: בֹּקֶר טוֹב אֲנִי רוֹצֶה לְהָמִיר דוֹלָרִים אָמֶרִיקָאִים לִשְׁקָלִים בְּבַקָּשָׁה מָה ? שַׁעַרהַחֲלִיפִין

(*boh*-kehr tohv. ah-*nee* roh-*tzeh* leh-hah-*meer* doh-lah-*reem* ah-mehr-ee-*kah*-neem leh-sh-*kah*-leem beh-vah-kah-*shah*. mah *shah*-ahr-ha-cha-lee-*feen?*)

Good morning. I want to exchange American dollars for shekels, please. What's the exchange rate?

Teller: בֹּקֶר אוֹר שַׁעַר הַחֲלִיפִין הוּא אַרְבָּעָה שְׁקָלִים לְדוֹלָר אֶחָד ▪

(*boh*-kehr ohr. *shah*-ahr ha-cha-lee-*feen* hoo ahr-bah-*ah* sheh-*kah-leem* leh-*doh*-lar e-*chad*.)

Morning light. The exchange rate is four shekels to the dollar.

Eric: יֹפִי אֲנִי רוֹצֶה לְהָמִיר אַרְבַּע מֵאוֹת דוֹלָרִים בְּהַמְחָאוֹת נוֹסְעִים לִשְׁקָלִים חֲדָשִׁים ▪

(*yoh*-fee. ah-*nee* roh-*tzeh* leh-hah-*meer* ahr-*bah* meh-*oht* doh-lah-*reem* beh-hahm-chah-*oht* nohs-*eem* lehsh-*kah*-leem chah-dah-*sheem*.)

Great. I want to exchange $400 in traveler's checks to New Israeli Shekels.

Teller: אֵין בְּעָיָה יֵשׁ לְךָ תְּעוּדַת זֶהוּת ?

(ayn be-ah--*yah*. yehsh leh-*chah* teh-oo-*daht* zeh-*hoot?*)

No problem. Do you have ID?

Eric: כֵּן הִנֵּה הַדַּרְכּוֹן שֶׁלִּי ▪

(kehn. hee-*nay* hah-dahr-*kohn* sheh-*lee*.)

Yes. Here's my passport.

Teller: וְהִנֵּההַכֶּסֶף שֶׁלְךָ לְאַרְבַּע מֵאוֹת דוֹלָרִים מְקַבְּלִים אֶלֶף שֵׁשׁ מֵאוֹת שְׁקָלִים מִינוּס עֶשְׂרִים לְעַמְלָה אָז אַתָּה מְקַבֵּל אֶלֶף חָמֵשׁ מֵאוֹת וּשְׁמוֹנִים שְׁקָלִים חֲדָשִׁים

(veh-hee-*nay* hah-*keh*-sehf shel-*chah*. leh-ahr-*bah* meh-*oht* doh-lahr-*eem* meh-kah*bleem* eh-lehf veh-shaysh meh-*oht* shkah-*leem mee*-noos ehs-*reem* shkah-*leem* lah-ah-m-*lah*. ahz ah-*tah* meh-kah-*behl* eh-lehf, chah-*mehsh* meh-*oht* oosh-moh-*neem* sh-kah-*leem* chah-dah-*sheem*.)

And here is your money. For $400, you get 1,600 shekels minus 20 shekels for the transaction fee. So you get 1,580 New Israeli Shekels.

Eric:
.תּוֹדָה רַבָּה

(toh-*dah* rah-*bah*.)

Thanks a lot.

● ●

WORDS TO KNOW

הַמְחָאָה	ham-chah-*ah*	check
כַּרְטִיס אַשְׁרַאי	kahr-*tees* ahsh-*rye*	credit card
כַּסְפָּר	*kahs*-pahr	bank teller
עַמְלָה	ahm-*lah*	fee
כַּסְפּוֹמָט	kahs-*poh*-maht	ATM
שַׁעֲרֵי הַחֲלִיפִין	*shah*-ahr hah-**h**ah-*lee*-feen	exchange rates
תְּעוּדַת זָהוּת	teh-oo-*daht* zeh-*hoot*	ID

CULTURAL WISDOM

The Hebrew word for *philanthropic giving* is צְדָקָה (tzdah-*kah*; literally: *justice* or *righteous giving*). The Jewish concept of philanthropy is inherent in this word's meaning. Although the Latin root for *charity* means "love" and is based on the idea of giving out of the goodness of one's heart, the Jewish concept of צְדָקָה is based on equitable distribution of wealth. In Judaism, transferring wealth from those who earn it to those who need it is an obligation for everyone. Even those who depend on receiving צְדָקָה are obligated to give it.

Flowing with the Currency

If you're an avid traveler, you may have all kinds of currencies in your pocket, such as

» דִּינָר (dee-*nahr*; Jordanian dinar)

» דּוֹלָר (*doh*-lahr; American or Canadian dollar)

» יוּרוֹ (*yur*-oh; European Euro, pronounced *ey*-ro in Israel because *Europe* is pronounced ey-*ro*-pah)

» פְרַנְק (*frank*; Swiss franc) »

» כֶּתֶר (*keh*-tehr; Danish and Norwegian crown) »

- ‏לִירָה‎ (*lee*-rah; British, Lebanese, and Egyptian pound)

- ‏פֵּיסוֹ‎ (*pay*-soh; Mexican peso)

- ‏רַנְד‎ (*rand;* Saudi Arabian rand)

- ‏יֶן‎ (*yehn;* Japanese yen)

- ‏זְלוֹטִי‎ (*zloh*-tee; Polish zloty)

Using Credit Cards

Anywhere you go these days, you can pay for almost everything with ‏כַּרְטִיסֵי אַשְׁרַי‎ (kahr-tees-*ay* ahsh-*rye*; *credit cards*), and Israel is no exception. You can ask whether a particular establishment accepts ‏כַּרְטִיסֵי אַשְׁרַי‎ (kahr-tees-*ay* ahsh-*rye*; *credit cards*) by asking either of the following questions:

- ? ‏אַתֶּם מְקַבְּלִים כַּרְטִיסֵי אַשְׁרַי י‎ (ah-*tehm* meh-kahb-*leem* kahr-tee-*say* ahsh-rye; Do you accept credit cards?)

- ? ‏אֶפְשָׁר לְשַׁלֵם עִם כַּרְטִיס אַשְׁרַי‎ (ehf-*shahr* leh-shah-*lehm* eem *kahr*-tees ahsh-*rye;* May I pay with a credit card?)

Using Electronic and Digital Currency

‏כֶּסֶף מְזֻמָּן‎ (keh-*sehf* meh-zoo-*mahn;* cash) is becoming rarer these days. Even using ‏כַּרְטִיסֵי אַשְׁרַי‎ (kahr-tees-ay ahsh-*rei;* credit cards) is going the way of the dino-saur. Some people are using ‏מַטְבְּעוֹת דִּיגִיטָלִיִּים‎ (maht-bay-oht dee-*gee-tahl*-eem; *digital currency*) or ‏קְרִיפְּטוֹ‎ (krip-*toh;* cryptocurrency), whereas others ‏ע הַעֲבָרַת כֶּסֶף‎ (hah-ah-vah-*raht* keh-*seh-feem;* transfer money). In Israel, they don't have Zelle or Venmo; they have their own app, ‏בִּיט זֹאת‎ (Bit–Zot), but you need an Israeli telephone to use it.

Directing Your Objects

So, you've got your verbs. Then you've got your nouns. Often, when you put them together in a sentence, you add another word that receives the action of the verb: the goal or result of the verb. This word is the direct object. In the sentence "Molly kicked the ball," *ball* is the direct object — the thing that got kicked (received the action of the verb).

Sometimes, you place a preposition between the verb and a definite noun (a noun preceded by the word *the* — *the book* as opposed to *a book*, which would be an indefinite noun, but that's another story). Prepositions are one of the trickiest things in Hebrew for English speakers to master because the verbs that normally accompany prepositions in English aren't necessarily the same verbs that take prepositions in Hebrew.

The Hebrew prepositions are

>> עַל (*ahl; on*)

>> בֵּין (*bayn; between*)

>> בְּ (*buh; in* or *with*)

>> עִם (*eem; with*)

>> כְּ (*kuh; like*)

>> לְ (*luh; to*)

>> מְ (*muh; from*)

Another difficulty with prepositions is the fact that Hebrew has an article (אֶת; *eht*) for definite direct objects if the verb before it doesn't use a proposition. (There's no equivalent in English.) אֶת is placed between a verb and a definite direct object. In the sentence אֲנִי רוֹצֶה לִקְנוֹת אֶת הַכּוֹבַע (ah-*nee* roh-*tzeh* leek-*noht* eht hah-*koh*-vah; *I want to buy the hat*), לִקְנוֹת is the verb, and הַכּוֹבַע is the direct object. The אֶת between them tells you that the direct object is definite (*the* hat) and not indefinite (*a* hat). You don't use אֶת when the object is indirect. So, if you want to buy *a* hat, but not any particular hat, you wouldn't use the article אֶת.

You also place the article אֶת in front of proper nouns, such as the name of a country, as in אֲנִי אוֹהֵב אֶת יִשְׂרָאֵל (ah-*nee* oh-*hehv* eht yees-rah-*ehl; I love Israel*).

Think of אֶת as a road sign — Definite Direct Object Ahead (DDOA).

TIP

Finally, you can't assume that English verbs and their Hebrew equivalents take the same preposition. In English, you say, "That depends *on* blah, blah, blah," but in Hebrew, you say, "That depends *with* blah, blah, blah." Similarly, we're proud *of* something in English but proud *in/with* something in Hebrew. And so it is with many verbs, especially when the preposition refers to some abstract relationship, not something physical and concrete.

What verbs take which prepositions? As in English, the verb–preposition linking pattern is completely arbitrary. You just have to know this stuff. Table 13-1 includes a short list to get you started.

TABLE 13-1

Looking at Hebrew Prepositions

Hebrew Verb + Preposition	Pronunciation	Translation
לָשֶׁבֶת עַל	lah-*sheh*-veht al	to sit *on*
לָרֶדֶת מִ	lah-*reh*-deht meh	to descend *from*
לְפַחַד מִ׳	leh-fah-*chehd* meh	to be afraid *from*
לְהַקְשִׁיב לְ	leh-hahk-*sheev* leh	to listen *to*
לְהִסְתַּכֵּל בְּ׳	leh-his-tah-*kehl* beh	to look *in*
לָתֵת לְ	lah-*teht* leh	to give *to*
לַעֲזֹר לְ	lah-ah-*zohr* leh	to help *to*
לְחַקּוֹת לְ	leh-chah-*koht* leh	to wait *to*
לִבְחֹר בְּ׳	leev-*chohr* beh	to choose *in/with*
לְשַׁלֵּם לְ׳	leh-shah-*lehm* leh	to pay *to*
לְנַגֵּן בְּ׳	leh-nah-*gehn* beh	to play (a musical instrument) *with*
לְבַקֵּשׁ מִ ׳	leh-vah-*kehsh* meh	to request *from*
לִנְהֹג בְּ׳	leen-*hohg* beh	to drive *in*
לָגוּר בְּ׳	lah-*goor* beh	to live *in* a place or (on) a street
לִשְׁלֹחַ לְ׳	leesh-*loh*-ahch leh	to send *to*
לְ	leh-sah-*pehr* leh	to tell *to*
לִשְׁמֹר עַל	leesh-*mohr* ahl	to guard *on*
לְצַוּוֹת עַל	leh-tzah-*voht* ahl	to command *on*
לְהִסְתַּכֵּל עַל	leh-hees-tah-*kehl* ahl	to look *upon*
לְהַאֲמִין בְּ׳	leh-hah-ah-*meen* beh	to believe *in/with*
לֶאֱחֹז בְּ	leh-eh-*chohz* beh	to grasp *with/in*
לְאַיֵּם עַל	leh-ah-*yehm* ahl	to threaten *on*
לֶאֱסֹר עַל	leh-eh-*sohr* ahl	to forbid *on*
לְהַבְדִּיל בֵּין	leh-hahv-*deel* bein	to differentiate *between*
לְהִתְיַדֵּד עִם	leh-heet-yah-*dehd* eem	to befriend *with*

(continued)

TABLE 13-1 *(continued)*

Hebrew Verb + Preposition	Pronunciation	Translation
לְהִתְכַּתֵּב עִם	leh-heet-*kah*-tehv eem	to correspond *with*
לְהִתְמוֹדֵד עִם	leh-heet-moh-*dehd* eem	to cope *with*
לְהוֹדוֹת לְ	leh-hoh-*doht* leh	to thank *to*
לְהָגֵן עִם	leh-hah-*gehn* ahl	to protect *on*
לִדְאֹג לְ	leed-*ohg*	to worry *to*

FUN & GAMES

Write the correct English translation for the following Hebrew words:

1. תְּעוּדַת זֶהוּת _____

2. חֶשְׁבּוֹן _____

3. בֹּקֶר אוֹר _____

4. שַׁעֲרֵי הַחֲלִיפִין _____

For the answers, go to Appendix C.

Chapter **14**

Handling Emergencies

I nto each life some rain must fall, and sometimes, it turns into a full-blown storm in the form of an emergency, which is never fun. In this chapter, I talk about possible unfortunate incidents and give you the vocabulary to deal with them if the need arises.

In an emergency situation, you call out for help to anyone who may hear and let everyone know that you need help now! The following list of Hebrew phrases are useful when you need a helping hand:

> » ! דָחוּף (dah-*hoof*; *It's urgent!*)

> » ! הַצִּילוּ (hahtz-*ee*-loo; *Rescue!*)

> » ! הִתְקַשְׁרוּ לַמִּשְׁטָרָה (heet-kahsh-*roo* lah-meesh-tah-*rah*; *Contact the police!*)

> » ! תַּעַזְרוּ לִי בְּבַקָּשָׁה (tah-ahz-*roo* lee beh-vah-kah-*shah*; *Help me, please!*)

Tackling Your Uncooperative Car

Car trouble can be very frustrating. If your car is giving you fits, I hope you've just נִגְמַר הַדֶּלֶק (neeg-*mahr* hah-*deh*-lehk; *run out of gas*) or something minor (and annoying) like a פַּנְצֶ'ר (puhn-*ture*;). I hope you didn't have תְּאוּנַת דְּרָכִים (teh-oo-naht drah-*cheem*; *an accident*). Driving a car can be perilous. Fasten your חֲגוֹרַת

בְּטִיחוּת (ẖah-goh-*raht* be-tee-*choot*; *seat belt*)! Use these basic Hebrew phrases to describe what has happened to your car:

» הַמְּכוֹנִית שֶׁלִּי הִתְקַלְקְלָה . (hah-meh-**ẖoh**-*neet* sheh-*lee* heet-kahl-keh-*lah*; *My car broke down.*)

» הַמְּכוֹנִית שֶׁלִּי נִתְקְעָה . (hah-meh-choh-*neet* sheh-*lee* neet-keh-h-*ah*; *My car is stuck.*)

» הַמְּכוֹנִית שֶׁלִּי נִתְקְעָה . (hahy-*tah* te-oo-*naht* drah-*cheem*; *There was an accident.*)

» נִגְמַר לִי הַדֶּלֶק . . . (neeg-*mahr* lee hah-*deh*- lehk; *I ran out of gas.*)

» יֵשׁ לִי פַּנְצֶ'ר (yehsh lee puhn-*ture*) or . . . סֶקֶר בַּגַּלְגַּל (teh-*kehr* bah-*gahl*-gahl; *I have a flat tire.*)

You also may need to communicate to emergency workers or bystanders if someone has been hurt (or not):

» אֲנִי בְּסֵדֶר . (ah-*nee* beh-*seh*-dehr; *I'm okay.*)

» אֲנִי נִפְצַעְתִּי . (ah-*nee* neef-*tzah*-tee; *I've been injured.*)

» מִישֶׁהוּ נִפְצַע . (mee-sheh-*hoo* neef-*tzah*; *Someone's been injured.*)

CULTURAL WISDOM

Jews recite a special prayer called שִׁבְרְכַּת הַגּוֹמֵל (beer-*kaht* hah-goh-*mehl*) after surviving a dangerous situation. You can recite it immediately or go to a synagogue the very next Sabbath to recite it. The words are as follows:

בָּרוּךְ אַתָּה אֲדוֹנִי אֱלֹקֵנוּ מֶלֶךְ הָעוֹלָם הַגּוֹמֵל לְחַיָּים טוֹבוֹת שֶׁגְּמָלַנִי כָּל טוֹב .

(bah-*rooẖ* ah-*tah* ah-doh-*naye* eh-loh-*hay*-noo *meh*-leh**ẖ**hah-oh-*lahm* hah-goh-*mehl* leh-**ẖ**ah-yah-*veem* toh-*voht* sheh-gh-mah-*lah*-nee kohl tohv.)

Praised are you Eternal One our God, Ruler of the Cosmos, who does favors for those who need them, and has done so for me.

If you recite these words in the synagogue, at the traditional time during the Torah reading, the congregation will respond:

שֶׁגְּמָלְךָ כָּל טוֹב הוּא יִגְמְלְךָ כֹל טוֹב סֶלַע .

(mee sheh-guh-mahl-*chah* kohl tohv hoo yeeg-mahl-*chah* kohl tohv seh-lah.)

May the One who has granted you goodness continue to do so!

If you find yourself in an emergency situation in which you really need to talk shop with a מְכוֹנַי (meh-**ẖoh**-*nye*; *mechanic*), see Table 14-1 for words that you may need.

TABLE 14-1

Helpful Words to Use with a Mechanic

Hebrew	Pronunciation	Translation
סוֹלְלָה	soh-leh-*lah*	battery
בְּלָמִים	bla-*meem*	brakes
דַּבְשָׁה	dav-*shah*	Pedal
דֶּלֶק	*deh*-lehk	gas
גַּלְגַּלִּים	gahl-*gahl*-eem	wheels
הֶגֶה	*heh*-geh	steering wheel
הִלּוּכִים	hee-loo-*cheem*	gears
מַעֲנוֹף	*may*-neef mah-*nohf*	Jack
מַפְתֵּחַ	mahf-*tehay*-a**h**	key
מַגְּבִים	mah-gah-*veem*	windshield wipers
מָנוֹעַ	mah-*noh*-ah	engine
מַשָּׂאִית גְּרָר	mah-sah-*eet* gruh-ahr	tow truck
מַצְמֵד	mats-*med*	clutch
מוּסָךְ	moo-*sach*	garage
שִׁמְשָׁה קִדְמִית	sheem-*shah* keed-*meet*	windshield
שֶׁמֶן	*sheh*-mehn	oil
תִּמְסֹרֶת	teem-*soh*-reht	transmission
צְמִיגִים	tzmee-*geem*	tires

Talkin' the Talk

Tamir's car has broken down. He flags down a woman named Sigal for help.

Tamir: הַצִּילוּ הַצִּילוּ !

(hahz-*ee*-loo! hahz-*ee*-loo!)

Rescue! Rescue!

Sigal: מָה קָרָה ?

(mah kah-*rah*?)

What happened?

Tamir: הַמְכוֹנִית שֶׁלִּי הִתְקַלְקְלָה .

(hah-meh-choh-*neet* sheh-*lee* heet-kahl-keh-*lah*.)

My car has broken down.

Sigal: פְּתַח אֶת מְכַסֶּה מָנוֹעַ .

(pe-*tach* eht meech-*seh* hah-mah-*noh*-ah.)

Open the hood.

Tamir: אַתְּ יְכוֹלָה לְתַקֵּן אֶת זֶה ?

(aht yeh-choh-*lah* leh-tah-*kehn* eht zeh?)

Can you fix it?

Sigal: לֹא הָרְצוּעָה שֶׁלָּךְ נִקְרְעָה הִתְקַשֵּׁר לְמוּסָךְ

(loh. hah-chah-goh-*rah* shehl-chah neesh-beh-*rah*. heet-kah-*shehr* leh-moo-*sach*.)

No. Your fan belt is broken. Call a garage.

WORDS TO KNOW

בְּסֵדֶר	buh-sehd-*ehr*	okay
דָּחוּף	dah-*choof*	urgent
דֶּלֶק	deh-*lehk*	gasoline
עֶזְרָה	ehz-*rah*	help
גַּלְגַּלִּים	gahl-gahl-*eem*	wheels
הַצִּילוּ	hah-tzee-*loo*	rescue
מָנוֹעַ	mah-noh-*ah*	motor
מְכוֹנִית	meh-choh-*neet*	car
מוּסָף	moo-*sahch*	hood
שֶׁמֶן	sheh-*mehn*	oil
צְמִיגִים	tzee-mee-*geem*	tires

Doctor, Doctor, Give Me the News

Are you feeling a bit under the weather? Are you flummoxed and can't figure out what's wrong? Maybe you need to see the doctor. Doctors have studied medicine for many years and can help relieve your symptoms. Use these Hebrew words when talking to a doctor or nurse:

>> אָח (a**h**; *nurse*) (M)

אָחוֹת (ach-*hoht; nurse*) (F)

>> בֵּית חוֹלִים (bayt **h**oh-*leem; hospital*)

>> חֲדַר מִיּוּן (chah-*dahr* mee-*yoon; emergency room*) >>

>> רוֹפֵא (roh-*feh; doctor*) (M) >>

רוֹפָה (rohf-*ah; doctor*) (F)

The knee bone's connected to the leg bone: Identifying your body parts

GRAMMATICALLY SPEAKING

If you want to explain that some part of your body hurts, you can say . . . כּוֹאֵב לִי הַ (koh–*ehv lee* hah; *. . . hurts me*) and finish the sentence with the body part that hurts. Just take your pick of the Hebrew words in Table 14-2.

TABLE 14-2

Body Parts

Hebrew	Pronunciation	Translation
אַף	*ahf*	nose
עֵינַיִם	ay-*nah*-eem	eyes
בֶּרֶךְ	beh-*rech*	knee
בֶּטֶן	*beh*-tehn	stomach
חָזֶה	chah-*zeh*	chest
עֶצֶם	*ehtz*-ehm	bone
גַּב	*gahv*	back
קַרְסֹל	kahr-*sohl*	ankle
כָּתֵף	kah-*tehf*	Shoulder

(continued)

TABLE 14-2 *(continued)*

Hebrew	Pronunciation	Translation
לֵב	*lehv*	heart
אֹזֶן	*oh*-zehn	ear
פֶּה	*peh*	mouth
רֵאוֹת	reh-*oht*	Lungs
רֶגֶל	*reh*-gehl	leg
רֹאשׁ	*rohsh*	head
צַוָּאר	tzah-*vahr*	neck
זְרוֹעַ	*zroh*-ah	arm

GRAMMATICALLY SPEAKING

Be careful not to put the sentence in a different order, with the body part first. If you do, you have to conjugate the verb *aches* in the feminine form, because the names of most parts of the body are feminine (with the exception of breasts — go figure).

Describing your symptoms

Poor baby! Not feeling well? Do you have a כְּאֵב רֹאשׁ (keh-*ehv* rohsh; *headache*)? A כְּ (keh-*ehv* beh-tehn; *stomachache*)? A חֹם (*ḥom; fever*)? Have you הֲקֵיאָה (hee-*keh*-tah; *been throwing up*) (MS)? Oy vey. I hope you don't have the flu. Use some of these Hebrew words and phrases to describe your condition:

» אֲנִי חוֹלֶה. (ah-*nee* choh-*leh; I'm sick.*) (M)

   אֲנִי חוֹלָה. (ah-*nee* choh-*lah; I'm sick.*) (F)

» אֲנִי הֵקֵאתִי. (ah-*nee* hee-keh-*tee; I threw up.*)

» אֲנִיהִצְטַנַּנְתִּי. (ah-*nee* heez-tah-*nahn*-tee; *I caught a cold.*)

» אֲנִי לֹא מַרְגִּישׁ טוֹב. (ah-*nee* loh mahr-*geesh* tohv; *I don't feel well.*) (M)

   אֲנִי לֹא מַרְגִּישָׁה טוֹב (ah-*nee* loh mahr-gee-shah tohv; *I don't feel well.*) (F)

» אֲנִי אַלֶרְגִּי לְ . . . (ah-*nee* ah-*lehr*-gee leh; *I'm allergic to . . .*) (M)

   אֲנִי אַלֶרְגִּית לְ . . . (ah-*nee* ah-*leer*-geet leh; *I'm allergic to . . .*) (F)

» יֵשׁ לִי שִׁלְשׁוּל. (yaysh lee shil-*shool; I have diarrhea.*)

» יֵשׁ לִי חֹם. (yehsh lee hohm; *I have a fever.*)

Explaining your unique medical needs

Doctors have a hard time treating you if they can't see the full picture. You must fill your doctor in on your medical history. If you're allergic to medication or have any other medical conditions, tell your doctor. Otherwise, the results may be disastrous.

GRAMMATICALLY SPEAKING

The Hebrew phrase יֵשׁ לִי (yaysh–*lee*), which translates as "I have," literally means "there is to me." For this reason, the following phrases are gender–neutral. Anyone can use them without changing the conjugation:

» ב בְּהֵרָיוֹן אֲנִי. (ah-*nee* buh-hair-rah-*yohn; I'm pregnant.*)

» יֵשׁ לִי אַסְטְמָה. (yaysh lee ahst-*mah; I have asthma.*)

» יֵשׁ לִי מַחֲלַת נְפִילָה. (yaysh lee mah-chah-lah-*aht* neh-fee-*lah; I have epilepsy.*)

» יֵשׁ לִי קוֹצֵב לֵב . (yehsh lee kohtz-*ehv-lehv; I have a pacemaker.*)

» יֵשׁ לִי סֻכֶּרֶת. (yaysh lee sah-*kehr*-eht; *I have diabetes.*)

Receiving a thorough examination

After you walk into the examination room, usually the nurse comes in, weighs you, and takes your חֹם (hohm; *temperature*), דוֹפֶק (doh–fehk; *pulse*), and לַחַץ דָּם (lah-hahtz dahm; *blood pressure*). Then the doctor arrives and probably asks some of the following questions about your condition:

» אֵיךְ אַתָּה מַרְגִּישׁ ? (ehch ah-*tah* mahr-*geesh; How do you feel?*) (M)

אֵיךְ אַתְּ מַרְגִּישָׁה ? (ehch aht mahr-gee-*shah; How do you feel?*) (F)

» מָה מַפְרִיעַ לְךָ ? (mah mah-*free*-ah luhch*hah; What's bothering you?*) (M)

מָה מַפְרִיעַ לָךְ ? (mah mah-*free*-ah -*lach; What's bothering you?*) (F)

» ו כּוֹאֵב לְךָ מַשֶּׁהוּ? (koh-*ehv* leh-*hah* mah-sheh-hoo; *Does something hurt you?*) (M)

כּוֹאֵב לָךְ מַשֶּׁהוּ? (koh-*ehv* -*lach* mah-sheh-hoo; *Does something hurt you?*) (F)

» אֵיפֹה זֶה כּוֹאֵב לְךָ ? (ay-*foh* zeh koh-*ehv* leh-*chah; Where does it hurt you?*) (M)

אֵיפֹה זֶה כּוֹאֵב לָךְ ? (ay-*foh* zeh koh-*ehv* lach; *Where does it hurt you?*) (F)

» כּוֹאֵב לְךָ פֹּה? (koh-*ehv* luh-*chah* poh; *Does it hurt here?*) (M)

כּוֹאֵב לָךְ פֹּה ? (koh-*ehv* lach poh; *Does it hurt here?*) (F)

» כַּמָּה זְמַן הִרְגַּשְׁתָּ כָּכָה ? (kah-*mah* z-mahn heer-*gahsh*-tah kah-chah; *How long have you felt this way?*) (M)

? כַּמָּה זְמַן הִרְגַּשְׁתְּ כָּכָה (kah-*mah* z-*mahn* heer-*gahsht* kah-*chah*; *How long have you felt this way?*) (F)

>> ?הַאִם אַתָּה אָלֶרְגִּי (hah-*eem* ah-*tah* ah-*lehr*-gee leh-mah-sheh-*hoo*; *Are you allergic to anything?*) (M)

? הַאִם אַתְּ אָלֶרְגִּית לְמַשֶּׁהוּ (hah-*eem* ah-*aht* ah-*lehr*-geet leh-mah-sheh-*hoo*; *Are you allergic to anything?*) (F)

TIP

Take a look at Chapter 7, where I cover the days and weeks.

During the office visit, the doctor examines different body parts and asks for symptoms to determine a diagnosis. To prepare for the examination, they may ask you to do any of the following:

>> נָא לְהוֹרִיד אֶת הַחֻלְצָה . (nah leh-hoh-*reed* eht hah-chool-*tzah*; *Please take off your shirt.*)

>> נָא לִנְשֹׁם . (nah leen-*shom*; *Please breathe.*)

>> נָא לְהִשְׁתַּעֵל . (leh-hish-tah-*ehl*; *Please cough.*)

>> נָא לִשְׁכַּב עַל הַגַּב . (nah leesh-*kahv* ahl hah-*gahv*; *Please lie down.*)

>> תִּפְתַּח אֶת הַפֶּה . (teef-*tach* eht hah-*peh*; *Open your mouth.*) (M)

תִּפְתְּחִי אֶת הַפֶּה . (teef-teh-*chee* eht hah-*peh*; *Open your mouth.*) (F)

Paying attention to the diagnosis

After the doctor examines you, they give a אבחון (eev–*choon*; *diagnosis*). The following words are possible diagnoses:

>> אֲבַעְבּוּעוֹת רוּחַ (ah-*bah*-ah-boo-oht *roo*-ach; *chicken pox*)

>> דַּלֶּקֶת (dah-*leh*-keht; *an infection*)

>> הִצְטַנְּנוּת (heetz-tahn-neh-*noot*; *a cold*)

>> שַׁפַּעַת (shah-*pah*-aht; *the flu*)

>> צַהֶבֶת (tzah-*hehv*-eht; *jaundice*)

You may want to ask ? הַאִם זֶה מַדְבִּיק (hah-eem zeh-mahd–*beek*; *Is it contagious?*). I hope you don't need a זְרִיקָה (zree–*kah*; *injection*) or a תּוֹךְ וְרִידִי (tohch–vuh–ree–*dee*; *I.V.*).

CULTURAL WISDOM

When people are ill, wish them a רְפוּאָה שְׁלֵמָה (reh-foo-*ah* shuh-lay-*mah*; *a complete recovery*). If someone is quite ill, you can recite a לְחוֹלִים מִי שֶׁבֵּרַךְ (mee-sheh-bay-*rach* lehhoh-*leem*; *a special prayer for the sick*) during the Torah service in synagogue on Monday, Thursday, or Saturday morning.

Talkin' the Talk

Shulamit hasn't been feeling well. At the doctor's office, Shulamit asks her doctor whether she can figure out what's wrong.

Shulamit:	אֲנִי לֹא מַרְגִּישָׁה טוֹב .
	(ah-*nee* loh mahr-gee-*shah* tohv.)
	I don't feel well.
Doctor:	מָה מַפְרִיעַ לָךְ ?
	(mah maf-ree-*ah* lach?)
	What's bothering you?
Shulamit:	כּוֹאֵב לִי הַגָּרְעוֹן הָרֹאשׁ וְהַבֶּטֶן .
	(koh-*ehv* lee hah-gah-*rohn* hah-rohsh veh-hah-*beh*-tehn.)
	My ears, head, and stomach hurt.
Doctor:	מָה עוֹד ?
	(mah ohd?)
	What else?
Shulamit:	אֲנִי הֵקֵאתִי וְיֵשׁ לִי שִׁלְשׁוּל .
	(ah-*nee* hee-keh-tee veh-yesh lee shil-*shool*.)
	I threw up, and I also have diahrrea.
Doctor:	תִּפְתְּחִי אֶת הַפֶּה וּתְנַשְׁמִי בְּבַקָּשָׁה .
	(teef-*teh*-chee eht hah-*peh* veh-teen-sheh-*mee* beh-vah-kah-*shah*.)
	Open your mouth, and breathe, please.
Doctor:	יֵשׁ לָךְ שַׁפַּעַת אֲנַח רוֹשֶׁמֶת לָךְ מִרְשָׁם וְגַם אַתְּ צְרִיכָה לָנוּחַ שָׁבוּעַ .

(yehsh lach shah-*pah-aht*. Ah-nee roh-shem-*eht* lach meer-*shahm*. veh-gahm aht tz*ree*-chah lah-*noo*-ach shah-voo-*ah*.)

You have the flu. I'm writing you a prescription. And you also need to rest for a week.

● ●

Going to the pharmacy

Perhaps the doctor gives you a מִרְשָׁם (meer–*shahm*; *prescription*), and you need to go to the בֵּית מִרְקַחַת (bayt mehr–*kah*–chaht; *pharmacy*) to fill it. While you're there, you may want to pick up some of the following items:

➤➤ אֲקָלְמוֹל (ahk-ah-*mohl*; *Israeli nonaspirin*)

➤➤ אַסְפִּירִין (ahs-*preen*; *aspirin*)

➤➤ כַּדּוּרֵי שֵׁנָה (kah-dohr-*ay* shay-*nah*; *sleeping pills*)

➤➤ מַדְחֹם (m*ahd*-hohm; *thermometer*)

➤➤ שִׁעוּל תְּרוּפָה נֶגֶד (*troo*-fah *neh*-gehd shee-*ool*; *cough medicine*)

➤➤ תַחְבּוֹשֶׁת (tahch-*boh*-sheht; *bandage*)

➤➤ סוכריות מציצה טִפּוֹת נֶגֶד שִׁעוּל / (tee-*poht* shee-*ool*; *cough drops*)

➤➤ סֻכָּרִיּוֹת מְצִיצָה (soo-*kahr*-ee-oht meh-*tzee*-zah; *throat lozenges*)

➤➤ כַּדּוּרִים נֶגֶד חֻמְצִיּוּת (kah-*door*-eem neh-*gehd* choom-tzee-*yoot*; *antacid tablets*)

Talkin' the Talk

Prescription in hand, Shulamit goes to the nearest pharmacy to have her prescription filled.

Shulamit: שָׁלוֹם יֵשׁ לִי מִרְשָׁם מֵהָרוֹפֵא .

(shah-*lohm*. yesh li –meer-*shahm* mee-hah-roh-*feh*.)

Hello. I have a prescription from the doctor.

Pharmacist: תְּנִי לִי אֶת הַמִּרְשָׁם .

(th-*nee lee* eht hah-meer*shahm*.)

Give me the prescription.

Shulamit:	הִנֵּה אֶפְשָׁר לָקַחַת אָקָמוֹל גַּם כֵּן ؟

(hee-*nay* ehf-*shahr* lah-*kah*-chat ah-kah-*mohl* gahm kehn?)

Here it is. May I take Akamol (Israeli acedamenaphine), too?

Pharmacist:	בְּוַדַּאי הִנֵּה הַתְּרוּפוֹת שֶׁלָּךְ גְּבֶרֶת קְחִי שְׁנֵי כַּדּוּרִים שָׁלוֹשׁ פְּעָמִים בַּיוֹם בְּהֶמְשֵׁךְ הַשָּׁבוּעַ .

(beh-vah-*dai*. hee-*nay* haht-roo-*foht* sheh-*lach* ge-*ver*-eht. K*chee* sh-*nay* kah-doo-*reem* pah-ah-*mah*-yeem buh-*yohm* be-meh-*shech* -shah-*voo*-ah.)

Certainly. Here's your medicine, miss. Take two pills three times a day for a week.

Shulamit:	תּוֹדָה רַבָּה לְךָ .

(toh-*dah* rah-*bah* leh-*chah*.)

Thank you very much.

Doctor:	אֵין בְּעַד מָה תַּרְגִּישִׁי טוֹב וּרְפוּאָה שְׁלֵמָה .

(ayn be'ahd *mah*. tahr-*gee*-shee tohv veh-reh-foo-*ah* sh-lay-*mah*.)

No problem. Feel better, and have a complete recovery.

. . . .

CULTURAL WISDOM

THE RED SHIELD OF DAVID: REACHING OUT TO OTHERS IN NEED

The Israeli version of the Red Cross is the מָגֵן דָּוִד אָדֹם (mah-*gehn* dah-*veed* ah-*dohm*; *the Red Shield of David*). If you're in Israel, use the following emergency phone numbers:

- מִשְׁטָרָה (meesh-tah-*rah*; *police*): 100
- אַמְבּוּלַנְס (ahm-boo-*lahnce*; *ambulance*): 101
- מְכָאֵי אֵשׁ (meh-kah-*bay* aysh; *fire department*): 102

WORDS TO KNOW

אָח	ahh	nurse (MS)
אָחוֹת	ah-hoht	nurse (FS)
בֵּית חוֹלִים	bayt hoh-leem	hospital
בֵּית מִרְקַחַת	bayt mehr-kah-hat	pharmacy
חֵרוּם	chee-room	emergency
חוֹלָה	hoh-lah	sick (FS)
חוֹלֶה	hoh-leh	sick (MS)
חֹם	hohm	fever
דַּלֶקֶת	dah-lehk-eht	infection
דּוֹפֶק	doh-fehk	pulse
כַּדּוּרִים	kah-door-eem	pills
לַחַץ דָּם	lah-hahtz dahm	blood pressure
מִרְשָׁם	meer-shahm	prescription
רוֹפְאָה	roh-fah	doctor (FS)
רוֹפֵא	roh-feh	doctor (MS)
תְּרוּפוֹת	tuh-roo-foht	medicine
יֵשׁ לִי	yaysh lee	I have
זְרִיקָה h	zuh-ree-kah	shot

Getting Help After You've Been Robbed

If you've ever walked out to your car to see that it was broken into, you know the sinking feeling in your stomach. I hope you never have to experience it. But if someone steals something from you, you can say. . . . מִשֶּׁהוּ גָּנַב לִי אֶת הַ (mee-sheh-hoo gah-nahv lee eht hah . . .; *Someone stole my . . .*).

If someone breaks into your car or your house, you say

>> פָּרְצוּ לִי אֶת הַמְכוֹנִית . (pahr-*tzoo* lee eht hah-meh-choh-*neet; My car has been broken into.*)

>> פָּרְצוּ לִי ת לַבַּיֶת . (pahr-*tzoo* lee t lah-*bye*-yeet; My house has been broken into.*)

People will probably tell you to נָא לִפְנוֹת אֶל הַמִּשְׁטָרָה (nah leef-*noht* ehl hah-meesh-*tah-rah*; go to the police).

Or what if your house — חַס וְהַלִילָה (hahs veh-*ḥah*-lee-lah; *heaven forbid*) — catches on fire? Call the מְכַבֵּי אֵשׁ (meh-kah-bay *aysh; fire department*) for מַכַבֵּי אֵשׁ (meh-kah-baye ehsh; *firefighters*) to come and extinguish the אֵשׁ (aysh; *fire*).

Talkin' the Talk

Randy, an American tourist, was pickpocketed. Luckily, he sees a police officer and flags her down.

Randy:	סְלִיחָה שׁוֹטֶרֶת גָּנְבוּ לִי אֶת הָאַרְנָק .
	(slee-*chah* shoh-tair-*eht*, gahn-voo *lee* eht hah-ahr-*nahk*.)
	Excuse me, police officer. My wallet has been stolen.
Officer:	מָתַי זֶה קָרָה ?
	(mah-*tye* zeh kah-*rah*?)
	When did it happen?
Randy:	בְּדִיּוּק עַכְשָׁו .
	(beh-dee-*yook* ahch-*shahv*.)
	Just now.
Officer:	הֵם פָּגְעוּ בָּךְ ?
	(*hehm*, pah-*g-oo* buh-*chah?*)
	Did they hurt you?
Randy:	לֹא אֲנִי בְּסֵדֶר .
	(loh. ah-nee beh-*se*-dehr.)
	No. I'm all right.

WORDS TO KNOW

אַרְנָק	ahr-*nahk*	wallet
אֵשׁ	*aysh*	fire
לִפְרֹץ	lee-*frohtz*	to break into
לִגְנֹב	leeg-*nohv*	to steal
מַכַּבֵּי אֵשׁ	meh-kah-*bay* esh	fire fighters
מִשְׁטָרָה	meesh-ṭah-*rah*	police station
שׁוֹטֵר	shoh-*tair*	police officer (M)
שׁוֹטֶרֶת	shoh-tair-*ehet*	police officer (F)

FUN & GAMES

Using the words in the word bank, identify the body parts in Hebrew.

עֵינַיִם, בֶּטֶן, גַּב, כָּתֵף, אֹזֶן, רֶגֶל, רֹאשׁ, צַוָּאר, זְרוֹעַ

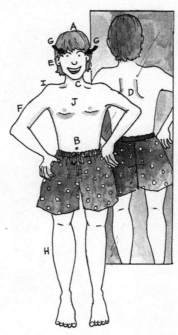

(A) _____

(B) _____

(C) _____

(D) _____

(E) _____

(F) _____

(G) _____

(H) _____

(I) _____

(J) _____

For the answers, go to Appendix C.

4

Diving Deeper into Hebrew Life

IN THIS PART . . .

Gauge the Israeli character.

Untangle the history of the Middle East.

Come to terms with war and peace.

Chapter **15**

An Introduction to Israel

t's hard to talk about the Hebrew language without also talking about where it's most widely spoken and the place where it all started: The Land and modern State of Israel. The story is a complex and exciting one.

Discovering Multicultural Israel

Israel is a multicultural, multifaith democratic country in הַמִּזְרָח הַתִּיכוֹן (hah-*meez-rah* hah-*tee*-ḥohn; *the Middle East*). Although it's a Jewish state, that connotation isn't religious; Israel has no official religion! Israel inherited the so-called "millet system" from the Ottoman Empire, which allows different religious groups to govern their own religious affairs. Matters of personal status (birth, marriage, divorce, and so on) are handled independently by the religious communities. The Israeli מֶמְשָׁלָה (mehm-*shah*-lah; *government*) allows for חֹפֶשׁ דָּת (ḥoh-fesh daht; *religious freedom*) and recognizes 14 religions and provides funding for their services. At the same time, Israel is a secular דֶּמוֹקְרַטְיָה (deh-moh-*krah-tee*-ah; *democracy*) with secular law — like the United States — that's separate from religious law.

Jewish-Israelis are a diverse bunch, hailing from every part of the globe where Jews wandered in their גָּלוּת (gah-*loot*; exile). About half of Jewish Israelis are מִזְרָחִי (Meez-*rah*-hee; *Mizrahi/Eastern*) Jews, which means that their recent ancestors migrated (and in many cases were expelled) from Arab lands following the 1948 Arab–Israeli War. The other half are אַשְׁכְּנַזִּים (ahsh-*kehn*-ah-zi; *Ashkenazi Jews*), which means that they are Jewish, and their ancestors ended up in Europe after they were expelled from ancient Judea way back when before migrating back to the Land of Israel — generally as refugees fleeing antisemitic violence.

A small group of Israeli Jews are אֶתְיוֹפִּים (eh-*tee-oo*-peem; *Ethiopian*) Jews. Some believe that they're descendants of the lost tribe of Dan; others attribute their origin to the offspring of the Israelite King Solomon and African Queen of Sheba.

Today in Israel, these distinctions are disappearing, as many Jewish Israelis have parents and grandparents from different groups. Most Israelis identify with one of four major Jewish religious subgroups, which fall on a spectrum of religious observance: חִלּוֹנִיִּים (*ḥee*-loh-*nee*-eem; *secular*), מְסָרְתִּיִּים (mah-*sohr-rah*-tee-eem) דתִי ם (*dah*-tee-eem; *religious or Torah-observant or Modern Orthodox*), and חרדי ם (Har-*eh*-deem; *ultra-Orthodox*). While there are some Israelis that affiliate with Reform and Conservative congregations, they are a minority as these denominations are a mostly an American phenomenon. Due to complicated politics, the Israeli government only recognizes Orthodox rabbis, so if you want to get married by a Reform rabbi in Israel, the Israeli government won't recognize it. There's a workaround, though: You can get married by mail in Argentina without ever setting foot there. And that the Israeli government will recognize. לֵךְ תֵּדַע (lehḥ *tey*-dah; *go figure*).

The largest ethnic minority in Israel is עֲרָבִים (ah-*rah*-veem; *Arabs*), the majority of whom are מֻסְלְמִים מ (moohs-*lah*-meem; *Muslim*) and the minority of whom are נוֹצְרִים (*nohtz*-reem; *Christian*). They're full Israeli אֶזְרָחִים (*ehz*-rah-ḥim; *citizens*) with equal rights under the law, with challenges in terms of equality of opportunity and discrimination that minorities in other countries also face. In 2015, the Israeli parliament passed Resolution 922, which earmarks billions of shekels to close the economic gap between the state's Jewish and Arab citizens. People in this latter group understand and describe their identity in different ways, including עֲרָבִי יִשְׂרָאֵל (*Ahr*-vey yees-*rah*-ehl; *Israeli Arabs*), פָלַסְטִינִי יִשְׂרָאֵלִי (Pah-*lehs-tee*-nah-ee yees-*rah-ehl*-ee; *Israeli–Palestinian*), and פָלַסְטִינִי אֶזְרַח יִשְׂרָאֵל (Pah-*lehs-tee-nah*-ee ehz-raḥ yees-*rah*-eh-leel; *Palestinian with Israeli citizenship*).

Other ethnic-minority Israeli citizens are the דְרוּזִים (duh-*rooz*-eem; *Druze*), בֶּדוּאִי (beh-*doh*-ee; *Bedouin*), אַרְמֶנִים (Ahr-*meh*-neem; *Armenians*), and צֶ'רְקֶסִים (Chehr-*kehs*-eem; *Circassians*). Add to the mix asylum seekers who found refuge in Israel from such far-flung places as Vietnam, Bosnia, and Eritrea, many of whom are naturalized citizens. Israel also has a sizable foreign-worker population — many from Thailand, West Africa, and the Philippines — that makes up 4 to 5 percent of its population; some of these workers eventually become Israeli citizens. Together, these groups make up the vibrant and diverse population that is Israel.

Touring Israeli Cities and Towns

They say that Jerusalem prays, Tel Aviv plays, and Haifa works. These are the three major cities in Israel.

The capital of the State of Israel is יְרוּשָׁלַיִם (yeh-*roo-sha*-lye-eem; *Jerusalem*). There, you will find Israel's כְּנֶסֶת (kuh-*nehs*-eht; *parliament*); בֵּית מִשְׁפָּט עֶלְיוֹן (*beyht meesh*-paht *ehl*-yohn; *Supreme Court*); and the קִרְיַת הַמֶּמְשָׁלָה (*Kahr*-yat Hah-*Mehm*-shah-lah; *Government Village*), which houses the Bank of Israel, along with government offices and ministries. In addition to all the government stuff, there's lots of fun stuff to do all over. You can hang out at the דרחוב מדרכה רחוב (ov meed-rah-hohv; *outdoor mall*) on Ben Yehuda Street, check out the cafes in the German Colony, or go to the עִיר עַתִּיקָה (*eer* ah-*tee*-kah; *Old City*) and wander through its four quarters: Christian, Armenian, Arab, and Jewish. While you're in the עִיר עַתִּיקָה (*eer* ah-*tee*-kah; *Old City*), of course, be sure to visit Judaism's holiest site, הַכֹּתֶל (hah-koh-tehl; *the Western Wall*), the last remnant of Solomon's בֵּית הַמִּקְדָּשׁ (*Beyht*-Hah-*Meek*-dahsh; *Temple*). [Technically, the wall was a retaining wall, not the בֵּית הַמִּקְדָּשׁ (*Beyht*- Hah-*Meek*-dahsh; *Temple*) itself.]

Jerusalem is also holy to two other monotheistic religions: אִסְלָאם (*ees*-lahm; *Islam*) and נַצְרוּת (*Nahtz*-root; *Christianity*). Islam teaches that the site of Judaism's בֵּית הַמִּקְדָּשׁ (*Beyht*- Hah-*Meek*-dahsh; *Temple*) was also the site where the prophet Muhammed ascended to heaven. In the seventh century, 700 years after the Jewish בֵּ הַמִּקְדָּשׁ (*Beyht*- Hah-*Meek*-dahsh; *Temple*) was destroyed; a mosque was built on that same spot. In the Christian quarter, דֶּרֶךְ הַיִּסּוּרִים (deh-*reh* hah-yee-*soor*-eem; *the Via Dolorosa*) and כְּנִיסַת הַקֶּבֶר (kuh-nee-*saht* hah-*keh*-vehr; *the Church of the Holy Sepulcher*) are holy to Christians.

תֵּל אָבִיב (*Tehl* ah-*veev*; Tel Aviv) is Israel's biggest city, known for its vibrant cultural scene. The city's proper name is תֵּל אָבִיב-יָפוֹ (*Tehl* ah-*veev* - *yah*-foh; Tel Aviv-Jaffa) as the cities merged in 1950, two years after the state was born. But locals still refer to these neighboring areas by their distinct names. Whatever you call this area, great hangouts include דִּיזֶנְגּוֹף) Dizengoff) Street; שׁוּק הַפִּשְׁפְּשִׁים (shook hah-peesh-peesh-eem; *the flea market*) in יָפוֹ (*yah*-foh; *Jaffa*); and the bohemian Florentine neighborhood in Tel Aviv known for its artist workshops, cafes, trendy restaurants, outdoor markets, and even graffiti tours!

Israel's third-largest city is חֵיפָה (*hee*-fah; *Haifa*), a progressive and mixed port city with large Jewish and Arab populations. A diverse and pluralistic city, חֵיפָה (*hee*-fah; *Haifa*) is also home to the Bahá'i World Center, the spiritual and cultural center of the Bahá'i religion. Once a year, the city hosts חַגִּים הַחַגִּים (*hah*-geem hah-hah-geem; *festival of festivals*), which celebrates חֲנֻכָּה (hah-*noo*-kah; *Hanukkah*) חַג הַמּוֹלָד, (hahg hah-*moh*-lahd; *Christmas*), and the Muslim עִיד (*eehd; Eid*).

Other Israeli cities include מוֹדִיעִין (moh-*dee*-een; *Modi'in*), Israel's largest planned city; נְצֶרֶת (nahtz-raht; *Nazareth*), an Arab Christian city with a sizable Muslim population; and אום אֶל-פַּחֶם (Um el-Faḥem.; Arabic: أم الفحم; literally: *Mother of Charcoal*), a majority Arab Israeli town that's considered to be a cultural and social capital of sorts for Arab Israelis in what's called the Triangle Region of Israel. Nearby, in the north, there are דָּלִיַת אֶל-כַּרְמֶל (dah-lee-*aht* hah-*kahr*-mehl; Arabic: دالية ٱلْكَرْمِل; *Daliyat al Karmel*), a Druze town; and רִיחָנִיָּה (ree-*ḥahn*-yah; *Rehaniya*), a Circassian town. To the south are the beach town אילת (aye-*loht*; *Eilat*), the major city in Israel's Negev Desert; בְּאֵר שֶׁבַע (buh-ehr-*sheh*-vah; *Beer-Sheva*); and a predominantly Bedouin city, רַהַט (rah-haht; Arabic: رهط; *Rahat*).

CULTURAL WISDOM

Israel is a multiparty democracy with a unicameral legislature called the כְּנֶסֶת (kuh-*nes*-eht; *Knesset*) with 120 seats; continual בְּחִירוֹת (buh-*ḥeer*-oht; *elections*); a free press; and an active, independent judiciary, including a Supreme Court that also acts as a high court of justice. Freedom House rates Israel as חוֹפְשִׁי (*ḥof*-shee; *free*), with a score of 76/100 (33/40 political rights, 43/60 civil liberties).

WORDS TO KNOW

הַמִּזְרָח הַתִּיכוֹן	hah-meez-*rah* hah-tee-*ḥ*ohn	the Middle East
מֶמְשָׁלָה	mehm-*shah*-lah	government
מִזְרָחִי	*Meez-rah*-hi	Middle Eastern Jews (literally: Eastern)
אַשְׁכְּנַזִּי	Ahsh-*keh*-nahz-ee	European Jews
חִלּוֹנִי	*ḥ*ee-*loh*-nee	secular
חֲרֵדִי	hah-rey-dee	ultra-Orthodox (literally: fearing)
מָסוֹרְתִּי	mah-*soh*-rah-tee	traditional
דָּתִי	*Dah*-tee	Torah-observant
עֲרָבִים	ah-*rah*-veem	Arabs
יְהוּדִים	yeh-*hoo*-dee	Jews
מֻסְלְמִי	*moos*-lah-mee	Muslim
נוֹצְרִי	*nohtz*-ree	Christian
עִירְעַתִּיקָה	eer ah-*tee*-kah	Old City (of Jerusalem)
הַכֹּתֶל	hah-*koh*-tehl	Western Wall (holiest site in Judaism)

אִסְלָאם	*ees*-lahm	Islam
נַצְרוּת	*nahtz*-root	Christianity
יַהֲדוּת	yah-*hah*-doot	Judaism
כְּנֶסֶת	kuh-*nehs*-eht	Israeli parliament
בְּחִירוֹת	beh-*hee*-roht	elections

Starting at the Beginning: A Brief History Lesson

Around the late Bronze Age (1200 BCE), small communities of people who would eventually be part of the Kingdom of Israel started to emerge in the hill country of Canaan, the land that is now the modern State of Israel and surrounding territories. Around 1050 BCE, the Israelite Kingdom arose. This kingdom managed to last for the reigns of three kings (Saul, David, and Solomon) before it split in the Northern Kingdom of Israel and the Southern Kingdom of Judah. Long story short, the Northern Kingdom was conquered by the Assyrian Empire in 722 BCE and its inhabitants scattered around the empire. (You may have heard about the Ten Lost Tribes; these people are those tribes.)

The Southern Kingdom of Judah held on until it was conquered by the next empire, the Babylonians, and its inhabitants were exiled in 586 BCE. The exile lasted about 70 years — long enough for Jews to remain cohesive and for their culture to evolve, but not so long that they forgot צִיּוֹן (*tzee*-ohn; *Zion*, another name for the Land of Israel).

Then along came the Persian Empire, the next bad boy on the block, which conquered everything and said, "Hey, all you peoples displaced by the last empire, now you can go back where you came from." So, the יְהוּדִים (yeh-*hoo*-deem; *Jews*) did.

Back to Judah they went, rebuilding their בֵּית הַמִּקְדָּשׁ (*Beyht- Hah-Meek-*dahsh; *Holy Temple*) in Jerusalem and resuming their sacrificial rites. There they stayed for 500 years or so, being independent, autonomous, semiautonomous, or subjugated.

Then along came the Romans. The Romans! The Romans! The Romans!

Romans tried to deal with the subjugated peoples they brought into their empire by letting them do their own thing (maintain their identity and culture), while letting them know just who was boss by levying מִסִּים (mee-*seem*; *taxes*), setting rules, and that kind of stuff. All stuff the Romans thought was perfectly reasonable and their subjects — in this case the Jews — didn't particularly like.

Things came to a head in 66 CE when the Jews revolted against the Romans, as documented in Josephus' *The Jewish Wars* and archaeological remains. To be honest, things didn't go well for the Jews. They lost, big-time. בֵּית הַמִּקְדָּשׁ (*Beyht-Hah-Meek-dahsh The Holy Temple*) in Jerusalem burned to a crisp. Thousands of deaths occurred. Jews were taken away to Rome's capital as slaves. So many slaves flooded the market that the price of slaves dropped throughout the empire. The Arch of Titus in Rome stands in testament to Rome's crushing victory.

Jews were exiled from their capital, which the Romans renamed Alia Capitolina. Those who didn't die or weren't taken away as slaves migrated to other parts of אֶרֶץ יִשְׂרָאֵל (*ehr*-rehtz yees-*rah*-ehl; *the Land of Israel*) and to other parts of the empire. Throughout the millennia, Jews always lived in אֶרֶץ יִשְׂרָאֵל (*ehr*-rehtz yees-*rah*-ehl; *the Land of Israel*), although it began to be called by different names. The Romans renamed the area Syria–Palestina, a name chosen to rub the Jews' faces in it. (They got the name from an ancient sea people, the Philistines, who gave the ancient Israelites (and a lot of other ancient peoples) a lot of grief.)

Here's where things get even more interesting. After this devasting event, the יהוּדִים (yeh-*hoo*-deem; *Jews*) didn't go away, as in disappearing into the fabric of other peoples and cultures in the ancient world. They held on to their identity and way of life, transforming their culture, once rooted in the Land of Israel and the sacrificial cult in Jerusalem, into a portable way of life based on the study of sacred writings, prayer, and law. This way of life is what today we call Judaism. יַהֲדוּת (yah-*hah*-doot; *Judaism*), one of the three monotheistic religions along with נַצְרוּת (*Nahtz*-root; *Christianity*) and אִסְלָאם (*ees*-lahm; *Islam*), is an *Orthopraxic* religion, one that emphasizes behavior over belief. It is also an ethnic religion, similar to, say, Hinduism or Shintoism, that doesn't seek adherents but is a system of beliefs, behavior, and belonging for a specific set of people — in this case, the יהוּדִים (yeh-*hoo*-deem; *Jews*). Judaism is more dispersed than other ethnic religions because . . . well, the הוּדִים (yeh-*hoo*-deem; *Jews*) are more dispersed. And there you go.

CULTURAL WISDOM Jews are from Judea and arrived in Europe due to enslavement or expulsion from their homeland in the Eastern Mediterranean. The map shown in Figure 15-1 shows how Jews were driven out of most areas of Europe over a 500-year period.

CULTURAL WISDOM Catherine the Great confined Jews in the Russian Empire to the Pale of Settlement in 1791. (See Figure 15-2.)

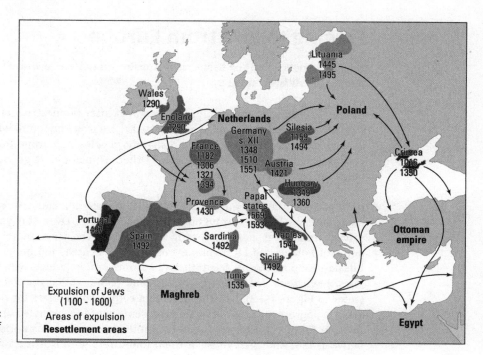

FIGURE 15-1:
The expulsion of the Jews.

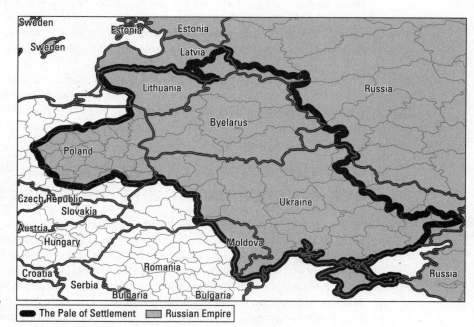

FIGURE 15-2:
The Pale of Settlement.

The Pale of Settlement Russian Empire

Fleeing to and from Europe

Now let's move from the Eastern Mediterranean (where Jews are from) to Europe (where many Jews ended up).

Jews were either brought to Europe as slaves after the destruction of the Second Temple in Jerusalem in 70 CE or migrated there over time. And when the Roman Empire collapsed, what knit the disparate peoples of Europe together was the Christian church. Jews were the great Other. Things didn't go well for them, to put it mildly.

Jews were vilified, segregated, harassed, murdered, and chased out of various places in Europe throughout the Middle Ages. Over 500 years, Jews were driven from their homes, fleeing eastward to the then-more-tolerant kingdoms of Poland and Lithuania. Eventually, these areas fell under the rule of the Russian Empire during the 18th and 19th centuries, which was less tolerant of Jews. Jews were confined to a geographic region called the Pale of Settlement (refer to Figure 15-2), which made them convenient targets for the violent antisemitic pogroms unleashed by popular sentiment (often fueled or directed by the Russian Empire's leaders). Some two million Jews fled this antisemitic violence between 1881 and 1914. Most of them found refuge in North America, but a tiny minority washed up in Ottoman Syria, a geographic entity at the time, which today is known as אֶרֶץ יִשְׂרָאֵל (ehr-ehtz yees-rah-ehl; *Land of Israel*) and also Historic Palestine. The גְּבוּלוֹת (gah-voo-loht; *borders*) of what we consider to be the modern State of Israel didn't exist yet; they came later. The plot thickens.

CULTURAL WISDOM

The map in Figure 15-3 shows how the Eastern Mediterranean under Ottoman administrative control was divided into districts. Jews called this area אֶרֶץ יִשְׂרָאֵל (*ehr*-ehtz yees-*rah*-ehl *the Land of Israel*), and the Arabs referred to the region as Syria or Palestine.

Wanting to be in charge: Nationalism, self-determination, and the Jewish State

While Jews in Eastern Europe were subject to pogroms which triggered a mass wave of migration, the Jews in Western Europe were being emancipated, let out of the ghettos, and allowed to take part in civilian life — at least legally; as far as the reality on the ground was concerned, not so much. Antisemitism continued to exist. A watershed moment was the infamous Dreyfuss trial, in which a French–Jewish army captain was erroneously convicted of treason. Although Dreyfuss was eventually exonerated, the mobs who gathered outside the courthouse chanting "Death to the Jews" made an impression on Austrian–Jewish journalist Theodor Herzl. Influenced by growing nationalism and the rise of emerging nation-states, Herzl concluded that the Jews would never be safe in Europe; they needed to get into the nation-state game with a nation-state of their own. He wasn't the first to make this observation or come up with the idea, but when he published his ideas in his 1896 pamphlet *The Jewish State*, it struck a chord, and Jewish nationalism, otherwise known as צִיּוֹנוּת (tzee-ohn-*noot*; *Zionism*), got organized.

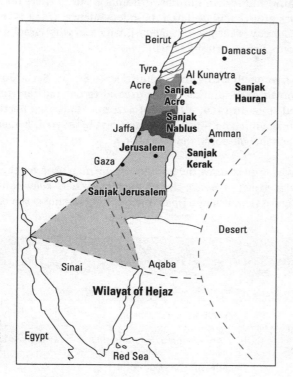

FIGURE 15-3: The Middle East under Ottoman control.

Jews weren't the only ones influenced by European nationalism; Arabs were as well. In fact, the first Zionist Congress and the First Arab Congress happened within a few years of each other, both in Europe. The First Zionist Congress convened in Basel, Switzerland, in 1897, and the First Arab Congress happened in 1903 in Paris, France, in 1903.

I think you can see that things were heading to a collision. with two nationalisms, two peoples, and one general area of land called by different names.

After World War I, the Ottoman Empire collapsed. Britain and France carved up the empire into territories known as *mandates*. With the collapse of the old world order of multinational empires, a new one of nation-states for different cultural groups emerged. Arab and Jewish nationalism — and eventually מְדִינַת יִשְׂרָאֵל (Meh-dee-*naht Yees*-rah-ehl; *the State of Israel*) — emerged from this global transformation.

Violence between Arab and Jewish populations in the British Mandate led in 1936 to the recommendation of partition, a common remedy to ethnic strife at the time. The plan was shelved and reintroduced in 1947 by the newly formed United Nations. With the passage of the partition plan, UN Resolution 181, war broke out between Arab and Jewish militias. Britain got out of there on May 15, 1948, a couple of hours after Israel declared its independence. (May 15 in 1948 was שַׁבָּת [Shah-baht; Saturday or the Jewish Sabbath], which is why Israel's announcement came a few hours before Britain's exit.)

Armies from five neighboring Arab countries — Egypt, Syria, Jordan, Lebanon, and Iraq — joined Arab militias on the ground to use military force against the newly declared state. In 1949, a series of agreements ceased hostilities and drew an armistice line, which became the de facto גְּבוּל (guh-vool; border) known as הַקַּו הַיָּרֹק (hah-kahv hah-yah-rohk; the Green Line).

CULTURAL WISDOM

The ink that was used to draw the borders on the map used for the 1949 armistice agreements was green — hence the name קַו הַיָּרֹק (hah-kahv hah-yah-rohk; The Green Line). Figure 15-4 is a מַפָּה (mah-pah; map) that shows the borders.

WORDS TO KNOW		
אֶרֶץ יִשְׂרָאֵל	eh-rehtz yees-rah-ehl	Land of Israel
בֵּית הַמִּקְדָּשׁ	beyt hah-meek-dahsh	Holy Temple
מְדִינַת יִשְׂרָאֵל	meh-dee-naht yees-rah-ehl	State of Israel
הַקַּו הַיָּרֹק	hah-kahv hah-yah-rohk	The Green Line
גְּבוּל	guh-vool	border
גְּבוּלוֹת	guh-vool-oht	borders
מַפָּה	mah-pah	map

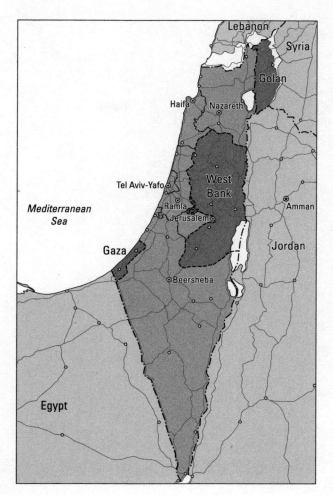

FIGURE 15-4:
Israel in 1948.

» **Acknowledging progress**

» **Seeing environmentalism as a path to peace**

Chapter **16**

War and Peace

War and peace. We're not talking about Tolstoy's famous novel, but the history of the Middle East. In this chapter, you'll get a chance to find out about Israel's wars and prospects for peace. There are some bright spots and reasons to be hopeful; not everything is doom and gloom.

In this chapter, I give you the Hebrew vocabulary to talk about what Israelis call הַמַּצָּב (hah-*mahtz*-ahv; *the situation*).

The Big Bang

Conflict in the Middle East between יְהוּדִים (yeh-*hoo*-deem; *Jews*) and עֲרָבִים (ah-*rah*-veem; *Arabs*) didn't start when יִשְׂרָאֵל (yees-*rah*-ehl; *Israel*) declared its independence; things had been brewing for some time. For centuries, Jews and Arabs lived in the Eastern Mediterranean as neighbors under the Ottoman Turks. Under Muslim rule, Jews were *dhimmis* — a Muslim–Arabic term meaning that they were both a protected and subjugated minority. As nationalism swept across Europe, Arabs and Jews were inspired to create their own movements for self-determination. The problem was that both groups envisioned their nation-state on the same piece of land. As part of their political strategy to create alliances to undermine the Ottoman Turks in World War I, the British, in a series of letters known as the Hussein McMann Correspondence, promised Arabs עַצְמָאוּת (ahtz-*mah*-oot; *independence*) if they would rise up against the Turks. The British also promised the Jews a national home in Palestine in the Balfour Declaration of 1917. Unbeknownst to both Arabs and Jews, the British had already made a secret agreement in 1916 with the French (the Sykes–Picot Agreement), in which the two Great Powers promised each other that they'd divide מִזְרָח הַתִּיכוֹן (*meez-*raḥ hah-*tee*-hon; *the Middle East*) between them after the Ottoman Empire collapsed.

WORDS TO KNOW		
הַמַּצָּב	hah-*mahtz*-ahv	the situation
עֲרָבִים	ah-*rah*-veem	Arabs
יְהוּדִים	yeh-*hoo*-deem	Jews
יִשְׂרָאֵל	yees-*rah*-ehl	Israel
עַצְמָאוּת	ahtz-*mah*-oot	independence
מִזְרָח הַתִּיכוֹן	meez-*rah*hah-tee-*hohn*	Middle East

War

In November 1947, the newly formed או"ם [(*oom; UN* United Nations)] passed Resolution 181, calling for the partition of the British Mandate of Palestine into two states: an Arab state and a Jewish state. With that announcement, a מִלְחָמָה (mil-ḥah-mah; *war*) of partition broke out between Arab and Jewish militias. In the shadow of the שׁוֹאָה (shoh-ah; *Holocaust*), Jews felt that they had nowhere else to go. At this point, the British Empire had essentially collapsed. Six months later, the British made a hasty retreat from their Mandate of Palestine. יִשְׂרָא (yees-*rah*-ehl; *Israel*) declared its independence on May 14, 1948, and armies from five neighboring Arab states joined the fighting to prevent the partition of Palestine and the emergence of a Jewish State. The war waged for more than a year and ended with an armistice and a line drawn in green ink on a map. This line formed the de facto גְּבוּלוֹת (guh-*voo*-loht; *borders*) of the new מְדִינַת יִשְׂרָאֵל (meh-dee-*naht* yees-*rah*-ehl; *State of Israel*).

During the war, about 750,000 Arab denizens of the area left, fled, or were forced out and became פְּלִיטִים (plee-*teem*; *refugees*). Land that was designated for the Arab State become part of Egypt and Jordan. About 10,000 Jews who found themselves on the other side of the Green Line (in territory that was occupied and later annexed by Transjordan) also left, fled, or were forced out. Jews who had been living in other areas of the former Ottoman Empire, now different Arab countries, found themselves unwelcome in lands where they had made their home for centuries. About 750,000 Jews in Arab lands left, fled, or were forced out. Most of them fled to the newly established מְדִינַת יִשְׂרָאֵל (meh-*dee*-naht yees-*rah*-ehl; *State of Israel*), where they were absorbed into and became citizens of the new state.

Israelis and Palestinians call this war by different names. For Jewish Israelis, the war was מִלְחֶמֶת עַצְמָאוּת (mil-*ḥeh*-meht hah-ahtz-*mah*-oot; *the War of Independence*) or מִלְחֶמֶת שִׁחְרוּר (mil-*ḥeh*-meht *shiḥ*roor; *War of Liberation*), but for Arab Palestinians, the event was a Nakba (*nahk*-bah Arabic: النكبة; *disaster*).

In 1956, Israeli army forces clashed with Egypt over the blockage of the Suez Canal and incursions across the Israeli border by armed non-state Arab militias. In Israel, these clashes are called מִבְצַע קָדֵשׁ (*Meev*-zah *Kah*-desh; *Suez Operation*) or מִלְחֶמֶת סִינַי (mil-*ḥeh*-meht *see*-nah-ee; *Sinai War*). Egypt and other Arab countries refer to this event as the Tripartite Aggression (ahl *ood*-wahn aht too-*laht*-tee; Arabic: العدوان الثلاثي; *Al-ʿUdwān aṭ-Ṯulāṯiyy*).

Tensions continued to brew and were brought to a boiling point in mid-1967. Egyptian and Syrian armed forces mobilized on Israel's borders to the south and to the north. Israeli decided to preempt what it saw as an inevitable מִלְחָמָה (mil-*ḥah*-mah; *war*) and strike first. Jordan got into the game firing over the גְּבוּל (guh-*vool*; *border*). Six days later, hostilities came to a halt, and Israel found itself in control of שְׁטָחִים (shtah-*ḥeem*; *territories*) that had previously been under Jordanian, Egyptian, and Syrian control. Israel began administering the territory as an occupying power, in accordance with the Geneva Convention. In Israel, this war is called מִלְחֶמֶת שֵׁשֶׁת הַיָּמִים (mil-*ḥeh*-meht *shay*-sheht hah-*yah*-meem; *the Six-Day War*). In the Arab world, the war is known as النكسة. (*Nak*-sah; *Setback*) or 1967 حرب, (*Harb* 1967; *War of 1967*).

In the wake of its נִצָּחוֹן (nee-tzah-*ḥohn*; *victory*), Israel declared that it would exchange land for שָׁלוֹם (shah-*lohm*; *peace*). Two months later, the fourth Arab League Summit convened in Khartoum and declared, "No, No, No": no peace, no negotiations, and no recognition of Israel.

הַשְּׁטָחִים (hah-*shtah*-heem; *the territories*) that came under Israeli control were רְצוּעַת עַזָּה (ree-*tzoo*-aht ah-*zah*; Arabic: قِطَاعُ غَزَّة *Qiṭāʿu Ġazzah*; *Gaza Strip*) and what is referred to as either the West Bank (as it's the West Bank of Jordan, which occupied and then annexed it in 1950) or its Biblical names יְהוּדָה (yeh-*hoo*-dah; *Judah*) and שֹׁמְרוֹן (shohm-*rohn*; *Samaria*).

In 1973, it was Israel's turn to be surprised when Egyptian and Syria forces blew past the Israeli צָבָא (tzah-vah; *army*) guarding the 1967 cease-fire lines and battled for nearly three weeks. Israelis refer to this event as מִלְחֶמֶת יוֹם כִּפּוּר (mil-heh-*meht* yohm *keh-poor*; *the Yom Kippur War*), as it began on Judaism's holiest day, יוֹם כִּפּוּר (yohm *keh-poor*; *Yom Kippur* or *Day of Atonement*). The war is referred in the Arab world as the Ramadan War, as it occurred during Ramadan, the holiest month in the Islamic calendar. The war ended in a truce, changing the power dynamics in the Middle East.

WORDS TO KNOW

מִלְחָמָה	meel-*hah*-mah	war
שׁוֹאָה	shoh-*ah*	Holocaust
גְּבוּל	guh-*vool*	border
גבולות	guh-*vool*-oht	borders
נִצָּחוֹן	neetz-ah-*hohn*	victory
הַשְׁטָחִים	hah-*shtah-h*eem	the territories
צָבָא	tzah-vah	army
פִּגוּעַ	pee-*goo*-ah	terrorist attack
כִּבּוּשׁ	*kee*-boosh	occupation
מַחְסוֹם	*mah*-sohm	checkpoint
שָׁלוֹם	*shah*-lohm	peace

Paths to Peace

Four years after the מִלְחֶמֶת יוֹם כִּפּוּר (mil-heh-*meht* yohm *keh-poor*; *Yom Kippur War*), the leader of מִצְרַיִם (meetz-*rah*-eem; *Egypt*) took a bold step: President Muhammad Anwar el-Sadat traveled to Israel's capital, יְרוּשָׁלַיִם (yeh-*roo*-shah-*lye*-eem; *Jerusalem*) and addressed the כְּנֶסֶת (keh-*nehs*-seht; *parliament*). His message: no more מִלְחָמָה (mil-*hah*-mah; *war*). U.S. President Jimmy Carter brokered a deal, and in 1979, מִצְרַיִם (meetz-*rah*-eem; *Egypt*) and יִשְׂרָאֵל (yees-*rah*-ehl; *Israel*) signed a peace treaty making Egypt the first Arab country to sign a peace treaty with Israel. In exchange, as promised, יִשְׂרָאֵל (yees-*rah*-ehl; *Israel*) delivered אֶרֶץ (ehr-ehtz; *land*) for שָׁלוֹם (shah-lohm; *peace*) and vacated the Sinai Peninsula, that had been under its control since the 1973 war. The peace treaty has held after all these years, and it wasn't the last. Israel signed a peace treaty with יַרְדֵּן (*yahr*-dehn; *Jordan*) in 1994 and with בַּחְרַיִן (bah-*rain*; Bahrain, the אִחוּד הָאֱמִירִיּוֹת הָעֲרָבִיּוֹת (ee-*hood* hah-ah-*meer*-oht hah-*ahr*-rah-vee-oht; United Arab Emirates), סוּדָן (*soo*-dahn; Sudan), and מָרוֹקוֹ (mah-*rahk*-oh; Morocco) in 2020.

Peace with the פָּלֶסְטִינִים (pah-lehs-tee-nye-eem; *Palestinians*) has proved to be elusive, but it isn't for lack of trying. In 1991, סְפָרַד (suh-*fah*-rahd; *Spain*) hosted a conference in Madrid, co-hosted by the אַרְצוֹת הַבְּרִית (ahrz-oht hah-*breet*; *the United States*) and בְּרִית הַמּוֹעָצוֹת (breet-hah-*moh*-ahz-oht; *the Soviet Union*), and attended by representative of יִשְׂרָאֵל (yees-*rah*-ehl; *Israel*), סוּרְיָה (soo-*ree*-yah; *Syria*), לְבָנוֹן (leh-*voh*-nohn; *Lebanon*), and the פָּלֶסְטִינִים (pah-lehs-*tee-nye*-eem; *the Palestinians*). This conference led to direct talks between representatives of the Israelis and the Palestinians, which in turn led to mutual recognition between Israel and the Palestinians, as represented by the Palestine Liberation Organization, also known as the אָשָ"ף (*ah*-ashaf; *PLO*). Then came the תַּהֲלִיךְ אוֹסְלוֹ (tah-ha-*leeh* ohs-loh; *Oslo Accords*) in 1993 and 1995.

The goal of the תַּהֲלִיךְ אוֹסְלוֹ (tah-ha-*leeh* ohs-loh; *Oslo Accords*) was שָׁלוֹם (shah-lohm; *peace*) and בִּטָּחוֹן (beeh-tah-*hohn*; *security*) for Israel and an independent מְדִינָה (meh-*dee*-nah; *state*) for the Palestinians — what is known as a two-state solution. To pave the way for that solution, the שְׁטָחִים (shtah-*heem*; *territories*) that came under Israeli control after the 1967 War were carved up into areas A, B, and C. Area A was under complete control of הָרָשׁוּת הַפָּלֶסְטִינִית (hah-rah-*shoot* hah-pah-lahs-ste-*nah-yeet*; *the Palestinian Authority*), B was under joint control of the Palestinian Authority and Israel, and C was under complete Israeli control. Most of the Palestinians in this territory, called by names including The West Bank (in reference to the West Bank of the Hashemite Kingdom of Jordan) and Biblical names, יְהוּדָה וְשֹׁמְרוֹן (yeh-*hoo*-dah veh-*shohm*-rohn; *Judea* and *Samaria*) live in areas A and B, which comprise about 40 percent of the territory.

The agreement was meant to be an interim step until a final solution was reached. But a final solution was never reached.

Offers were made in 2000 by Israeli Prime Minister Barak and rejected by Palestinian Authority Prime Minister Yasser Arafat. In 2008, Israeli Prime Minister Olmert offered Palestinian Authority Prime Minister Mahmoud Abbas 94 percent of the territories, withdrawal from Jerusalem's Holy Basin (where sites important to three monotheistic religions are), and a land swap for the last 6 percent. This offer was rejected.

But there's תִּקְוָה (teek-vah; *hope*). Palestinian Authority Chairman Mahmoud Abbas and Israeli Defense Minister Benny Gantz met in early 2022. As David Broza sings in his revised edition of his song יִהְיֶה טוֹב (yeh-*hee*-yeh tohv; *It Will Be OK*): עוֹד נִלְמַד לִחְיוֹת בְּיַחַד (ohd neel-*mahd* lee-*hee-yoht* beh-*yah*-hahd; *one day we will learn to live together*).

Environmental Cooperation May Be the Key

Look at מִזְרַח הַתִּיכוֹן (meez-rahah-tee-hohn; the Middle East) on a topographical map, and something will jump out at you immediately: Not a lot of מַיִם (mai-eem; water) is there. That's right. The Middle East is a lot of מִדְבָּר (meed-bahr; desert). It won't surprise you that water scarcity is a source of סִכְסוּךְ (seeh-sooh; conflict) in the region. Here's what might surprise you: It also may be part of the פִּתָּרוֹן (pee-tah-rohn; solution). Experts note that countries that cooperate over water conservation never go to war with each other. Israel is a world leader in הַתְפָּלַת מַיִם (heet-pah-aht mai-yeem; desalination), wastewater reuse, and treatment, as well as agricultural water conservation. And here's the good news: A lot of שִׁתּוּף פְּעֻלָּה (shee-toof peh-oo-lah; cooperation) is happening on water issues in the Middle East.

The organization EcoPeace Middle East https://ecopeaceme.org) is composed of Israeli, Jordanian, and Palestinian אֵיכוּת הַסְּבִיבָה (ee-hoot hah-suh-vee-vah; conservation) activists. One of its signature programs is called מַיִם וּשְׁכֵנוּת טוֹבָה (mah-yeem oo-shee-hah-noot toh-vah; Good Water Neighbors) (website: https://old.ecopeaceme.org/projects/community-involvement/). The program brings Israeli, Palestinian, and Jordanian communities together to discuss their shared water concerns. An even more ambitious proposal is the Green Blue Deal for the Middle East, (https://ecopeaceme.org/wp-content/uploads/2021/03/A-Green-Blue-Deal-for-the-Middle-East-EcoPeace.pdf), which advocates using the sun and the oceans to create energy and water security for the entire region. As part of this vision, Israel, Jordan, and the United Arab Emirates signed a deal in November 2021 to swap desalinated מַיִם (mah-yeem; water) and אֶנֶרְגְיָה סוֹלָארִית (eh-nehr-gee-ah soh-lahr-eet; solar energy).

WORDS TO KNOW		
פָּלַסְטִינִים	Pah-lees-tee-nye-eem	Palestinians
אָשָׁ"ף	Ah-shaf	PLO
הָרָשׁוּת הַפָּלַסְטִינִית	Hah-ree-shoot hah-pah-lees-tee-nah-yeet	The Palestinian Authority
מְדִינָה	meh-dee-nah	state
מִצְרַיִים	Meetz-rah-yeem	Egypt
תַהֲלִיךְ אוֹסְלוֹ	tah-hah-leeh ahs-loh	Oslo Accords

תִּקְוָה	*teek*-vah	hope
מַיִם	*Mah*-yeem	water
מִדְבָּר	*Meed*-bahr	desert
סִכְסוּךְ	see**h**-soo**h**	conflict
פִּתָרוֹן	peh-*tah*-rohn	solution
שִׁתּוּף פְּעֻלָּה	shee-*toof* peh-oo-*lah*	cooperation
אֶנֶרְגְּיָה סוֹלָארִית	eh-nehr–*gee*-ah soh-*lahr*-eet	solar energy

5

Sacred Hebrew

Chapter **17**

Let's Get Biblical

The Hebrew Bible comprises three parts: תּוֹרָה (*Toh*-rah *Torah*), which consists of the five books of Moses (Genesis, Exodus, Leviticus, Numbers, and Deuteronomy); נְבִיאִים (neh-vee-*eem*; *Prophets*), which includes Judges, Joshua, Samuel, and Kings as well as books of prophets such as Isaiah, Jeremiah, and Amos; and כְּתוּבִים (keh-too-*veem*; *The Writings*), which includes the Psalms, the Song of Songs, and Ruth. Together, these sections are called the תָּנָ"ך (tah-*nahh*) in Hebrew. Calling the Hebrew Bible the Old Testament is a misnomer because the concept is Christian. Refer to the Jewish Biblical canon by its Hebrew name, תָּנָ"ך, or simply the Hebrew Bible.

Although the modern Hebrew you may hear spoken on the streets of Tel Aviv and around the world bears much similarity to its biblical progenitor, you can notice a few differences. Comparing modern Hebrew with biblical Hebrew is like comparing modern English with its Shakespearian cousin — the same language, but different.

In this chapter, I introduce you to a few of the key features of biblical Hebrew to help you understand the world's best-selling book in its original language.

Figuring Out the Word Order in Biblical Hebrew

The first difference in biblical Hebrew is word order. Although in modern Hebrew, the noun or pronoun often starts a sentence, in biblical Hebrew, a verb often takes the lead. Table 17-1 shows a couple of examples.

TABLE 17-1

Checking Out Biblical Word Order

Modern Hebrew	Biblical Hebrew
הַשֵׁם אָמַר אֶל בְּנֵי יִשְׂרָאֵל (hah-*shem* ah-*mahr* ehl buh-*nay* yees-rah-*ehl; The Eternal One Said to the Children of Israel)*	... וַיֹּאמֶר הַשֵּׁם אֶל בְּנֵי יִשְׂרָאֵל לֵאמֹר (vah-yoh-*mehr* hah-*shehm* ehl buh-*nay* yees-rah-*ehl* leh-eh-*mohr*; (Literally: *Said the Eternal One to the Children of Israel, saying)*
מֶלֶךְ חָדָשׁ קָם בְּמִצְרַיִם שֶׁלֹּא יָדַע אֶת יוֹסֵף (meh-lehch chah-dahsh kahm buh-meez-rah-yeem sheh-loh-yah-dah eht yoh-sehf; *a new king arose in Egypt that did not know Joseph)*	וַיָּקָם מֶלֶךְ־חָדָשׁ עַל־מִצְרָיִם אֲשֶׁר לֹא־יָדַע אֶת־יוֹסֵף: (vah-yah-kahm meh-lehch-chah-dahsh ahl-meetz-rah-yeem ah-sherloh-yah-dah eht yoh-sehf; *(There) Arose a new king over Egypt that did not know Joseph)* (Exodus 1:8)

GRAMMATICALLY SPEAKING

Biblical Hebrew possesses something unique called the וָו הַהִפּוּךְ (vahv hah-hee-*pooch*), which I like to call *the amazing reversing Vav* (ו). You place the וָו הַהִפּוּךְ (vahv hah-hee-*pooch*) in front of a past-tense verb, and the verb magically changes to future tense. Place it in front of a future-tense verb, and the verb amazingly changes to the past tense. הֲקִמֹתִי (hah-kee-*moh*-tee) means "I established," for example. But if you put the amazing reversing **Vav** (ו) in front, וַהֲקִמֹתִי (veh-kee-moh-*tee*) means, "I will establish," as in this verse:

... וַהֲקִמֹתִי אֶת־בְּרִיתִי בֵּינִי וּבֵינֶךָ וּבֵין (veh-hah-kee-moh-*tee* eht *bree*-tee bay-*nee* oo-*vayn*-chah; *I will establish my covenant between me and you . . .*) (Genesis: 17:7)

Look at another example. שִׁנַּנְתָּם means "taught them." But with the amazing reversing **Vav** (ו) in front, וְשִׁנַּנְתָּם becomes "you shall teach them," as in this verse:

וְשִׁנַּנְתָּם לְבָנֶיךָ (veh-shee-nahn-*tahm* leh-vah-*neh*-chah; *You shall teach them to your children . . .*) (Deuteronomy 6:7)

Note: Sometimes, in addition to its role in changing verb tense, the וָו הַהִפּוּךְ does double duty and means "and."

Clipped verbs are another phenomenon in biblical texts. You get a clipped verb when the end letter ה (*hey*) disappears, which happens often when a verb is paired with a וָו הַהִפּוּךְ.

The Hebrew verb for "he will see," for example, is (*yeer-eh"*). An example of this verb's getting clipped with a וָו הַהִפּוּךְ being placed in front of it is וַיַּרְא (vah-*yahr*; *he saw*). Watch closely, because three things happen:

1. The ה (*hey*) drops off.

2. Because the ה (*hey*) dropped off, the vowel below the י (*yod*) changes from an *ee* sound to an *ah* sound.

3. Finally, an amazing reversing **Vav** (ו) is added to the front of the word, changing it from past tense to future tense.

Table 17-2 shows some common biblical verbs with וָו הַהִפּוּךְ (vahv hah-hee-*pooch*). I put an asterisk next to clipped verbs.

TABLE 17-2

Looking at Biblical Verbs

Hebrew	Pronunciation	Translation
וַיֵּלֶךְ	vah-yee-*lech*	he went
וַיַּרְא *	vah-*yahr*	he saw
וַיְהִי	vah-yeh-*hee*	it came to pass
וַיַּעַשׂ *	vah-*yah*-ahs	he made
וַיְבָרֶךְ	vah-*yah*-reḥ	he blessed
וַיַּעַן *	vah-*yah*-ahn	he answered
וַתַּעַן	vah-tah-*ahn*	she answered
וַיְצַו *	vah-yeh-*tzahv*	he commanded
וַיֵּצֵא	vah-yeh-*tzeh*	he went out
וַיְדַבֵּר	vah-yeh-*dah*-behr	she went out
וְאָהַבְתָּ	vuh-ah-hahv-*tah*	you shall love
וְשִׁנַּנְתָּם	vuh-shee-nahn-*tahm*	you (MP/FP) shall teach
וְשָׁמְרוּ	vuh-shahm-*roo*	they will guard
וַהֲקִמֹתִיו	veh-hah-kee-moh-*tee*	I will establish
וַיֹּאמֶר	Va-*yoh*-mehr	he said

WORDS TO KNOW

בְּנֵי יִשְׂרָאֵל	uh-nay yees-rah-*ehl*	children of Israel
בְּרִיתִי	bree-*tee*	my covenant
לְבָנֶיךָ	leh-vah-*neh*-ḥah	to your children
מֶלֶךְ	*meh*-lehch	king
מִצְרַיִם	meetz-*rah*-yeem	Egypt
וְשִׁנַּנְתָּם	vah-shee-*nahn*-tam	you shall teach
וַיָּקָם	vah-yah-*kahm*	arose
וַיֹּאמֶר	vah-yoh-*mehr*	he said
יִשְׂרָאֵל	yees-rah-*ehl*	Israel

Emphasizing When God Really Meant It

Sometimes when the Bible says something, it *really* means it. And because the Bible doesn't have italics, it uses a special tense called the *emphatic tense* (or emphatic verb construct) to show when God meant business. The word to be emphasized is repeated, and during the second repetition, the suffix וּן (*oon*) or וֹת (*ot*) is added. See whether you can find them in the following passages:

> שָׁמוֹר תִּשְׁמְרוּן אֶת־מִצְוֹת יְהֹוָהאֱלֹקיכֶם (sha-*mohr* teesh-mah-*roon* eht meetz-*voht* hah-shehm eh-loh-hay-*chehm*; *You shall surely keep the commandments of the Eternal One your God.*) (Deuteronomy 6:17)

> וַיֹּאמֶר הַנָּחָשׁ אֶל־הָאִשָּׁה לֹא־מוֹת תְּמֻתוּן (vah-*yoh*-mehr hah-nah-*chahsh* ehl hah-ee-*shah* loh moth teh-moot-*toon*; *The snake said to the woman, you are absolutely not going to die.*) (Genesis 3:4)

Biblical text also demonstrates emphasis by placing the command form of a verb in front of the future–tense verb. (See Appendix A for more examples of future tense.) Here's an example:

> וַיְצַו יְהֹוָה אֱלֹהִים עַל־הָאָדָם לֵאמֹר מִכֹּל עֵץ־הַגָּן אָכֹל תֹּאכֵל׃וּמֵעֵץ הַדַּעַת טוֹב וָרַע לֹא תֹאכַל מִמֶּנּוּ כִּי בְּיוֹם אֲכָלְךָ מִמֶּנּוּ מוֹת תָּמוּת

vah-yay-*tzahv* hah-*shehm* eh-loh-*heem* ahl-hah-ah-*dahm* leh-eh-*mohr* mee-*kohl* aytz hah-*gahn* ah-*chohl* toh-*chehl*, oo-mey-*aytz* hah-dah-*aht* tohv vah-*rah* loh toh-*chahl* mee-*meh*-noo kee buh-*yohm* och-leh-*chah* mee-*meh*-noo moht tah-*moot*.

God the Eternal One commanded the human being saying from all the trees in the garden you can absolutely eat. But from the Tree of Knowing Good and Evil you shall not eat from it, for on the day of your eating (it) you will absolutely die. (Genesis 2:16-17)

CULTURAL WISDOM

The Hebrew word for the first human being אָדָם (ah–*dahm*) is connected to the Hebrew word for earth אֲדָמָה (ah–dah–*mah*), from which the human being was created. According to rabbinic wisdom, this being was initially neither male nor female and was actually a hermaphrodite. Hence, calling this creature "a man" is a bit of a misnomer. Better translations are "human being" or "earthling."

WORDS TO KNOW

עֵץ	aytz	tree
הַגָּן	hah-*gahn*	the garden
אִשָּׁה	ee-*shah*	woman
לֵאמֹר	leh-eh-*mohr*	saying
מִצְוֹת	meetz-*voht*	commandments
מוֹת	*moht*	you shall die
נָחָשׁ	nah-*chahsh*	snake
שָׁמוֹר	shah-*mohr*	you shall keep, guard
תֹּאכֵל	toh-*chehl*	you shall eat
וַיְצַו	vah-yay-*tzahv*	commanded
וַיֹּאמֶר	vah-yoh-*mehr*	said

NAMING THE BOOKS OF THE BIBLE

The books of the Hebrew Bible have Hebrew names, of course! Although this list is by no means exhaustive, here are the Hebrew names of the books with which you may be most familiar:

* בְּרֵאשִׁית	buh-ray-*sheet*	Genesis
* שְׁמוֹת	sh-*moht*	Exodus
* וַיִּקְרָא	vah-yee-*krah*	Leviticus
* בְּמִדְבָּר	bah-meed-*bahr*	Numbers
* דְּבָרִים	duh-vahr-*eem*	Deuteronomy
* יְהוֹשֻׁעַ	yeh-hoh-shoo-*ah*	Joshua
* שׁוֹפְטִים	shohf-*teem*	Judges
* מְלָכִים	muh-lah-*cheem*	Kings
* יְשַׁעְיָהוּ	yeh-sha-ah-*yah*-hoo	Isaiah
* יִרְמְיָהוּ	yeer-mee-*ya*-hoo	Jeremiah
* תְּהִלִּים	teh-hee-*leem*	Psalms
* מִשְׁלֵי	meesh-*lay*	Proverbs
* שִׁיר הַשִּׁירִים	sheer hah-sheer-*eem*	The Song of Songs
* קֹהֶלֶת	koh-*hehl*-eht	Ecclesiastes

Wishing, Intending, and Prohibiting

GRAMMATICALLY SPEAKING

In Biblical texts, when the text wants to indicate the speakers' wishes or intends something to happen (as in *and it shall come to pass*), an *ah* or an *eh* is added at the end of the word. This tense is called *cohortive*. Here's an example:

אֶתֵּן (eh-*tehn*; *I will give*) becomes אֶתְּנָה, which is hard to translate into English but means "I really intend to give." When you see the *a* or *ah* at the end of the verb, it means, "I really intend to do this thing I'm saying I'm gonna do!" Don't be confused by the וְ in the following passage. It's not an amazing reversing **Vav** but a regular old וְ, which translates as "and":

וְאֶתְּנָה בְרִיתִי בֵּינִי וּבֵינֶךָ וְאַרְבֶּה אוֹתְךָ בִּמְאֹד מְאֹד: (veh-eht-*nah* vree-*tee* bay-*nee* oo-vayn-neh-**h**ah . . .; *And I really will give my covenant between me and you [between your children]* . . .) (Genesis 17:2)

In another example, הַגֵּיד (hah–*geed; tell*) is in a command form. You add two things to this verb. First, add the ה at the end; again, it's hard to translate into English but basically means "I really want you to do this thing I'm asking you to do!" To soften it, נָא is added in this case, which means "please." (How very polite!) Take a look at an example of this phenomenon in action:

וַיֹּאמְרוּ אֵלָיו הַגִּידָה־נָּא לָנוּ בַּאֲשֶׁר לְמִי־הָרָעָה הַזֹּאת . . . (hah-gee-*dah-nah* lah-*noo* bah-ah-*shehr* leh-*mee* hah-rah-*ah* hah-*zoht; Tell us please on whose account is this evil* . . .) (Jonah 1:8)

Biblical Hebrew expresses prohibitions by using the Hebrew word for "no," לֹא (*loh*) or אַל (*ahl*) plus the imperfect tense, as in: לֹא תִּרְצָ֖ח (loh teertz-*ah; don't murder*) (Exodus 20:13). In general, לֹא is for general prohibitions (such as *don't murder*), whereas אַל is used for forbidding a specific action, such as אַל־תִּשְׁלַח יָדְךָ (ahl teesh-*lah*h yahd-*hah; do not lay*; literally: *stretch out your hand*) (Genesis 22:12).

Deciphering One-Word Wonders

Sometimes, words occur or appear once in the Hebrew Bible. These words are called **Hapax Legomena** (hah-*pahx* leh-goh-meh-*nah*). They're special because if they occur only once, we can't be certain what they mean in their biblical contexts, which of course leaves plenty of room for the imagination! Some of the most famous **Hapax Legomena** include.

➤➤ תֹּהוּ וָבֹהוּ (toh-*hoo*-vah-voh-*hoo*): From Genesis 1:2: The earth was תֹּהוּ וָבֹהוּ over the surface of the deep and a wind from God sweeping over the water."

What does תֹּהוּ וָבֹהוּ mean? Scholars have written many volumes about it, but no one knows for sure. The New Jewish Publication Society translates it as "unformed and void."

➤➤ סֻלָּם (soo-*lahm*): Genesis 28:12: He had a dream; a סֻלָּם was set on the ground and its top reached to the sky, and angels of God were going up and down on it.

What's a סֻלָּם? Nobody knows, as it appears just once in the Hebrew Bible, but the New Jewish Publication Society translates it as "stairway." Gunther Plaut's commentary in *The Torah: A Modern Commentary* (UAHC Press) indicates that the word can also be translated as "ladder" or "ramp" and notes, "The סֻלָּם in Jacob's dream reflects an ancient belief in a cosmic bond between heaven and earth."

TIP

You can search up more one-word wonders in an amazing reference book called *A New Concordance of the Bible,* compiled by Avraham Even-Shoshan (Kiryat-Sefer Ltd, Jerusalem), which lists every word and phrase in the Hebrew Bible in alphabetical order and shows exactly where it appears throughout the תנ"ך (*Tanach; Hebrew Bible*). If you want to go into further depth with biblical Hebrew, I recommend the *Grammatical Concepts 101 for Biblical Hebrew: Learning Biblical Hebrew Grammatical Concepts through English Grammar,* by Gary A. Long (Hendrickson Publishers).

Counting Down the Greatest Biblical Hits

Many people have a list of their favorite biblical quotations. In the following list, I share some of mine with you:

» אֶת־עַמִּי וְיַעַבְדֻנִי (shuh-*lacht* eht ah-*mee* vuh-yah-ahv-*doo*-nee; *Let My people go, so that they might serve Me.*) (Exodus 9:1)

» וְשָׁמְרוּ בְנֵי־יִשְׂרָאֵל אֶת־הַשַּׁבָּת לַעֲשׂוֹת אֶת־הַשַּׁבָּת לְדֹרֹתָם בְּרִית עוֹלָם (veh-shahm-*roo* buh-nay yees-rah-*ehl* eht hah-shah-*baht* bay-*nee* oo-vayn buh-*nay* yees-rah-*ehl* oht hee leh-oh-*lahm; The Children of Israel shall guard the Sabbath, making the Sabbath for generations. Between Me and the Children of Israel, it shall be a sign forever.*) (Exodus 31:16)

» זְאֵב וְטָלֶה יִרְעוּ כְאֶחָד וְאַרְיֵה כַּבָּקָר יֹאכַל־תֶּבֶן וְנָחָשׁ עָפָר לַחְמוֹ לֹא־יָרֵעוּ וְלֹא־יַשְׁחִיתוּ בְּכָל־הַר קָדְשִׁי (zuh-*ehv* vuh-tah-*leh* yeer-*oo* keh-eh-*hahd* veh-ahr-*yeh* kuh-bah-*kahr* yoh-*hahl* teh-vehn . . . loh yah-*reh*-oo veh-loh-yash-*hee*-too buh-*hohl* har kohd-*shee; The wolf and the lamb shall eat together, And the lion shall eat straw like the fox. . . . You shall not hurt or destroy in all my Holy Mountain.*) (Isaiah 65:25)

» וְכִתְּתוּ חַרְבוֹתָם לְאִתִּים וַחֲנִיתוֹתֵיהֶם לְמַזְמֵרוֹת (vuh-*hee*-teh-*too* *hahr*-voh-*tahm* leh-ee-*teem* veh-hah-*nee*-toh-*thei*-hehm leh-mahz-*mehr*-oht; *They shall beat their swords into plowshares, their spears into pruning hooks.*) (Isaiah 2:4)

» כַּמַּיִם מִשְׁפָּט וּצְדָקָה כְּנַחַל אֵיתָן (vah-yee-*gahl* kuh-*mah*-yeem meesh-*paht* oo-tzeh-dah-*kah* kuh-*nah*-hahl ay-*tahn; Let law and order flow like water, justice like a strong stream.*) (Amos 5:24)

» שֶׁמָּצָאתִי אֵת שֶׁאָהֲבָה נַפְשִׁי (sheh-mah-tzah-*tee* eht sheh-ah-hah-*vah* nahf-*shee; I have found the one my soul loves.* (Song of Songs 3:4)

» אֲנִי לְדוֹדִי וְדוֹדִי לִי (ah-*nee* leh-doh-*dee* vuh-doh-*dee* lee; *I am my beloved's, and my beloved is mine.*) (Song of Songs 6:3)

» מַיִם רַבִּים לֹא יוּכְלוּ לְכַבּוֹת אֶת־הָאַהֲבָה וּנְהָרוֹת לֹא יִשְׁטְפוּהָ (*mah*-yeem rah-*beem* loh yooch-*loo* leh-chah-*boht* eht hah-hah-*vah* oo-neh-hah-*rot* loh yeesh-teh-*foo*-hah; *Many waters cannot extinguish love, nor can rivers drown it out.*) (Song of Songs 8:7)

» כִּי אֶל־אֲשֶׁר תֵּלְכִי אֵלֵךְ וּבַאֲשֶׁר תָּלִינִי אָלִין עַמֵּךְ עַמִּי וֵאלֹהַיִךְ אֱלֹהָי (kee ehl ah-*shehr* til-*chee* ay-*laych* oo-vah-ah-*shehr* tah-*lee-nee* ah-*leen* ah-*mech* ah-*mee* veh-eh-loh-*hye-eech* eh-loh-*hye*; *For wherever you go, I will go, wherever you lodge I will lodge, your people shall be my people, and your God, my God.*) (Ruth 1:16)

» לַכֹּל זְמָן וְעֵת לְכָל־חֵפֶץ תַּחַת הַשָּׁמָיִם (lah-*kohl* zuh-*mahn* veh-*ayt* leh-**h**ohl cheh-fehtz tah-**h**aht hah-shah-*mye-eem*; *For everything there is a season, and there is a time for every purpose under heaven.*) (Ecclesiastes 3:1)

WORDS TO KNOW

אַהֲבָה	ah-hah-*vah*	love
עַם	*ahm*	people
דּוֹד	*dohd*	beloved (M)
לְעוֹלָם	leh-oh-*lahm*	forever
מַיִם	mah-*yeem*	water
מִשְׁפָּט	meesh-*paht*	law
נַחַל	nah-**h**ahl	river
נֶפֶשׁ	*neh*-fehsh	soul
אוֹת	*oht*	sign
רַב	*rahv*	great
צְדָקָה	tzuh-dah-*kah*	justice

FUN & GAMES

I've hidden the Hebrew names of the following (English) books of the Bible in this word search for you to track down. The answers are in Appendix C.

Deuteronomy	Joshua	Numbers
Exodus	Judges	Proverbs
Genesis	Leviticus	Psalms

```
M  B  A  M  I  D  B  A  R  T
I  A  R  K  I  Y  A  V  I  E
S  H  O  F  T  I  M  E  S  H
H  A  U  H  S  O  H  E  Y  I
L  S  C  B  M  S  F  B' A  L
E  D' H  L  I  H  M  H  F  I
I  A  G  E  R  E  T  C  T  M
D' V  R  H  A  M  S  V  O  E
T  E  F  S  V  O  H  D  C  Y
B  M  H  I  D' T  M  B  S  A
```

Chapter **18**

Like a Prayer

Most people yearn to respond to the wonders around them. Jews express this yearning in prayer and blessings directed to God. Judaism has prayers and blessings for almost every occasion and event, from the ridiculous to the sublime. This fact reveals a core teaching of Judaism: that even the daily and seemingly mundane tasks of our lives offer opportunities for encountering the Divine.

In this chapter, I give you some basic vocabulary so you can understand these prayers and blessings, and I tell you how to navigate the Jewish prayer book. Finally, I give you some tips on ways to make all the blessings and prayers more meaningful.

Blessing: The Basics

Rabbis have taught that the nature and purpose of blessing can be found in under-standing the word itself. The Hebrew word for "blessing," בְּרָכָה (brah–*hah*), comes from the root that contains the characters ב (*beit*), ר (*resh*), and כ (*haf*). Other Hebrew words that share this root are

» בְּרְכַּיִם (beer-*kah*-yeem; *knees*)

» בְּרֵכָה (bray-*chah*; *pool*)

What's the connection? We bend our בִּרְכַּיִם (beer-*kah*-yeem; *knees*) to honor an important dignitary, such as a king, queen, or president. A בְּרָכָה (brah-*ḥah; bless-ing*) is similar because it's a way of honoring God. When we jump into a בְּרֵכָה (bray-*chah; pool*), the water can shock us and wake us up. It also surrounds us. So, too, when we recite a בְּרָכָה (brah-*ḥah*), we wake up to blessings around us and remind ourselves that the Divine is everywhere. We must acknowledge God's presence around us: here, between you, others, the tree, the rock, and everywhere!

Judaism teaches that all creation — humanity, nature, animals, and the cosmos — emanate from One Divine Source. All is connected. Judaism teaches that to enjoy anything — food, beauty in nature, or a momentous occasion — without acknowledging its Divine Source in the form of a blessing is akin to thievery!

Deciphering the blessing formula

Judaism, being the ritualized religion that it is, has a formula on which blessings are built. Most blessings start with three basic parts:

>> בָּרוּךְ (bah-*rooch*; *Blessed* or *Praised*): The first part of the blessing, which offers blessings and praise.

>> אַתָּה יְיָ (ah-*tah* ah-doh-*naye*; *You God*): The second part of the blessing formula, which includes God's ineffable name.

>> אֱלֹקֵינוּ מֶלֶךְ הָעוֹלָם (eh-loh-*hay*-noo *meh*-le**ḥ** hah-oh-*lahm*; *Our God and Ruler of the Cosmos*): The third part of the blessing formula, which acknowledges that our God is a universal God, a God of all peoples. This portion of the blessing reminds us that because all people are connected to God, they all must be treated justly.

After the בָּרוּךְ אַתָּה יְיָ מֶלֶךְ אֱלֹקֵינוּ מֶלֶךְ הָעוֹלָם, you can add whatever blessing is specific to the occasion. See "Identifying some basic blessings" later in this chapter for examples of blessings that can follow this beginning.

Scholar Marcia Falk came up with an egalitarian version of the blessing formula: נְבָרֵךְ אֶת עֵין הַחַיִּים (neh-vahr-*ehḥ* eht ayin hah-*ḥah*-*yeem*; *Let us bless the Source of Life*).

CULTURAL WISDOM

In Jewish tradition, Jews no longer pronounce the name of God. During the times when the ancient Temple stood in Jerusalem, only once a year, on Yom Kippur, would the High Priest utter God's name. Today, in fact, God's name — spelled with the four Hebrew characters י (*yud*), ה (*hey*), ו (*vav*,) and another ה (*hey*) — is considered to be so holy that it's rarely written, instead abbreviated with the characters י (*yud*) and י (*yud*). So how do you pronounce it? Many Jewish communities opt to address God as אֲדֹנָי (ah-doh-*naye*), which literally means "My Lord" or

"My Master." Other traditions speak of God as יָהּ (*yah*) or שְׁכִינָה (sh**ḥ**eh-**ḥ**ee-*nah*), which means "God's presence." Some say that the four letters of God's name correspond to the various tenses of the verb *to be*: the infinitive, present, past, and future. In other words, God is the Eternal One, beyond all time and space. I use this translation of God's name in this book.

WORDS TO KNOW		
אַתָּה	ah-*tah*	You (divine)
בָּרוּךְ	bah-*rooch*	bless/praise
אֱלֹקֵינוּ	eh-loh-*hey*-noo	our God
הָעוֹלָם	hah-oh-*lahm*	the Cosmos
מֶלֶךְ	meh-leh**ḥ**	Ruler (divine)

CULTURAL WISDOM

Millenia before Albert Einstein (who was Jewish, by the way) posited his theory of relativity and the time–space continuum, the Hebrew language intuited this universal truth. The Hebrew word עוֹלָם (oh-*lahm*), which I translate as "cosmos," contains the concepts of infinity in both time and space. In modern Hebrew, לְעוֹלָם (leh-oh-*lahm*) means "forever," and עוֹלָם (oh-*lahm*) means "world" or "universe." The concepts of time and space are embedded in the Hebrew word עוֹלָם, revealing an understanding that time and space are indeed connected.

Identifying some basic blessings

Judaism has a blessing for almost everything. Again, most blessings begin with the same basic blessing formula, . . . בָּרוּךְ אַתָּה יְיָ מֶלֶךְ אֱלֹקֵינוּ מֶלֶךְ הָעוֹלָם (bah-*rooḥ* ah-*tah* ah-doh-*naye* eh-loh-*hey*-noo meh-leh hah-oh-*lahm* meh-le hah-oh-*lahm*; *Praised are You Eternal One Ruler of the Cosmos*), and conclude with words specific to a particular blessing, depending on the circumstance. The following sections tell you some common times to say blessings and the words you need to say them.

Before eating bread

Before eating bread, you follow the basic blessing with הַמּוֹצִיא לֶחֶם מִן הָאָרֶץ (hah-moh-*tzee leh*-em meen hah-*ah*-rehtz; *who brings forth bread from the Earth*). So, the entire blessing looks like this.

בָּרוּךְ אַתָּה יְיָ מֶלֶךְ אֱלֹקֵינוּ מֶלֶךְ הָעוֹלָם הַמּוֹצִיא לֶחֶם מִן הָאָרֶץ

(bah-rooḥ ah-tah ah-doh-naye eh-loh-hey-noo meh-leḥ hah-oh-lahm meh-lech hah-oh-lahm hah-moh-tzee leh-ḥem meen hah-ah-rehtz.)

Blessed are You, Eternal One our God, Universal Presence, who brings forth bread from the Earth.

Before drinking wine

Before you drink wine, you finish the basic blessing with בּוֹרֵא פְּרִי הַגֶּפֶן (boh-reh puh-ree hah-gah-fehn; *who creates the fruit of the vine*). The whole blessing in Hebrew is

בָּרוּךְ אַתָּה יְיָ אֱלֹקֵינוּ מֶלֶךְ הָעוֹלָם בּוֹרֵא פְּרִי הַגֶּפֶן

(bah-rooḥ ah-tah ah-doh-naye eh-loh-hey-noo meh-leḥ hah-oh-lahm meh-leḥ hah-oh-lahm boh-ray puh-ree hah-gah-fehn.)

Blessed are You, Eternal One our God, Universal Presence, who creates the fruit of the vine.

Over Sabbath candles

Over Sabbath candles, you follow the basic blessing phrase with אֲשֶׁר קִדְּשָׁנוּ בְּמִצְוֹתָיו וְקִדְּשָׁנוּ לְהַדְלִיק נֵר שֶׁל שַׁבָּת (ah-shair keed-shah-noo buh-meetz-voh-tahv veh-keed-shah-noo leh-hahd-leek nair shehl shah-baht; *who made us holy with Divine commandments and commanded us to kindle Shabbat lights*). It looks like this in Hebrew:

בָּרוּךְ אַתָּה יְיָ אֱלֹקֵינוּ מֶלֶךְ הָעוֹלָם אֲשֶׁר קִדְּשָׁנוּ בְּמִצְוֹתָיו וְקִדְּשָׁנוּ לְהַדְלִיק נֵר שֶׁל שַׁבָּת

(bah-rooch ah-tah ah-doh-naye eh-loh-hey-noo meh-lech hah-oh-lahm meh-lech hah-oh-lahm ah-shair keed-shah-noo buh-meetz-voh-tahv veh-keed-shah-noo leh-hahd-leek nair shehl shah-baht.)

Blessed are You, Eternal One our God, Universal Presence, who sanctifies us with paths of holiness and gives us the festival lights.

For special occasions

On special occasions — birthdays, holidays, upon eating the first fruit of its season, and so on — you conclude the basic blessing with שֶׁהֶחֱיָנוּ וְקִיְּמָנוּ הִגִּיעָנוּ לִזְמַן הַזֶּה (scheh-he-chee-yahn-noo ve-kee-yah-mah-noo veh-heeg-ee-ah-noo lahz-mahn hah-zeh; *who has kept us alive, sustained us, and enabled us to reach this season*). This blessing looks like this in Hebrew:

בָּרוּךְ אַתָּה יְיָ אֱלֹקֵינוּ מֶלֶךְ הָעוֹלָם שֶׁהֶחֱיָנוּ וְקִיְּמָנוּ הִגִּיעָנוּ לִזְמַן הַזֶּה

(bah-*rooch* ah-*tah* ah-doh-*noye* eh-loh-hay-*noo* meh-*lech* hah-oh-*lahm* sheh-cheh-chee-ah-*noo* veh-kee-ayh-mahn-*oo* veh-hee-gee-ah-*noo* lahz-*mahn* hah-*zeh*.)

Blessed are You, Eternal One our God, Universal Presence, who keeps us in life always, who supports the unfolding of our uniqueness, and who brings us to this very moment for blessing.

Before reading the Torah

During a regular שַׁבָּת (*shah*–baht; *Shabbat*) service, anyone in the congregation can be asked to recite a blessing before the reading of the Torah. (Don't worry; usually, you know in advance that you'll be asked.) Usually, this blessing is chanted responsively with the other members of the congregation.

If you're called to recite the blessing, walk up to the בִּימָה (*bee*–mah; *podium*) when the rabbi calls your name. If you're wearing a טַלִּית (tah–*leet*; *prayer shawl*), the rabbi or Torah reader will point to the word of the Torah scroll where the reader will be reading. In most traditional services, you're supposed to take the צִיצִית (*tzee*–tzeet; *fringes*) of the corner of your טַלִּית (tah–*leet*; *prayer shawl*) and touch them to the word in the scroll and then to your lips as an expression of your love for the Torah before beginning the blessing.

Recite the first line and listen for the congregation's response. Then repeat their response and recite the last line of the blessing.

[Person saying the blessing]

בָּרְכוּ אֶת ה' הַמְבֹרָךְ

(bahr-*choo* eht ah-doh-*noye* hahm-voh-*rahch*.)

Praise the Eternal One, the one who is blessed!

[Congregation]

בָּרוּךְ ה' הַמְבֹרָךְ לְעוֹלָם וָעֶד

(bah-*rooch* ah-doh-noye ham-voh-*rahch* leh-oh-*lahm* vah-*ehd*.)

The Eternal One is blessed forever and ever.

[Person saying the blessing]

בָּרוּךְ ה' הַמְבֹרָךְ לְעוֹלָם וָעֶד

בָּרוּךְ אַתָּה ה' אֱלֹהֵינוּ מֶלֶךְ הָעוֹלָם אֲשֶׁר בָּחַר בָּנוּ מִכָּל הָעַמִּים וְנָתַן לָנוּ אֶת תּוֹרָתוֹ. בָּרוּךְ אַתָּה ה' נוֹתֵן הַתּוֹרָה:

(bah-*rooch* ah-*tah* ah-doh-*noye* eh-loh-hay-*noo* meh-*lehch* hah-oh-*lahm* ah-*shehr* bah-*chahr* bah-*noo* mee-*kohl* hah-ah-*meem* veh-nah-*tahn* lah-*noo* eht toh-*raht-oh*. Bah-*rooch* ah-*tah* ah-doh-*noye* noh-*tayn* hah-toh-*rah*.)

בָּרוּךְ אַתָּה ה' אֱלֹהֵינוּ מֶלֶךְ הָעוֹלָם אֲשֶׁר נָתַן

Praised are You, Eternal One, Our God Ruler of the Cosmos, who chose us from among the nations, and gave us Divine (literally: his) Torah. Praised are You Eternal One, giver of Torah.

After reading the Torah

When the Torah reading is finished, the rabbi or reader points to the final word of the passage. Once again, you touch the scroll with the צִיצִית (tzee-tzeet; *fringes*) of your טַלִּית (*tah*-leet; *prayer shawl*) and bring the צִיצִית (tzee-tzeet; *fringes*) to your lips before reciting the following blessing in its entirety:

בָּרוּךְ אַתָּה ה' אֱלֹהֵינוּ מֶלֶךְ הָעוֹלָם אֲשֶׁר נָתַן לָנוּ תּוֹרַת אֱמֶת וְחַיֵּי עוֹלָם נָטַע בְּתוֹכֵנוּ.

בָּרוּךְ אַתָּה ה' נוֹתֵן הַתּוֹרָה:

(bah-*rooch* ah-*tah* ah-doh-*noye* eh-loh-hay-*noo* meh-*lehch* hah-oh-*lahm* ah-*shehr* nah-*tahn* lah-noo toh-*raht* eh-*meht* veh-chah-*yay* oh-*lahm* nah-*tah* beh-toh-chay-*noo* bah-*rooch* ah-*tah* ah-doh-*noye* noh-*tayn* hah-toh-*rah.*)

Praised are You Eternal One, Our God Ruler of the Cosmos, Who chose us from all the nations, and gave us Divine (literally: his) Torah. Praised are You, Eternal One, giver of Torah.

When witnessing the wonder of nature

Finally, when witnessing the wonder of nature, such as lightning, high mountains, or great rivers, finish the blessing with עוֹשֶׂה מַעֲשֶׂה בְּרֵאשִׁית (oh-*seh* mah-ah-*seh* buh-ray-*sheet*; *maker of works of creation*). Try this prayer:

בָּרוּךְ אַתָּה יְיָ אֱלֵקֵינוּ הָעוֹלָם עוֹשֶׂה מַעֲשֶׂה בְּרֵאשִׁית

(bah-*rooch* ah-tah ah-doh-*noye* eh-loh-hay-*noo* meh-*lehch* hah-oh-*lahm* oh-seh mah-ah-*say* veh-ray-*sheet.*)

Blessed are You, Eternal One our God, Universal Presence, who makes the works of creation.

After a meal

The traditional blessing after a meal is called בִּרְכַּת הַמָּזוֹן (beer-*kaht* hah-mah-*zohn*; *the blessing for nourishment*). Often referred to in the United States as simply the בִּרְכַּת (**beer-***kaht*), this blessing celebrates the experience of being filled, nourished, and supported by food and by the universe in which the food grows. The purpose of בִּרְכַּת הַמָּזוֹן (beer-*kaht* hah-mah-*zohn*) is to express the wish that this experience be universalized and experienced by everyone. (**Note:** This version is shortened.)

בָּרוּךְ אַתָּה

יְיָ, אֱלֹהֵינוּ מֶלֶךְ הָעוֹלָם
הַזָּן אֶת־הָעוֹלָם כֻּלּוֹ בְּטוּבוֹ בְּחֵן בְּחֶסֶד
וּבְרַחֲמִים, הוּא נוֹתֵן לֶחֶם לְכָל־בָּשָׂר
כִּי לְעוֹלָם חַסְדּוֹ. וּבְטוּבוֹ הַגָּדוֹל
תָּמִיד לֹא חָסַר לָנוּ, וְאַל יֶחְסַר לָנוּ
מָזוֹן לְעוֹלָם וָעֶד. בַּעֲבוּר שְׁמוֹ הַגָּדוֹל
כִּי הוּא אֵל זָן וּמְפַרְנֵס לַכֹּל וּמֵטִיב לַכֹּל,
וּמֵכִין מָזוֹן לְכָל־בְּרִיּוֹתָיו אֲשֶׁר בָּרָא.
בָּרוּךְ אַתָּה יְיָ, הַזָּן אֶת־הַכֹּל.

(bah-*rooch* ah-*tah* ah-doh-*noye* eh-loh-hey-*noo* meh-*lehch* hah-oh-*lahm* hah-*zahn* eht hah-oh-*lahm* buh-koo-*loh* buh-too-*voh* buh-*chehn*-buh-cheh-*sehd* oo-vah-rah-chah-*meem*, hoo noh-*tayn* leh-*chehm* luh-*chol* bah-*sahr* kee leh-oh-*lahm* chahs-*doh*. Oov-too-*voh* hah-gah-*dohl* tah-*meed* loh chah-*sahr* lah-*noo* veh-ahl yehch-*sahr* lah-*noo* mah-*zohn* leh-oh-*lahm* vah-*ehd*. Bah-ah-*voor* sh-*moh* hah-gah-*dohl* kee-hoo ahl zahn oo-fahr-*nehs* buh-ree-oh-*tahv* ah-*shehr* bah-*rah*. Bah-*rooch* ah-*tah* ah-doh-*noye* hah-*zahn* eht hah-*kohl*.)

Blessed are You, Eternal One our God, Ruling Presence of the Universe, who nourishes the entire universe in Goodness; who with grace, with loving kindness, and with mercy, provides nourishment for all flesh, with everlasting loving kindness. In that great goodness we have not lacked and may we never lack nourishment evermore. For the sake of God's great name, because God nourishes and sustains all, and prepares food for all creatures which God created. Blessed are You, Eternal One, who nourishes all.

WORDS TO KNOW

בּוֹרֵא	boh-*reh*	creates
בְּרִית	*breet*	covenant
דּוֹר	*dohr*	generation
אֶחָד	eh-*ḥahd*	one
אֵל	*ehl*	God
הָאֲדָמָה	hah-ah-dah-*mah*	the earth
הַגֶּפֶן	hah-gah-*fehn*	the vine
הַלְלוּיָהּ	hah-leh-loo-*yah*	praise God
קָדוֹשׁ	kah-*dohsh*	holy

מְזוֹנוֹת	mee-zoh-*noht*	foods
נֵר	*nehr*	candle
שֵׁם	*shehm*	name
יִשְׂרָאֵל	yees-rah-*ehl*	Israel
זְכוֹר	zuh-*hohr*	remember

Spiritually Speaking: Figuring Your Way around the Prayer Book

You may understand a little Hebrew now, but you still may not know heads from tails when you walk into services at your local synagogue. In this section, I cover some of the basic rubrics of the Jewish prayer service. I talk about the שְׁמַע (shuh-*mah*) prayer, which Jews recite daily in the morning and evening prayer services. I also spend some time on the central Jewish prayer of עֲמִידָה (ah-mee-*dah*), known also as הַתְּפִלָּה (hah-tfee-*lah*; *the prayer*), which appears in the three prayer services — morning, noon, and evening — and has both weekday and Sabbath versions. Finally, I take a look at some concluding prayers recited in all the services.

Hebrew is an incredibly easy language to read. The hardest part, after getting used to the letters, is remembering to read from right to left. In most cases, you read the consonant letter first and the vowel below it; then you go back up to the consonant again. See Chapter 1 for a discussion of the Hebrew alphabet.

The Sh'ma and her blessings

The שְׁמַע (shuh-*mah*) is known as the watchword of the Jewish faith, as it affirms the unity of the universe, rooted in the belief in One God. The prayer originates in the Torah and literally speaks to the Jewish people, saying "Listen up, people of Israel! The Eternal One is our God, the Eternal One is One!"

שְׁמַע יִשְׂרָאֵל יְהֹוָה אֱלֹהֵינוּ יְהֹוָה אֶחָד:

(sh-*mah* yees-rah-*ehl* ah-doh-*noye* eh-loh-hay-*noo* ah-doh-*noye* eh-*chahd*.)

Listen, Israel: The Eternal is our God, the Eternal is One.

THE CHOREOGRAPHY OF PRAYER

If you ever attended football games in high school, you're probably familiar with the chant, "Lean to the left, lean to the right, stand up, sit down, fight, fight, fight!" Jewish prayer services are somewhat similar (with respect to standing up and sitting down at least). At times you stand, at other times you sit, and you even turn to the left and the right. You stand whenever the ark containing the Torah scrolls is open and during the בָּרְכוּ (bahr-ḥoo; *the call to worship*), during the silent recitation of the עֲמִידָה (ah-mee-*dah*), and for the first three blessings during the repetition of those prayers. You also stand during the עָלֵינוּ (ah-ley-*noo*), which is part of the concluding prayers of the service.

During the קְדֻשָּׁה kuh-doo-shah; *sanctification*), which is the third blessing in the prayer, you not only get to stand, but also to stand on your toes and sway from side to side, like the angels of which the prayer speaks. You also stand during the חֲצִי קַדִּישׁ (chah-*tzee* kah-*deesh*; a prayer that Jews say when transitioning from one portion of the service to another). During the קַדִּישׁ יָתוֹם (kah-deesh yah-*tohm*; *the mourner's Kaddish*), those not mourning the loss of a close relative usually sit down while those in mourning rise. But some Reform congregations have all the congregants rise and recite the prayer in memory of those who lost their lives in the Holocaust and have no one to recite the prayer for them.

You can say the שְׁמַע (shuh-*mah*) any time throughout the day. These words are the last expressions that a Jew is to speak before dying, and these words are contained in daily prayers and are included in the prayer upon retiring for the night. This prayer calls on people to hear that which awakens the deeper love and compassion of their beings — to hear the deeper message that all is one.

REMEMBER

When you want to say these prayers in Hebrew, keep in mind that the *ḥ* transliteration is a guttural sound, like clearing your throat. When you see the letter *i*, it's pronounced *ee*, as in the word *feet*. The *e* sounds like *eh*, and the *o* is a short *o*.

The שְׁמַע (shuh-*mah*) is introduced by the call to worship, the בָּרְכוּ (bahr-*choo*), and is surrounded by different blessings in the morning and evening services. In the morning, the יוֹצֵר אוֹר (yoh-*tzehr* ohr) prayer, which speaks of how Divine Energy creates the world anew each day, precedes the שְׁמַע (shuh-*mah*). The אַהֲבָה רַבָּה (ah-hah-*vah* rah-*bah*), which speaks of God's love for the people of Israel, as demonstrated by revealing to them Divine law, follows. In the evening, the blessings before the שְׁמַע (shuh-*mah*) are on similar themes.

The second paragraph of the שְׁמַע (shuh-*mah*) is often referred to as the וְאָהַבְתָּ (ve-ah-*hahv*-tah; *you shall love*), although it's technically part of the same prayer. (*Note:* The following prayer is an abridged version.)

וְאָהַבְתָּ אֵת יְהֹוָה אֱלֹהֶיךָ בְּכָל־לְבָבְךָ וּבְכָל־נַפְשְׁךָ וּבְכָל־מְאֹדֶךָ: וְהָיוּ הַדְּבָרִים הָאֵלֶּה אֲשֶׁר אָנֹכִי מְצַוְּךָ הַיּוֹם עַל־לְבָבֶךָ: וְשִׁנַּנְתָּם לְבָנֶיךָ וְדִבַּרְתָּ בָּם בְּשִׁבְתְּךָ בְּבֵיתֶךָ וּבְלֶכְתְּךָ בַדֶּרֶךְ וּבְשָׁכְבְּךָ וּבְקוּמֶךָ: וּקְשַׁרְתָּם לְאוֹת עַל־יָדֶךָ וְהָיוּ לְטֹטָפֹת בֵּין עֵינֶיךָ: וּכְתַבְתָּם עַל־מְזֻזוֹת בֵּיתֶךָ וּבִשְׁעָרֶיךָ:

(veh-ah-hahv-*tah* ah-doh-*noye* eh-lo-cheh-*chah* buh-*chohl* leh-vahv-*chah* oov-*chohl* nahf-sheh-*chah* oov-*chohl* meh-oh-deh-*chah*. veh-hah-yoo hahd-vah-*reem* ha-ay-leh ah-*shehr* ah-noh-*chee* meetz-ahv-*chah* hah-yohm ahl leh-vah-veh-*chah*. veh-shee-nahn-*tam* leh-vah-neh-*chah* veh-dee-bahr-tah-*bahm*, buh-sheev-teh-*chah* buh-vay-teh-*chah* oo-vee-shah-ah-ray-*chah*.)

Then you will love The Eternal One your God with all your heart, with all your soul, and with all your resources. Let these words, which I command you today, be upon your heart. Repeat them to your children and speak of them when you sit in your house, when you walk on the way, when you lie down and when you rise up. Bind them as a sign upon your arm and let them be for frontlets between your eyes. Write them on the doorposts of your house and upon your gates.

The וְאָהַבְתָּ (veh-ah-*hahv*-tah, "you shall love" prayer) contains commandments to affix a מְזוּזָה (me-zoo-*zah*; words from the Torah written on a parchment and placed within a container) to one's door, to pray with תְּפִלִּין טַלִּית (tah-*leet*; *prayer shawl*), and to teach one's children about God and God's laws. The prayer also talks about the causal relations between actions and fate. If you follow the natural and Divine laws of the universe, you'll surely enjoy prosperity. But if you don't, misery is sure to follow. To put it another way, our actions have consequences, and everything is more connected than you think.

The מִי־כָמֹךָ (mee-chah-*moh*-chah), a prayer that recalls God's redemption of the Hebrew slaves from Egypt, follows the שְׁמַע (she-mah, "hear o Israel prayer") in both the morning and evening. In the evening, the מִי־כָמֹךָ (mee-kah-*moh*-hah; "Who is like you" prayer) is followed by an additional prayer called the הַשְׁכִּיבֵנוּ (hahsh-kee-*vay*-noo), which asks that God shelter us under their Divine wing, keep us safe throughout the night, and grant us peace.

CULTURAL WISDOM

Jews recite certain prayers, such as the בָּרְכוּ (bahr-*choo*) and the עֲמִידָה (ah-mee-*dah*), facing east toward Zion. When you're in Israel, you face Jerusalem. And when you're in Jerusalem, you face הַר הַבַּיִת (hahr hah-*bah*-yeet; *the Temple Mount*), the remnant of the ancient Holy Temple of Jerusalem. Jewish tradition has it that הַר הַבַּיִת (hahr hah-*bah*-yeet; *the Temple Moun*) is not only the site of the ruins of the Holy Temple, but also was the site upon which Abraham, Judaism's patriarch, nearly sacrificed his son Isaac and the spot upon which creation of the world began. Some legends claim that on this spot, Jacob had his famous dream of a ladder ascending to heaven with angels on it. In the Talmud, this spot is called the טַבּוּר הָאָרֶץ (tah-*boor* hah-ah-*rehtz*; *navel of the world*) and is considered to be the connecting point between the earthly and heavenly worlds. The site remains the most holy site in the Jewish world today and the focus of many Jewish prayers.

WORDS TO KNOW

בָּרְכוּ	*bahr*-choo	raise
חֹשֶׁךְ	**ḥ**oh-shehch	darkness
אֶחָד	eh-**ḥ**ahd	one
לֵב	*lehv*	heart
לְעוֹלָם וָעֶד	oh-lahm vah-*ehd*	forever and ever
נֶפֶשׁ	neh-fehsh	soul
אוֹר	ohr	light
שְׁמַע	sheh-*mah*	listen
יוֹצֵר	*yoh*-tzair	creates

PRAYER GEAR

During prayer services, men (and in some liberal congregations, women) may wear a head covering called a כִּפָּה (kee-*pah*), which demonstrates reverence to God. During morning services, adults in the congregation — just men in traditional settings, and men and women in more liberal settings — may wear a טַלִּית (tah-*leet*), which is a four-cornered garment with fringes on its corners. The fringes are tied in such a way that they number 613, the number of מִצְווֹת (meetz-*voh, commandments*) a Jew is commanded to observe. The basis for this custom is the Torah (Numbers 15:38) itself, which states, "וְעָשׂוּ לָהֶם צִיצִת עַל־כַּנְפֵי בִגְדֵיהֶם לְדֹרֹתָם וְנָתְנוּ עַל־צִיצִת הַכָּנָף פְּתִיל תְּכֵלֶת" (veh-ah-*soo* lah-*hem* tzeet-*tzeet* ahl kahn-*fey* beeg-day-*hem* leh-doh-roh-*tam; and you shall make for yourself fringes on the corners of your garments for all generations*). During weekday morning services, but not on the Sabbath, men — and in more liberal settings, women — don תְּפִלִּין (teh-fee-*leen*), which are little boxes containing biblical verses strapped to the head and forearm. The origins of this custom can also be found in the Torah (Exodus 13:19), which states, "וְהָיָה לְאוֹת עַל־יָדְכָה וּלְטוֹטָפֹת בֵּין עֵינֶיךָ" (veh-hah-yah le'*oht* ahl yahd-*chah* veh-oo- leh-toh-tah-*foht* bayn aye-neh-*chah; And you shall make them as a sign upon your hand, as a symbol between your eyes*).

Dissecting the Standing Prayer

Known as the Standing Prayer, the עֲמִידָה (ah-mee-*dah*) consists of three parts:

>> שֶׁבַח (*sheh*-vach; *praise*)

>> בַּקָשָׁה (bah-kah-*shah*; *petition*)

>> הוֹדָאָה (hoh-dah-*yah*; *thanks*)

The שֶׁבַח (*sheh*-vach; *praise*) section consists of a prayer called the אָבוֹת (ah-*voht*) that invokes the Jewish ancestors. In Orthodox prayer books, אַבְרָהָם (ahv-rah-*hahm*; *Abraham*), יִצְחָק (yeetz-*chahk*; *Isaac*), and יַעֲקֹב (yah-ah-*kohv*; *Jacob*) are mentioned. In Conservative, Reform, Reconstructionist, and Renewal prayer books, the matriarchs שָׂרָה (sah-*rah*; *Sarah*), רִבְקָה (reev-*kah*; *Rebecca*), רָחֵל (rah-*chehl*; *Rachel*), and לֵאָה (lay-*ah*; *Leah*) are also invoked.

The second blessing in the שֶׁבַח section praises God as a mighty hero, healer of the sick and redeemer of captives. The third blessing, the קְדֻשָׁה (keh-doo-*shah*), speaks of God's holiness.

On weekdays, the בַּקָשָׁה (bah-kah-*shah*; *petition*) section asks God for all sorts of goodies: בִּינָה (bee-*nah*; *wisdom*), תְּשׁוּבָה (tuh-shoo-*vah*; *repentance*), סְלִיחָה (suh-lee-*chah*; *forgiveness*), גְּאֻלָּה (geh-oo-*lah*; *redemption*), רְפוּאָה (reh-foo-*ah*; *healing*), קִבּוּץ גָּלֻיוֹת (kee-*bootz* gahl-loo-*yoht*; *the ingathering of the Jewish exiles to Israel*), and צֶדֶק (*tzeh*-dehk; *justice*), to name a few. On the Sabbath, Jews replace the petitionary prayers with a blessing praising the Sabbath day.

The עֲמִידָה (ah-mee-*dah*) concludes with the הוֹדָאָה (hoh-dah-*yah*; *thanks*) section, words of gratitude to God, a beseeching to God to hear our prayer, and a prayer for peace.

Concluding prayers

The עָלֵינוּ (ah-*lay*-noo), which affirms the unique destiny of the Jewish people and looks forward to the day when all peoples of the world are united in peace and harmony, and the קַדִּישׁ יָתוֹם (kah-*deesh* yah-*tohm*; *mourner's prayer*) conclude Jewish prayer services. This prayer is actually in Aramaic, which is also written in Hebrew letters. Many congregations also add prayers for the State of Israel and prayers for peace.

CHOOSING THE SITE FOR THE HOLY TEMPLE OF JERUSALEM

A Jewish legend tells of two siblings who farmed a plot of land together. One of the siblings was married, with children; the other sibling was single and had no children. One night after the wheat harvest, the married sibling sat awake deep in thought. "I am married with children," the married sibling thought. "But my sibling is all alone. It's not fair that I should have all this wheat to myself when I have so many people to take care of me. I am going to sneak some of my wheat into my sibling's pile." So, in the darkness of the night, the married sibling did so.

Coincidentally, that same night, the single sibling sat up pondering way into the night. "I am single, I've got just myself to worry about," the single sibling thought. "But my sibling has to worry about a spouse and children! It's not fair that I should have so much just for me. I am going to sneak some of my wheat into my sibling's pile." So, in the darkness of the night, the single sibling did so.

In the morning, both siblings were puzzled when their piles of wheat were unchanged. So, the process repeated itself again, and again, night after night, until the siblings finally ran into each other carrying sheaves of wheat to the other's side of the field. When they realized what the other had done, they embraced and wept.

God looked down upon this scene of love, harmony, and sharing, and decreed that on the Holy Temple of Jerusalem should be built on that very spot as a symbol of such values. That spot remains the most venerated spot in the Jewish world.

Praying for peace

Because peace is such a central concept in Judaism, you can choose among many prayers for peace. The morning, afternoon, and evening עֲמִידָה (ah-mee-*dah*; *standing prayer* all conclude with a prayer for peace. Many congregations in Israel and across the Jewish Diaspora include a prayer for peace during the Torah service or at the conclusion of the morning prayer service.

TIP

To see and hear these prayers, check out https://www.learnhebrewprayers.com.

A PRAYER FOR PEACE

At the beginning of the 19th century, Rabbi Nachman of Bratslav wrote one particularly moving prayer for peace. Many synagogues in Israel and the Jewish Diaspora recite it, and Israeli children study it as part of their third-grade curriculum:

תְּפִלָּה לְשָׁלוֹם / רַבִּי נַחְמָן מִבְּרֶסְלַב

אֲדוֹן הַשָּׁלוֹם, מֶלֶךְ שֶׁהַשָּׁלוֹם שֶׁלּוֹ, עוֹשֶׂה שָׁלוֹם וּבוֹרֵא הַכֹּל. יְהִי רָצוֹן מִלְּפָנֶיךָ שֶׁתְּבַטֵּל מִלְחָמוֹת וּשְׁפִיכוּת דָּמִים מִן הָעוֹלָם וְתַמְשִׁיךְ שָׁלוֹם גָּדוֹל וְנִפְלָא בָּעוֹלָם וְלֹא יִשָּׂא גּוֹי אֶל גּוֹי חֶרֶב וְלֹא יִלְמְדוּ עוֹד מִלְחָמָה.

עָזְרֵנוּ וְהוֹשִׁיעֵנוּ כֻּלָּנוּ שֶׁנִּזְכֶּה תָּמִיד לֶאֱחֹז בְּמִדַּת הַשָּׁלוֹם, וְיִהְיֶה שָׁלוֹם גָּדוֹל בֶּאֱמֶת בֵּין כָּל אָדָם לַחֲבֵרוֹ, וּבֵין אִישׁ לְאִשְׁתּוֹ וְלֹא יִהְיֶה שׁוּם מַחֲלֹקֶת אֲפִלּוּ בַּלֵּב בֵּין כָּל בְּנֵי אָדָם.

וְיִהְיֶה כָּל אָדָם אוֹהֵב שָׁלוֹם וְרוֹדֵף שָׁלוֹם תָּמִיד בֶּאֱמֶת וּבְלֵב שָׁלֵם, וְלֹא נַחֲזִיק בְּמַחֲלֹקֶת כְּלָל לְעוֹלָם וַאֲפִלּוּ נֶגֶד הַחוֹלְקִים עָלֵינוּ וְלֹא נְבַיֵּשׁ שׁוּם אָדָם בָּעוֹלָם מִקָּטֹן וְעַד גָּדוֹל וְנִזְכֶּה לְקַיֵּם בֶּאֱמֶת מִצְוֹת וְאָהַבְתָּ לְרֵעֲךָ כָּמוֹךָ בְּכָל לֵב וָגוּף וָנֶפֶשׁ וּמָמוֹן, וִיקֻיַּם בָּנוּ מִקְרָא שֶׁכָּתוּב, וְנָתַתִּי שָׁלוֹם בָּאָרֶץ וּשְׁכַבְתֶּם וְאֵין מַחֲרִיד וְהִשְׁבַּתִּי חַיָּה רָעָה מִן הָאָרֶץ וְחֶרֶב לֹא תַעֲבֹר בְּאַרְצְכֶם. ה' שָׁלוֹם, בָּרְכֵנוּ בְשָׁלוֹם

Yehi Ratzon Milfanecha Adonoi Eloheinu V'Elohei Avoteinu
SheTevtel Milchamot U'Shifihut Damim Min HaOlam.
V'Tamshich Shalom Gadol V'Niflah Ba'Olam
V'Lo Yisa Goi El Goi Cherev V'Lo Yilmadu Od Milchamah
Rak Yakiru V'Yedu Kol Yoshvei-Tevel Ha'Emet La'Amito.
Asher La Banu LaZeh Ha'Olam Bishveil Riv U'Machloket
V'Lo Bishveil Sinah V'Kinah, V'Kintur U'Shfichut Damim,
Rak Banu La'Olam K'dai Le'Hakir Otcha Titbarech LaNetzach.
U'V'Chen Trachem Aleinu, Vikuyam Banu Mikra SheKatuv:
VeNatati Shalom Ba'Aretz U'Sh'chavtem V'Ayn Machrid
V'Hishbati Chaya Ra'ah Min Ha'Aretz V'Cherev Lo Ta'Avor B'Artzchem
VaYigal KaMayim Mishpat, U'Tzadakah K'Nachal Eitan.
Ki Mal'ah Ha'Aretz De'ah Et-Adonoi KaMayim LaYam M'chasim.

May it be your will Eternal One our God and God of our ancestors that war and bloodshed will cease.
That a great, wonderful peace will envelope the whole world,
And nation will not lift up sword against nation, and neither shall they learn war any more.
Only will all the inhabitants of the earth will become acquainted with and know this truth:
We did not come into this world for fighting or quarrels,
And not for hatred, zelotry, destruction or spilling of blood.
Rather, we have only come into the world to know you God and to praise you forever.
So, please have mercy upon us, and fulfill the promise written in Scriptures:

> *I will grant peace to the land. You shall lie down and none shall be afraid.*
> *I will rid the land of vicious beasts and the sword shall not cross your lands.*
> *Justice will swell up like water, righteousness like a mighty stream.*
> *And all of the earth shall be filled with the knowing of the Eternal One as the water fills the sea.*

Making Prayer Meaningful

If you've mastered the Hebrew in the Jewish prayers, you've won half the battle. The other half of the battle is finding meaning in those prayers, and it isn't always easy. The rabbi of my synagogue in Jerusalem, Rabbi Levi Weiman-Kelman of the Jerusalem synagogue *Kol HaNeshamah,* said in his essay "An Introduction to Prayer," "Praying is a lot like playing jazz. Sometimes we all pray in harmony, other times we pray at our own rhythm, at our own volume. Jewish tradition explores the inner meaning of the words through interpretation, and ancient sacred texts stay alive when each generation reinterprets them."

Although the focus of this book is עִבְרִית (eev-*reet; Hebrew*) rather than תְּפִלָּה (tuh-fee-*lah; prayer*), I want to guide you to some books that may make your prayer experience more spiritually satisfying. Some books I suggest are

>> *To Pray as a Jew,* by Rabbi Hayim Halevy Donin (Basic Books): This classic work covers the basic structure of the Orthodox prayer service and explains what to do when.

>> *The Way into Jewish Prayer,* by Lawrence Hoffman (Jewish Lights): This book reveals the spirituality and wisdom inherent in Jewish prayer, as well as the who, what, why, when, and how of Jewish prayer.

>> *Making Prayer Real: Leading Jewish Spiritual Voices on Why Prayer Is Difficult and What to Do about It,* Rabbi Mike Commins (Jewish Lights): This book is a collection of writings by 50 people who bring their wisdom to bear on the joys and challenges of Jewish prayer.

>> *The Path of Blessing,* by Rabbi Marcia Prager (Jewish Lights): This book discusses the potent meaning one can find in Jewish blessings.

FUN & GAMES

Pick your favorite blessing or prayer of the ones I present in this chapter. Take a shot at writing it in Hebrew on the following lines:

_____

_____

_____

_____

Chapter 19

Sacred Time, Sacred Space

I n Judaism, a blessing exists that praises God for distinguishing between the holy and the everyday (or *profane*). Both the holy and the everyday are important in life. Much of this book focuses on the everyday stuff, but at times, the holy and the everyday converge. In this chapter, I talk a bit about the sacred places of Jewish worship, and I give you some Hebrew vocabulary to use during sacred times of the year.

Going to a Synagogue

In Hebrew, a *synagogue* is called a בֵּית כְּנֶסֶת (bayt knehs-eht; literally: *house of gathering*). In traditional synagogues, you may find a מְחִצָּה (meh-chee-tzah; *divider*) between the men and women's sections, but in other synagogues, men and women sit together. The *pulpit* is called a בִּימָה (bee-mah). The אֲרוֹן הַקֹּדֶשׁ (ah-*rohn* hah-*koh*; *holy ark*) is the special ark, or closet, that holds the Torah scrolls at the front of the synagogue. The ark is placed on the eastern side of the synagogue, facing Zion and Jerusalem. The "eternal light" hanging above the אֲרוֹן הַקֹּדֶשׁ (ah-*rohn* hah-*koh*; *holy ark*) is called the נֵר תָּמִיד (nehr tah-*meed*). The נֵר תָּמִיד (nehr tah-*meed*) is always lit, symbolizing the eternity of God.

LOOKING AT CHRISTIAN CHURCHES IN ISRAEL

Many כְּנֵסִיּוֹת (kneh-see-*yoht; churches*) dot the landscape in Israel, including כְּנֵסִיַּת הַקֶּבֶר (kneh-see-*yaht* hah-keh-*vehr; the Church of the Holy Sepulcher*) in the Old City of Jerusalem, where the Christian faithful believe that Jesus was buried. Adherents of many streams of נַצְרוּת (nahtz-*root; Christianity*) share this כְּנֵסִיָּה (Kneh-see-*yah; church*). You can see them all in action if you visit this church on חַג הַמּוֹלָד (ahg hah-*moh*-lahd; *Christmas*), one of the holiest days of the הַשָּׁנָה הַנּוֹצְרִית (hah-shah-*nah* hah-nohtz-*reet; Christian year*). The Hebrew word for "Christian" is נוֹצְרִי (nohtz-*ree*), which comes from נָצְרַת (nahtz-*raht; the city of Nazareth*).

You can find synagogues on almost every street corner in Israel, as well as in the Diaspora (Jewish communities around the world). Synagogues are primarily places of worship, but as the name implies, they're the center of much of Jewish communal life. Congregants go to synagogues not only for prayer and religious study, but also for meals, celebrations, and community events. Traditionally, on weekdays, three prayer services are held each day: שַׁחֲרִית (shah-*ḥah-reet; the morning service*), מִנְחָה (meen-*chah; the afternoon service*), and מַעֲרִיב (mah-ah-*reev; the evening service*). Additionally, Torah services are held on Monday, Thursday, and Sabbath (Saturday) mornings, when the Torah is read out loud.

Checking Out Holy Words for Holy Days

The calendar you're probably most familiar with — the Gregorian or civil calendar — is a solar calendar based on the number of days necessary for the Earth to revolve around the sun. The Jewish לוּחַ (loo-*ahch; calendar*) is both a lunar and a solar calendar, officially called *luni–solar,* which sounds just about right because it's kinda loony. Each month follows the phases of the moon. A month begins when the moon is just a sliver facing left in the night sky. A full moon occurs on the 15th of every month; toward the end of each month, the moon shrinks back into a sliver and disappears again.

The Jewish year consists of 12 months, which are 29 or 30 days long. A pure lunar calendar is 354 days, 11 days short of a complete solar rotation. So, the Jewish calendar adds an extra month to 7 of every 19 years, which allows it to be guided by the patterns of the moon but still keep pace with the seasons of the sun so that the Jewish holidays always fall roughly in the same season. That's why רֹאשׁ הַשָּׁנָה (rohsh-hah-*shah*-nah; *Jewish New Year*) always falls roughly in the fall, חֲנֻכָּה

(ḥah-noo-*kah*; *Hanukah*) falls generally in the winter, and פֶּסַח (pay-*sahch*; *Passover*) comes each year in the spring.

In the following sections, I provide a brief introduction to important Jewish holidays and some of the Hebrew vocabulary that accompanies them. To find out more about Jewish holidays, check out *Judaism For Dummies,* 2nd Edition, by Rabbi Ted Falcon and David Blatner (John Wiley & Sons, Inc.).

Shabbat: The Sabbath

Of central importance to the Jewish week, שַׁבָּת (shah-*baht*; *Jewish Sabbath*) is ushered in with הַדְלָקַת נֵרוֹת (hahd-lah-kaht neh-*roht*; *candle-lighting*), בְּרָכוֹת (brah-*choht*; *blessings*), and **a** שִׁירָה (shee-*rah*; *song*). The dinner table is covered with a מַפָּה לְבָנָה (mah-*pah* leh-vah-*nah*; *white tablecloth*), and people recite בְּרָכוֹת (brah-*choht*; *blessings*) *over the* חַלָּה (chah-*lah*; *braided egg bread*) and יַיִן (yah-yin; *wine*) at the beginning of אֲרֻכַּת הַשַּׁבָּת (ah-roo-*chaht* hah-shah-*baht*; *the festive Sabbath meal*).

The lighting of candles ushers in many Jewish holidays, including the Jewish New Year and Passover. Candle-lighting marks the transitional moment between the profane and the sacred. Candles also serve a practical purpose: According to traditional practice, turning on a light or striking a match after the holiday begins is forbidden. יַיִן (yah-yin; *wine*), a symbol of joy in Judaism, is also used to usher in holy days. The two loaves of חַלָּה (chah-*lah*; *braided egg bread*) symbolize the two portions of manna that Jews were given on Fridays in the Sinai wilderness so they wouldn't need to search for food on the Sabbath day. The table itself is considered to be a mini-altar, reminiscent of the altar in the בֵּית הַמִּקְדָּשׁ (bayt hah-meek-*dahsh*; *Holy Temple*) that stood in Jerusalem many years ago. Jews dip their חַלָּהi (chah-*lah*; *braided egg bread*) in מֶלַח (meh-*lahch*; *salt*) just as the priests in the בֵּית הַמִּקְדָּשׁ (bayt hah-meek-*dahsh*; *Holy Temple*) once did during the ritual offerings that took place there.

שַׁבָּת (shah-*baht*; *Jewish Sabbath*) is devoted to מְנוּחָה (meh-noo-*chah*; *rest*), תְּפִלָּה (tuh-fee-*lah*; *prayer*), הִתְיַשְּׁבוּת (heet-chahsh-*voot*; *contemplation*), and זְמַן מִשְׁפַּחְתִּי (z-mahn meesh-*pahch*-tee; *family time*). The traditional greeting on the Jewish Sabbath is שַׁבָּת שָׁלוֹם (shah-*baht* shah-*lohm*; *A peaceful Sabbath*). שַׁבָּת (shah-*baht*; *Jewish Sabbath*) lasts for 25 hours, from sunset Friday evening until sundown Saturday night, when the sun has completely set and three כּוֹכָבִים (koh-chahv-*eem*; *stars*) are visible in the night sky.

The holy day of שַׁבָּת (shah-*baht*; *Jewish Sabbath*) is ushered out with a ceremony called הַבְדָּלָה (hahv-dah-*lah*; literally: *differentiation*), in which בְּרָכוֹת (brah-*choht*; *blessings*) are said over בְּסָמִים (beh-sah-*meem*; *spices*), a נֵר הַבְדָּלָה (nehr hahv-dah-*lah*; *braided Havdallah candle*), and יַיִן (yah-yin; *wine*), or another "important drink of the society." (So, this rule means that, while traditionally you use wine or grape juice, you can also use a drink that is considered "important" in your society. Lots of room for interpretation there. So in Japan, that drink could be sake. Here in the United State, I like to use beer. Other Jewish Americans use orange juice, coffee, or even hard liquor.) The braided candle, with its many wicks, represents the complexity of the regular workweek, which is returning and beginning anew. The sweet smell of the בְּסָמִים (beh-sah-*meem*; *spices*) is meant to comfort us as the peaceful שַׁבָּת (shah-*baht*; *Jewish Sabbath*) departs and to tide us over until it returns. When שַׁבָּת (shah-*baht*; *Jewish Sabbath*) is over, it's customary to wish people a שָׁבוּעַ טוב (shah-voo-*ah tohv*; *good week*).

Rosh HaShanah: The Jewish New Year

רֹאשׁ הַשָּׁנָה (rohsh hah-shah-*nah*; *Jewish New Year*) literally means "the head of the year". This holiday is also called יוֹם הַזִּכָּרוֹן (yohm hah-zee-*kah*-rohn; *Day of Memory*) and יוֹם הַדִּין (yohm hah-*deen*; *Day of Judgment*). The Jewish New Year ushers in a ten-day contemplative period known as יָמִים הַנּוֹרָאִים (yah-*meem* noh-rah-*eem*; *Awesome Days*). Jews mark רֹאשׁ הַשָּׁנָה (rohsh hah-shah-*nah*; *Jewish New Year*) with a festive meal during which they serve a round חָלָה (chah-*lah*; *braided egg bread*) and other symbolic foods, such as דָּג (*dahg*; *fish*), גֶּזֶר (geh-*zehr*; *carrots*), and רִמּוֹנִים (ree-mohn-*eem*; *pomegranates*). These foods symbolize the fertility, luck, and plenty that we hope will be ours in the new year. The all-time-favorite tradition, dipping תַּפּוּחִים (tah-poo-*cheem*; *apples*) in דְּבַשׁ (duh-*vahsh*; *honey*), symbolizes hope for a sweet new year.

During this holy and intense time of the year, folks engage in acts of תְּפִלָּה (tuh-fee-*lah*; *prayer*), תְּשׁוּבָה (teh-shoo-*vah*; *repentance*), and צְדָקָה (tzeh-dah-*kah*; *righteous acts and giving*). Traditional greetings include שָׁנָה טוֹבָה (shah-*nah* toh-*vah*; *A good year*), שָׁנָה טוֹבָה וּמְתוּקָה (shah-*nah* toh-*vah* oo-meh-too-*kah*; *A good and sweet year*), and לְשָׁנָה טוֹבָה תִּכָּתֵבוּ (leh-shah-*nah* toh-*vah* tee-kah-*tay-voo*; *A good year and may we be written in the Book of Life*).

Yom Kippur: The Day of Atonement

יוֹם כִּפּוּר (yohm keh-*poor*; *Day of Atonement*) caps יָמִים נוֹרָאִים (yah-*meem* noh-rah-*eem*; *Awesome Days*). (Check out "Rosh HaShanah: The Jewish New Year" earlier in this chapter.) יוֹם כִּפּוּר (yohm keh-*poor*; *D a* צוֹם (*tzohm*; *fast*) and סְלִיחוֹת (slee-*choht*; *penitential prayers*), and ends with a long, loud שׁוֹפָר (shoh-*fahr*; *blast*) traditionally sounded with a ram's horn. The traditional greeting for this holy day is גְּמַר חֲתִימָה טוֹבָה (guh-*mahr* chah-tee-*mah* toh-*vah*; *May you be sealed in for a good year*).

Sukkot: The Fall Harvest Festival

The holiday of סֻכּוֹת (soo-*koht*; *holiday of booths*), which falls five days after Yom Kippur, has many names that reflect its many meanings. It's called סֻכּוֹת in honor of the סֻכּוֹת (soo-koht literally: *booths*) that Jews build on this holiday to commemorate the ancient Hebrews who lived in these makeshift structures in the Sinai wilderness for 40 years after the exodus from Egypt.

After breaking the fast of כִּפּוּר (yohm keh-*poor*; *Day of Atonement*), the tradition is to rush outside and begin building a סֻכָּה (soo-*kah*; *temporary hut)* for סֻכּוֹת (soo-koht; *booths*). People generally build these סֻכּוֹת (soo-*kah*; *temporary huts*) in their backyard or on their patio, by themselves or with the help of friends and family members. Building a סֻכָּה (soo-*kah*; *temporary hut*) and living in it for the duration of this seven-day festival is among the central observances, along with gathering אַרְבַּעַת הַמִּינִים (ahr-bah-*aht* hah-mee-*neem*; *four species*): a לוּלָב (loo-*lahv*; *palm branch*), an עֲרָבָה (ahr-ah-*vah*; *willow branch*), הֲדַס (hah-*dahs*; *myrtle*), and אֶתְרוֹג (eh-*trohg*; *citron*) — and shaking them. You can buy these four species already bound together in a Jewish store; then you can ritually shake them each day and carry them in the parades that take place in the synagogue each morning of this holiday.

This holiday is also called חַג הָאָסִיף (ḥahg hah-ah-*seef*; *harvest holiday*) because it celebrates the fall harvest, זְמַן שִׂמְחָתֵנוּ (z-*mahn* seem-chaht-tay-noo; *season of our joy*), or simply הֶחָג (heh-*ḥahg*; *the holiday*).

On this holiday, you traditionally greet fellow celebrants with a hearty חַג שָׂמֵחַ (ḥahg sah-*may*-ach; *Happy holiday*) during the first two days and the last day of the festival. During the in-between days, known as חֹל הַמּוֹעֵד (ḥohl hah-moh-*ehd*), you wish others a מוֹעֵד טוֹב (moh-*ehd tohv*; *Good holiday*; literally: *good time*).

Sh'mini Atzeret and Simchat Torah: Praying for Rain and Rejoicing in the Torah

שְׁמִינִי עֲצֶרֶת (shuh-mee-*nee* ahtz-air-*reht*; *Sh'mini Atzeret*) and שִׂמְחַת תּוֹרָה (seem-*chat* toh-*rah*; *Simchat Torah*) cap the weeklong סוּכּוֹת (soo-koht; *booths*) festival (refer to "Sukkot: The Fall Harvest Festival" earlier in this chapter). שְׁמִינִי עֲצֶרֶת (shuh-mee-*nee* ahtz-air-*reht*; *Sh'mini Atzeret*) ushers in the rainy season in Israel with a special תְּפִלַּת הַגֶּשֶׁם (teh-fee-*laht* hah-*geh*-shem; *prayer for rain*) asking God for just enough rain to be a בְּרָכָה (brah-*chah*; *blessing*) but not so much that it's a קְלָלָה (klah-*lah*; *curse*).

שִׂמְחַת תּוֹרָה (shuh-mee-*nee* ahtz-air-*reht*; *Sh'mini Atzeret*) marks the end and beginning of the yearly Torah reading cycle. In Israel and the Reform Jewish communities of the Diaspora, folks celebrate שְׁמִינִי עֲצֶרֶת (shuh-mee-*nee* ahtz-air-*reht*; *Sh'mini Atzeret*) and שִׂמְחַת תּוֹרָה (seem-*chat* toh-*rah*; *Simchat Torah*) as one holiday, but in Orthodox and Conservative Jewish communities in the Diaspora, they're celebrated as two different holidays on two consecutive days. The traditional greeting for these holidays is חַג שָׂמֵחַ (ḥahg sah-*may*-ach; *Happy holiday*).

Celebrating Sigd: The Holiday of Ethiopian Jews

For centuries, the Ethiopian Jewish community lived isolated from the rest of worldwide Jewry, believing that they were the last remaining Jews in the world. Some people trace the lineage of this community to the offspring of the Queen of Sheba and King Solomon; others trace it to the Israelites who were exiled from the Northern Kingdom of Israel after the Assyrian Kingdom conquered it in 722 BCE. In the 1980s and 1990s, Ethiopian Jews were airlifted to safety in their מוֹלֶדֶת (moh-*lehd*-eht; *homeland*) in Israel. They brought with them a holiday called סִגְד (suh-*geed*; *Sigd*), which is now an official holiday in the State of Israel and also catching on with הַתְּפוּצוֹת Diaspora Jewry worldwide. The holiday is celebrated 50 days after יוֹם כִּפּוּר (yohm *kee*-poor; *Yom Kippur*) on the 29th of the Hebrew month of Heshvan. This date is commemorated as the date in which God revealed themselves to Moses. In Ethiopia, סִגְד (suh-*geed*; *Sigd*) was a time for Ethiopian Jews to express their longing for יְרוּשָׁלַיִם (Yeh-roo-*shah-lye*-eem; *Jerusalem*) now that they have returned home to יִשְׂרָאֵל (Yis-*rah*-ehl; *Israel*), סִגְד (suh-*geed*; *Sigd*) is a celebration of that חֲלוֹם (ḥah-lohm; *dream*) come true and is marked by festivals around the country. It's also a holiday to celebrate the culture and contribution of Ethiopian Jewry to Israel and the Jewish people.

	WORDS TO KNOW	
חַג	*ḥahg*	holiday
נֵרוֹת	nehr-*oht*	candles
רֹאשׁ הַשָּׁנָה	rohsh hah-shah-*nah*	Jewish New Year
שַׁבָּת	shah-*baht*	Sabbath
תְּפִלָּה	tuh-fee-*lah*	prayer
תְּשׁוּבָה	tuh-shoo-*vah*	repentance
צְדָקָה	tzeh-dah-*kah*	righteous giving
יַיִן	*yah*-yin	wine
יוֹם כִּפּוּר	yohm keh-*poor*	Day of Atonement

Ḥanukkah: The Jewish Festival of Lights

During the darkest nights of the year shines one of the most beloved Jewish holidays, חֲנֻכָּה (ḥah-noo-kah; literally: dedication), otherwise known as חַג אוּרִים (ḥahg oo-reem; Festival of Light). חֲנֻכָּה (ḥah-noo-kah; Hanukkah) celebrates the victory of the Jews over their Assyrian rulers who desecrated the Holy Jewish Temple and sought to outlaw the practice of Judaism. חֲנֻכָּה (ḥah-noo-kah: Hanukkah) also celebrates the Jewish rededication of the Holy Temple and dedication to Jewish values and ways of life. Jews celebrate the eight-day holiday by lighting נֵרוֹת (nay-roht; candles) in a special חֲנֻכָּה (ḥah-noo-kah; candelabra called a חֲנֻכִּיָּה (ḥah-noo-kee-yah), adding one each night of the festival.

The candles symbolize the container of oil found in the Temple, which was enough to burn for one day in the מְנוֹרָה (meh-noh-rah;) but instead burned for eight days. The נֵרוֹת (nay-roht; candles) are lit by a helper candle called the שַׁמָּשׁ (shah-mahsh). The שַׁמָּשׁ (shah-mahsh\ gives light to the other candles without diminishing its own, which reveals an important spiritual truth: When you share, you create abundance.

Traditional foods include לְבִיבוֹת (leh-vee-voht; latkes, which are potato pancakes) and סֻפְגָּנִיּוֹת (soof-gahn-ee-yoht; jelly doughnuts), reminiscent of the container of oil found in the Temple. Spinning the סְבִיבוֹן (seh-vee-vohn; dreidle, which is the special Ḥanukkah top) is also part of the celebration. In Israel, the סְבִיבוֹן (seh-vee-vohn; dreidel) has four sides with the Hebrew letters nun, gimmel, hey, and peh, which stand for the words נֵס (nehs; miracle), גָּדוֹל (gah-dohl; great), הָיָה (hah-yah; happened), and פֹּה (poh; here), spelling out "A great miracle happened here." But in the Jewish Diaspora, the peh is replaced by shin because a great miracle happened שָׁם (shahm; there) — in Israel.

Traditional greetings for this holiday include חַג חֲנֻכָּה שָׂמֵחַ (ḥahg ḥah-noo-kah sah-may-ach; Happy Chanukkah) and חַג אוּרִים שָׂמֵחַ (ḥahg oo-reem sah-may-ach; Happy Holiday of Lights).

HaHag shel HaHagim: The Festival of Festivals

Haifa, a city on Israel's northern coast, is known for its diversity as well as the peaceful coexistence among its Israeli citizens of many faiths: יַהֲדוּת (Yah-hah-doot; Judaism), נַצְרוּת (Nahtz-root; Christianity), אִסְלַאם (ees-lahm; Islam), and בְּהַאי (bah-hai; Baháʼi). In celebration of this coexistence, Haifa hosts הֶחָג שֶׁל חַגִּים (hah-hahg shehl hah-hahg-eem; the Festival of Festivals) on weekends in December that mark חֲנֻכָּה (ḥah-noo-kah; Hanukkah), רְמָדָאן (rah-mah-dahn; Ramadan) and חַג הַמּוֹלָד (ḥahg hah-moh-lahd; Christmas). The holiday was founded in 1914 by Haifa's first רֹאשׁ הָעִיר (rohsh hah-eer; mayor), and each year it grows in size and renown. People come from all over Israel to enjoy food, music, theater, and crafts and to celebrate Israel's הֶטֶרוֹגֶנִיּוּת (heh-troh-*gehn-ee*-oot; *diversity*), and דּוּ-קִיּוּמִיּוֹ (doo-*kee-oom-ee*-oot; *coexistence*).

Tu BiShevat: The Birthday of the Trees

Even the trees have a holiday on the Jewish calendar! This postbiblical holiday, known by its date, בִּשְׁבָט (tu-bee-sheh-*vaht*), the 15th of שְׁבָט (sheh-*vaht*; *the Hebrew month of Shevat*), was originally a holiday for tax purposes. Today, it has grown into a holiday celebrating עֵצִים (aytz-*eem*; *trees*) and טֶבַע (teh-*vah*; *nature*).

Of growing popularity are טוּ בִּשְׁבָט (*seders*; *ritual meals*) modeled after the traditional Passover meal. These ritual meals, conceptualized by Jewish mystics, involve eating different types of fruits and nuts, and drinking from four different-colored cups of wine and grape juice. The first cup is white wine, symbolizing winter. The second cup is white wine with a drop of red wine, symbolizing the Earth's awakening with spring. The third cup is half red and half white wine, symbolizing the ripening harvest during summertime. And the final cup is a cup of red wine, symbolizing the fullness of the fall harvest.

In Israel, schoolchildren plant trees to celebrate טוּ בִּשְׁבָט (tu-bee-sheh-*vaht*; *Tu Bishvat/the 15th of Shevat*). If you're not in Israel, it's customary to buy a tree in Israel that the קֶרֶן קַיֶּמֶת לְיִשְׂרָאֵל (keh-rehn kah-yehm-*eht* leh-yees-rah-*ehl*; *Jewish National Fund*) plants. You can buy one by calling the Jewish National Fund at (800) 542-8733 or visiting the organization's website at https://www.jnf.org.

Purim: A Jewish Mardi Gras

פּוּרִים (poo-*reem*; *Purim*) is a favorite among children because they get to dress up in תַּחְפּוֹשׂוֹת (tahch-poh-*soht*; *costumes*) when they come to synagogue. Adults in the congregation chant from the מְגִלַּת אֶסְתֵּר (meh-gee-*laht* ehs-*tehr*; *Scroll of Esther*), telling the story of the wicked Haman (*hah*-mahn) and the brave Queen Esther (ehs-*tahr*). Pandemonium reins in the synagogue as children and adults alike drown out the villain's name with רַעֲשָׁנִים (rah-ah-shah-*neem*; *noisemakers*).

Other hallmarks of פּוּרִים (poo-*reem*; *Purim*) include a festive סְעוּדָה (seh-oo-*dah*; *meal*), מַתָּנוֹת לָאֶבְיוֹנִים (mah-tah-*noht* leh-ehv-yoh-*neem*; *gifts to the poor*), and מִשְׁלוֹחַ מָנוֹת (meesh-loh-*ach* mah-*noht*; *little gift packages*) containing the traditional Purim pastry, אָזְנֵי הָמָן (ohz-*nay* hah-*mahn*) and other tasty treats. אָזְנֵי הָמָן (ohz-*nay* hah-*mahn*) literally translates as "Haman's ears" (although in other traditions, they're considered to be Haman's hat) as a way of making fun of the villain of the Purim story. These customs originate from the Scroll of Esther itself, which states that the day the Jewish people were saved from the wicked Haman was to be a day of feasting and gift-giving.

WORDS TO KNOW

חֲנֻכָּה	ḥah-noo-*kah*	Hanukkah
עֵץ	*aytz*	tree
נֵס	*nehs*	miracle
פּוּרִים	poo-*reem*	Purim
רַעֲשָׁן	rah-ah-*shahn*	noisemaker
סְבִיבוֹן	seh *vee*-vohn	dreidle
טֶבַע	teh-*vah*	nature

Pesach: Passover

פֶּסַח (pay-*sahch*; *Passover*) is a springtime holiday that celebrates the Hebrew Exodus from מִצְרַיִם (*meetz*-rah-eem; *Egypt*), when they fled the oppression of the Egyptian pharaoh and began their return to אֶרֶץ יִשְׂרָאֵל (ahr-*ehtz* yees-rah-*ehl*; *the Land of Israel*) by crossing the Sinai wilderness.

A frenzied spring-cleaning project with a spiritual component in which traditional Jewish households rid themselves of חָמֵץ (ḥah-*maytz*; *leavened food products*) ushers in this holiday of renewal. The night before the holiday begins, adults hide pieces of חָמֵץ (ḥah-*maytz*; *leavened food products*) throughout the house. Then children search the darkened house for חָמֵץ (ḥah-*maytz*; *leavened food products*) with the aid of a candle, feather, and spoon in a ritual called בְּדִיקַת חָמֵץ (beh-dee-*kaht* chah-*maytz*). The candle provides light in a darkened house; the feather is used to sweep the חָמֵץ (ḥah-*maytz*; *leavened food products*) into the spoon. Then the חָמֵץ (ḥah-*maytz*; *leavened food products*) are thrown away or burned the next day.

Families hold a traditional Passover meal called the סֵדֶר (seh-*dehr*; literally: *order*) in which participants read the Passover story from a book called the הַגָּדָה (hah-*gahd*-ah; literally: *the telling*); drink four cups of יַיִן (yah-yeen; *wine*); and eat other symbolic foods, such as מַצָּה (mahtz-*ah*; *unleavened bread*), כַּרְפַּס (kahr-*pahs*; *parsely*), חֲרֹסֶת (ḥah-roh-*seht*; a food symbolic of brick mortar that different Jewish communities make with different ingredients, including apples, walnuts, and dates), בֵּיצָה (bay-*tzah*; *egg*), and מָרוֹר (mah-*rohr*; *bitter herbs*). The מַצָּה מַצָּה (mahtz-*ah*; *unleavened bread*) is reminiscent of the bread that the Hebrew slaves quickly made before their departure from Egypt and therefore didn't have time to let rise. The מָרוֹר (mah-*rohr*; *bitter herbs*) recall the bitterness of slavery. The חֲרֹסֶת (ḥah-roh-*seht*; *Haroset*), which is quite tasty, recalls the mortar that the enslaved Hebrews used to make bricks. And the בֵּיצָה (bay-*tzah*; *egg*), and the כַּרְפַּס (kahr-*pahs*; *parsely*) evoke the hope of this springtime holiday.

Yom HaShoah V'Ha'G'vurah: Holocaust Remembrance Day

יוֹם הַשּׁוֹאָה (yohm hah-shoh-*ah*; *Holocaust Remembrance Day*) memorializes the tragedy of the Jews who were systematically murdered as part of Hitler's Final Solution. The Holocaust killed six million Jewish people (including a million and half children), destroying one third of world Jewry. World Jewry chose to commemorate this dark time in our history on the Hebrew date of the 27th of נִיסָן (Nissan is a Hebrew month in the spring), the date of the 1943 Warsaw Ghetto uprising against the Nazis, when Jews fought back against their oppressors.

Jews mark the day with solemn speeches, memorial candles, and a special טֶקֶס (*teh*-kehs; *ceremony*) that features the reading of victims' names at Israel's Holocaust memorial, יַד וָשֵׁם (yahd vah-*shehm*; *Yad Vashem*). In Israel, a siren sounds at 10 a.m., and the Israeli population stops all activities and stands at attention for the duration of the siren. Each year, Jewish youths from around the world conduct a March of the Living at the death camps in Poland and follow it with a trip to Israel for Israel's Independence Day the following week.

Yom HaZikaron: Israeli Memorial Day

יוֹם הַזִּכָּרוֹן (yohm hah-zee-kah-*rohn*; *Yom HaZikaron*) is a solemn and sad day on the Jewish calendar. This day memorializes those who fell in Israel's מִלְחָמוֹת (meel-chah-*moht*; *wars*) or were killed in פִּגּוּעִים (pee-*goo*-eem; *terrorist attacks*). Ceremonies and visits to הַר הֶרְצֵל (hahr *hehr*-tzehl; *Mount Hertzl*), Israel's main military cemetery, mark this remembrance. This holiday falls one week after וֹם הַשּׁוֹאָה (yohm hah-shoh-*ah*; *Holocaust Remembrance Day*). As on וֹם הַשּׁוֹאָה (yohm hah-shoh-*ah*; *Holocaust Remembrance Day*), a siren wails at 10 a.m. At this time, all of Israel stands silently at attention in memory of the lives that were lost.

Yom HaAtzma'ut: Israeli Independence Day

Like so much in Jewish history, the bitter is mixed with the sweet. At the close of ם הַזִּכָּרוֹן (yohm hah-zee-kah-*rohn*; *Yom HaZikaron*), a siren sounds marking the end of the day of mourning and ushering in the celebration of Israel's independence. In Israel, יוֹם הָעַצְמָאוּת (yohm hah-ahtz-*mah*-oot; *Independence Day*) the day is marked by זִקּוּקִין (zee- *koo*-keen; *fireworks*), עַל הָאֵשׁ (ahl hah-*aysh*; *barbecues*), dancing in the streets, and general revelry.

Lag B'Omer: The 33rd Day of the Omer

A somewhat obscure day on the Jewish calendar, this date is the 33rd day of a counting period between פֶּסַח (*pay*-sahḥ; *Passover*) and שָׁבוּעוֹת (shah-voo-*oht*; *Festival of Weeks*) called the עֹמֶר (*oh*-mehr). לַ"ג בָּעֹמֶר (*lahg* bah-*oh*-mehr; *Lag B'Omer*) is a traditional time for a ceremonial first cutting of a baby's hair called חֲלָקָה (ḥah-lah-*kah*) and חֲתֻנּוֹת (hah-too-*noht*; *weddings*). The day also commemorates the end of a plague that sickened many students of a famous first-century rabbi, Rabbi Akiva. As such, outdoor revelry and that Israeli favorite, עַל הָאֵשׁ (ahl hah-*aysh*; *barbecues*), mark the day.

Shavuot: The Festival of Weeks

שָׁבוּעוֹת (shah-voo-*oht*), often translated as the "Feast of Weeks," celebrates the high point of the Jewish calendar year: the giving of the תּוֹרָה (toh-*rah*; *Torah*) on הַר סִינַי (hahr see-*naye*; *Mount Sinai*) to the עַם יִשְׂרָאֵל (ahm yees-rah-*ehl*; *Jewish people*). Jews celebrate the holiday with an all-night study session called תִּקּוּן לֵיל שָׁבוּעוֹת (tee-*koon* layl shah-voo-*oht*) and the reading of the עֲשֶׂרֶת הַדִּבְּרוֹת (ah-sehr-*eht* hah-dee-*broht*; *Ten Commandments*) at a sunrise service. Dairy products are the food of choice for this holiday. Flowers and greenery decorate the synagogue in this happy late-spring holiday, which also celebrates the חִטָּה (ḥee-*tah*; *wheat harvest*) and the בִּקּוּרִים (bee-koo-*reem*; *first fruit of the season*) in Israel. On many secular kibbutzim in Israel, שָׁבוּעוֹת (shah-voo-*oht*; *Shavuot/literally: weeks*) is a time of parades, wearing white, and decorating tractors for parades that celebrate the harvest — including one featuring all the babies who were born on the kibbutz in the past year.

Tisha B'Av: The Ninth of Av

A somber day on the Jewish calendar, תִּשְׁעָה בְּאָב (teesh-*ah* beh-*ahv*; *the ninth of Av*) commemorates the destruction of the בֵּית הַמִּקְדָּשׁ (bayt hah-meek-*dahsh*; *Holy Temple*) in Jerusalem in 356 BCE and 70 CE. Other calamities that occurred on this day include the expulsion of the Jews from England in 1290 CE; the expulsion of the Jews from Spain in 1492 CE; and when Tsar Nicholas II ordered a mobilization of the Russian army in 1914, which led to Germany declaring war on Russia and eventually World War I (which some people believe ultimately led to the Holocaust and the destruction of a third of the Jews in the world).

A dawn-to-dusk צוֹם (*tzohm*; *fast*), readings of the אֵיכָה (ay-*chah*; *Book of Lamentations*), and other rituals of אֵבֶל (eh-*vehl*; *mourning*) mark the day. On this solemn day, it's traditional *not* to greet anyone. As Rabbi Ted Falcon and David Blatner note in *Judaism For Dummies*, 2nd Edition (John Wiley & Sons, Inc.), "This day raises important themes for today's Jews — loss, exile, and the desire to return home."

Tu B'Av: The Holiday of Love

Six days after תִּשְׁעָה בְּאָב (tee-*shah* beh-*ahv; the ninth of Av*) comes טוּ בְּאָב (too beh-*ahv; the 15th of Av*), a joyous holiday of hope and love. Tradition holds that during the time of the בֵּית הַמִּקְדָּשׁ (bayt hah-meek-*dahsh; Holy Temple in ancient Jerusalem*), young women who wanted to marry exchanged white garments (so that no one could tell the rich women from the poor women) and danced in the light of the full יָרֵחַ (yah-*ray-ach; moon*), while men who wanted to get married danced after them in search of a כַּלָּה (kah-*lah; bride*).

Today in Israel, a musical "love festival" on the shores of the כִּנֶּרֶת (kee-*neh*-reht; *Sea of Galilee*) marks the day. This holiday signals the beginning of the end of the year, רֹאשׁ הַשָּׁנָה (rohsh hah-shah-nah; *Jewish New Year*) being a mere six weeks away. At this time, people begin to sign cards and other correspondences with the traditional New Year's greeting, לְשָׁנָה טוֹבָה תִּכָּתֵבוּ (leh–shah-*nah* toh-*vah* tee-kah-tay-*voo; May you be written and sealed for a good year*).

WORDS TO KNOW		
חָמֵץ	**h**ah-*maytz*	leaven
חִטָּה	**h**ee-*tah*	wheat
אֵבֶל	eh-*vehl*	mourning
הַר סִינַי	hahr see-*nah*-ye	Mount Sinai
מָרוֹר	mah-*rohr*	bitter herbs
צוֹם	*tzohm*	fast

All My Life's a Circle: Jewish Life-Cycle Events

Much of Jewish practice is about inculcating a sense of belonging to the Jewish people. Judaism is like a good friend, along with you on your life's journey, comforting you during life's sorrows, and deepening those times of joy. One way Jewish peoplehood is expressed is through various life-cycle ceremonies.

Brit/Simchat Bat: Welcome to the family

Judaism teaches that all Jews are in a covenantal relationship with God. In other words, there's stuff that Jews have gotta do, and stuff that God will do, and each side is supposed to live up to its end of the bargain. So, when a baby is teeny-tiny, they' re welcomed into the covenant between God and the Jewish people in a ceremony. For boys, this ceremony happens on the eighth day and is called a בְּרִית מִילָה (breet *mee*-lah *Brit Milah*), which means "covenant" and involves ritual circumcision. Some (not many) Jewish families elect to conduct a covenant ceremony without circumcision, called בְּרִית שָׁלוֹם (breet *shah*-lohm; *Brit Shalom*). For girls, several practices with different names have emerged: שִׂמְחַת בַּ (seem-*ḥaht* baht; *Simchat Bat*, or *joy of a daughter*) בְּרִית בַּת (*Brit Bat*, or *daughter's covenant*), זֶבֶד הַבַּת (*zeh*-veht hah-*baht Zeved HaBat*, or *Gift of the Daughter*, or בְּרִיתָה (bree-*tah*; *Britah*, or *covenant/female conjugation*). These ceremonies can be conducted on the 8th, 18th, or 30th day of life, or whenever.

B'nai Mitzvah: Coming of Age

One of the best-known Jewish life-cycle ceremonies is the בַּר מִצְוָה bahr *meetz*-vah; *Bar Mitzvah* (ceremony in which a Jewish boy comes of age). For girls, the ceremony is a בַּת מִצְוָה (baht *meetz*-vah; *Bat Mitzvah*), and the emerging term for nonbinary children is בֵּת מִצְוָה (beht *meetz*-vah; *Bet Mitzvah*). A child becomes a *Bar/Bat/Bet Mitzvah* when they come of age: 13 for boys, or 12 or 13 for girls. The טֶקֶס (the-*kehs*; *ceremony*) marks the occasion but doesn't change status (like a wedding ceremony, for example.) So a person doesn't "get Bar Mitzvahed" the way that they "get married." That said, most families mark the occasion with a טֶקֶס (the-*kehs*; *ceremony*) that usually — but not always — takes place in a בֵּית כְּנֶסֶת (beit-kuh-*nehs*-seht; *synagogue*). The lucky *mitzvah* kiddo usually leads תְּפִלּוֹת (teh-*fee*-loht; *prayers*), chants בְּרָכוֹת (brah-*ḥoht*; *blessings*) over the ritual תּוֹרָה (*Torah reading*), chants the תּוֹרָה (*Torah reading*) publicly, and gives a speech on the פָּרָשַׁת הַשָּׁבוּעַ (pah-rah-*shaht* hah-shah-*voo*-ah; *weekly Torah portion*). And then there's the festive party. Wahoo!

Kiddushin: Sacred Partnership

One of life's most meaningful events — and important choices — is finding your intended — בְּשֶׁאֵרְט (bah-shehrt; *besharte*, or "intended one") — and getting married. In Hebrew, this ceremony is called קִדּוּשִׁין (kee-*doo*-sheen; *Kiddushin*, or no English translation, that's what it is called, comes from the root for holy), which comes from the Hebrew word קָדוֹשׁ (kah-*dohsh*; *Kadosh*, or *Holy*). The idea is the two people are creating a sacred partnership — one built on the fact that they're sacred to each other in a way that they aren't to anyone else. The wedding ceremony is called חֲתֻנָּה (hah-*too*-nah; *Hatunah*, or *wedding*). Traditionally, the כַּלָּה

(Kah-*lah*; *bride*) and חָתָן (*ḥah-tahn*; *groom*) (or bride and bride, groom and groom) stand under a חֻפָּה (*Huppah*, or *wedding canopy*) with four open sides symbolic of the home they're building together. Traditionally, the כַּלָּה (Kah-*lah*; *bride*) circles the חָתָן (*ḥah-tahn*; *groom*), and in egalitarian ceremonies, the spouses circle each other. יַיִן (yah-*yeen*; *wine*) is blessed and sipped, and שֶׁבַע בְּרָכוֹת (*sheh*-vah brah-*ḥoht*; *shevah brachot*, or *seven blessings*) are recited. The כְּתוּבָה (keh-*too*-bah; *marriage contract*) is read. (It's signed before the wedding in a separate ceremony.) A glass is broken in memory of the destruction of the בֵּית מִקְדָּשׁ (Beit Hah-Meek-*dahsh*; *ancient Temple in Jerusalem*) and in acknowledgment of the fact that in life, we take the bitter with the sweet. מַזָּל טוֹב (mah-*zahl* tohv; *Mazal Tov*, or *congratulations*; literally: *a good sign*)!

Baruḥ Dayan HaEmet: End of Life

One of the most painful parts of life is being separated from your loved ones by death. Judaism offers a series of practices and rituals that walk the mourner through mourning. Phrases traditionally recited upon hearing of someone's loss are בָּרוּךְ דַּיַּן הָאֱמֶת (*bah-rooḥ dah-yahn hah-eh-meht*;; *blessed is the true judge*), זִכְרוֹנוֹ\זִכְרוֹנָהּ לִבְרָכָה (*zeeḥ-roh-no/nah leev-rah-ḥah*; *may their memory be a blessing*), and שֶׁלֹּא תֵּדַע עוֹד צַעַר (*sheh-lo-teh-deh/ee ohd tzah-ahr may you know no more sorrow*). After the funeral, families observe שִׁבְעָ (*shee*-vah; *shiva*, or *seven days of mourning*) in which they're supported by their community with visits, food, and communal prayer. Jews recite a life-affirming prayer called the קַדִּישׁ (*kah*-deesh; *Kaddish*) for the next 11 months after a close relative has died. These practices are meant to bring comfort to the living.

FUN & GAMES

Now it's time to see how festive you're feeling. Match the holiday in the first column with the English term in the second column by drawing a line between the terms. The answers are in Appendix C.

יוֹם הַזִּכָּרוֹן	Jewish New Year
פֶּסַח	Awesome Days
שָׁבוּעוֹת	Israeli Memorial Day
רֹאשׁ הַשָּׁנָה	Day of Atonement
יוֹם כִּפּוּר	Holocaust Remembrance Day
יוֹם הַשּׁוֹאָה	Festival of the Weeks
שַׁבָּת	The Jewish Sabbath
יָמִים נוֹרָאִים	Passover

6

The Part of Tens

IN THIS PART . . .

Stock your Hebrew library.

Liven up your conversation with classic Hebrew expressions.

Chat like an Israeli.

Chapter **20**

Ten Books on Hebrew You Just Gotta Have

I f you're like me, you're a real book fiend. Although I wrote *Hebrew For Dummies* to fulfill your every basic Hebrew need, I also want to help you take your Hebrew to the next level. Check out these amazing books if you want to delve even deeper into the wonderful world of Hebrew language.

Hebrew Roots. Jewish Routes: A Tribal Language in a Global World

Hebrew Roots, Jewish Routes: A Tribal Language in a Global World (by Dr. Jeremey Benstein, Behrman House) explains why Hebrew is absolutely the coolest! Benstein explains how Hebrew is both one of the oldest and one of the newest languages in the world, its incredible story and its amazing significance. I'm in love with this language and if you aren't already in love with Hebrew, then after this book you will be too.

Hebrew: The Eternal Language

Hebrew: The Eternal Language (by William Chomsky, Jewish Publication Society) is a gem of a book that tells the amazing story of the Hebrew language from its birth in the Near Eastern cradle of civilization to its use as a modern, thriving language in the state of Israel today. This fascinating story illuminates how Hebrew encapsulates the unique experiences and ideas of the Jewish people.

The Tongue of the Prophets: The Life Story of Eliezer Ben Yehuda

The Tongue of the Prophets: The Life Story of Eliezer Ben Yehuda (by Robert St. John, Greenwood) reads like a novel, and it should. The story of Eliezer Ben Yehuda seems almost too incredible to be true. Meet the man who revived Hebrew into the modern, spoken language it is today.

The Hebrew Alphabet: A Mystical Journey

This beautiful little book, *The Hebrew Alphabet: A Mystical Journey* (by Edward Hoffman, illustrations by Karen Silver, Chronicle Books), unlocks the mysteries of the Hebrew letters. Accompanied by stunning illustrations of the Hebrew alphabet, this book reveals how the Hebrew letters can be used as tools for spiritual development, based on the work of 11th-century Jewish mystic Rabbi Abraham Abulafia.

Hebrew Talk: 101 Hebrew Roots And The Stories They Tell

In his *Hebrew Talk: 101 Hebrew Roots and the Stories They Tell* (EKS Publishing), Joseph Lewin, executive director of the National Center for the Hebrew Language, delves into the 101 Hebrew roots — those three letters that form the core of every Hebrew word. Each root tells a story, and together this exploration reads like a *tour de force* of Jewish history. A testament to the vitality of the Hebrew language and the incredible journeys of the Jewish people.

Aleph-Bet Yoga: Embodying the Hebrew Letters for Physical and Spiritual Well-Being

Feel stressed out? *Aleph Bet Yoga: Embodying the Hebrew Letters for Physical and Spiritual Well-Being* (by Steven A. Rapp, Jewish Lights) will help calm your nerves. Yoga meets Hebrew in this work that combines the poses of Hatha yoga with the shapes of the Hebrew alphabet. Each position is shown with a Hebrew verse and an English reflection for meditation.

The Word: The Dictionary that Reveals the Hebrew Source of English

Some say Hebrew is the mother of all languages. *The Word: The Dictionary that Reveals the Hebrew Source of English* (by Isaac E. Mozenson, SPI Books) sets out to prove it. By tracing the etymology of hundreds of everyday words, Mozenson exposes the possible Hebrew origins of these words. A fascinating journey.

How the Hebrew Language Grew

How the Hebrew Language Grew (by Edward Horowitz, KTAV) not only tells the great history of the Hebrew language, but it also explains the basic structure and vocabulary. An easy and fascinating read.

The Story of Hebrew

The Story of Hebrew (by Lewis Glinert, Princeton University Press) recounts the history of the Hebrew language from its Biblical beginnings to its modern expression in Israel. Glinert also explores the ways this remarkable language remained alive long after it ceased to be anyone's mother language, serving as a conduit of Jewish culture and history and a bridge between civilizations. A scholarly read, and a remarkable story.

Poems of Jerusalem and Love Poems

Poems of Jerusalem and Love Poems (by Yehuda Amichai, Sheap Meadow Press) is a gorgeous collection of poems about the two favorite subjects Israel's premier poet, Yehuda Amichai's — love and Jerusalem. This bilingual edition can help you pick up some Hebrew and expose you to Israel's most beloved poet. A gifted poet and a talented teacher, Yehuda Amichai taught foreign students at the Hebrew University of Jerusalem in the latter part of his career. I had the pleasure of studying with him. Yehuda Amichai died in September 2000. May his memory be a blessing.

In the words of the great sage Shammai, "Make your study a fixed habit; otherwise, you will never study." And in the words of his rival, the great sage Hillel, "Now, go and study!"

Chapter **21**

Ten Favorite Hebrew Expressions

Even outside Israel, Hebrew is an important part of Jewish life. Throughout history, the Jewish people have continued to hold on to the language of their native land. Today, although most of the world's Hebrew speakers live in Israel, there are about a million Hebrew speakers living elsewhere, most of them in North America. Even if they don't speak Hebrew fluently, most Jews know a Hebrew phrase or two. Here are ten Hebrew phrases you're likely to hear in Jewish communities both inside and outside Israel.

Mazal Tov

מַזָּל טוֹב (mah-*zahl tohv*; literally: *A good sign*)

This phrase is used to mean "Congratulations." Guests shout it at Jewish weddings when the groom stomps on a glass, breaking it in memory of the destruction of the Temple in Jerusalem and as a reminder that the world is still broken today. You can also say מַזָּל טוֹב to someone on other happy occasions — a birthday, a Bar or Bat Mitzvah, a new job, or an engagement. Here's something funny: In Israel, whenever someone accidentally breaks a glass or a dish in a restaurant, the entire restaurant shouts מַזָּל טוֹב in unison.

B'Karov Etzlehḥ

בְּקָרוֹב אֶצְלֵךְ (buh-kah-*rohv* ehtz-*lehḥ*; literally: *Soon so shall it be by you*) (F)

This expression is a good way to respond when someone wishes you a hearty מַזָּל טוֹב. Its most common use is by brides in response to their single women friends congratulating them on their wedding, but you can use it in any circumstance. If you want to say בְּקָרוֹב אֶצְלֵךְ to a guy, you should say בְּקָרוֹב אֶצְלֵךְ (buh-kah-*rohv* ehtz-leh-*ḥah*).

Titchadesh

תִּתְחַדֵּשׁ (teet-*ḥah*-*dehsh*; literally: *You shall be renewed*) (M)

This is a nice thing to say to males when they make a new purchase, whether they've bought clothing, a car, or a house. If you're speaking to a girl or woman, you should say תִּתְחַדְּשִׁי (teet-hahd-*shee*). To a group of people, say תִּתְחַדְּשׁוּ (teet-hahd-*shoo*).

B'Teavon

בְּתֵאָבוֹן (buh-tay-ah-*vohn*; literally: *With appetite*)

בְּתֵאָבוֹן is the Hebrew equivalent of "Bon appetit!" A host may say this when presenting a dish, and a waiter or waitress may say it to customers in a restaurant. When you dine with someone, you can say this phrase to each other before digging in. When I was at Jewish camp as a child, the counselors used this phrase at the beginning of meals to signal to the campers that we could begin eating. Ah, yummy camp food . . . ! בְּתֵאָבוֹן

B'Ezrat HaShem

בְּעֶזְרַת הַשֵּׁם (beh-ehz-*raht* hah-*shehm*; literally: *With help of the Name*)

In religiously observant circles, Jews often refer to the Holy One (God, that is) as הַשֵּׁם, (hah-*shem*; The Name/God), which means "the Name." Because God's name is so precious, you never even recite it in prayer, let alone in conversation. But sometimes, you do want to talk about God in the course of conversation, so religiously observant folks mention God by referring to הַשֵּׁם. People often use this phrase when they speak about the future and want God's help. This book will be successful, בְּעֶזְרַת הַשֵּׁם.

Yishar Koahḥ

יָשָׁר כֹּחַ (yih-shahr koh-*ach*; literally: *Straight power*)

You can use this expression when you want to say "Good for you," "Way to go," or "More power to you" when someone has accomplished something. People often use this phrase in the synagogue after someone receives an honor such as leading a portion of the prayer service or reading Torah. The proper response to this phrase is בָּרוּךְ תִּהְיֶה (bah-*rooḥ*-teeh-hee-*yeh*) to a guy and בְּרוּכָה תִּהְיִי (bh-roo-*ḥah* tee-hee-*yee*) to a girl or a woman. Both phrases mean "You shall be blessed."

Dash

ד"ש (*dahsh*)

ד"ש is an acronym for תִּדְרִישַׁת שָׁלוֹם (duh-*ree*-shaht *shah*-lohm), which literally means "wishings or demands of peace." ד"ש is used to mean "Regards." You ask someone to send ד"ש just as you'd ask to someone to send your regards. For the full Hebrew phrase, use either of the following:

» תִּמְסֹר לוֹ ד"ש מִמֶּנִּי (teem-*sohr* loh dahsh mee-*mehn*-nee; *Send him my regards*)

» תִּמְסוֹרִי לָהּ ד"ש מִמֶּנִּי (teem-sah-*ree* lah dahsh mee-*mehn*-nee; *Send her my regards*)

You can also send warm regards with ד"ש חַם (dahsh *ḥahm*).

Nu

נוּ (nuuuuuuu)

This phrase has no literal translation into English. After a friend has gone out on a hot date the night before, when your mother has an important interview, or when your child has a big test at school, you'll probably want to inquire about how everything went. So, you ask נוּ? expectantly and wait for a reply.

Kol HaKavod

כָּל הַכָּבוֹד (kohl hah-kah-*vohd*; literally: *All the respect*)

You can use this little phrase when you want to say "All right," "Way to go," or "A job well done." You've almost finished reading this chapter. כָּל הַכָּבוֹד!

L'Ḥaim

לַחַיִּים (lecha'*im*; literally: *To life*)

לַחַיִּים is one of my favorite Jewish expressions because I believe that it reveals a lot about the Jewish approach to life. The phrase isn't "to a good life," "to a healthy life," or even "to a long life"; it's simply "to life," recognizing that life is indeed good and precious and that it should always be celebrated and savored. לַחַיִּים!

» Eating ice cream

» Keeping a positive attitude

Chapter 22

Ten Great Israeli Phrases

Modern Hebrew is a wonderfully colorful language, and the expressions I list in this chapter demonstrate that fact. If you want to sound like a real native speaker, use these phrases correctly, and you're sure to impress.

Mah Pitom

מָה פִּתְאֹם (mah peet-*ohm*; literally: *What suddenly*)

This expression is the Hebrew equivalent of "What'cha talkin' 'bout, Willis?" Use it to express surprise and disagreement. You can also use it to object modestly to a complement. So, if someone says to you, "You must be the greatest Hebrew speaker who ever lived," you can reply with מה פתאם.

Yesh G'vul L'Chol Ta'alul

יֵשׁ גְּבוּל לְכֹל תַּעֲלוּל (yaysh guh-*vool* leh-ḥohl tah-ah-*lool*; literally: *There's a limit to all mischievousness*)

Truer words have never been spoken. Frequently used with children when their behavior has gotten out of hand, this phrase can also be used with adults — particularly politicians. What do you think of the antics of the mayor? Out of control? יֵשׁ גְּבוּל לְכָל תַּעֲלוּל. You can also use the beginning of this phrase, יֵשׁ גְּבוּל, which means "There's a limit," to mean simply "Enough, already."

Pa'am Shlishit Glidah

פַּעַם שְׁלִישִׁית גְּלִידָה (pah-*ahm* shlee-*sheet* glee-*dah*; literally: *The third time, ice cream!*)

I first heard this phrase from my Hebrew professor at University of California-Los Angeles, Yonah Sabar, when I ran into him on campus twice in the same day. Apparently, you say this phrase when you run into someone unexpectedly twice in one day, suggesting that if this coincidence happens a third time, you'll both sit down to ice cream. Israel is a small country, so you'd expect to see people sitting and chowing down on ice cream all the time.

Im K'var, Az K'var

אִם כְּבָר אָז כְּבָר (eem-*kvahr*, ahz *kvahr*; literally: *If already, then already*)

This little number is the Israeli equivalent of "Just do it" or "You might as well do it." You're planning a trip to Paris, France, but while you are already on the Continent, but then you decide to extend your trip to Germany, Italy, and Spain. After all, you're already in Europe, so בְּאִם כְּבָר אָז כְּבָר.

B'Shum Panim VaOfen Lo

בְּשׁוּם פָּנִים וָאֹפֶן לֹא (buh-*shoom* pah-*neem* vah-oh-*fehn* loh; literally: *In no face and manner*)

This phrase is the Israeli equivalent of "No way, José" or "In no way, shape, or form." Say it when you really mean it — such as when your teenage son or daughter wants to go to an all-night coed slumber party (with no parents around) at the school troublemaker's house. Yeah, right. בְּשׁוּם פָּנִים וָאֹפֶן לֹא.

Stam

סְתָם (stahm; literally: *Plain*)

This phrase is one of those Hebrew phrases I wish we had in English. It's so useful. Israelis usually pronounce it by stretching out the *a*, as in *staaaaaaaam*. In response to the question "Why did you do that?", you can say סְתָם (*staaaaaahm*; *just because*). You can use it to emphasize a word, as in the phrase הוּא סְתָם תִּפֵּשׁ (hoo stahm tee-*pehsh*; *He's just plain stupid.*) You can use this phrase to mean "Nothing," as in "What are you doing?" סְתָם. (stahm; nothing) Or you can use it as "just kidding." "Hey, did you know the sky is falling?" סְתָם (*staaaaaaaahm*; just kidding!)! It's a great all-purpose word.

Betaḥḥ

בֶּטַח (beh-*tahch*; literally: *Certainly*)

Here's an expression that's classically Israeli. Like סְתָם (*stahm*), Israelis pronounce it by elongating the *a*, as in *betaaaahḥ*. Use it emphatically when the answer is obvious, and you want to say something like "But of course." Did you enjoy reading *Hebrew For Dummies?* בֶּטַח!

Ḥaval Al HaZ'man

(ḥa-*val* al-haz-*mahn*; literally: *A waste of time*)

This one's a little counterintuitive. Although it means "a waste of time," Israelis use it to mean the opposite: Something is great, huge, or fantastic. I didn't believe it either until I heard it all over Israel. So, what do you think of this book? I hope reading that it has been figuratively, but *not* literally חֲבָל עַל הַזְּמַן!

Ḥazak V'Amatz

חֲזַורק וְאָמַץ (ḥah-*zahk* veh-aeh-*mahtz*; literally: *Be strong and courageous*)

This phrase is one of my favorite Israeli expressions because it comes straight from the Bible — a true testament to the power those ancient words have over our lives today. It's from the first chapter of the Book of Joshua (Joshua 1:6), where God speaks to Joshua, who's getting ready to lead the people of Israel over the river Jordan and into the Promised Land. חֲזַק וֶאֱמַץ כִּי תַּנְחִיל אֶת הָעָם (ḥah-*zahk* veh-eh-*mahtz* kee ah-*tah* tahn-*heel* eht hah-*ahm*; *Be strong and courageous, for you shall lead the nation!*). Incidentally, President Bill Clinton quoted these words in one of his speeches in the fall of 1995. Today, Israelis use it like "You can do it." I say this to my friends when they're going through a rough time or facing a big challenge.

Yehiyeh Tov

יְהְיֶה טוֹב (yih-hee-*yeh* tohv; literally: *It will be good* or *Things will get better*)

This quintessential Israeli phrase has been used since before Israel was officially declared a state. Israelis have seen tough times, but through them all, they continue to hold on to their optimism and belief that even in the most difficult of times, things will get better. Jews throughout the world share the dream of an Israel at peace with its neighbors. The dream and phrase are rooted in the Judaic vision of a world where peace and harmony exist among all peoples, countries, and regions. יְהְיֶה טוֹב

Appendix A

Verb Tables

For each verb in this appendix, I give you its infinitive form, present tense, past tense, future tense, and imperative (command form). This list isn't exhaustive, but you can make yourself understood if you use any of the common verbs in the following tables.

You may wonder why the present tense in the following tables has only four forms. Traditionally, Hebrew had no present tense per se, but under the influence of European languages and because 19th-century Jewish immigrants felt a need for a present tense, modern Hebrew developed something to serve as present tense: the four forms I show in these tables. When you use the present tense, keep in mind that it expresses continuous action or state of being, such as "I am writing" rather than simply "I write."

The 's you see in the following tables indicate where the Hebrew character you would use to write that syllable would be silent (if you were writing in Hebrew characters). This list is in Hebrew alphabetical order according to the first letter of the root.

לֶאֱהֹב Le'ehov (to love)

Present Tense

אוֹהֵב / 'ohev (MS)	אוֹהֲבִים / 'ohavim (MP)
אוֹהֶבֶת / 'ohevet (FS)	אוֹהֲבוֹת / 'ohavot (FP)

	Past Tense	**Future Tense**	**Imperative**
I	אָהַבְתִּי / 'ahavti	אוֹהַב / 'ohav	
You (MS)	אָהַבְתָּ / Ahavta	תֹּאהַב / T'ohav	אֱהֹב / Ehov
You (FS)	אָהַבְתְּ / Ahavt	תֹּאהֲבִי / Tohavi	אַהֲבִי / Ahavi
He	אָהַב / Ahav	יֹאהַב / Yohav	
She	אָהֲבָה / Ahava	תֹּאהַב / Tohav	
We	אָהַבְנוּ / Ahavnu	נֹאהַב / Nohav	

	Past Tense	Future Tense	Imperative
You (MP)	אֲהַבְתֶּם / Ahavtem	תֹּאהֲבוּ / Tohavu	אֲהַבְנוּ / Ahavu
You (FP)	אֲהַבְתֶּם / Ahavten	תֹּאהֲבוּ / Tohavu	אָהֲבוּ / Ahavu
They	אָהֲבוּ / Ahavu	יֹאהֲבוּ / Yohavu	

לֶאֱכֹל Le'Eḥol (to eat)

Present Tense

אֹכֵל / 'oḥel (MS)	אוֹכְלִים / 'oḥlim (MP)	
אוֹכְלִים / 'oḥelet (FS)	אוֹכְלוֹת / 'oḥlot (FP)	

	Past Tense	Future Tense	Imperative
I	א אָכַלְתִּי / 'aḥalti	אוֹכַל / 'oḥal	
You (MS)	אָכַלְתָּ / 'aḥalta	תֹּאכַל / To'ḥal	אֱכֹל / Eḥol
You (FS)	אָכַלְתְּ , / ' aḥlt	אִכְלִי / To'ḥli	אִכְלִי / Iḥli
He	הוּא אָכַל / 'aḥ	יֹאכַל / Yo'ḥal	
She	אָכְלָה / 'aḥla	תֹּאכַל / To'ḥal	
We	אָכַלְנוּ / 'aḥalnu	נֹאכַל / No'ḥal	
You (MP)	אֲכַלְתֶּם / 'aḥaltem	תֹּאכְלוּ /To'ḥlu	אִכְלוּ / Iḥlu
You (FP)	אֲכַלְתֶּן / 'aḥalten	תֹּאכְלוּ / To'ḥlu	אִכְלוּ / Iḥlu
They	אָכְלוּ / 'aḥlu	ה יֹאכְלוּ / Yo'ḥlu	

לְאוֹמַר Lo'mar

Present Tense

אוֹמֵר / 'omer (MS)	אוֹמְרִים / 'omrim (MP)	
אוֹמֶרֶת / 'omeret (FS)	אוֹמְרוֹת / 'omrot (FP)	

	Past Tense	Future Tense	Imperative (Command)
I	אָמַרְתִּי / 'amarti	אֹמַר / 'omar	
You (MS)	אָמַרְתָּ / 'amarta	תֹּאמַר / To'mar	אֱמֹר / 'emor
You (FS)	אַתְּ אָמַרְתְּ / 'amart	תֹּאמְרִי / To'mri	אִמְרִי / 'imri
He	אָמַר / 'amar	יֹאמַר / Yo'mar	
She	אָמְרָה / 'amra	תֹּאמַר / To'mar	
We	אָמַרְנוּ / 'amarnu		נֹאמַר / No'mar
You (MP)	אַתֶּם / 'amartem	תֹּאמְרוּ / To'mru	אִמְרוּ / 'imru
You (FP)	אֲמַרְתֶּן / 'amarten	אַתֶּם תֹּאמְרוּ / To'mru	אִמְרוּ / 'imru
They	אָמְרוּ / 'amru	יֹאמְרוּ / Yo'mru	

לָבוֹא LaVoh (to come, to arrive)

Present Tense

בָּא / Ba' (MS)	בָּאִים / Ba'im (MP)
בָּאָה / Ba'a (FS)	בָּאוֹת / Ba'ot (FP)

	Past Tense	Future Tense	Imperative (Command)
I	בָּאתִי / Ba'ti	אָבוֹא / 'avo	
You (MS)	בָּאתָ / Ba'ta	תָּבוֹא / Tavo'	בּוֹא / Bo
You (FS)	בָּאַתְּ / Ba't	תָּבוֹאִי / Tavo'i	בּוֹאִי / Boi
He	בָּא / Ba'	יָבוֹא / Yavo'	
She	בָּאָה / Ba'a	תָּבוֹא / Tavo	
We	בָּאנוּ / Ba'nu	נָבוֹא / Navo	
You (MP)	בָּאתֶם / Ba'tem	תָּבוֹאוּ / Tavo'u	בּוֹאוּ / Bomu
You (FP)	בָּאתֶן / Ba'ten	תָּבוֹאוּ / Tavo'u	תָּבוֹאוּ / Bo'u
They	בָּאוּ / Ba'u	יָבוֹאוּ / Yavo'u	

לָגוּר LaGur (to live, to dwell)

Present Tense

גָּר / Gar (MS)	גָּרִים / Garim (MP)
גָּרָה / Garah (FS)	גָּרוֹת / Garot (FP)

	Past Tense	Future Tense	Imperative (Command)
I	גַּרְתִּי / Garti	אָגוּר / Agur	
You (MS)	גַּרְתָּ / Garta	תָּגוּר / Tagur	גּוּר / Gur
You (FS)	גַּרְתְּ / Gart	תָּגוּרִיי / Taguri	גּוּרִי / Guri
He	גָּר / Gar	יָגוּר / Yagur	
She	גָּרָה / Gara	תָּגוּר / Tagur	
We	גַּרְנוּ / Garnu	נָגוּר / Nagur	
You (MP)	גַּרְתֶּם / Gartem	תָּגוּרוּ / Taguru	גּוּרוּ / Guru
You (FP)	גַּרְתֶּן / Garten	תָּגוּרוּ / Taguru	גּוּרוּ / Guru
They	גָּרוּ / Garu	יָגוּרוּ / Yaguru	

לָלֶכֶת Lalaḥet (to go, to walk)

Present Tense

הוֹלֵךְ / Holeḥ (MS)	הוֹלְכִים / Holḥim (MP)
הוֹלֶכֶת / Holeḥet (FS)	הוֹלְכוֹת / Holḥot (FP)

	Past Tense	Future Tense	Imperative (Command)
I	הָלַכְתִּי / Halaḥti	אֵלֵךְ / 'eleḥ	
You (MS)	הָלַכְתָּ / Halaḥta	תֵּלֵךְ / Teleḥ	לֵךְ / Leḥ
You (FS)	הָלַכְתְּ / Halaḥt	תֵּלְכִי / Telḥi	לְכִי / Leḥi
He	הָלַךְ / Halaḥ	יֵלֵךְ / Yeleḥ	
She	הָלְכָה / Halḥa	תֵּלֵךְ / Teleḥ	
We	הָלַכְנוּ / Halaḥnu	נֵלֵךְ / Neleḥ	
You (MP)	הָלַכְתֶּם / Halaḥtem	תֵּלְכוּ / Telḥu	לְכוּ / Leḥu

	Past Tense	Future Tense	Imperative (Command)
You (FP)	הֲלַכְתֶּן / Halaḥten	תֵּלְכוּ / Telḥu	לְכוּ / Leḥu
They	הָלְכוּ / Halḥu	יֵלְכוּ / Yelḥu	

לִזְכֹּר Lizkor (to remember)

Present Tense

זוֹכֵר / Zoḥer (MS)	זוֹכְרִים / Zoḥrim (MP)
זוֹכֶרֶת / Zoḥeret (FS)	זוֹכְרוֹת / Zoḥrot (FP)

	Past Tense	Future Tense	Imperative (Command)
I	זָכַרְתִּי / Zaḥarti	אֶזְכֹּר / 'ezkor	
You (MS)	זָכַרְתָּ / Zaḥarta	תִּזְכֹּר / Tizkor	זְכוֹר / Zaḥor
You (FS)	זָכַרְתְּ / Zaḥart	תִּזְכְּרִי / Tizkeri	זִכְרִי / Ziḥri
He	זָכַר / Zaḥar	יִזְכֹּר / Yizkor	
She	זָכְרָה / Zaḥra	תִּזְכֹּר / Tizkor	
We	זָכַרְנוּ / Zaḥarnu	נִזְכֹּר / Nizkor	
You (MP)	זָכַרְתֶּם / Zaḥartem	תִּזְכְּרוּ / Tizkeru	זִכְרוּ / Ziḥru
You (FP)	זָכַרְתֶּן / Zaḥarten	תִּזְכְּרוּ / Tizkeru	זִכְרוֹ / Ziḥru
They	זָכְרוּ / Zaḥru	יִזְכְּרוּ / Yizkeru	

לַחֲזֹר Laḥzor (to return)

Present Tense

חוֹזֵר / Ḥozer (MS)	חוֹזְרִים / Ḥozrim (MP)
חוֹזֶרֶת / Ḥozeret (FS)	חוֹזְרוֹת / Ḥozrot (FP)

	Past Tense	Future Tense	Imperative (Command)
I	חָזַרְתִּי / **H**azarti	אֶחֱזוֹר / **Eh**zor	
You (MS)	חָזַרְתָּ / **H**azarta	תַּחֲזוֹר / **Tah**zor	חֲזוֹר / **H**azor
You (FS)	חָזַרְתְּ / **H**azart	תַּחְזְרִי / **Tah**zeri	חִזְרִי / **H**izri
He	חָזַר / **H**azar	יַחֲזוֹר / **Yah**zor	
She	חָזְרָה / **H**azra	תַּחֲזוֹר / **Tah**zor	
We	חָזַרְנוּ / **H**azarnu	נַחֲזוֹר / **Nah**zor	
You (MP)	חֲזַרְתֶּם / **H**azartem	תַּחְזְרוּ / **Tah**zeru	חִזְרוּ / **H**izru
You (FP)	חֲזַרְתֶּן / **H**azarten	תַּחְזְרוּ / **Tah**zeru	חִזְרוּ / **H**izru
They	חָזְרוּ / **H**azru	וַיַחְזְרוּ / **Yah**zeru	

לַחֲשֹׁב La**h**shov (to think)

Present Tense

חוֹשֵׁב / **H**oshev (MS)	חוֹשְׁבִים / **H**oshvim (MP)
חוֹשֶׁבֶת / **H**oshevet (FS)	חוֹשְׁבוֹת / **H**oshvot (FP)

	Past Tense	Future Tense	Imperative (Command)
I	חָשַׁבְתִּי / **H**ashavti	אֶחֱשֹׁב / **Eh**shov	
You (MS)	חָשַׁבְתָּ / **H**ashavta	תַּחֲשֹׁב / **Tah**shov	חֲשֹׁב / **H**ashov
You (FS)	חָשַׁבְתְּ / **H**ashvt	תַּחְשְׁבִי / **Tah**shevi	חִשְׁבִי / **H**ishvi
He	חָשַׁב / **H**ashav	יַחֲשֹׁב / **Yah**shov	
She	חָשְׁבָה / **H**ashva	תַּחֲשֹׁב / **Tah**shov	
We	וְחָשַׁבְנוּ / **H**ashavnu	נַחֲשֹׁב / **Nah**shov	
You (MP)	חֲשַׁבְתֶּם / **H**ashavtem	תַּחְשְׁבוּ / **Tah**shevu	חִשְׁבוּ / **H**ishvu
You (FP)	חֲשַׁבְתֶּן / **H**ashavten	תַּחְשְׁבוּ / **Tah**shevu	תַּחְשְׁבוּ / **H**ishvu
They	חָשְׁבוּ / **H**ashvu	וַיַחְשְׁבוּ / **Yah**shevu	

לָדַעַת Lada'at (to know)

Present Tense

יוֹדֵעַ / Yode'a (MS)	יוֹדְעִים / Yod'im (MP)
יוֹדַעַת / Yoda'at (FS)	יוֹדְעוֹת / Yod'ot (FP)

	Past Tense	Future Tense	Imperative (Command)
I	יָדַעְתִּי / Yada'ti	אֵדַע / 'eda	
You (MS)	יָדַעְתָּ / Yada'ta	תֵּדַע / Teda'	דַּע / Da'
You (FS)	יָדַעְתְּ / Yada't	תֵּדְעִי / Ted'i	דְּעִי / D'ee
He	יָדַע / Yada'	יֵדַע / Yeda'	
She	יָדְעָה / Yad'ah	תֵּדַע / Teda'	
We	יָדַעְנוּ / Yada'nu	נֵדַע / Neda'	
You (MP)	יְדַעְתֶּם / Yada'te	תֵּדְעוּ / Ted'u	דְּעוּ / D'u
You (FP)	יְדַעְתֶּן / Yada'ten	תֵּדְעוּ / Ted'u	דְּעוּ / D'u
They	יָדְעוּ / Yad'u	יֵדְעוּ / Yed'u	

לִנְסֹעַ Linso'a (to travel)

Present Tense

נוֹסֵעַ / Nose'ah (MS)	נוֹסְעִים / Nos'im (MP)
נוֹסַעַת / Nosa'at (FS)	נוֹסְעוֹת / Nos'ot (FP)

	Past Tense	Future Tense	Imperative (Command)
I	נָסַעְתִּי / Nasa'ti	אֶסַּע / 'esa'	
You (MS)	נָסַעְתָּ / Nasa'ta	תִּסַּע / Tisa'	סַע / Sa'
You (FS)	נָסַעְתְּ / Nasa't	תִּסְעִי / Tis'i	סְעִי / S'i
He	נָסַע / Nasa'	יִסַּע / Yisa'	
She	נָסְעָה / Nas'ah	תִּסַּע / Tisa'	
We	נָסַעְנוּ / Nasa'nu	נִסַּע / Nisa'	
You (MP)	נָסַעְתֶּם / Nasa'tem	תִּסְעוּ / Tis'u	סְעוּ / S'u

	Past Tense	Future Tense	Imperative (Command)
You (FP)	נְסַעְתֶּן / Nasa'ten	תִּסְעוּ / Tis'u	סְעוּ / S'u
They	נָסְעוּ / Nas'u	יִסְעוּ / Yis'u	

לִקְנוֹת Liknot (to buy)

Present Tense

קוֹנֶה / Koneh (MS)	קוֹנִים / Konim (MP)
קוֹנָה / Konah (FS)	קוֹנוֹת / Konot (FP)

	Past Tense	Future Tense	Imperative (Command)
I	קָנִיתִי / Kaniti	אֶקְנֶה / 'ekneh	
You (MS)	קָנִיתָ / Kanita	תִּקְנֶה / Tikneh	קְנֵה / Kneh
You (FS)	קָנִית / Kanit	תִּקְנִי / Tikni	קְנִי / K'ni
He	קָנָה / Kanah	יִקְנֶה / Yikneh	
She	קָנְתָה / Kan'ta	תִּקְנֶה / Tikneh	
We	קָנִינוּ / Kanu	נִקְנֶה / Nikneh	
You (MP)	קְנִיתֶם / Kanitem	תִּקְנוּ / Tiknu	קְנוּ / K'nu
You (FP)	קְנִיתֶן / Kaniten	תִּקְנוּ / Tiknu	קְנוּ / K'nu
They	קָנוּ / Kanu	יִקְנוּ / Yiknu	

לִקְרֹא Likro (to read, to call, to call out)

Present Tense

קוֹרֵא / Kore' (MS)	קוֹרְאִים / Kor'im (MP)
קוֹרֵאת / Kore't (FS)	קוֹרְאוֹת / Kor'ot (FP)

	Past Tense	Future Tense	Imperative (Command)
I	קָרָאתִי / Kara'ti	אֶקְרָא / 'ekrah	
You (MS)	קָרָאתָ / Kara'ta	תִּקְרָא / Tikrah	קְרָא / Kra
You (FS)	קָרָאת / Kara't	תִּקְרְאִי / Tikre'i	קִרְאִי / Kir'i
He	קָרָא / Kara'	יִקְרָא / Yikra'	
She	קָרְאָה / Kara'	תִּקְרָא / Tikra'	
We	קָרָאנוּ / Kara'nu	נִקְרָא / Nikra'	
You (MP)	קָרָאתֶם / Kara'tem	תִּקְרְאוּ / Tikre'u	קִרְאוּ / Kir'u
You (FP)	קָרָאתֶן / Kara'ten	תִּקְרְאוּ / Tikre'u	קִרְאוּ / Kir'u
They	קָרְאוּ / Kar'u	יִקְרְאוּ / Yikre'u	

לִשְׁמֹעַ Lishmo'a (to hear)

Present Tense

שׁוֹמֵעַ / Shome'a (MS)	שׁוֹמְעִים / Shom'im (MP)
שׁוֹמַעַת / Shoma'at (FS)	שׁוֹמְעוֹת / Shom'ot (FP)

	Past Tense	Future Tense	Imperative (Command)
I	שָׁמַעְתִּי / Shama'ti	אֶשְׁמַע / 'eshma	
You (MS)	שָׁמַעְתָּ / Shama'ta	תִּשְׁמַע / Tishma	שְׁמַע / Shema'
You (FS)	שָׁמַעְתְּ / Shama't	תִּשְׁמְעִי / Tishme'i	שִׁמְעִי / Shim'i
He	שָׁמַע / Shama'	יִשְׁמַע / Yishma'	
She	שָׁמְעָה / Sham'ah	תִּשְׁמַע / Tishma'	
We	ו שָׁמַעְנוּ / Shama'nu	נִשְׁמַע / Nishma'	
You (MP)	שָׁמַעְתֶּם / Shama'tem	תִּשְׁמְעוּ / Tish'me'u	שִׁמְעוּ / Shim'u
You (FP)	שָׁמַעְתֶּן / Shama'ten	תִּשְׁמְעוּ / Tish'me'u	שִׁמְעוּ / Shim'u
They	שָׁמְעוּ / Sham'u	יִשְׁמְעוּ / Yish'me'u	

לִשְׁתּוֹת Lishtot (to drink)

Present Tense

שׁוֹתֶה / Shoteh (MS)	שׁוֹתִים / Shotim (MP)
שׁוֹתָה / Shotah (FS)	שׁוֹתוֹת / Shotot (FP)

	Past Tense	Future Tense	Imperative (Command)
I	שָׁתִיתִי / Shatiti	אֶשְׁתֶּה / 'shteh	
You (MS)	שָׁתִיתָ / Shatita	תִּשְׁתֶּה / Tishteh	שְׁתֵה / Shteh
You (FS)	שָׁתִית / Shatit	תִּשְׁתִּי / Tishti	שְׁתִי / Shti
He	שָׁתָה / Shata	יִשְׁתֶּה / Yishteh	
She	שָׁתְתָה / Shatetah	תִּשְׁתֶּה / Tishteh	
We	שָׁתִינוּ / Shatinu	נִשְׁתֶּה / Nishteh	
You (MP)	שְׁתִיתֶם / Shatitem	תִּשְׁתּוּ / Tishtu	שְׁתוּ / Shtu
You (FP)	שְׁתִיתֶן / Shatiten	תִּשְׁתּוּ / Tishtu	שְׁתוּ / Shtu
They	שָׁתוּ / Shatu	יִשְׁתּוּ / Yishtu	

Appendix B

Hebrew–English Mini-Dictionary

A

אבא/abba (ah-bah) m: father

אָח/ach (ahḥ) m.: brother

ארוחת ערב/arḥat erev (ah-roo-ḥaht eh-rehv) f: dinner

א/aruchat tzohorayim (ah-roo-chaht tzoh ho-rah-yeem) f: lunch

אחות ach/aḥot (ahḥ/aḥ-oht) m/f: nurse

אחות/achyanit (ah-yahn-eet) f: niece

אחות/achot (ah-hoht) f: sister

אחיין/אחיינית/ahyan (ach-yahn) m: nephew

עדי/עדינה/adin/adina (ah-deen/ah-deen-ah) m/f: gentle

אדון/adon (ah-dohn) m: sir

אַף/af (ahf): nose

אפרסק/afarsek (ah-fahr-sehk) m: peach

אפודה/afudah:(ah-foo-dah) f: sweater

אגם/agam (ah-gahm) m: lake

עגבנייה/agvania (ahg-vah-nee-yah) f: tomato

עכביש/akavich (ah-kah-veesh) m: spider

על יד/al-yad (ahl-yahd): next to

אמבטיה/ambatia (ahm-baht-yah) f: bathroom

ענן/anan (ah-nahn) m: cloud

אננס/ananas (ah-nah-nahs) m: pineapple

אנגלית/anglit (ahn-gleet): English (language)

עניבה/anivah (ah-nee-vah) f: necktie

ערבית/aravit (ah-rah-veet) f: Arabic

אריה/arieh (ahr-yeh) m: lion

ארון/aron (ah-rohn) m: closet

ארצות הברית/artzot habrit (ahr-tzoht hah-breet) f: United States

ארוחת בוקר/aruchat boker (ah-roo-chaht boh-kehr) f: breakfast

עשירה/ עשיר/ashir/ashira (ah-sheer/ah-shee-rah) m/f: rich

עצוב/עצובה atzuv/atzuvah (ah-tzoov/ah-tzoo-vah) m/f: sad

אוטובוס/autobus (oh-toh-boos) m: bus

אבטיח/avatiach (ah-vah-tee-ach) m: watermelon

אביב/aviv (ah-veev) m: spring (season)

עבודה/avodah (ah-voh-dah) f: work

עין/ayin (ah-yeen) f: eye

אין/ayn (ayn): there isn't

B

בעל/ba'al (bah-ahl) m: husband

בחוץ/bahutz (bah-**h**ootz): outside

ברק/barak (bah-rahk) m: lightning

בריא/bari/b'ri'ah (bah-ree/buh-ree-ah) m/f: healthy

בשר/basar (bah-sahr) m: meat

בן דוד/bat-dod (baht-dohd) f: cousin

בבקשה/bavakasha (bah-vah-kah-shah): please

בית/bayit (bah-yeet) m: house

בגדים/begadim (beh-gah-deem:) m: clothes

בגד ים/beged yam (beh-gehd yahm) m: bathing suit

בית חולים/beit cholim (bayt choh-leem) m: hospital

ביצים/beitzim (baytz-eem) f: eggs

בן דוד/ben-dod (behn-dohd) m: cousin

ברך/berech (behr-ech) f: knee

בטן/beten (beh-tehn) f: stomach

בין/bin (been) m: between

בניין/binyan (been-yahn) m: building

ביטחון/bitachon (beh-tah-chohn) m: security

בוקר/boker (boh-kehr) m: morning

בריכה/breiha (buh-ray-**h**ah) f: pool

בסדר/b'seder (buh-sehd-her): okay

בתיאבון/b'teavon! (beh-tay-ah-vohn): good appetite!

בובה/bubah (boo-bah) f: doll

בול/bul (bool) m: stamp

C

חכם/חכמה/chacham/chachamah (**hah**-hahm/hah-**hah**-mah) m/f: smart

חגורה/chagorah (**hah**-gohr-ah) f: belt

חלב/chalav (**hah**-lah) m: milk

חליפה/chalifa (**hah**-lee-fah) f: suit

חלון/chalon (**hah**-lohn) m: window

חם/חמה/cham/chamah (**hahm**/ **chahm**-ah) m/f: hot

חנות/chanut (**hah**-noot) f: store

חטיף/chatif (**hah**-teef) m: snack

חתימה/chatimah (**hah**-tee-mah) f: signature

חתול/chatul (**hah**-tool) m: cat

חצאית/chatza'it (**hah**-tzah-eet) f: skirt

חיות/chayot (**hah**-yoht) f: animals

חזק/חזקה/chazak/chazakah (chah-zahk/ chah-zahk) m/f: strong

חזיה/chazia (hahz-ee-ah) f: bra

חדר שינה/chadar sheinah (heh-dahr shay-nah) m: bedroom

חשבון/cheshbon (**hehsh**-bohn) m: bill

חוף ים/chof yam (**hohf** yahm) m: beach

חופש/חופשה/chofesh, **h**ufsha (**hoh**-fehsh, hoof-shah) m/f: vacation

חורף/choref (hoh-rehf) m: winter

חולצה/chulzah (hool-tzah) f: shirt

D

דחוף/dahuf (dah-*ḥof*): urgent

דג/dag (*dahg*) m: fish

דקה/dakah (ah-*kah*) f: minute

דרקון/darkon (dahr-*kohn*) m: passport

דרום/darom (dah-*rohm*) m: south

דווקא/davka (dahv-*kah*): ironically

דלק/delek (deh-*lehk*) m: fuel

דלת/delet (deh-*leht*) f: door

דבק/devek (deh-*vehk*) m: glue

דירה/dira (deer-*ah*) f: apartment

דלי/d'li (duh-*lee*) m: bucket

דואר/doar (doh-*ahr*) m: mail

דוד/dod (*dohd*) m: uncle

דודה/dodah (doh-dah) f: aunt

דוב/dov (*dohv*) m: bear

E

אפס/efes (eh-*fehs*): zero

איך/eich *ech*): how

איפה/eifo (ay-*foh*): where

איזה/eizeh (ay-*zeh*): which

עמק/emek (eh-*mehk*) m: valley

אמשemesh eh-*mehsh*) m: last night

אמת/emet (eh-*meh*) m: truth

עשר/esek (eh-*sehk*) m: business

עט/et (*ayt*) m: pen

אתמול/etz/etmol (eht-*mohl*) m: yesterday

עץ/etz (*aytz*) m: tree

G

גדר/gader (gah-*dehr*) m: fence

גג/gag (*gahg*) m: roof

גלגליות/galgiliot (gahl-gee-lee-*oht*) f: inline skates

גן חיות/gan hayot (gahnhah-*yoht*) m: zoo

גר גרה/gar/garah (gahr/gahr-*ah*) m/f: live (dwell)

גרביים/garbayim (gahr-baye-*eem*) m: socks

גרעינים/garinim (gah-ree-*neem*) m: seeds

גב/gav (*gahv*) m: back

גזר/gezer (geh-*zehr*) m: carrot

גיס/gis (*gees*) m: brother-in-law

גיסה/gisa (gee-*sah*) f: sister-in-law

גלידה/glidah (guh-lee-*dah*) f: ice cream

גבינה/g'vinah (guh-vee-*nah*) f: cheese

גבול/g'vul (guh-*vool*) m: border

H

הנחה/hanacha (hah-nah-hah) f: discount

הר/הרים/har (*hahr*) m: mountain

הינה/henei (hee-*nay*): here is

הודעה/hoda'a (hoh-dah-*ah*): message

הורים/horim (hoh-*reem*) m: parents

I

אמא/ima (ee-*mah*) f: mother

עיפרון/iparon (ee-pahr-*ohnv*) m: pencil

עיר בירה/ir bira (eer beer-*ah*) f: capital city

עיר/עירים/ir (*eer*) f: city

אישה/ishah (ee-*shah*) f: wife

עיתון/iton (ee-*tohn*) m: newspaper

itona'i/itona'it (ve-tohn-ah-ee/ee-toh-ah-*eet*) m/f: journalist

מיץ תפוזים/itz tapuzim (meetz tah-poo-*zeem*) m: orange juice

עברית/ivrit (eev-*reet*) f: Hebrew

J

ג'וק/ג'וקים/juke (*jook*) m: bug

K

ככה – ככה/kacha-kacha (kah-*chah* kah-*chah*): so-so

כחול/kachol (kah-*chohl*) m: blue

כדורסל/kadur-sal (kah-door *sahl*) m: basketball

כף/kaf (*kahf*) m: tablespoon

כף/כפפ/כפפות/kafa'fa/k'fafot (kah-fah-*fah*/kuh-*fah-foht*) f: glove, gloves

כאן/kan (*kahn*): here

קניון/kanyon (kan-*yohn*) m: shopping mall

קבוצה/kapit (kah-*peet*) f: team

קר/קרה/kar/karah (kahr/kahr-*ah*) m/f: cold

כרטיס אשראי/kartis ashrei (kahr-*tees* ahsh-*rye*) m: credit card

כרטיס/kartis (kahr-*tees*) m: ticket

כספומט/kaspomat (kahs-poh-*maht*) m: ATM

קצת/katan/k'tanah (kah-*tahn*/kuh-*tah-nah*) m/f: little

כתף/katef (kah-*tehf*) f: shoulder

תפוז/katom (kah-*tohm*) m: orange (fruit)

קיץ/kayitz (kah-*yeetz*) m: summer

כייף/kef (kehf) m: fun

קהילה/kehilla (keh-hee-*lah*) f: community

כלב/kelev (keh-*lehv*) m: dog

כן/ken (kehn): yes

כסף/kesef (keh-*sehf*) m: money

שירותים/keshet (keh-*sheht*) m: restroom

כיור/kior (kee-*ohr*) m: sink

כיפה/kipah (kee-*pah*) f: yarmulke

קיר/kir (keer) m: wall

כיס/kis (kees) m: pocket

כיסא/kisei (kee-say) m: chair

קסילופון/kislofon (kees-loh-fohn) m: xylophone

כוכב/kochav (koh-chahv) m: star

קוף/kof (kohf) m: monkey

קורות חיים/korot ḥaim (koh-roht ḥah-yeem) m: résumé

כוס/kos (kohs) m: cup

כובע/kovah (koh-vah) m: hat

קטן/ktzat (kuh-tzaht): (a) little

כביסה/k'visa (kuh-vee-sah) f: laundry

L

למה/lamah (lah-mah): why

לבן/lavan (lah-vahn) m: white

לאן/lean (leh-ahn): (to) where

למעלה/lemala (leh-mahl-ah): up

למטה/lematah (leh-mah-tah): down

לב/lev (lehv) m: heart

לפני/lifnei (leef-nayv): before

לא/lo (loh): no

לוח/luah (loo-ahh) m: calendar

M

מאפיה/ma'afiah (mah-ah-fee-ah) f: bakery

מעלית/ma'alit (mah-ah-leet) f: elevator

מערב/ma'arav (mah-ah-rahv) m: west

מחק/machak (mah-hahk) m: eraser

מחר/mahar (mah-hahr) m: tomorrow

מחרתיים/mahartayim (mah-hahr-tye-eem) m: day after tomorrow

מחברת/mahberet (mahh-behr-eht) f: notebook

מחשב/mahshev (mahh-shehv) m: computer

למה/maduah (mah-doo-ah): why

מפתח/mafteah (mahf-tay-ah) m: key

מגפיים/magafayim (mah-gah-fah-yeem) m: boots

מגבת/magevet (mah-gehev-eht) f: towel

מגבת/mah (mah): what

מלון/malon (mah-lohn) m: hotel

שקט/mamash (mah-mahsh): quite

מפה/mapah (mah-pah) f: tablecloth

מפית/mapit (mah-pete) f: napkin

מרק/marak (mah-rahk) m: soup

מסקינטייפ/mas (mahs) m: tape

משכורת/maskoret (mahs-koh-reht) f: salary

מסרק/masrek (mahs-rehk) m: comb

מתי/matai (mah-tye): when

מטאטא/matateh (mah-tah-tay) f: broom

מטוס/matos (mah-*tohs*) m: airplane

מים/mayim (mye-*eem*) m: water

מַזְגָן/mazgan (mahz-*gahn*) m: air
conditioner

מזלג/mazleg (mahz-*lehg*) m: fork

מכנסיים/mechansayim (mech-nah-*sah-
yeem*) m: pants

מעיל/me'il (meh-*eel*) m: coat

מלפפון/melafafon (meh-lah-fah-*fohn*) m:
cucumber

מלצר/meltzar (mehl-*tzahr*) m: waiter

מלצרית/meltzarit (mehl-*tzahr-eet*) f:
waitress

מאד/me'od (meh-*ohd*): very

מטרייה/metria (mee-tree-*ah*) f: umbrella

מאוחר/me'uchar (meh-oo-*chahr*) m: late

מזג אוויר/mezeg avir (meh-zehg ah-*veer*)
m: weather

מי/mi (*mee*): who

מדבר/midbar (meed-*bahr*) m: desert

מיקרוגל/mikrogal (meek-roh-*gahl*) m:
microwave

משקפי שמש/mishkafay shemesh (meesh-
kah-*fay* sheh-*mehsh*) m: sunglasses

משקפיים/mishkafayim (meesh-kah-
fah-*yeem*) m: eyeglasses

משמש/mish-mish (meesh-*meesh*) m:
apricot

משפחה/mishpaha (meesh-pah-*hah*) f:
family

מספר/mispar (mees-*pahr*) m: number

משרד/misrad (mees-*rahd*) m: office

מתחת/mitahat (mee-tah-*haht*): under

מיטה/mitah (mee-*tah*) f: bed

מטבח/mitbach (meet-*bahch*) m: kitchen

מצריים/mitzaryim (meetz-rye-*eem*) f:
Egypt

מצויין/mitzuyan (meh-tzoo-*yahn*) m:
excellent

מברשת/mivreshet (meev-resh-*eht*) f:
brush

מזרח/mizrach (meez-*rahch*): east

מזבדה/mizvada (meez-vah-*dah*) f:
suitcase

מכונית/mochonit (meh-cho-*neet*) f: car

מורה/moreh/morah (moh-*reh*/moh-*rah*)
m/f: teacher

מוצאי שבת/motzay shabbat (mohtz-*ay*
shah-*baht*): Saturday night

מוקדם/mukdam (mook-*dahm*): early

מוסך/musach (moo-*sahch*) m: garage

N

נא/na (*nah*): please

נעל/na'al/na'alyim (nah-*ahl*/nah-ahl-*lye-eem*) f: shoe, shoes

נכון/nahon (nah-*hohn*): correct

נהר/nahar (nah-*hahr*) m: river

נקניקה/naknikiah (nahk-nee-kee-*ah*) f: hot dog

נמל התעופה/namal ha'teufa (nah-*mahl* hah-tef-oo-*fah*) m: airport

נקודה/nehda (neh-*dah*) f: granddaughter

נכד/nehed (neh-*hehd*) m: grandson

נודניק/nudnik/nudnikit (nood-*neek*/nood-nee-*keet*) m/f: pest

O

אוכל/ohel (oh-*hehl*) m: food

עוף/of (*ohf*) m: chicken

עור/or (*ohr*) m: skin

עורך דין/orech din/orachat din (oh-rehch *deen*/oh-rah- chaht *deen*) m/f: lawyer

אורז/orez (oh-*rehz*) m: rice

אוזן/ozen (oh-*zehn*) f: ear

עוזב/ozev/ozevet (oh-*zehv*/oh-*zehv*-eht) m/f: depart

P

פנים/panim (pah-*neem*) f: face

פרבר/parvar (pahr-*vahr*) m: suburb

פה/peh (*peh*) m: mouth

פלאפון/pelafon (peh-leh-*fohn*) m: cellphone

פיל/peel (*peel*) m: elephant

פינה/pinah (pee-*nah*) f: corner

פה/poh (*poh*): here

פרח/prachim (puh-rah-*cheem*) m: flowers

פסנתר/p'santer (puh-sahn-*tehr*) m: piano

R

רחוק/rahok/raokah (rah-*chohk*/rah-*chohk*-ah) m/f: far

רחוב/rahov (rah-*hohv*) m: street

רע/rah (*rah*) m: bad

רק/rak (*rahk*): only

רמזור/ramzor (rahm-*zohr*) m: traffic light

רנטגן/rantgen (rahnt-*gehn*) m: X-ray

רבה/רב rav/raba (rahv/rah-*bah*) m/f: rabbi

רגל/regel (reh-*gehl*) f: leg

רהיט/rehut (ree-*hoot*) m: furniture

רוכסן/ריץ׳ רץ/rich-rach (reech-*rahch*) m: zipper

ריקוד/rikud (ree-*kood*) m: dance (noun)

רצפה/ritzpa (reetz-*pah*) f: floor

רופא/רופה/rofeh/rofah (roh-*feh*/roh-*fah*) m/f: doctor

ראש/rosh (*rohsh*) m: head

רוטב/rotev (roh-*tehv*) m: sauce

רוח/ruach (roo-*ach*) m: wind

S

סבא/saba (sah-*bah*) m: grandfather

שפה/safa (sah-*fa*) f: language

ספסל/safsal (sahf-*sahl*) f: bench

סכין/sakin (sah-*keen*) m: knife

סל/sal (*sahl*) m: basket

סלט/salat (sah-*laht*) m: salad

שמחות/שמחים/שמחה/שמח/sameach/s'micha (suh-may-*ach*/suh-may-*chah*) m/f: happy

סנדלים/sandalim (sahn-dahl-*eem*) m: sandals

ספה/sapah (sah-*pah*) f: couch

סבתא/savta (sahv-*tah*) f: grandmother

סגול/segol (seh-*gohl*) m: purple

סלע/sela (she-*lah*) f: rock

סרט דבק/seret devik (seh-*reht* deh-*veek*) m: tape

סרט/seret (seh-*reht*) m: movie

שעה/sha'ah (shah-*ah*) f: hour

שבת/shabbat (shah-*baht*) f: Saturday

שחור/shahor (shah-*ḥohr*) m: black

שלום/shalom (shah-*lohm*): peace

שם/sham (*shahm*): there

שמיים/shamayim (shah-mye-*eem*) m: sky

שנה/shanah (shah-*nah*) f: year

שעון/sha'on (shah-*ohn*) m: watch

שטיח/shatiah :(shah-tee-*ah*) m: rug

שבוע/shavua (shah-voo-*ah*) m: week

שזיף/shazif (shah-*zeef*) m: plum

שקדים/shekdim (shuh-kay-*deem*) f: almonds

שקט/sheket (sheh-*keht*): quiet

שלג/sheleg (sheh-*lehg*) m: snow

שם/shem (*shehm*) m: name

שמש/shemesh (sheh-*mehsh*) f: sun

שלשום/shilshon (shil-*shohn*) m: day before yesterday

שיר/shir (*sheer*) m: song

שנייה/shniyah (shuh-nee-*yah*) f: second (in time)

שוטר/שוטרת/שוטרים/שוטרות/shoter/shoteret (shoh-*tehr*/shoh-tehr-*eht*) m/f: police officer

סוודר/shulchan (shool-*chahn*) m: sweater

שיחה/sicha (see-*chah*) f: conversation

שמלה/simla (seem-*lah*) f: dress

סיור/siur (see-*ohr*) m: tour

סליחה/sliha (slee-*hah*): excuse (me)

גשם/smartoot (suh-mahr-*toot*) m: rain

שמאל/s'mol (suh-*mohl*) m: left

סוף שבוע/sof hashavua (sohf hah-shah-voo-*ah*): weekend

סתיו/stav (*stahv*): fall (season)

סתיו/sukaria (soo-kahr-ee-*ah*) f: candy

סוס/sus (*soos*) m: horse

T

תכשיטים/tachsheetim (tahch-shee-*teem*) f: jewelry

תחתונים/tachtonim (tahch-toh-*neem*) m: underwear

תפריט/tafrit (tahf-*reet*) f: menu

טעים/ta'im (tah-*eem*) m: delicious

תנור/tanor (tah-*noor*) m: oven

תפוח אדמה/tapuach adamah (tah-poo-*ahch* ah-dah-*mah*) m: potato

תפוח/tapuah (tah-poo-*ah*) m: apple

תפוז/tapuz (tah-*pooz*) m: orange (color)

טרי/tari/t'riah (tah-*ree*/tuh-*ree-ah*) m/f: fresh

טלפון/telefone :(the-leh-*fohn*) m: telephone

טלוויזיה/televizia (the-leh-veez-*ee-ah*) f: television

תירס/teras (tee-*rahs*) m: corn

תר/tered (teh-*rehd*) m: spinach

טבע/teva (teh-*vah*) m: nature

תקר/tikra (teek-*rah*) f: ceiling

טיפש/טיפשה/tipesh/tipshah (teep-*esh*/teep-*shah*) m/f: stupid

טיול/tiyul (tee-*yool*) m: hiking

תמונות/t'munot (tuh-moo-*noht*) f: pictures

תודה/todah (toh-*dah*): thanks

טוב/tov/tovah (*tohv*/tohv-*ah*) m/f: good

צפון/tzafon (tzah-*fohn*): north

צהוב/tzahov (tzah-*hohv*) m: yellow

צעיף/tza'if (tzah-*eef*) m: scarf

צעיר/צעירה tza'ir/tza'irah (tzah-*eer*/tzah-ee-*rah*) m/f: young

צלחת/tzalahat (tzah-lah-*haht*) f: plate

צמא/צמיא/tza'meh/tze'me'ah (tzah-*meh*/tzah-*meh-ah*) m/f: thirsty

צוואר/tzavar (tzah-*vahr*) m: neck

צות/tzevet (tzeh-*veht*) f: team

צפור/tzipur (tzee-*pohr*) m: bird

צוהוריי/tzohorayim (tzoh-hoh-rah-*yeem*) m: noon

U

עוגה/ugah (oo-*gah*) f: cake

עוגייה/ugiah (oo-gee-*ah*) f: cookie

V

ורד/vered (veh-*rehd*) m: rose

ורוד/verod (veh-*rohd*) m: pink

Y

יד/yad (*yahd*) f: hand

יפה/yafeh/yahfa (yah-*feh*/yah-*fah*) m/f: pretty

יקר/יקרה/yakar/yakara (yah-*kahr*/yah-*khar-ah*) m/f: expensive

ים/yam (*yahm*) m: ocean

ימין/yamin (yah-*meen*) m: right

ירוק/yarok (yah-*rohk*) m: green

ישר/yashar (yah-*shahr*) m: straight

יין/yayin (yah-*yeen*) m: wine

ירקות/yerakot (yeh-rah-*koht*) m: vegetables

יש/yesh (*yaysh*): there is

ישראל/yisrael (yees-rah-*ehl*) f: Israel

יום חמישי/yom chamishi (yohm chah-mee-*shee*): Thursday

יום רביעי/yom revi'i (yohm reh-vee-*ee*) m: Wednesday

יום שישי/yom shishi (yohm shee-*shee*) m: Friday

יום שלישי/yom shlishi (yohm shuh-lee-*shee*) m: truth

יום/yom (*yohm*) m: day

Z

זול/zol (*zohl*) m: inexpensive

English–Hebrew Mini-Dictionary

A

air conditioner: מזגן/mazgan (mahz-*gahn*) m

airplane: מטוס/matos (mah-*tohs*) m

airport: נמל תעופה/namal ha'teufa (nah-*mahl* hah-tef-oo-*fah*) m

almonds: שקדים/shekdim (shuh-kay-*deem*) f

animals: חיות/chayot (chah-*yoht*) f

apartment: דירה/dira (deer-*ah*) f

apple: תפוח/tapuach (tah-poo-*ach*) m

apricot: משמש/mish-mish (meesh-*meesh*) m

Arabic: ערבית/aravit (ah-rah-*veet*) f

ATM: כספומט/kaspomat (kahs-poh-*maht*) m

aunt: דודה/dodah (doh-dah) f

B

back: גב/gav (*gahv*) m

bad: רע/rah (rah) m

bakery: מאפייה/ma'afiah (mah-ah-fee-ah) f

ball: כדור/kadur (kah-*door*) m

basketball: כדורסל/kadur-sal (kah-door *sahl*) m

basket: סל/sal (*sahl*) m

bathing suit: בגד ים/beged yam (beh-*gehd yahm*) m

bathroom: אמבטיה/ambatia (ahm-bah-*tee*-ah) f

beach: חוף ים/chof yam (chohf *yahm*) m

bear: דוב/dov (*dohv*) m

bed: מיטה/mitah (mee-*tah*) f

bedroom: חדר שינה/chedar sheinah: (cheh-*dahr* shay-*nah*) m

before: לפני/lifnei (leef-*nayv*)

belt: חגורה/chagorah (chah-gohr-*ah*) f

bench: ספסל/safsal (sahf-*sahl*) f

between: בין/bin (*been*) m

bill: חשבון/cheshbon (chehsh-*bohn*) m

bird: ציפור/tzipur (tzee-*pohr*) m

black: שחור/shachor (shah-*chohr*) m

blue: כחול/kachol (kah-chohl) m

boots: מגפיים/magafayim (mah-gah-fah-*yeem*) m

border: גבול/g'vul (guh-*vool*) m

bra: חזייה/chazia (chahz-*ee*-ah) f

breakfast: ארוחת בוקר/aruchat boker: (ah-roo-*chaht* boh-*kehr*) f

broom: מטאטא/matateh (mah-tah-*tay*) f

brother: גבול/ach (*ahch*) m

brother-in-law: גיס/gis (*gees*) m

brush: מברשת/mivreshet (meev-resh-*eht*) f

bucket: דלי/d'li (duh-*lee*) m

bug: וק/juke (*jook*) m

building: בניין/binyan (been-*yahn*) m

bus: אוטובוס/autobus (ah-toh-*boos*) m

business: עסק/esek (eh-*sehk*) m

C

cake: עוגה/ugah (oo-*gah*) f

calendar: לוח/luach (loo-*ahch*) m

candy: סוכריה/sukaria (soo-kahr-ee-*ah*) f

capital city: עיר בירה/ir bira (eer beer-*ah*) f

car: מכונית/mochonit (meh-cho-*neet*) f

carrot: גזר/gezer (geh-*zehr*) m

cat: חתול/chatul (chah-*tool*) m

ceiling: תקרה/tikra (teek-*rah*) f

cellphone: מלפפון/pelafon (peh-leh-*fohn*) m

chair: כיסא/kisei (kee-*say*) m

cheese: גבינה/g'vinah (guh-vee-*nah*) f

chicken: עוף/of (*ohf*) m

city: עיר/ir (*eer*) f

closet: ארון/aron (ah-*rohn*) m

clothes: בגדים/begadim (beh-gah-*deem*) m

cloud: ענן/anan (ah-*nahnv*) m

coat: מעיל/me'il (meh-*eel*) m

cold: קרה/kar/karah (kahr/kahr-*ah*) m/f

comb: מסרק/masrek (mahs-rehk) m

community: קהילה/kehilla (keh-hee-*lah*) f

computer: מחשב/machshev (mahch-*shehv*) m

conversation: סליחה/sicha (see-*chah*) f

cookie: עוגייה/ugiah (oo-gee-*ah*) f

corn: תירס/teras (tee-*rahs*) m

corner: פינה/pinah (pee-*nah*) f

correct: נכון/nachon (nah-*chohn*)

couch: ספה/sapah (sah-*pah*) f

cousin: בת דוד/bat-dod (baht-*dohd*) f

cousin: ben-dod (behn-*dohd*) m

credit card: כרטיס אשראי/kartis ashrei (kahr-*tees* ahsh-*rye*) m

cucumber: מלפפון/melafafon (meh-lah-fah-*fohn*) m

cup: כוס/kohs (*kohs*) m

D

dance: (noun) ריקוד/rikud (ree-*kood*) m

day: יום/yom (yohm)

day after tomorrow: מחרתיים/machartayim (mah-chahr-tye-*eem*) m

day before yesterday: שלשום/shilshon (shil-*shohn*) m

delicious: טעים/ta'im (tah-*eem*) m

depart: עוזב/עוזבת/ozev/ozevet (oh-*zehv*/oh-*zehv-eht*) m/f

desert: מדבר/midbar (meed-*bahr*) m

dinner: ארוחת ערב/aruchat erev (ah-roo-chaht eh-*rehv*) f

discount: הנחה/hanacha (hah-nah-*chah*) f

doctor: רופא/rofeh/rofah (roh-*feh*/roh-*fah*) m/f

dog: כלב/kelev (keh-*lehv*) m

doll: בובה/bubah (boo-*bah*) f

door: דלת/delet (deh-*leht*) f

down: למטה/lematah (leh-mah-*tah*)

dress: שמלה/simla (seem-*lah*) f

E

ear: אוזן/ozen (oh-*zehn*) f

early: מוקדם/mukdam (mook-*dahm*)

east: מזרח/mizrach (meez-*rahch*)

eggs: ביצים/beitzim (baytz-*eem*) f

Egypt: מצריים/mitzaryim (meetz-rye-*eem*) f

elephant: פיל/pil (*peel*) m

elevator: מעלית/ma'alit (mah-ah-*leet*) f

English (language): אנגלית/anglit (ahn-*gleet*)

eraser: מחק/machak (mah-*chahk*) m

excellent: מצויין/mitzuyan (meh-tzoo-*yahn*) m

excuse (me): סליחה/slicha (slee-*chah*)

expensive: יקר/יקרה/yakar/yakara (yah-kahr/yah-khar-ah) m/f

eye: עין/ayin (ah-*yeen*) f

eyeglasses: משקפיים/mishkafayim (meesh-kah-fah-*yeem*) m

F

face: פנים/panim (pah-*neem*) f

fall (season): סתיו/stav (*stahv*)

family: משפחה/mishpacha (meesh-pah-*chah*) f

far: רחוק/רחוקה/rachok/rachokah:(rah-*chohk*/rah-*chohk*-ah) m/f

father: אבא/abba (ah-*bah*) m

fence: גדר/gader (gah-*dehr*) m

fish: דג/dag (*dahg*) m

floor: רצפה/ritzpa (reetz-*pah*) f

flowers: פרחים/prachim (puh-rah-*cheem*) m

food: אוכל/ochel (oh-*chehl*) m

fork: מזלג/mazleg (mahz-*lehg*) m

fresh: טרי/tari/t'riah (tah-*ree*/tuh-*ree*-ah) m/f

Friday: יום שישי/yom shishi (yohm shee-*shee*) m

fuel: דלק delek (deh-*lehk*) m

fun: כייף/kef (kehf) m

furniture: ריהוט/rehut (ree-*hoot*) m

G

garage: מוסך/musach (moo-*sahch*) m

gentle: עדין/adin/adina (ah-*deen*/ah-*deen*-ah) m/f

glove, gloves: כפפה/כפפות/kafa'fa/k'fafot (kah-fah-*fah*/kuh-fah-*foht*) f

glue: דבק/devek (deh-*vehk*) m

good appetite!: בתיאבון/b'teavon! (beh-tay-ah-*vohn*)

good: טוב/טובה/tov/tovah (*tohv*/tohv-*ah*) m/f

granddaughter: נכדה/nechda (nech-*dah*) f

grandfather: סבא/saba (sah-*bah*) m

grandmother: סבתא/savta (sahv-*tah*) f

grandson: נכד/neched (neh-*chehd*) m

green: ירוק/yarok (yah-*rohk*) m

H

hand: יד/yad (*yahd*) f

happy: שמח/שמחה/sameach/s'micha: (suh-may-*ach*/suh-may-*chah*) m/f

hat: כובע/kovah (koh-*vah*) m

head: ראש rosh (*rohsh*) m

healthy: בריא בריאה/bari/b'ri'ah (bah-*ree*/buh-ree-*ah*) m/f

heart: לב/lev (*lehv*) m

Hebrew: עברית/ivrit (eev-*reet*) f

here is: הנה/henei (hee-*nay*)

here: כאן/kan (*kahn*)

here: פה/poh (*poh*)

hiking: טיול/tiyul (tee-*yool*) m

horse: סוס/sus (*soos*) m

hospital: בית חולים/beit holim (bayt hoh-*leem*) m

hot dog: נקניקיה/naknikiah (nahk-nee-kee-*ah*) f

hot: חם/חמה/ham/hamah (*hahm*/hahm-*ah*) m/f

hotel: מלון/malon (mah-*lohn*) m

hour: שעה/sha'ah (shah-*ah*) f

house: בית/bayit (bah-*yeet*) m

how: איך/eich (*ech*)

husband: בעל/ba'al (bah-*ahl*) m

ice cream: גלידה/glidah (guh-lee-*dah*) f

inexpensive: זול/zol (*zohl*) m

inline skates: גלגליות/galgiliot (gahl-gee-lee-*oht*) f

ironically: דווקא/davka (dahv-*kah*)

Israel: ישראל/yisrael (yees-rah-*ehl*) f

jewelry: תכשיטים/tachsheetim (tahch-shee-*teem*) f

journalist: עיתונאי עיתונאית/itona'i/itona'it (ve-tohn-ah-ee/ee-toh-ah-*eet*) m/f

key: מפתח/mafteach (mahf-tay-*ach*) m

kitchen: מטבח/mitbach (meet-*bahch*) m

knee: ברך/berech (behr-*ech*) f

knife: סכין/sakin (sah-*keen*) m

lake: אדם/agam (ah-*gahm*) m

language: שפה/safa (sah-*fa*) f

last night: אמש/emesh (eh-*mehsh*) m

late: מאוחר/me'uchar (meh-oo-*chahr*) m

laundry: כביסה/k'visa (kuh-vee-*sah*) f

lawyer: עורך דין/עורכת דין/orech din/orachat din (oh-rehch *deen*/oh-rah-chaht *deen*) m/f

left: שמאל/s'mol (suh-*mohl*) m

leg: רגל/regel (reh-*gehl*) f

lightning: ברק/barak (bah-*rahk*) m

(a) little: קצת/ktzat (kuh-*tzaht*)

little: קטן/katan/k'tanah (kah-*tahn*/kuh-*tah-nah*) m/f

lion: אריה/arieh (ahr-yee-*eh*) m

live: (dwell) גר/גרה/gar/garah (gahr/gahr-*ah*)

lunch: ארוחת צהריים/aruchat tzohorayim (ah-roo-*chaht* tzoh-ho-rah-*yeem*) f

M

mail: דואר/doar (doh-*ahr*) m

meat: בשר/basar (bah-*sahr*) m

menu: תפריט/tafrit (tahf-*reet*) f

message: הודעה/hoda'a (hoh-dah-*ah*)

microwave: מיקרוגל/mikrogal (meek-roh-*gahl*) m

milk: חלב/chalav (chah-*lah*) m

minute: דקה/dakah (ah-*kah*) f

money: כסף/kesef (keh-*sehf*) m

monkey: קוף/kof (*kohf*) m

morning: בוקר/boker (boh-*kehr*) m

mother: אמא/ima (ee-*mah*) f

mountain: הר/har (*hahr*) m

mouth: פה/peh (*peh*) m

movie: סרט/seret (seh-*reht*) m

N

name: שם/shem (*shehm*) m

napkin: מפית/mapit (mah-*pete*) f

nature: טבע/teva (teh-*vah*) m

neck: צבר/tzavar (tzah-*vahr*) m

necktie: עניבה/anivah (ah-nee-*vah*) f

nephew: אחיין/achyan (ach-*yahn*) m

newspaper: עיתון/iton (ee-*tohn*) m

next to: על/al-yad (ahl-*yahd*)

niece: אחיינית/achaynit (ach-yahn-*eet*) f

no: לא/lo (loh)

noon: צהריים/tzohorayim (tzoh-hoh-rah-*yeem*) m

north: צפון/tzafon (tzah-*fohn*)

nose: אף/af (*ahf*)

notebook: מחברת/machberet (mahch-behr-*eht*) f

number: מספר/mispar (mees-*pahr*) m

nurse: אח/אחות/ach/achot (*ahch*/ach-oht) m/f

O

ocean: ים/yam (*yahm*) m

office: משרד/misrad (mees-*rahd*) m

okay: בסדר/b'seder (buh-sehd-*her*)

only: רק/rak (*rahk*)

orange juice: מיץ תפוזים/mitz tapuzim (meetz tah-poo-*zeem*) m

orange (fruit): כתום/katom (kah-*tohm*) m

orange (color): תפוז/tapuz (tah-*pooz*) m

outside: תפוח/bachutz (bah-*chootz*)

oven: תנור/tanor (tah-*noor*) m

P

pants: מכנסיים/mechansayim (mech-nah-*sah-yeem*) m

parents: הורים/horim (hoh-*reem*) m

passport: דרכון/darkon (dahr-*kohn*) m

patio: מרפסת/mirpeset (meer-peh-*seht*) f

peace: שלום/shalom (shah-*lohm*)

peach: אפרסק/afarsek (ah-fahr-*sehk*) m

pen: עט/et (*ayt*) m

pencil: עיפרון/iparon (ee-pahr-*ohnv*) m

pest: נודניק/nudnik/nudnikit (nood-*neek*/nood-nee-*keet*) m/f

piano: פסנתר/p'santer (puh-sahn-*tehr*) m

pictures: תמונות/t'munot (tuh-moo-*noht*) f

pineapple: אננס/ananas (ah-nah-*nahs*) m

pink: וורוד/verod (veh-*rohd*) m

plate: צלחת/tzalachat (tzah-lah-*chaht*) f

please: בבקשה/bavakasha (bah-vah-kah-*shah*)

please: נא/na (*nah*)

plum: שזיף/shazif (shah-*zeef*) m

pocket: כיס/kis (*kees*) m

police officer: שוטר/שוטרת/shoter/shoteret (shoh-*tehr*/shoh-tehr-*eht*) m/f

pool: בריכה/breicha (buh-ray-*chah*) f

potato: תפוח אדמה/tapuach Adamah (tah-poo-*ahch* ah-dah-*mah*) m

pretty: פה/יפה/יפים/יפות/yafeh/yahfa (yah-*feh*/yah-*fah*) m/f

purple: סגול/segol (seh-*gohl*) m

Q

quiet: שקט/sheket (sheh-*keht*)

quite: ממש/mamash (mah-*mahsh*)

R

rabbi: רב/רבה/rav/raba (rahv/rah-*bah*) m/f

rag: סמרטוט/smartoot (suh-mahr-*toot*) m

rain: גשם/geshem (geh-*shehm*) m

rainbow: קשת/keshet (keh-*sheht*) m

red: אדום/adom (ah-*dohm*) m

refrigerator: מקרר/makrair (mahk-*rahr*) m

restroom: שרותים/sherutim (sheh-roo-*teem*) m

resume: קורות חיים/korot chaim (koh-*roht* chah-*yeem*) m

rice: אורז/orez (oh-*rehz*) m

rich: עשיר/עשירה ashir/ashira (ah-*sheer*/ah-*sheer-ah*) m/f

right: ימין/yamin (yah-*meen*) m

river: נהר/nahar (nah-*hahr*) m

rock: סלע/sela (she-*lah*) f

roof: גג/gag (*gahg*) m

rose: וורד/vered (veh-*rehd*) m

rug: שטיח/shatiah (shah-tee-*ah*) m

S

sad: עצוב/עצובה/עצובים/עצובות/atzuv/atzuvah (ahtz-*oov*/ahtz-*oov*) m/f

salad: סלט/salat (sah-*laht*) m

salary: משכורת/maskoret (mahs-koh-*reht*) f

sandals: סנדלים/sandalyim (sahn-dah-lye-*eem*) m

Saturday night: מוצאי שבת/motzay shabbat (mohtz-*ay* shah-*baht*)

Saturday: שבת/shabbat (shah-*baht*) f

sauce: רוטב/rotev (roh-*tehv*) m

scarf: צעיף/tza'if (tzah-*eef*) m

second: (in time) שנייה/shniyah (shuh-nee-*yah*) f

security: ביטחון/bitachon (beh-tah-*chohn*) m

seeds: גרעינים/garinim (gah-ree-*neem*) m

shirt: חולצה/chulzah (chool-*tzah*) f

shoe, shoes: נעל/נעליים/na'al/na'alyim (nah-*ahl*/nah-ahl-*lye-eem*) f

shopping mall: כתף/kanyon (kan-*yohn*) m

shoulder: כתף/katef (kah-*tehf*) f

signature: חתימה/chatimah (chah-tee-*mah*) f

sink: כיור/kior (kee-*ohr*) m

sir: אדון/adon (ah-*dohn*) m

sister: אחות/achot (ah-*choht*) f

sister-in-law: גיסה/gisa (gee-*sah*) f

skin: עור/or (*ohr*) m

skirt: חצאית/chatza'it (chah-tzah-*eet*) f

sky: שמיים/shamayim (shah-mye-*eem*) m

smart: חכם/חכמה/חכמים/חכמות/chacham/chachamah (chah-*chahm*/chah-*chah-mah*) m/f

snack: חטיף/chatif (chah-*teef*) m

snow: שלג/sheleg (sheh-*lehg*) m

soccer: כדורגל/kadur regel (kah-*door* reh-*gehl*) m

socks: גרביים/garbayim (gahr-baye-*eem*) m

song: שיר/shir (*sheer*) m

so-so: ככה ככה/kacha-kacha (kah-*chah* kah-*chah*)

soup: מרק/marak (mah-*rahk*) m

south: מרק/darom (dah-*rohm*) m

spider: עכביש/akavich (ahk-ah-*veech*) m

spinach: תרד/tered (teh-*rehd*) m

spring (season): אביב/aviv (ah-*veev*) m

stairs: מדרגות/madregot (mahd-dray-*goht*) f

stamp: בול/bul (*bool*) m

star: כוכב/kochav (koh-*chahv*) m

stomach: בטן/beten (beh-*tehn*) f

store: חנות/chanut (chah-*noot*) f

straight: ישר/yashar (yah-*shahr*) m

street: רחוב/rachov (rah-*chohv*) m

strong: חזק/חזקה/chazak/chazakah (chah-*zahk*/chah-*zahk*) m/f

stupid: טיפש טיפשה/tipesh/tipshah (teep-esh/teep-*shah*) m/f

suburb: פרבר/parvar (pahr-*vahr*) m

suit: חליפה/chalifa (chah-lee-*fah*) f

suitcase: מזוודה/mizvada (meez-vah-dah) f

summer: קיץ/kayitz (kah-*yeetz*) m

sun: שמש/shemesh (sheh-*mehsh*) f

sunglasses: משקפי שמש/mishkafay shemesh (meesh-kah-*fay* sheh-*mehsh*) m

sweater: אפוד/afudah (ah-foo-*dah*) f

T

table: שולחן/shulhan (shool-*ḥahn*) m

tablecloth: מפה/mapah (mah-*pah*) f

tablespoon: כף/kaf (*kahf*) m

tape: סרט דבק/seret devik (seh-*reht* deh-*veek*) m

teacher: מורה/מורה/moreh/morah (moh-reh/moh-*rah*) m/f

team: צוות/tzevet (tzeh-*veht*) f

teaspoon: כפית/kapit (kah-*peet*) f

telephone: טלפון/telefone (the-leh-*fohn*) m

television: טלויזיה/televizia (the-leh-veez-*ee-ah*) f

thanks: תודה/todah (toh-*dah*)

there is: יש/yesh (*yaysh*)

there isn't: אין/ayn (*ayn*)

there: שם/sham (*shahm*)

thirsty: צמא/צמאה/tza'meh/tze'me'ah (tzah-*meh*/tzah-*meh-ah*) m/f

Thursday: יום חמישי/yom chamishi (yohm chah-mee-*shee*)

ticket: כרטיס/kartis (kahr-*tees*) m

tomato: עגבנייה/agvania (ahg-vah-nee-*ah*) f

tomorrow: מחר/machar (mah-*chahr*) m

tour: סיור/siur (see-*ohr*) m

towel: מגבת/magevet (mah-gehev-*eht*) f

traffic light: רמזור/ramzor (rahm-*zohr*) m

tree: עץ/etz (*aytz*) m

truth: אמת/emet (eh-*meh*) m

Tuesday: יום שלישי/yom shlishi (yohm shuh-lee-*shee*)

U

umbrella: מטרייה/metria (mee-tree-*ah*) f

uncle: דוד/dod (*dohd*) m

under: מתחת/mitachat (mee-tah-*chaht*)

underwear: תחתונים/tahtonim (tahḥ-toh-*neem*) m

United States: ארצות הברית/artzot habrit (ahrtz-oht hah-*breet*) f

up: למעלה/lemala (leh-mahl-*ah*)

urgent: דחוף/dahuf (dah-*ḥof*)

V

vacation: חופשה/hofesh, hufsha (ḥoh-*fehsh*, ḥoof-*shah*) m/f

valley: עמק/emek (eh-*mehk*) m

vegetables: ירוק/yerakot (yeh-rah-*koht*) m

very: מאוד/me'od (meh-*ohd*)

W

waiter: מלצר/meltzar (mehl-*tzahr*) m

waitress: מלצרית/meltzarit (mehl-*tzahr-eet*) f

wall: קיר/kir (*keer*) m

watch: שעון/sha'on (shah-*ohn*) m

water: מים/mayim (mye-*eem*) m

watermelon: אבטיח/avatiach (ah-vah-tee-*ach*) m

weather: מזג אויר/mezeg avir (meh-zehg ah-*veer*) m

Wednesday: יום רביעי/yom revi'i (yohm reh-vee-*ee*) m

week: שבוע/shavua (shah-voo-*ah*) m

weekend: סוף שבוע/sof hashavua (sohf hah-shah-voo-*ah*)

west: מערב/ma'arav (mah-ah-*rahv*) m

what: מה/mah (*mah*)

when: מתי/matai (mah-*tye*)

where: איפה/eifo (ay-*foh*)

(to) where: לאן/lean (leh-*ahn*)

which: איזה/eizeh (ay-*zeh*)

white: לבן/lavan (lah-*vahn*) m

who: מי/mi (*mee*)

why: למה/lamah (lah-*mah*)

why: מדוע/maduah (mah-doo-*ah*)

wife: אישה/ishah (ee-*shah*) f

wind: רוח/ruach (roo-*ach*) m

window: חלון/chalon (chah-*lohn*) m

wine: יין/yayin (yah-*yeen*) m

winter: חורף/choref (choh-*rehf*) m

work: עבודה/avodah (ah-voh-*dah*) f

X

X-ray: רנטגן/rantgen (rahnt-*gehn*) m

xylophone: קסילופון/kislofon (kees-loh-*fohn*) m

Y

yarmulke: כיפה/kipah (kee-*pah*) f

year: שנה/shanah (shah-*nah*) f

yellow: צהוב/tzahov (tzah-*hohv*) m

yes: כן/ken (*kehn*)

yesterday: אתמול/etmol (eht-*mohl*) m

young: צעיר/צעירה/tza'ir/tza'irah (tzah-eer/tzah-ee-*rah*) m/f

Z

zero: אפס/efes (eh-*fehs*)

zipper: ריץ'רץ'/rich-rach (reech-*rahch*) m

zoo: גן חיות/gan hayot (gahn ḥah-*yoht*) m

Answer Key

Chapter 1: You Already Know Some Hebrew

ב (B) _____ Makes a B sound as in boat.

ג (G) _____ Makes a G sound as in girl.

ל (L) _____ Makes an L sound as in lemon.

ב (V) _____ Makes a V sound as in video.

ד (D) _____ Makes a D sound as in door

ה (H) _____ Makes a strong guttural H sound

ר (R) _____ Makes the R sound as in round. Roll it like a Spanish R and pronounce it from the back of your throat.

א (silent) _____ Makes a Sh sound as in show.

Chapter 2: The Nitty Gritty: Basic Hebrew Grammar

1. הוּא רוֹצֶה אֶת הַמְּכוֹנִית נָכוֹן?/הַאִם הוּא רוֹצֶה אֶת הַמְּכוֹנִית?

2. יֵשׁ מַגֶּבֶת נָכוֹן?/הַאִם יֵשׁ מַגֶּבֶת?

Chapter 3: Shalom, Shalom! Meeting and Greeting

1. how   **2.** where   **3.** why   **4.** what   **5.** when   **6.** who

Chapter 4: Getting to Know You: Making Small Talk

A. אַבָּא / Aba (father)   **B.** אִמָּא / Ima (mother)   **C.** אָחוֹת / Aḥot (sister)

D. אָח / Aḥ (brother)   **E.** סָבְתָא Savtah (grandmother)

Chapter 5: Eat! Eat! You're So Thin!

כַּפִּית / Kapit (spoon), מַפָּה / Mapah (tablecloth), מַפִּית / Mapit (napkin), מָרָק / Marak (soup), מַזְלֵג / Mazleg (fork), עוֹף / Of (chicken), סַכִּין / Sakin (knife), יַיִן / Yayin (wine)

Chapter 6: Going Shopping

A. כּוֹבַע / Kovah (hat)

B. צָעִיף / Tza'if (scarf)

C. כְּפָפוֹת / Kfafot (gloves)

D. מַגָּפַּיִם / Megafayim (boots)

E. מִטְרִיָּה / Mitria (umbrella)

F. שִׂמְלָה / Simla (dress)

G. חֻלְצָה / Hultzah (shirt)

H. מְעִיל קָצָר / Me'il Katzar (jacket)

I. חֲגוֹרָה / Ḥagorah (belt)

J. מִכְנָסַיִם / Miḥnasyim (pants)

K. גַּרְבַּיִם / Garbayim (socks)

L. נַעֲלַיִם / Na'alyim (shoes)

M. מִשְׁקְפֵי שֶׁמֶשׁ / Mishkafay-Shemesh (sunglasses)

N. בֶּגֶד יָם / Beged Yam (bathing suit)

O. סַנְדָּלִים / Sandalim (sandals)

Chapter 7: Having Fun Hebrew Style

כֶּלֶב / Kelev (dog), חָתוּל / Hhatul (cat), אַרְיֵה / Arieh (lion), פִּיל / Peel (elephant), צִפּוֹר / Tzipor (bird), פָּרָה / Parah (cow), סוּס / Sus (horse), תַּרְנְגוֹל / Tarnegol (rooster), דָּג / Dag (fish), סוּס יְאוֹרשכשי / Sus Ha'Ye'or (hippo)

Chapter 8: Enjoying Your Free Time: Hobbies, Sports, and Other Fun Activities

שְׂחִיָּהS / S'hiya (swimming), כַּדּוּר רֶגֶל / Kadur–Regel (soccer), רִקּוּד / Rikud (ballet), טִיּוּל / Tiyul (hiking), כַּדּוּר בָּסִיס / Kadur–Basis (baseball)

Chapter 9: Talking on the Phone

1. C (Speaking.) **2.** B (Certainly.) **3.** A (He's not here right now.)

Chapter 10: At the Office and Around the House

A. אַמְבַּטְיָה / Ambatia **B.** חֲדַר שֵׁנָה / Ḥadar Sheinah

C. מִטְבָּח / Mitbach **D.** סָלוֹן / Salon

Chapter 11: Planning and Taking a Trip

1. לִנְסֹעַ / Linso'a **2.** לְטַיֵּל / L'Tayel **3.** לְהַפְלִיג / Lehaflig

4. יַמְרִיא / Yamrie **5.** דַּרְקוֹן / Darkon

Chapter 12: Getting Around: Flying, Driving, and Riding

1. B **2.** G **3.** A **4.** F **5.** E

Chapter 13: Money, Money, Money

1. traveler's checks **2.** I.D.

3. account **4.** Morning light (good morning)

5. exchange rate

Chapter 14: Handling Emergencies

A. רֹאשׁ / Rohsh **B.** בֶּטֶן / Beten

C. צַוָּאר / Tzavar **D.** גַּב / Gav

E. אֹזֶן / Ozen **F.** זְרוֹעַ / Zro'a

G. עֵינַיִם / Aynayim **H.** רֶגֶל / Regel

I. כָּתֵף / Katef

Chapter 17: Let's Get Biblical

Chapter 18: Like a Prayer

There's no correct answer for this one. Hope you had fun trying to write in Hebrew! Keep practicing and it'll get easier.

Chapter 19: Sacred Time, Sacred Space

יוֹם הַזִּכָּרוֹן Yom HaZikaron (Israeli Memorial Day)

פֶּסַח Pesach (Passover)

שָׁבוּעוֹת Shavuot (Festival of the Weeks)

רֹאשׁ הַשָּׁנָה Rosh HaShanah (Jewish New Year)

יוֹם כִּפּוּר Yom Kippur (Day of Atonement)

יוֹם הַשּׁוֹאָה Yom HaShoah (Holocaust Remembrance Day)

שַׁבָּת Shabbat (The Jewish Sabbath)

יָמִים נוֹרָאִים Yamim Noraim (Awesome Days)

Index

A

Abulafia, Abraham, 334
Abulafia, Abraham ben Samuel, 23
Academy for Hebrew Language, 11, 157
activity terms and phrases
  art galleries, 129
  dancing, 153–154
  live entertainment, 130–135
  movies, 129–130
  museums, 129
  music, 135–136
  outdoor, 152–153
  sports
    baseball, 147–150
    basketball, 147
    other, 149–152
    soccer, 146–147
    swimming, 149
  zoo, 136–137
adjectives
  adverbs and, 137–138
  matching nouns to, 90–94
  overview, 36–37
  sentence-structure and, 209
adverbs, 40–41, 137–138
Airbnb, 211–212
airport terms and phrases, 221–223
Aleph-Bet Yoga: Embodying the Hebrew Letters for Physical and Spiritual Well-Being (Rapp), 335
Almagor, Gila, 131
alphabet, 19–21
Amichai, Yehuda, 336
animal terms and phrases, 136–137
antisemitism in Europe, 272–274
apartment terms and phrases
  decorations, 185
  furnishing, 181–182
  housecleaning, 182
  hunting for, 183–185
  overview, 183
  rooms, 180–181
  safety, 185–186
appliance terms and phrases, 182
apps, phone, 211
Arab citizens, 268
Arab-Israeli wars, 267–268, 276, 279–282
Arad, Ya'el, 149
Arafat, Yasser, 283
arrive (verb), conjugation table for, 347
Ashkenazi Jews, 18, 82, 267–268
Aviya's Summer (film), 131

B

Balfour Declaration of 1917, 280
banking terms and phrases
  common vocabulary, 239
  currency, 236–237
  dialogue, 238
  exchanging money, 240–242
  talking to tellers, 235–236
Barak, Ehud, 283
Baruḥ Dayan HaEmet, 328
baseball terms and phrases, 147–150
basketball terms and phrases, 147
be (verb), conjugation table for, 125
Beauty Queen of Jerusalem, The (TV show), 132
Benstein, Jeremey, 333
Ben-Yehuda, Eliezer, 13, 334
Betahḥ, 343
B'Ezrat HaShem (phrase), 339
Bialik, Hayyim Nahman, 230
Bible, Hebrew
  cohortive tense, 294–295
  emphatic tense, 292–294
  Hapax Legomena, 295–296
  history of Israel in, 271
  overview, 289
  prayer before and after reading, 303–304
  quotes from, 296–297
  word order in, 290–292

L

M

N

W

Y

About the Author

Jill **Suzanne** Jacobs is a writer and educator. She holds a graduate degree in Israel Education from George Washington University and an MA in Jewish Education from Hebrew Union College-Jewish Institute of Religion. She writes and educates from Southern California, where she lives with her daughter — a second-generation Diaspora Hebrew speaker — and their dog, who knows some Hebrew (and some Yiddish) too.

Dedication

This book is dedicated to my daughter, love and light of my life. Aria, this one's for you.

Author's Acknowledgments

This second edition was written exactly 18 years after I wrote the first. In Judaism, 18 is חַי, which means "life." And it has been a lifetime.

My first thanks go to Sue Mellen and Barb Cahoon, indominable leaders of YourWriters.com (https://www.yourwriters.com), who brought me this project 18 years ago and insisted that I could do it, even when I said I couldn't. Then they found me again 18 years later, after I'd relocated to the West Coast. It's such a blessing to have them in my life again, and I'm so grateful to them for bringing me this rewarding project. שָׁלוֹם (*shalom*), سلام (*salaam*), peace!

An incredible debt of gratitude goes to the wonderful team at Wiley: to Kelsey Baird, associate acquisitions editor, for her vision of a second edition of *Hebrew For Dummies* and for reaching out; and to Paul Levesque, the project editor, for his hard work, patience, sense of humor, interest in Hebrew, and good cheer.

To Shir Geshvindman, fellow mom, fellow educator, and reviewer of this manuscript, who answered my many Hebrew queries for the past six months.

רַב תּוֹדוֹת (rav todot; *many thanks*) to Eran Ben-Yemini, my Israeli Hebrew informant, and my fellow students at the iCenter, George Washington University's graduate program in Israel Education, for answering my Hebrew and Israel-related queries, helping ensure that the Hebrew represented here is indeed reflective of the Hebrew spoken in its native land, the modern-day State of Israel.

And אַחֲרוֹן אַחֲרוֹן חָבִיב (Aḥaron, aḥaron, ḥaviv: roughly: *last but certainly not least*), I humbly offer my sincere thanks to G-d: Unifying Force of the Cosmos, Source of All Harmony. Thank you for the incredible blessings and random good luck I've had in my life. Who else can I possibly thank? מוֹדָה אֲנִי (Modah Ani; *I am grateful*). I offer this book as prayer: a prayer for שָׁלוֹם (shalom; *peace and wholeness*) for Israel, the Middle East, and indeed for all peoples who inhabit the Earth. כֵּן יִהְיֶה רָצוֹן (Ken Yehiye Ratzon; *that it be so*).

Publisher's Acknowledgments

Acquisitions Editor: Kelsey Baird
Senior Project Editor: Paul Levesque
Copy Editor: Keir Simpson
Tech Editor: Shir Geshvindman

Production Editor: Mohammed Zafar Ali
Cover Image: © ChameleonsEye/Shutterstock